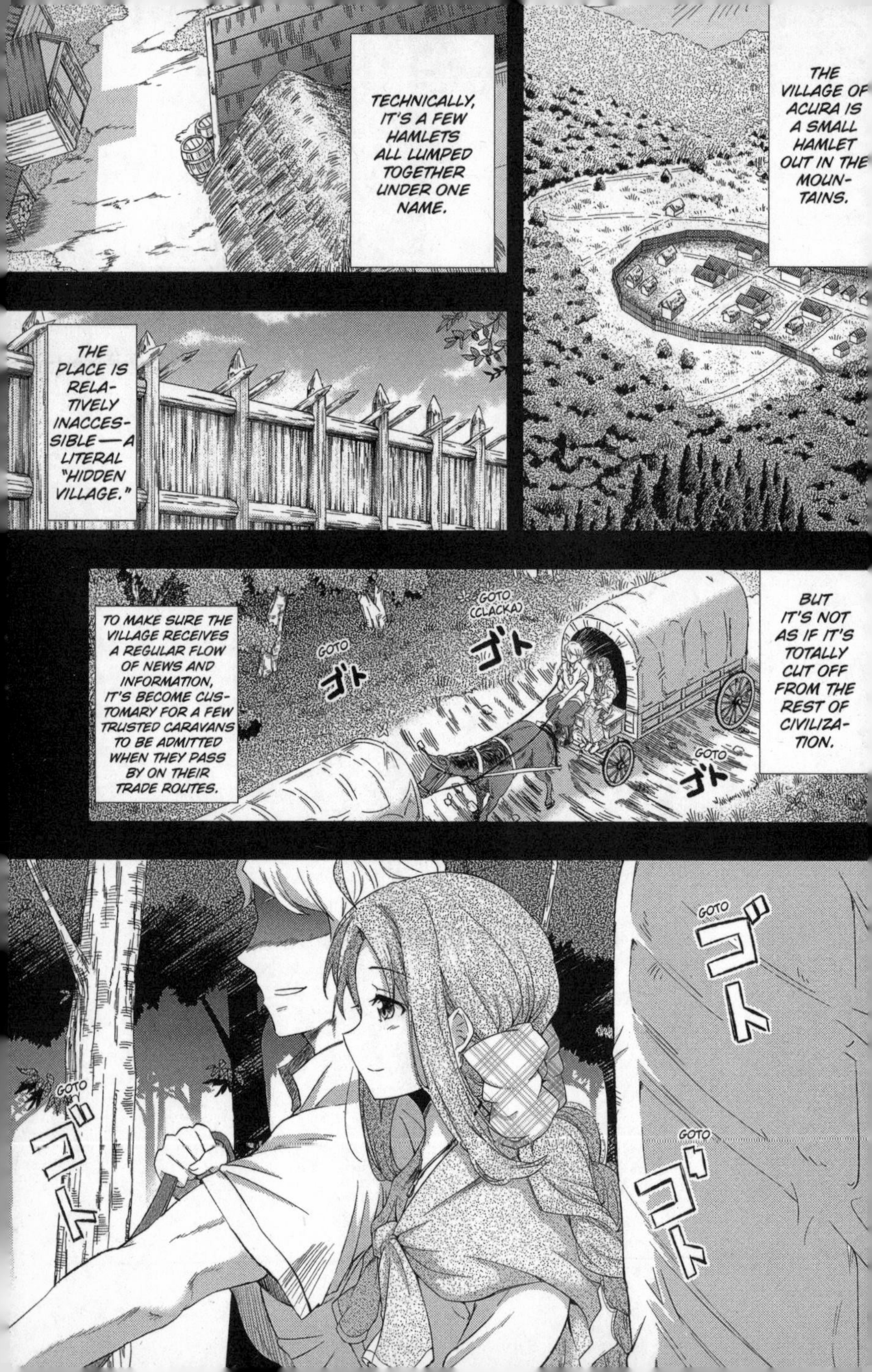
THE VILLAGE OF ACURA IS A SMALL HAMLET OUT IN THE MOUN-TAINS.
TECHNICALLY, IT'S A FEW HAMLETS ALL LUMPED TOGETHER UNDER ONE NAME.
THE PLACE IS RELA-TIVELY INACCES-SIBLE—A LITERAL "HIDDEN VILLAGE."
BUT IT'S NOT AS IF IT'S TOTALLY CUT OFF FROM THE REST OF CIVILIZA-TION.
GOTO (CLACKA)
ゴト
GOTO
ゴト
TO MAKE SURE THE VILLAGE RECEIVES A REGULAR FLOW OF NEWS AND INFORMATION, IT'S BECOME CUS-TOMARY FOR A FEW TRUSTED CARAVANS TO BE ADMITTED WHEN THEY PASS BY ON THEIR TRADE ROUTES.
GOTO
ゴト
GOTO
ゴト
GOTO
ゴト
GOTO
ゴト

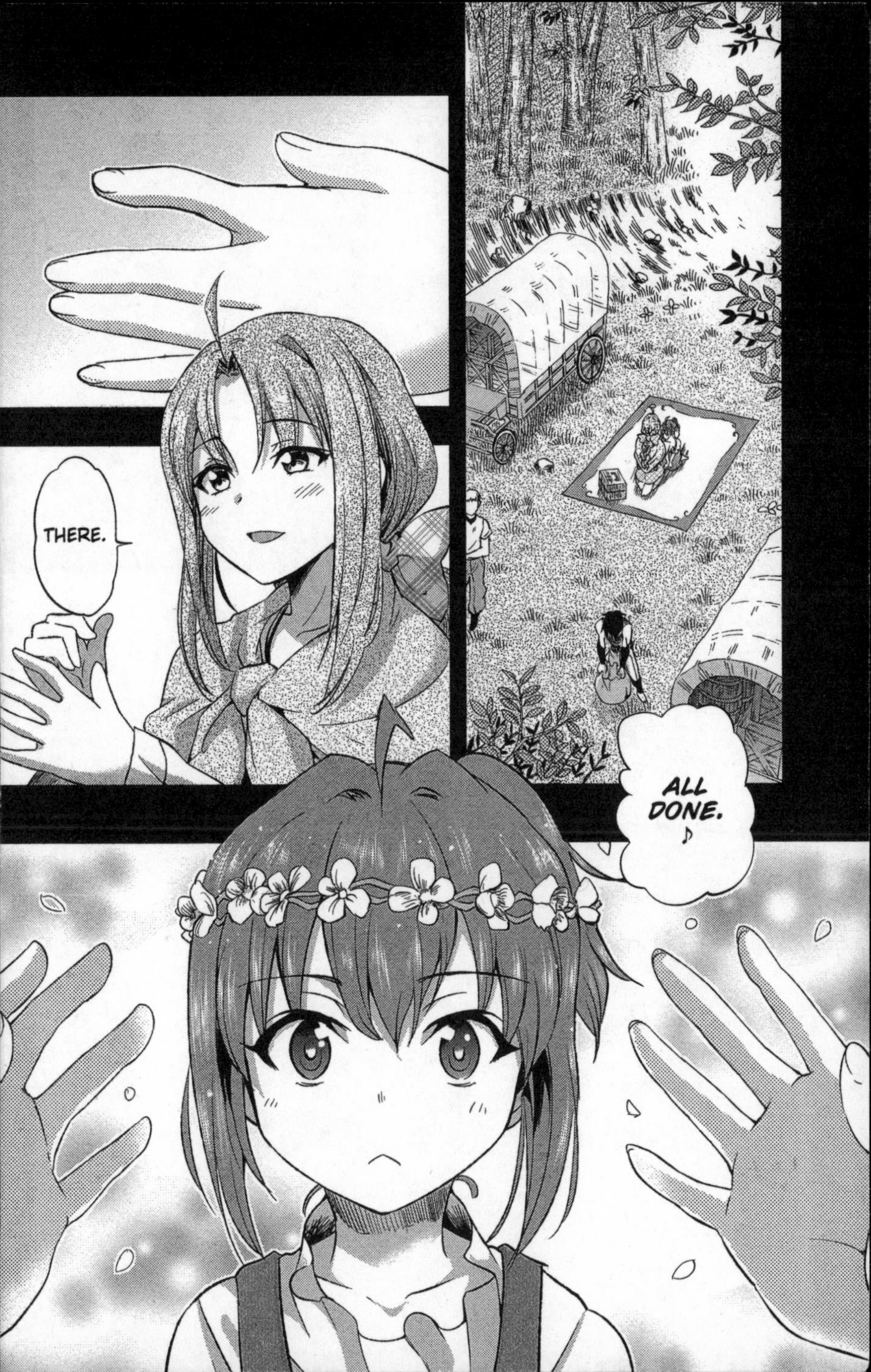
THERE.
ALL DONE. ♪

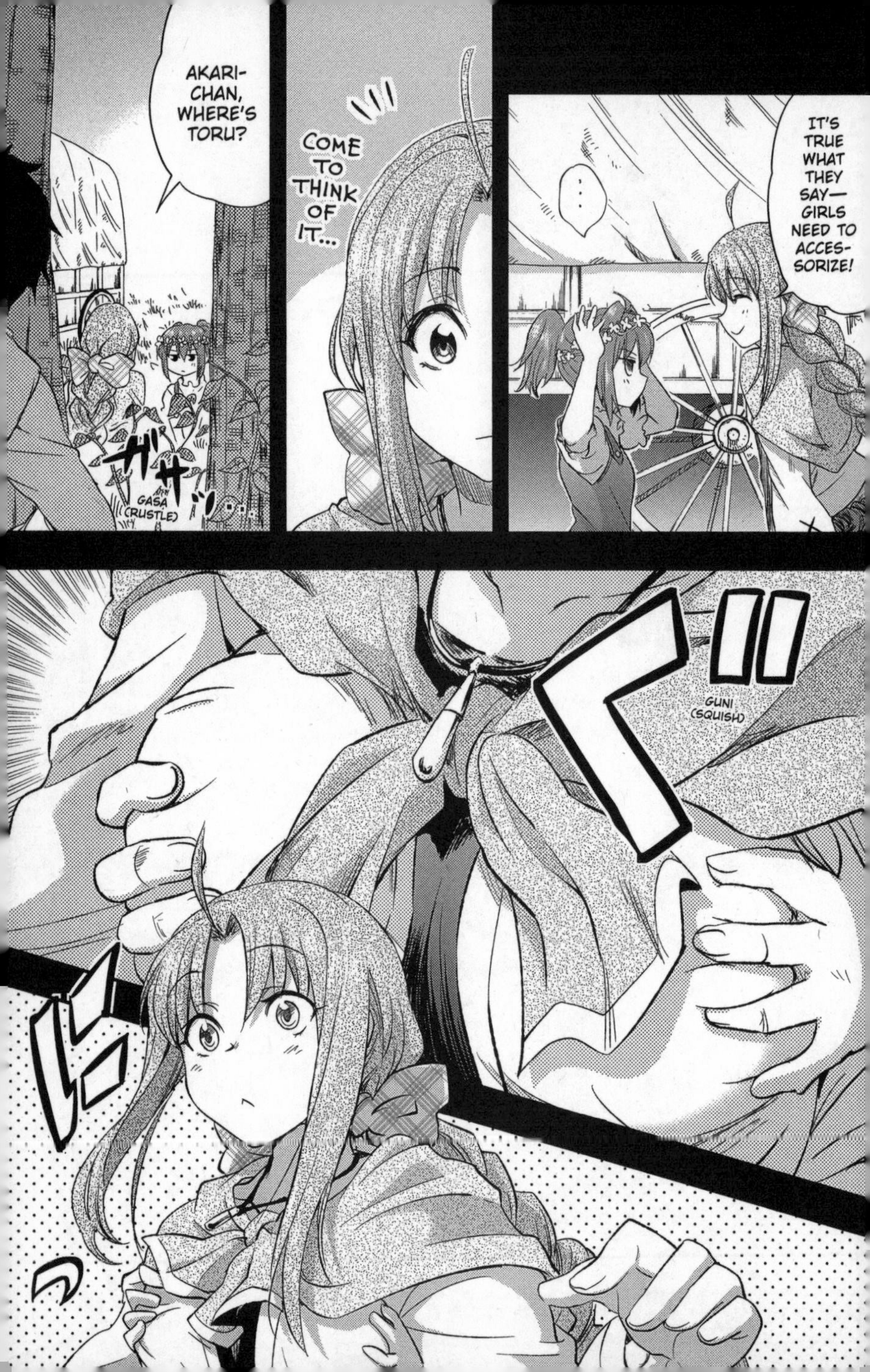
IT'S TRUE WHAT THEY SAY— GIRLS NEED TO ACCES-SORIZE!
...
COME TO THINK OF IT...
AKARI-CHAN, WHERE'S TORU?
GASA (CRUSTLE)
GUNI (SQUISH)

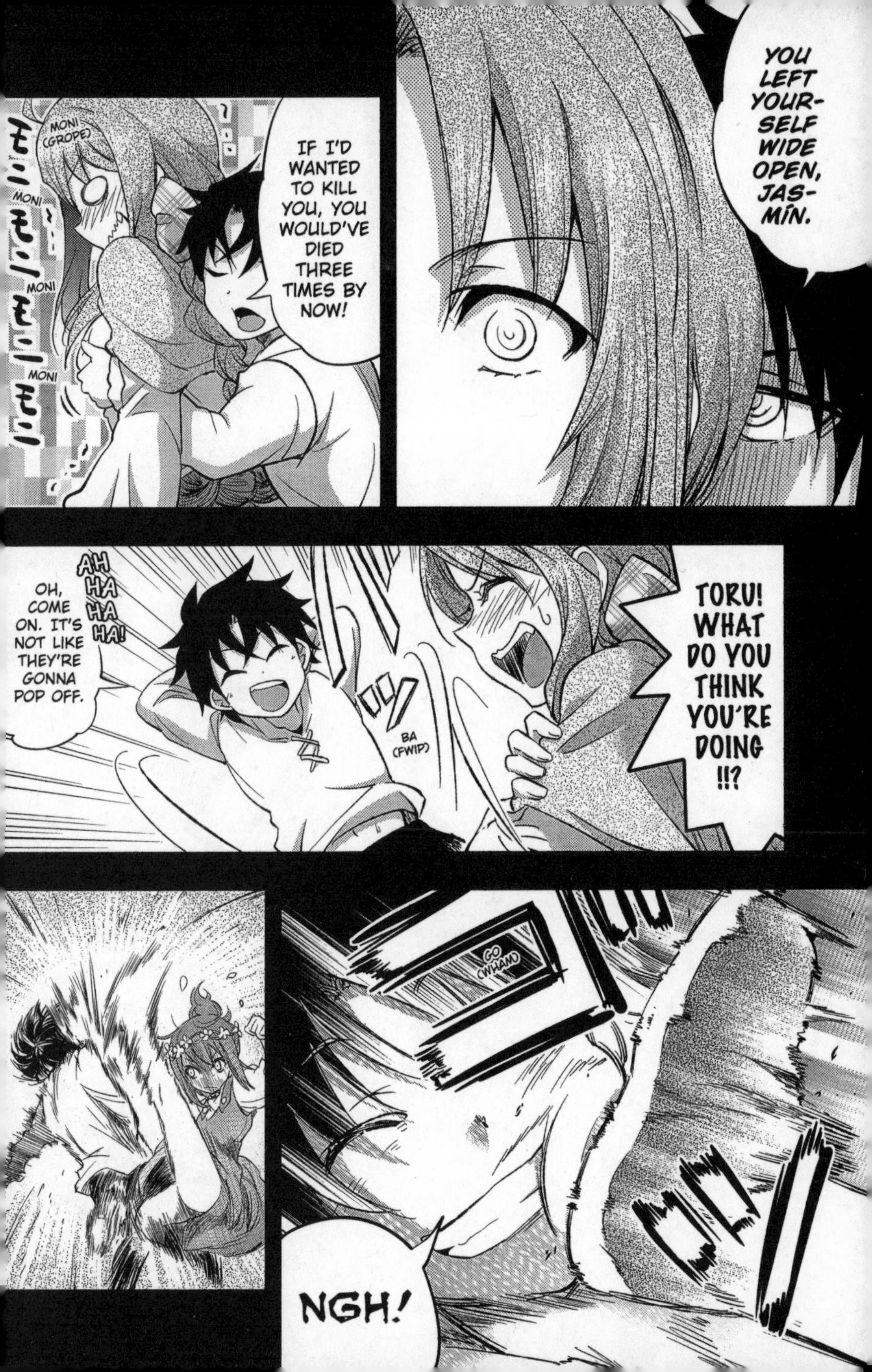
YOU LEFT YOURSELF WIDE OPEN, JASMÍN.
MONI (GROPE)
MONI
MONI
MONI
IF I'D WANTED TO KILL YOU, YOU WOULD'VE DIED THREE TIMES BY NOW!
TORU! WHAT DO YOU THINK YOU'RE DOING!!?
BA (FWIP)
AH HA HA HA HA!
OH, COME ON. IT'S NOT LIKE THEY'RE GONNA POP OFF.
GO (WHAM)
NGH!

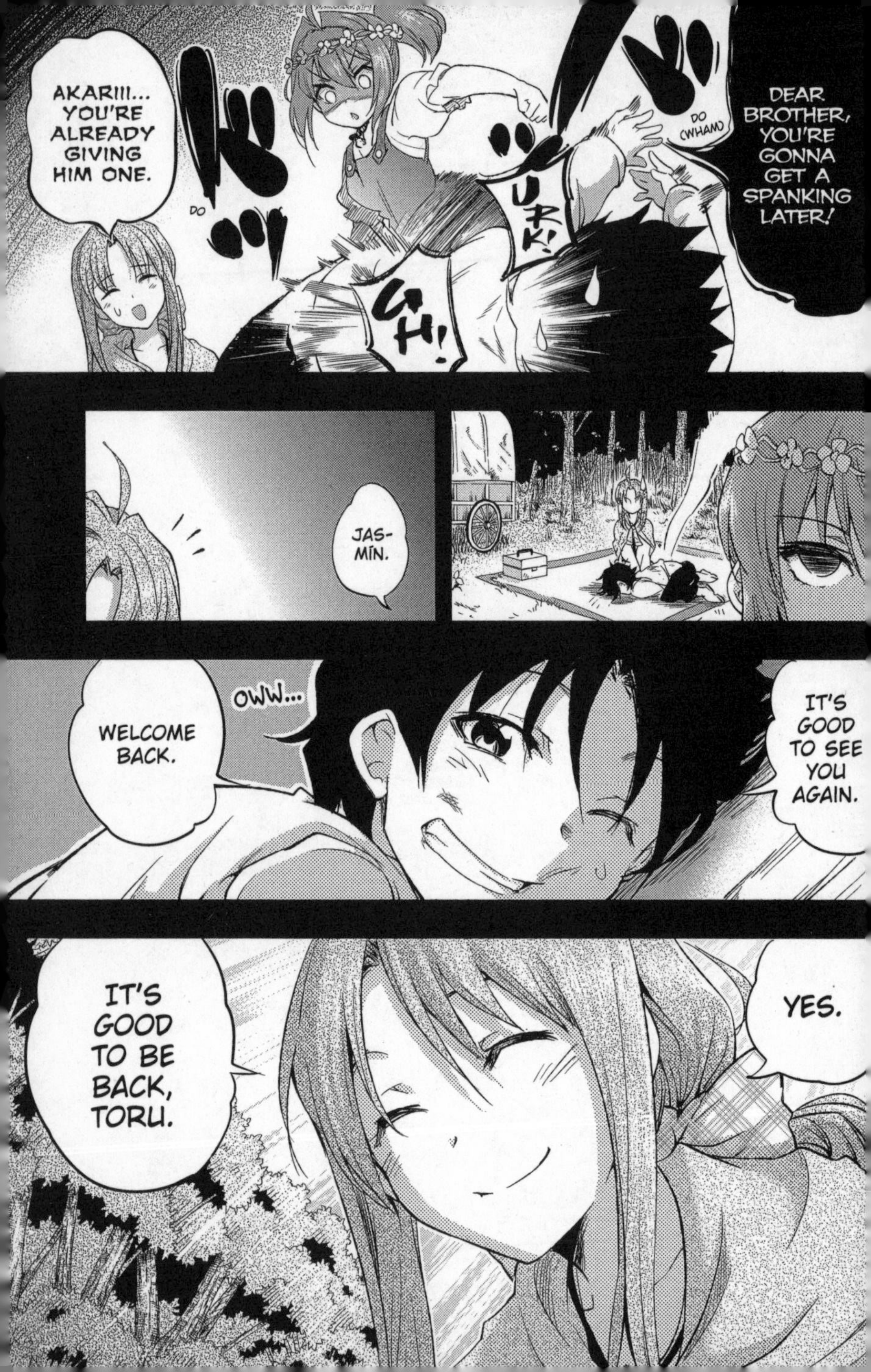
DEAR BROTHER, YOU'RE GONNA GET A SPANKING LATER!
DO (WHAM)
URK!
UH!
DO
AKARIII... YOU'RE ALREADY GIVING HIM ONE.
JAS-MÍN.
IT'S GOOD TO SEE YOU AGAIN.
OWW...
WELCOME BACK.
YES.
IT'S GOOD TO BE BACK, TORU.

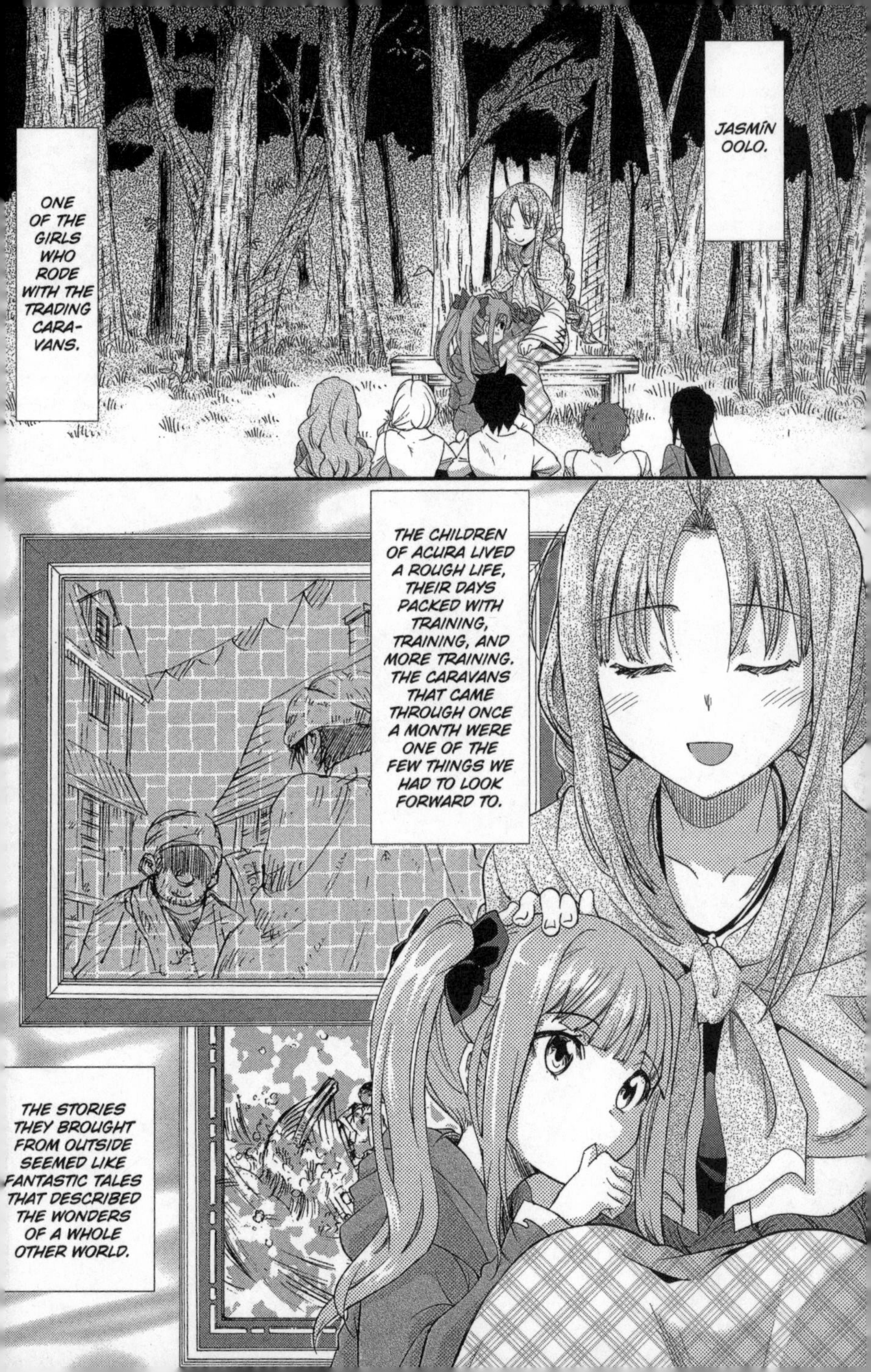
JASMÍN OOLO.
ONE OF THE GIRLS WHO RODE WITH THE TRADING CARA- VANS.
THE CHILDREN OF ACURA LIVED A ROUGH LIFE, THEIR DAYS PACKED WITH TRAINING, TRAINING, AND MORE TRAINING. THE CARAVANS THAT CAME THROUGH ONCE A MONTH WERE ONE OF THE FEW THINGS WE HAD TO LOOK FORWARD TO.
THE STORIES THEY BROUGHT FROM OUTSIDE SEEMED LIKE FANTASTIC TALES THAT DESCRIBED THE WONDERS OF A WHOLE OTHER WORLD.

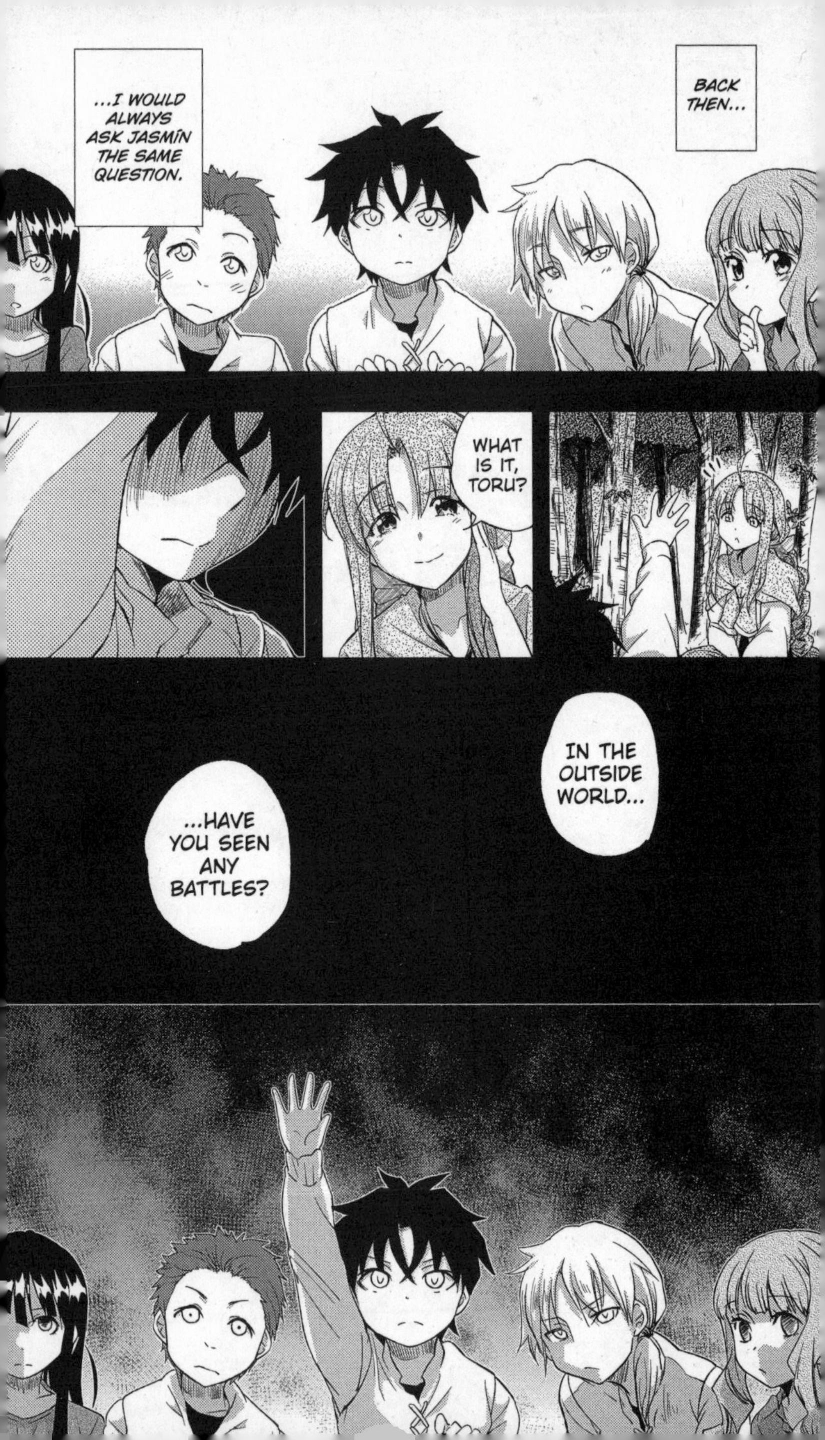
BACK THEN...
...I WOULD ALWAYS ASK JASMÍN THE SAME QUESTION.
WHAT IS IT, TORU?
IN THE OUTSIDE WORLD...
...HAVE YOU SEEN ANY BATTLES?

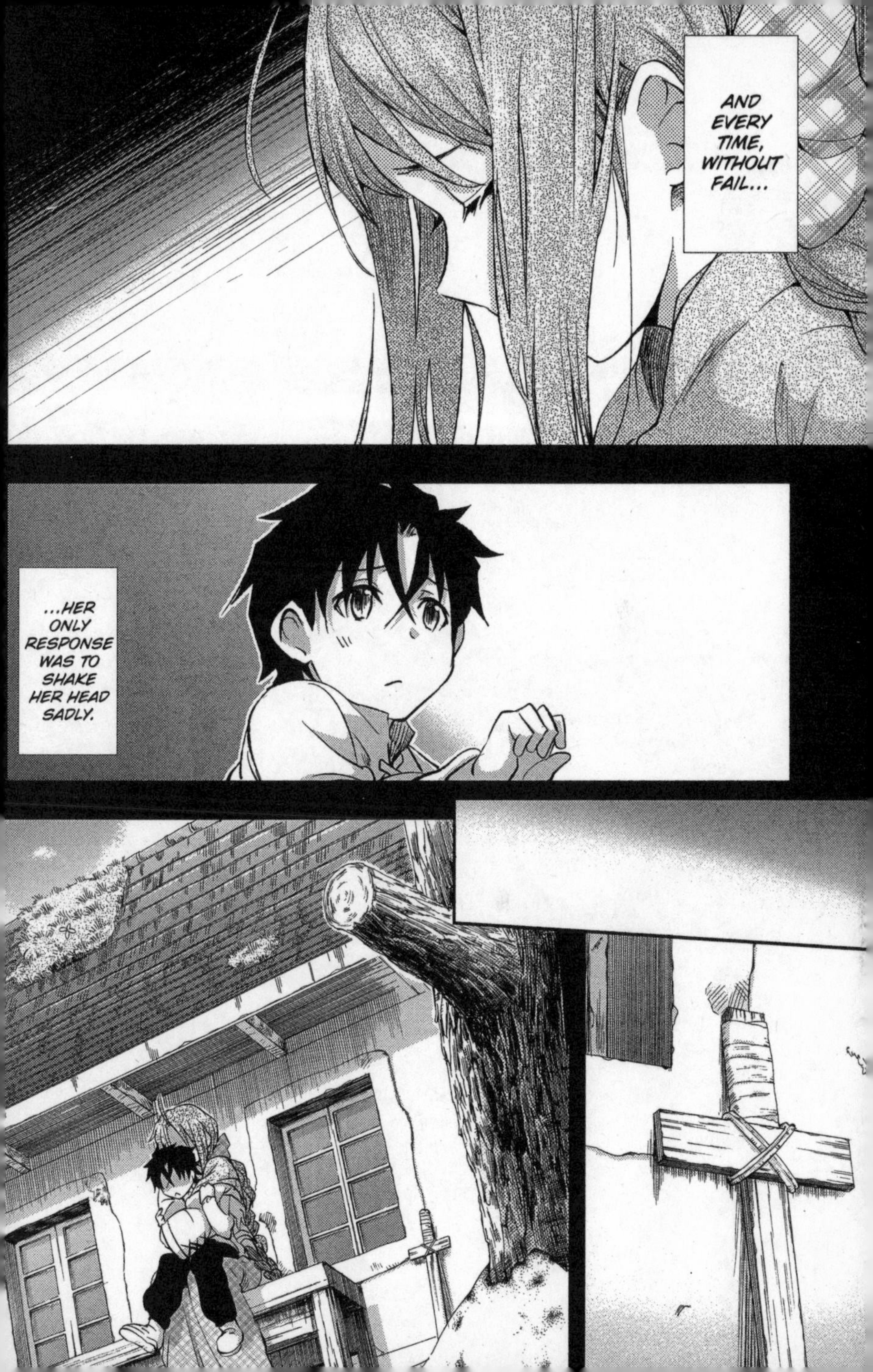
AND EVERY TIME, WITHOUT FAIL...
...HER ONLY RESPONSE WAS TO SHAKE HER HEAD SADLY.

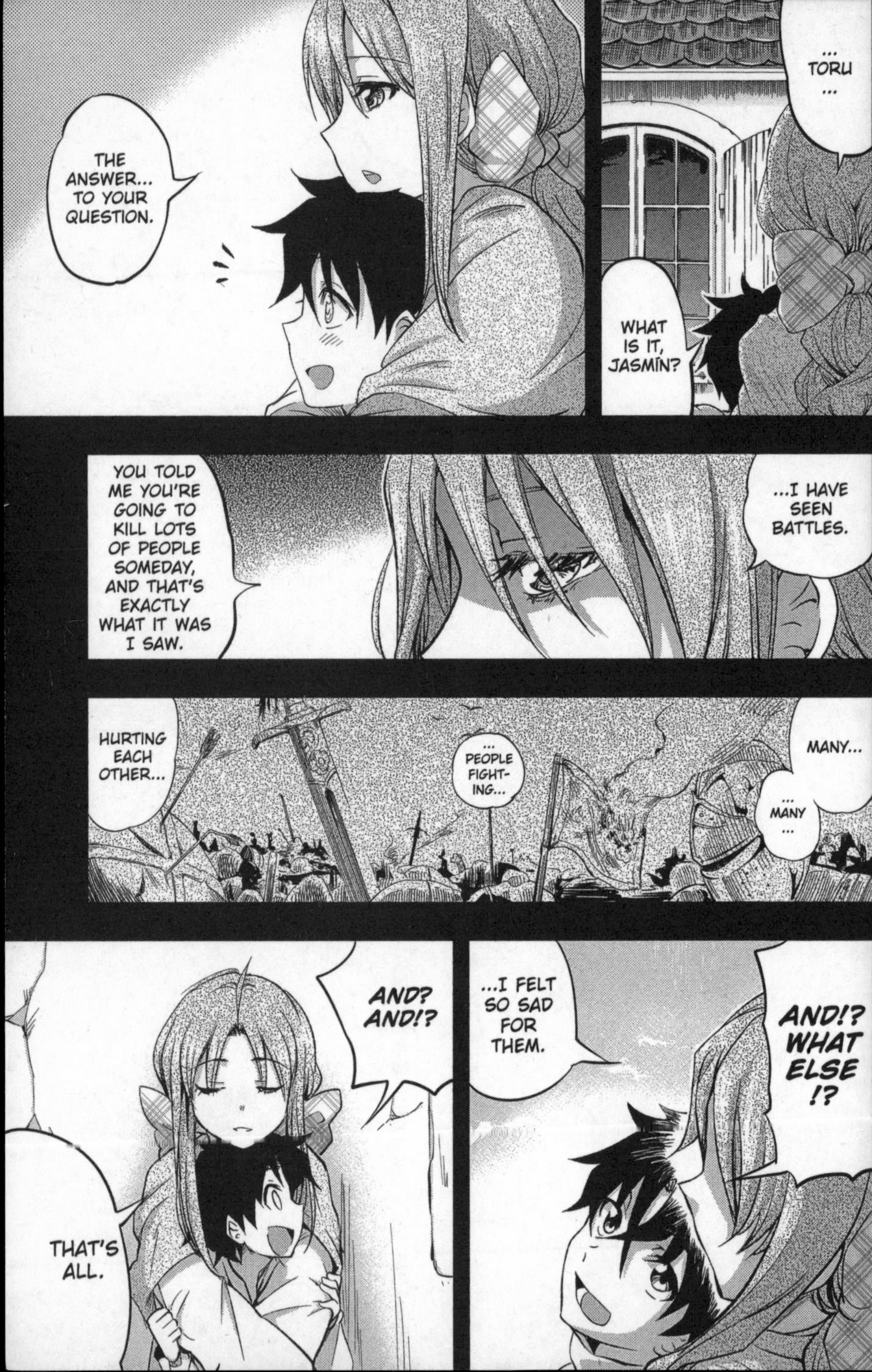
... TORU ...
WHAT IS IT, JASMÍN?
THE ANSWER... TO YOUR QUESTION.
...I HAVE SEEN BATTLES.
YOU TOLD ME YOU'RE GOING TO KILL LOTS OF PEOPLE SOMEDAY, AND THAT'S EXACTLY WHAT IT WAS I SAW.
MANY...
... MANY ...
... PEOPLE FIGHTING...
HURTING EACH OTHER...
AND!? WHAT ELSE !?
...I FELT SO SAD FOR THEM.
AND? AND!?
THAT'S ALL.

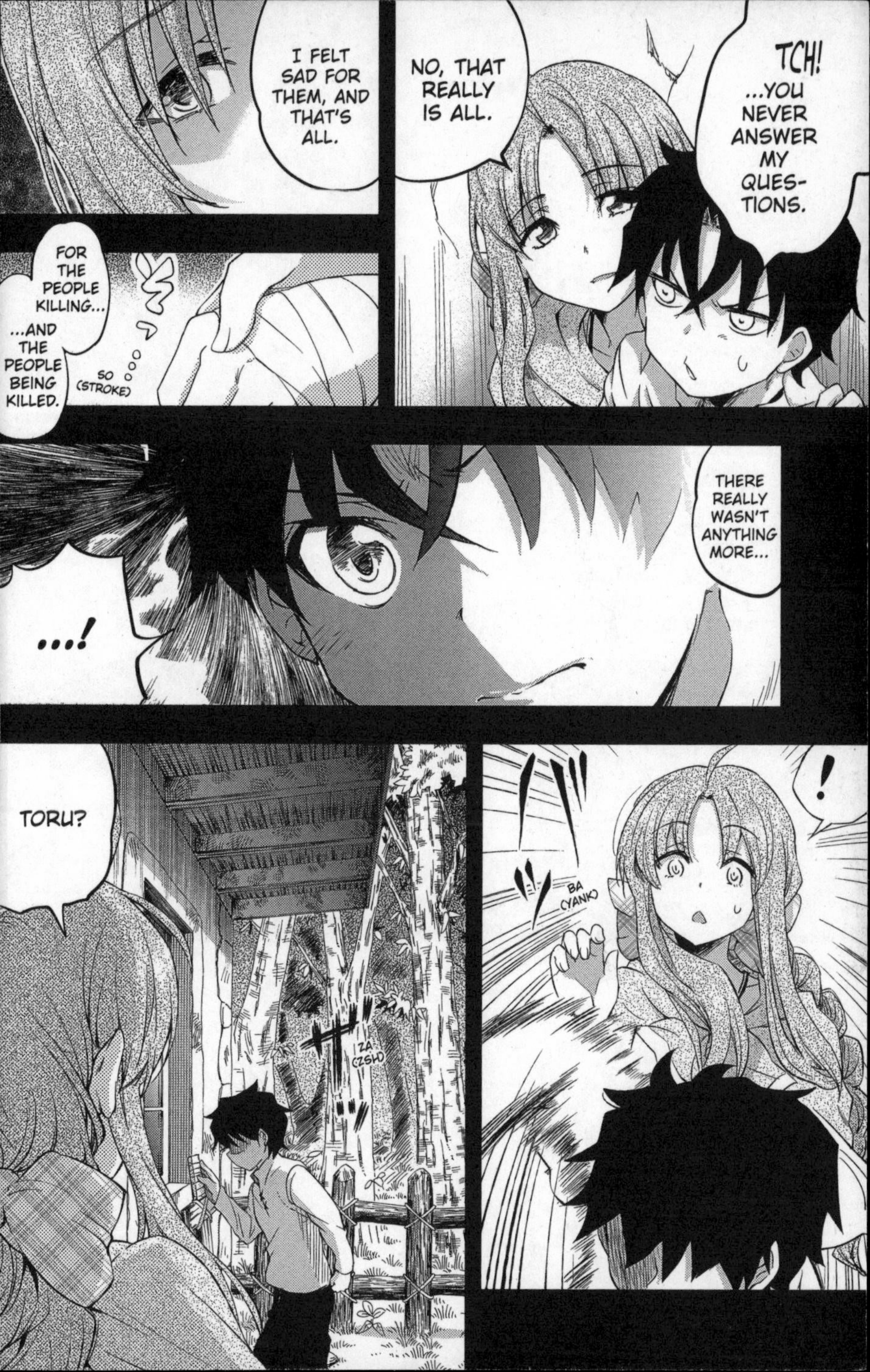
TCH!
...YOU NEVER ANSWER MY QUES-TIONS.
NO, THAT REALLY IS ALL.
I FELT SAD FOR THEM, AND THAT'S ALL.
FOR THE PEOPLE KILLING...
...AND THE PEOPLE BEING KILLED.
SO (STROKE)
THERE REALLY WASN'T ANYTHING MORE...
...!
!
BA (YANK)
TORU?
ZA (ZSH)

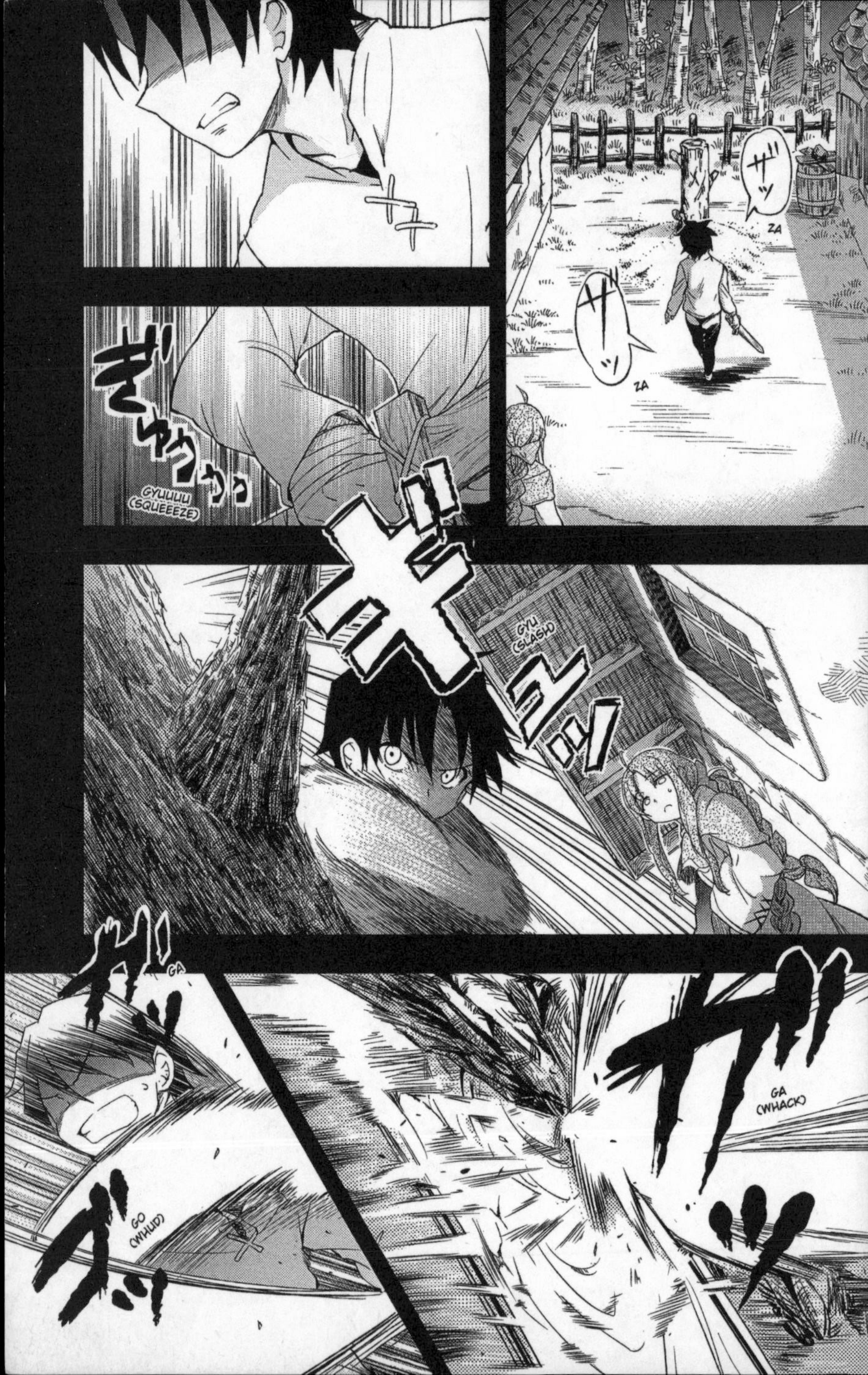
ZA
ZA
GYUUUU (SQUEEEZE)
GYU (SLASH)
GA (WHACK)
GA
GO (WHUD)

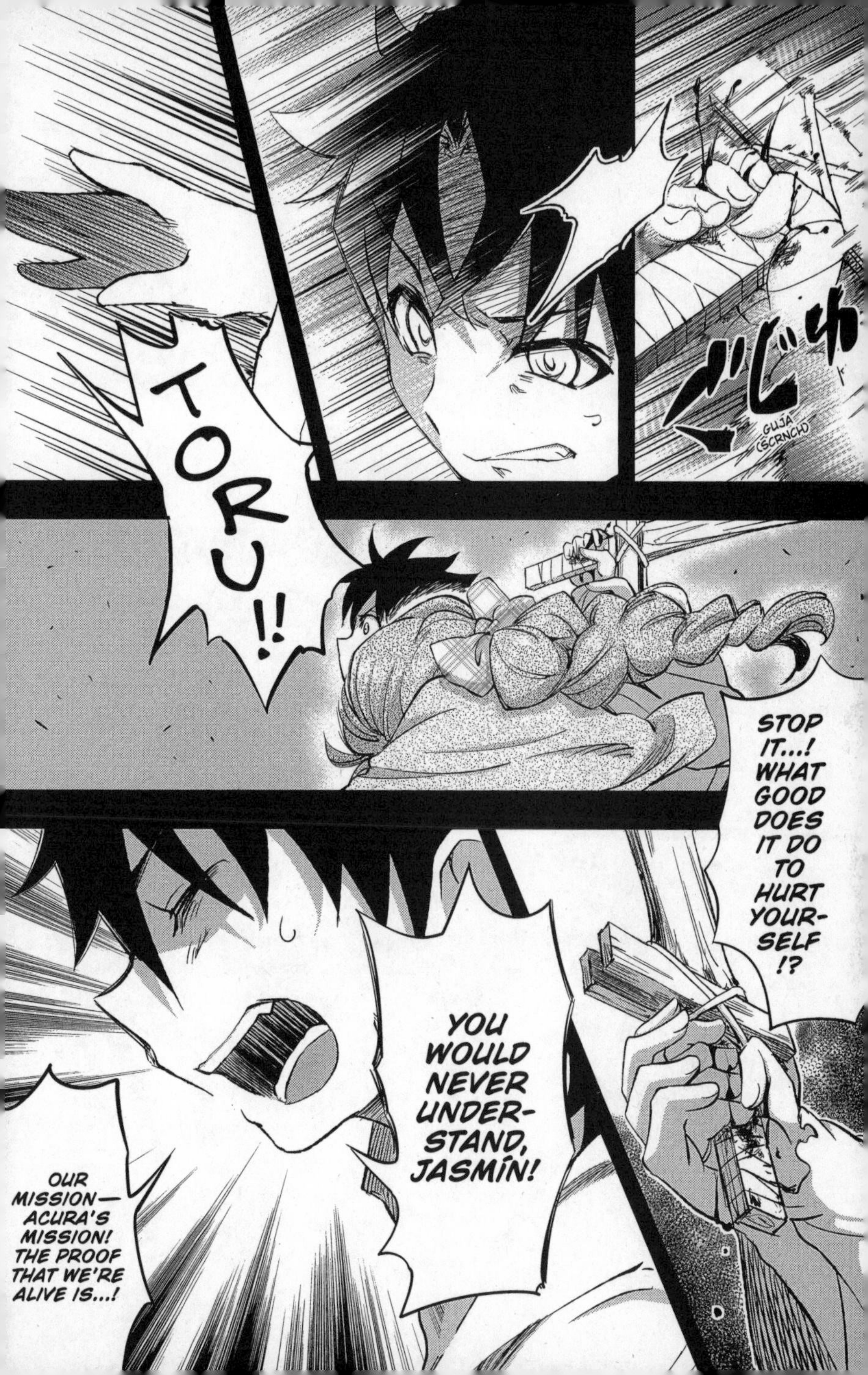
GUJA (SCRNCH)
TORU!!
STOP IT...! WHAT GOOD DOES IT DO TO HURT YOURSELF!?
YOU WOULD NEVER UNDERSTAND, JASMÍN!
OUR MISSION—ACURA'S MISSION! THE PROOF THAT WE'RE ALIVE IS...!

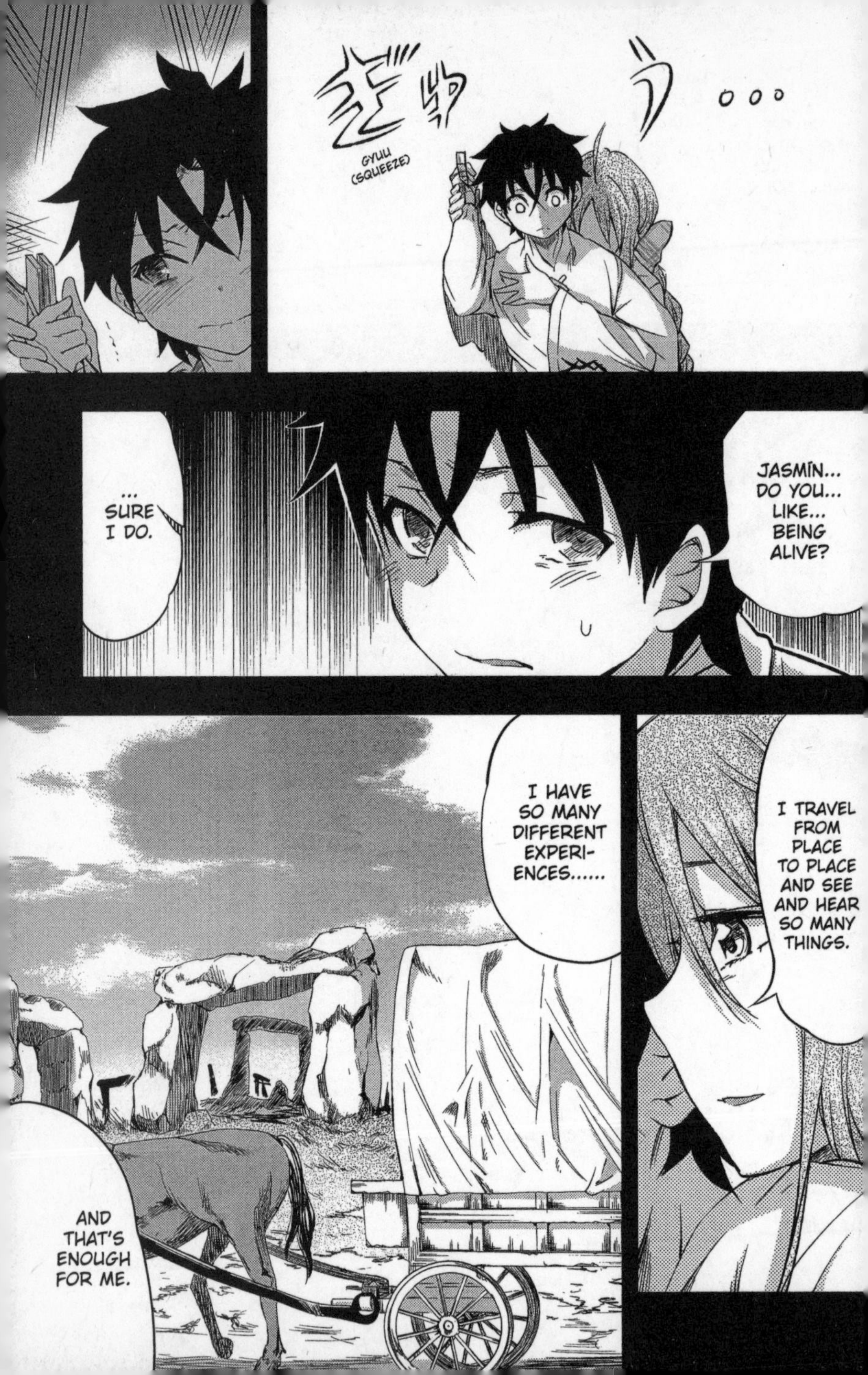
GYUU (SQUEEZE)
JASMÍN... DO YOU... LIKE... BEING ALIVE?
... SURE I DO.
I TRAVEL FROM PLACE TO PLACE AND SEE AND HEAR SO MANY THINGS.
I HAVE SO MANY DIFFERENT EXPERI- ENCES......
AND THAT'S ENOUGH FOR ME.

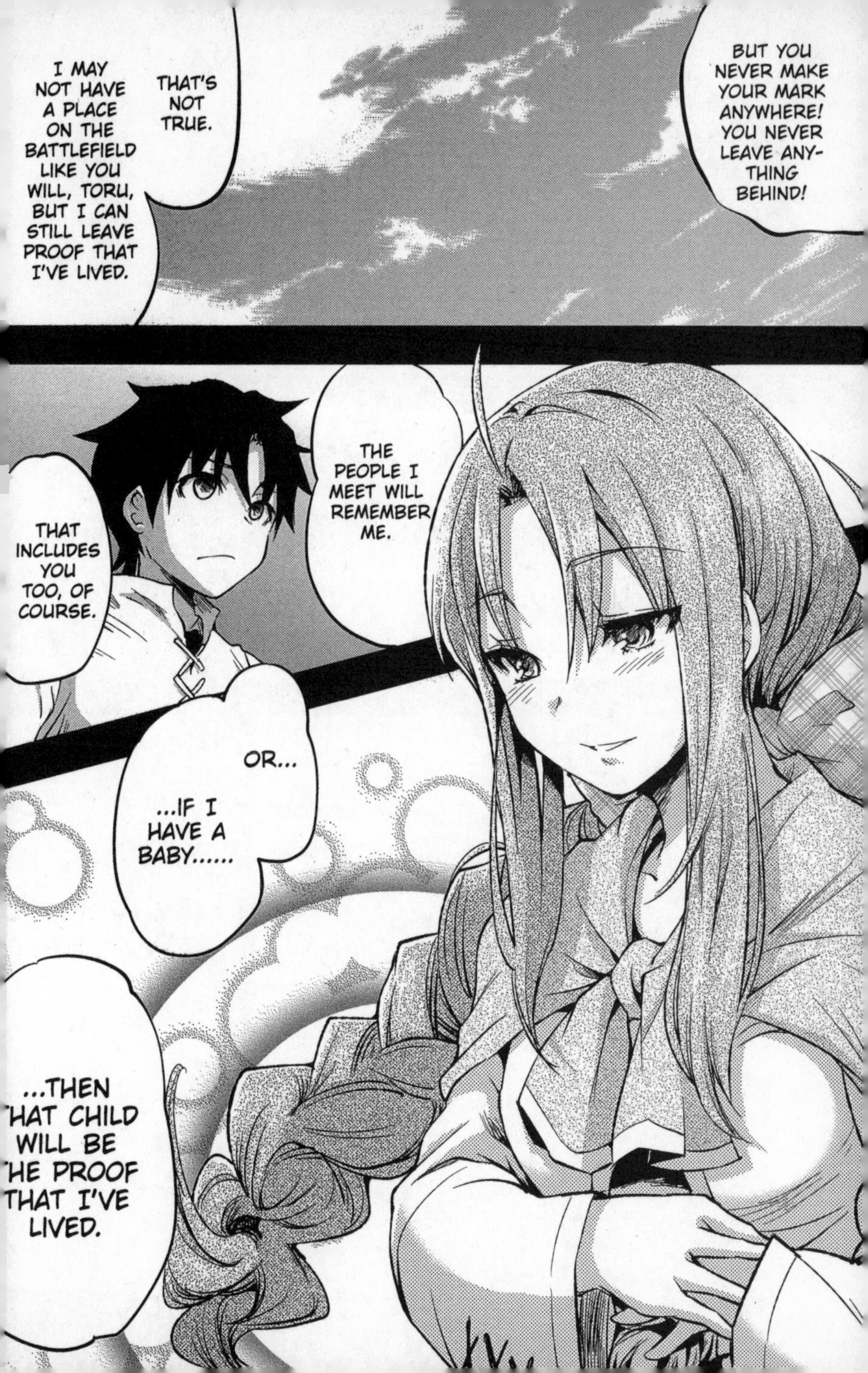
BUT YOU NEVER MAKE YOUR MARK ANYWHERE! YOU NEVER LEAVE ANY-THING BEHIND!
THAT'S NOT TRUE.
I MAY NOT HAVE A PLACE ON THE BATTLEFIELD LIKE YOU WILL, TORU, BUT I CAN STILL LEAVE PROOF THAT I'VE LIVED.
THE PEOPLE I MEET WILL REMEMBER ME.
THAT INCLUDES YOU TOO, OF COURSE.
OR...
...IF I HAVE A BABY......
...THEN HAT CHILD WILL BE HE PROOF THAT I'VE LIVED.

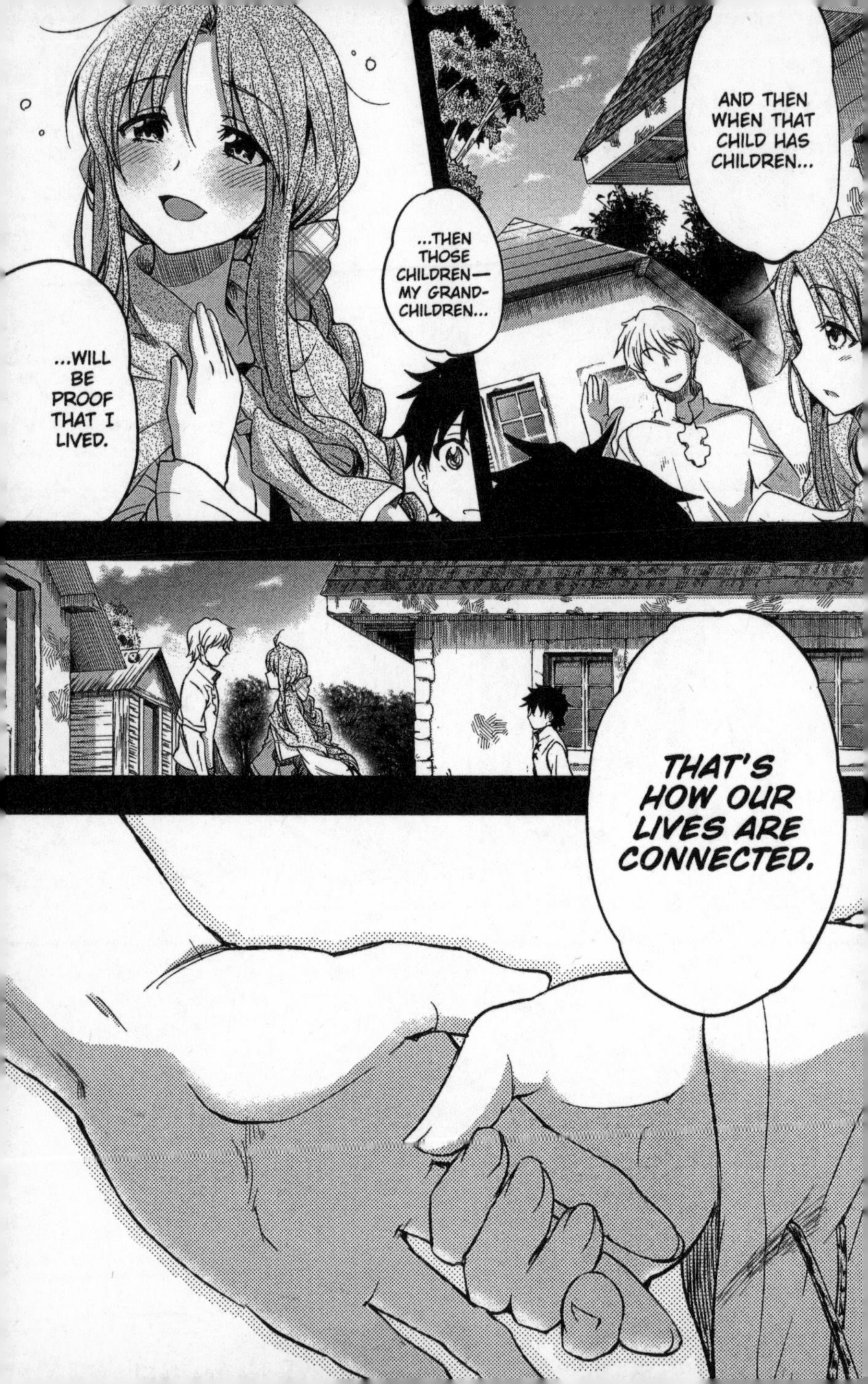
AND THEN WHEN THAT CHILD HAS CHILDREN...
...THEN THOSE CHILDREN—MY GRAND-CHILDREN...
...WILL BE PROOF THAT I LIVED.
THAT'S HOW OUR LIVES ARE CONNECTED.

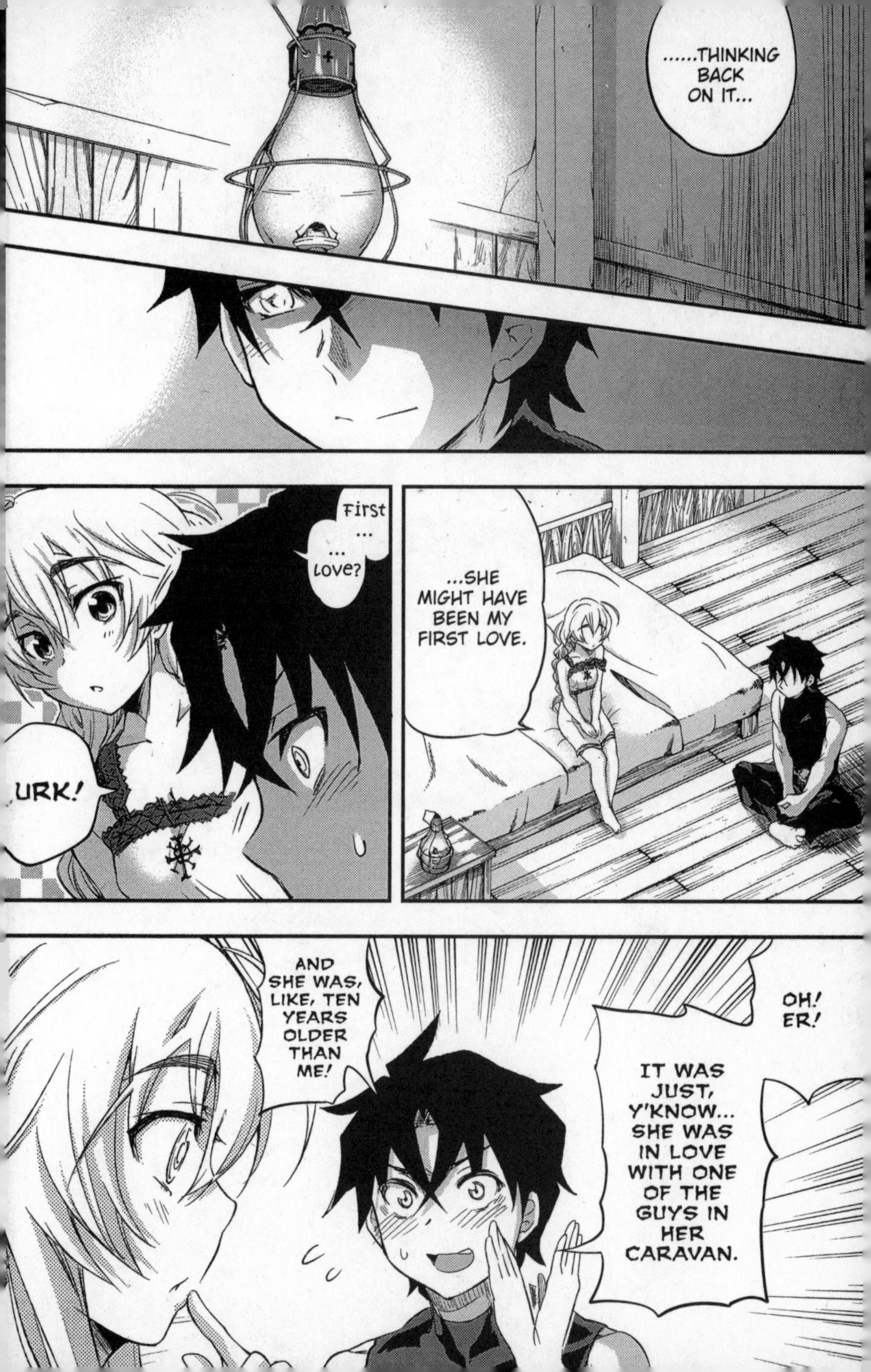

......THINKING BACK ON IT...
...SHE MIGHT HAVE BEEN MY FIRST LOVE.
First ... ... Love?
URK!
OH! ER!
IT WAS JUST, Y'KNOW... SHE WAS IN LOVE WITH ONE OF THE GUYS IN HER CARAVAN.
AND SHE WAS, LIKE, TEN YEARS OLDER THAN ME!

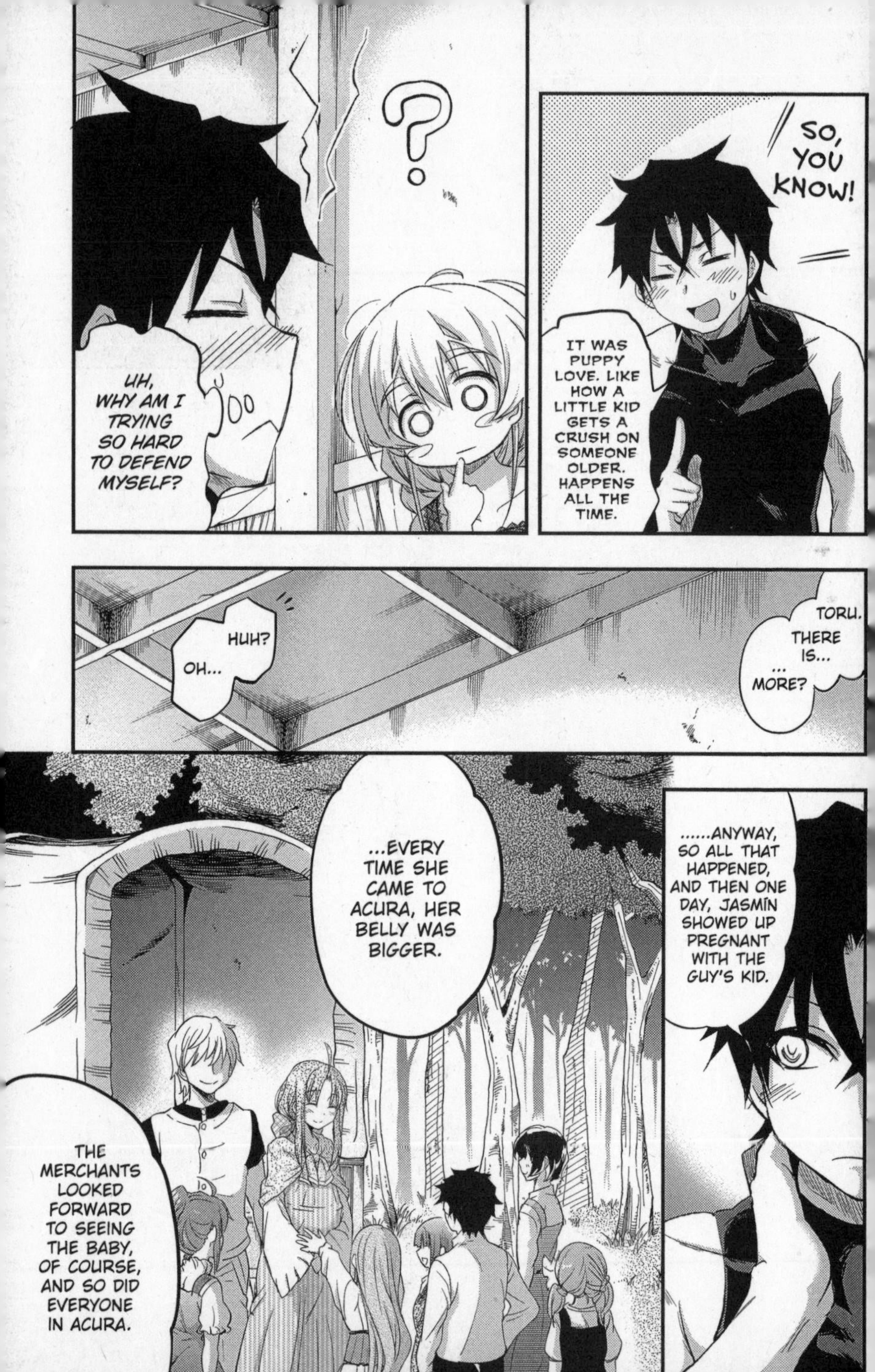
SO, YOU KNOW!
IT WAS PUPPY LOVE. LIKE HOW A LITTLE KID GETS A CRUSH ON SOMEONE OLDER. HAPPENS ALL THE TIME.
?
UH, WHY AM I TRYING SO HARD TO DEFEND MYSELF?
TORU. THERE IS... ...MORE?
HUH? OH...
......ANYWAY, SO ALL THAT HAPPENED, AND THEN ONE DAY, JASMÍN SHOWED UP PREGNANT WITH THE GUY'S KID.
...EVERY TIME SHE CAME TO ACURA, HER BELLY WAS BIGGER.
THE MERCHANTS LOOKED FORWARD TO SEEING THE BABY, OF COURSE, AND SO DID EVERYONE IN ACURA.

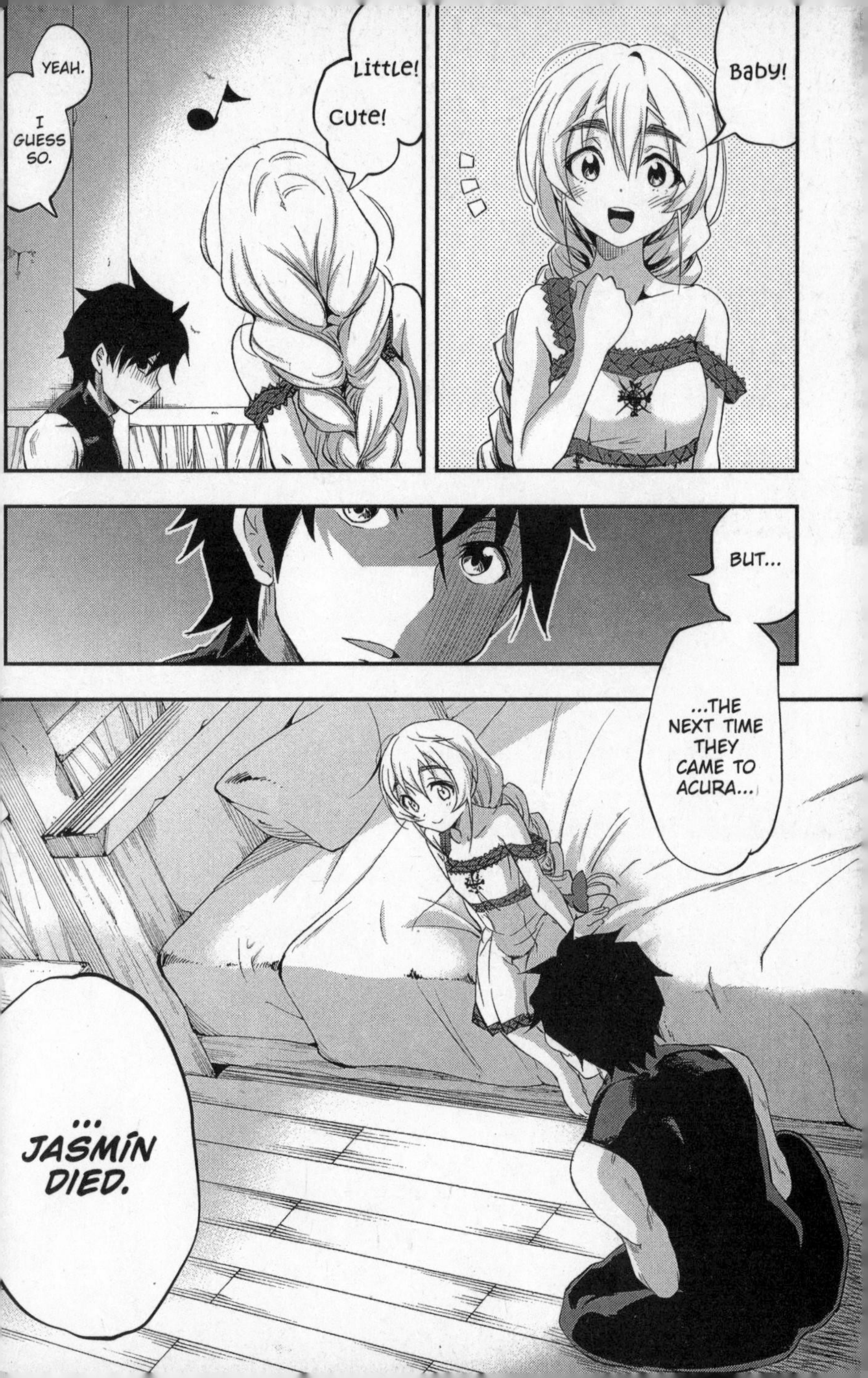
Baby!
Little!
Cute!
YEAH.
I GUESS SO.
BUT...
...THE NEXT TIME THEY CAME TO ACURA...
...JASMIN DIED.

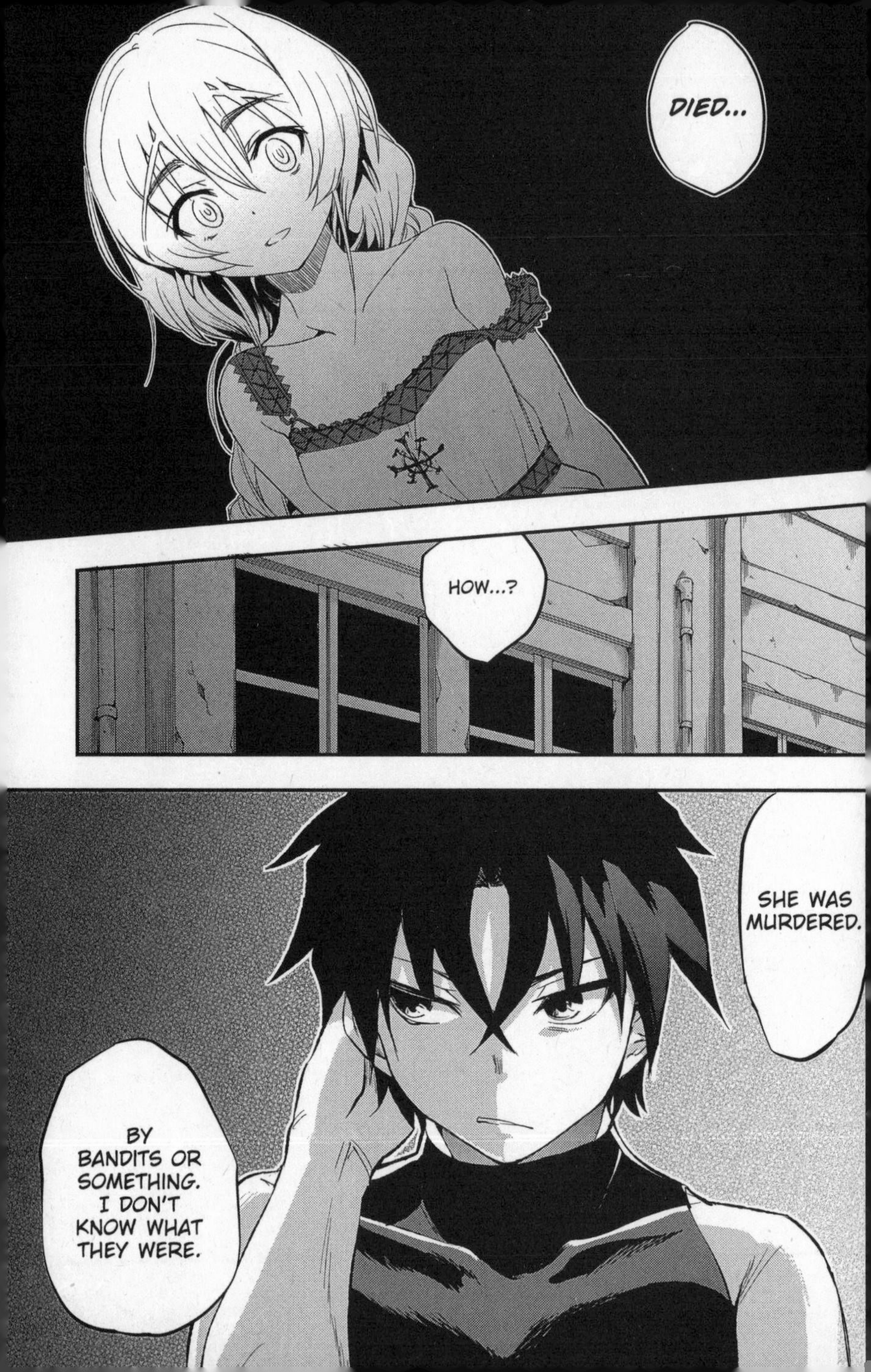
DIED...
HOW...?
SHE WAS MURDERED.
BY BANDITS OR SOMETHING. I DON'T KNOW WHAT THEY WERE.

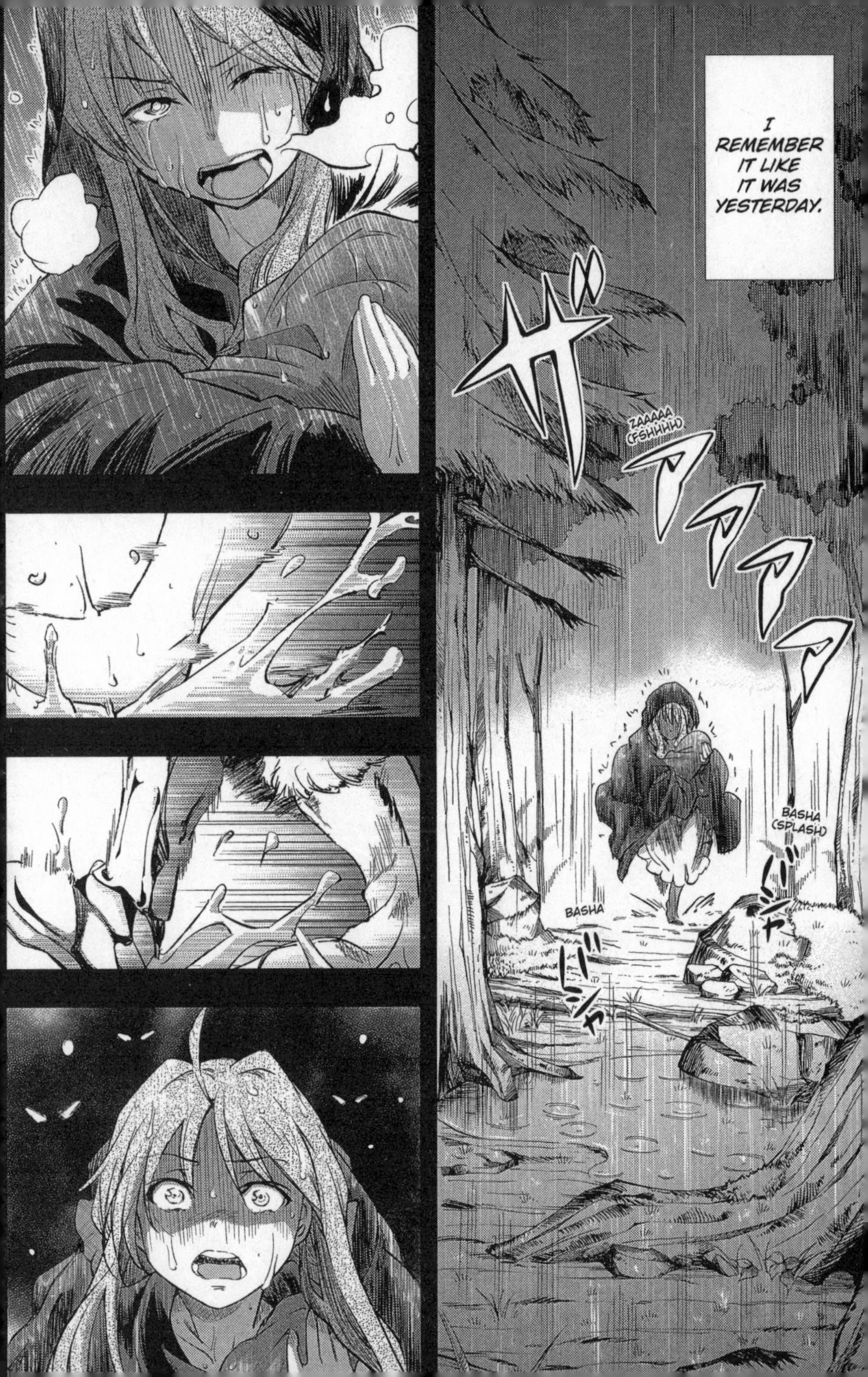
I REMEMBER IT LIKE IT WAS YESTERDAY.
ザアアアア
ZAAAAA (FSHHHH)
BASHA (SPLASH)
バシャ
BASHA
バシャ

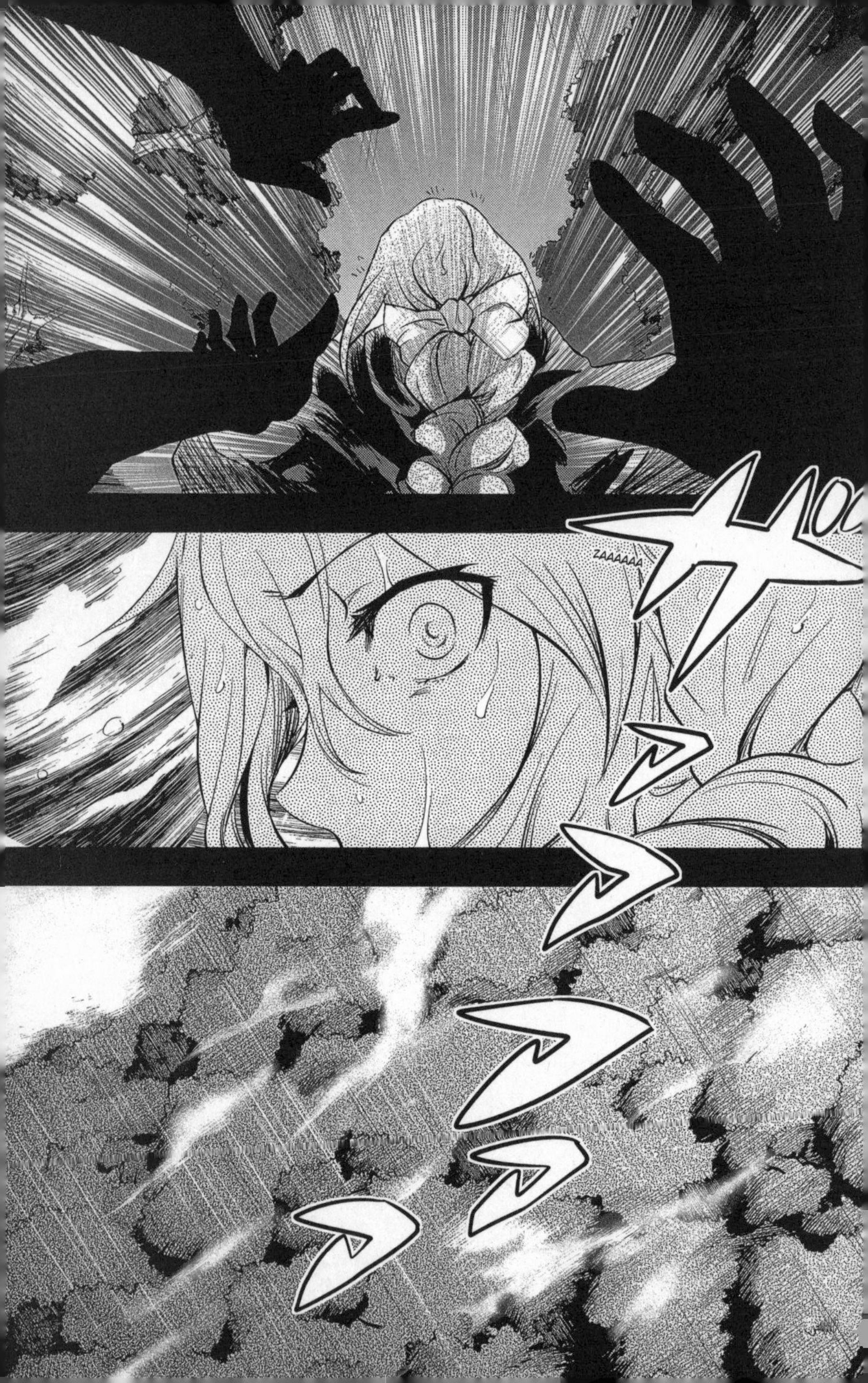
ZAAAAAA

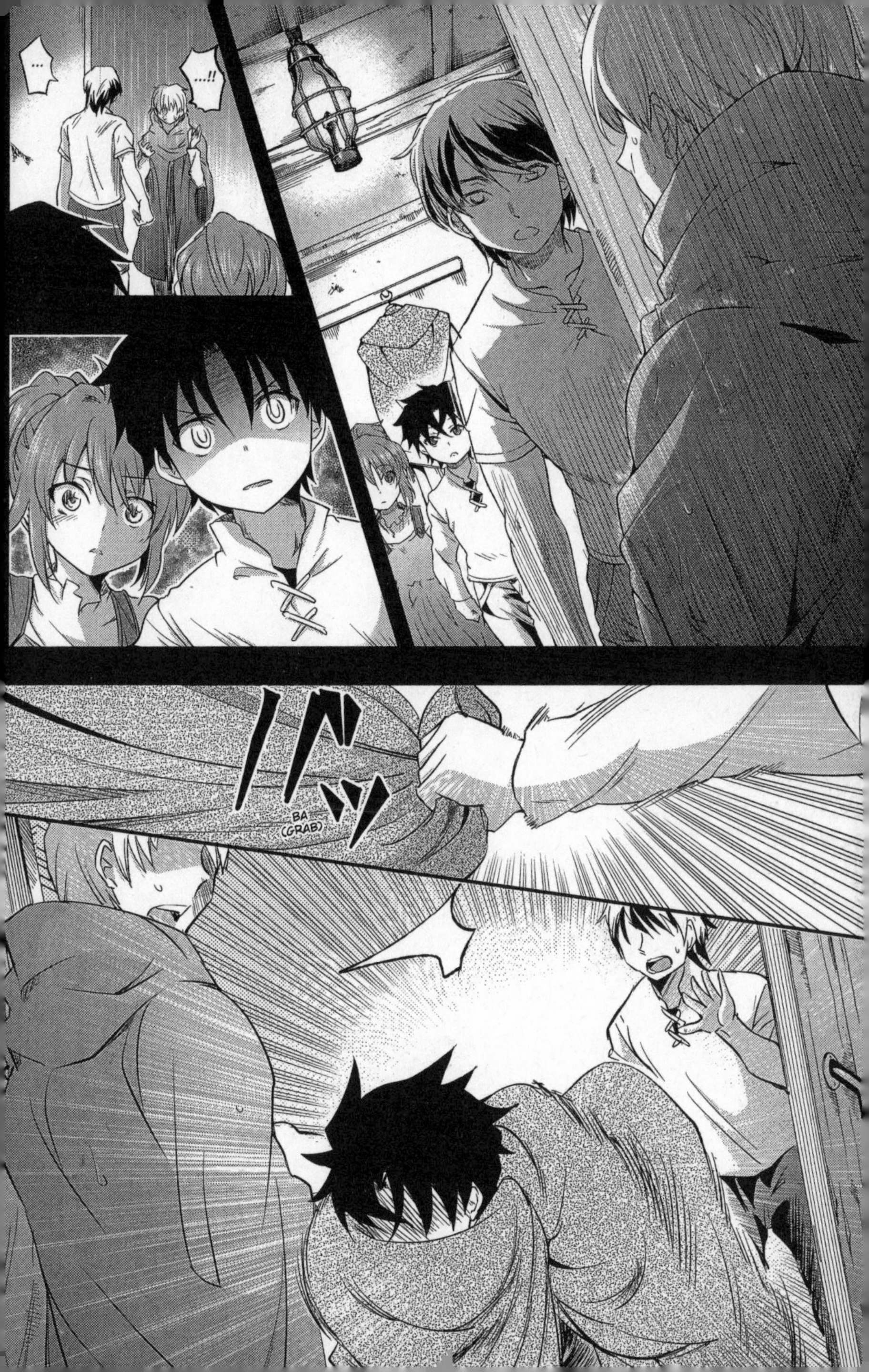
...!!
...
バッ
BA
(GRAB)

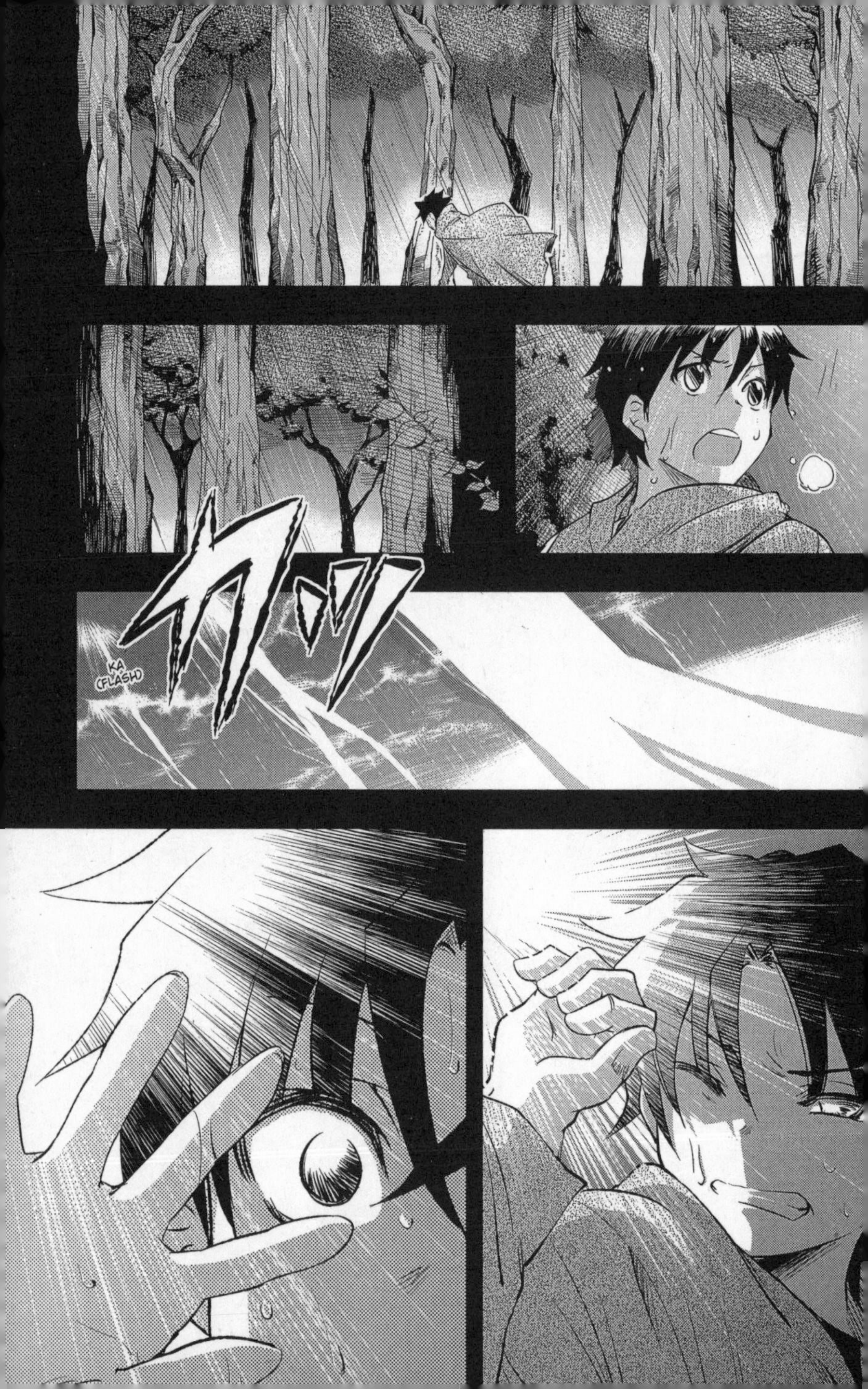
KA
(FLASH)

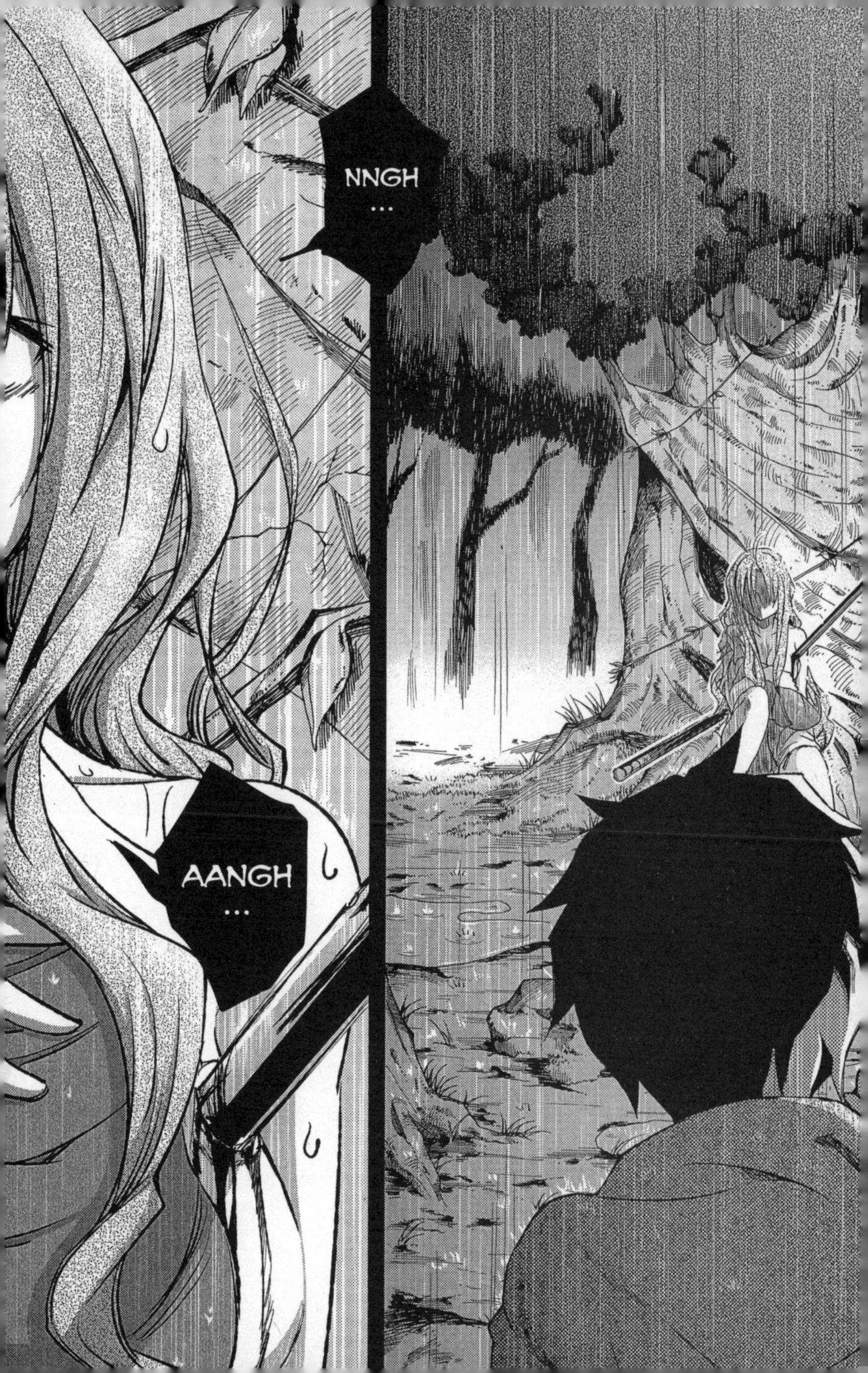
NNGH ...
AANGH ...

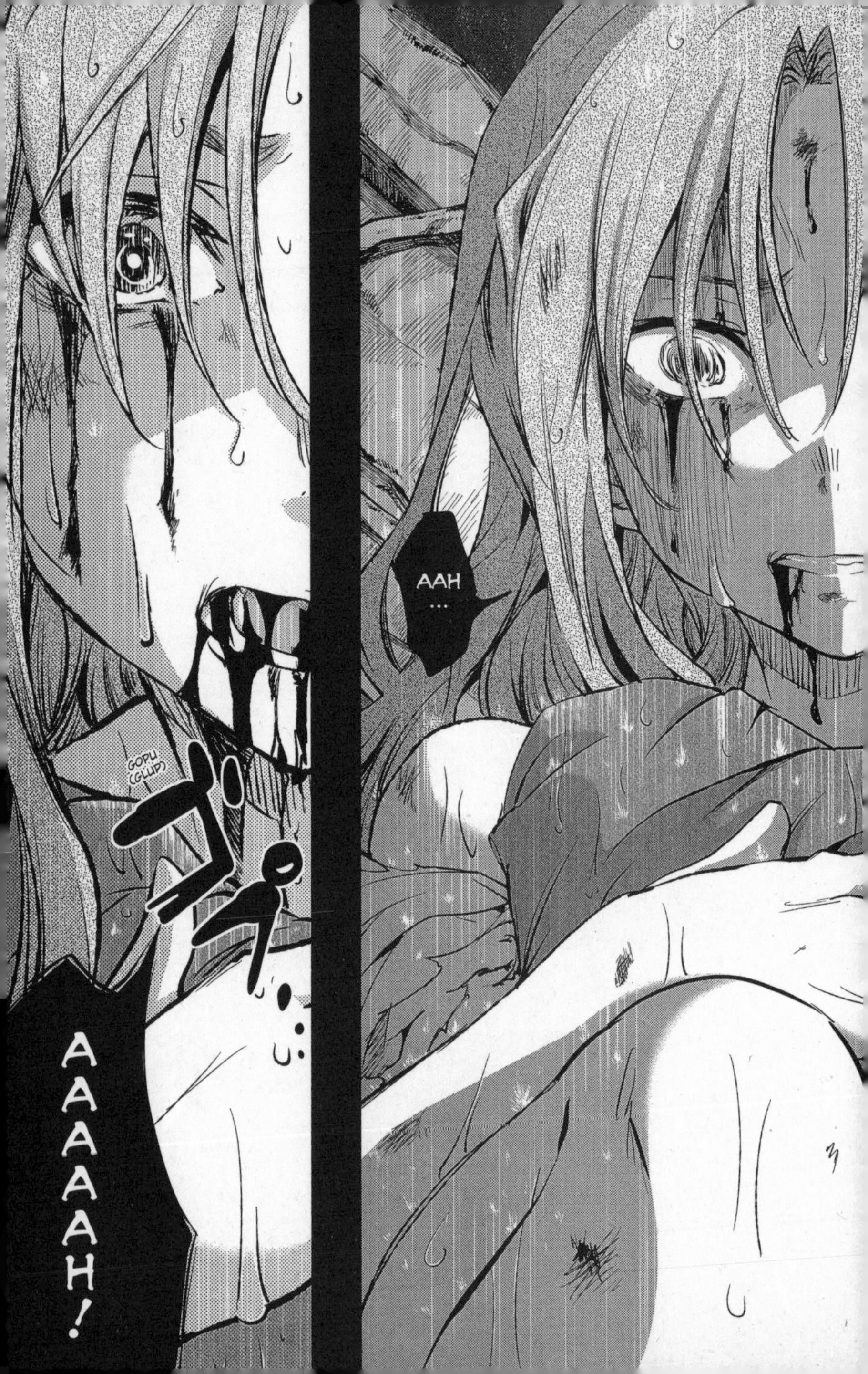
AAH ...
GOPU (GLUP)
AAAAAH!

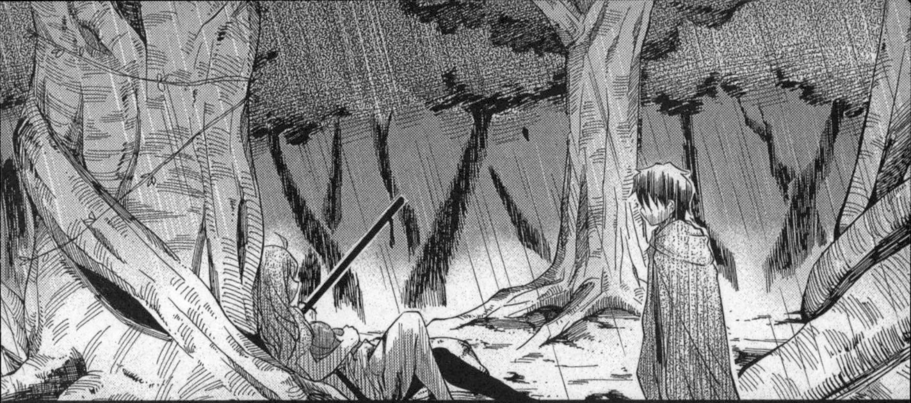

THE ONLY SOUND OUT OF HER MOUTH WAS SOME UNINTELLIGIBLE GROANING.

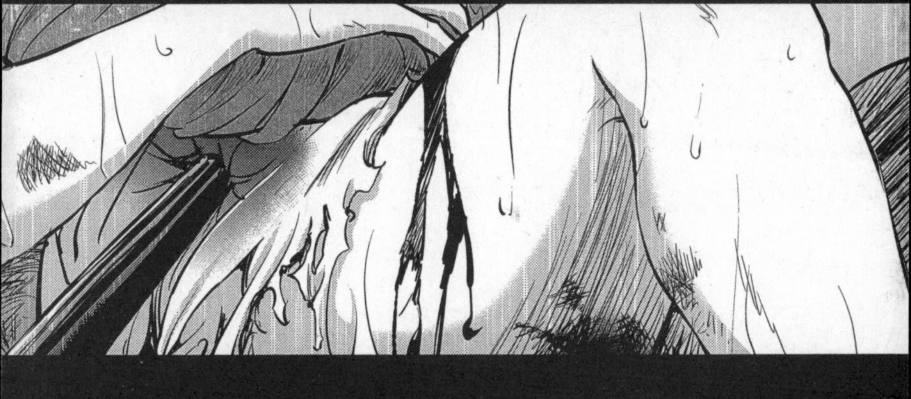

SHE HAD BEEN RUN THROUGH. THE SPEAR OR WHATEVER IT WAS WAS STILL STICKING OUT OF

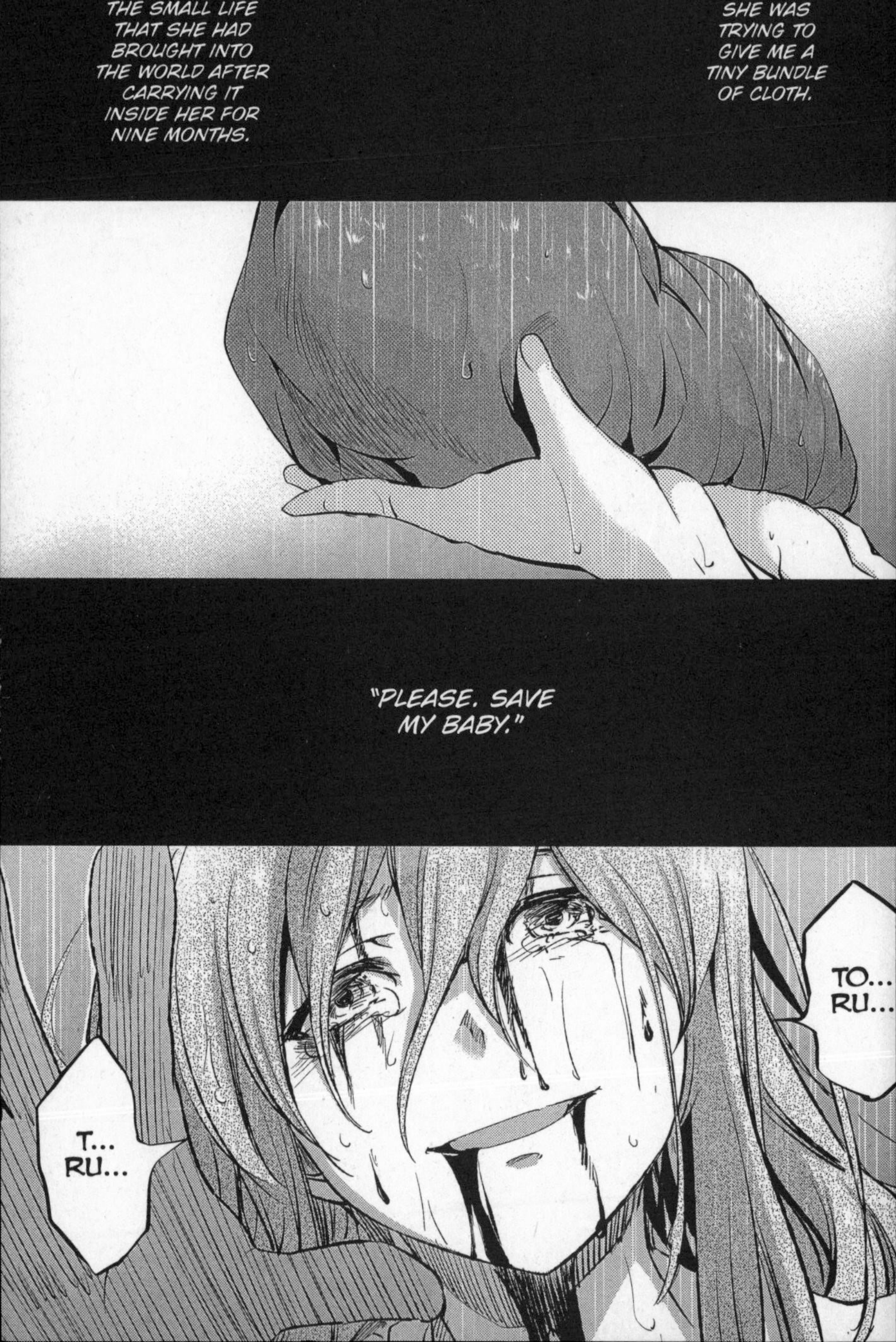
SHE WAS TRYING TO GIVE ME A TINY BUNDLE OF CLOTH.
THE SMALL LIFE THAT SHE HAD BROUGHT INTO THE WORLD AFTER CARRYING IT INSIDE HER FOR NINE MONTHS.
"PLEASE. SAVE MY BABY."
TO... RU...
T... RU...

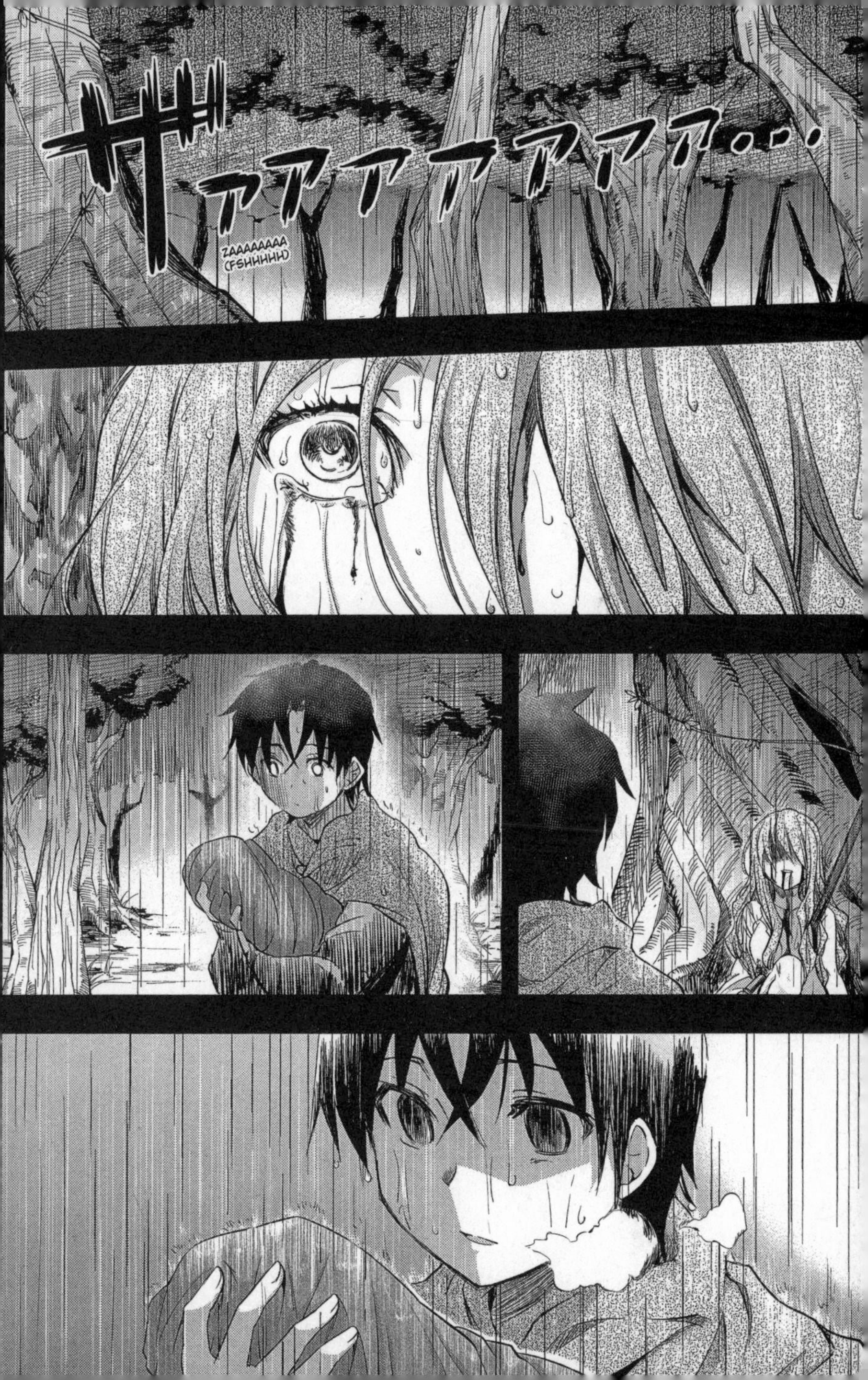
ザァァァァァァァ…
ZAAAAAAAA
(FSHHHHH)

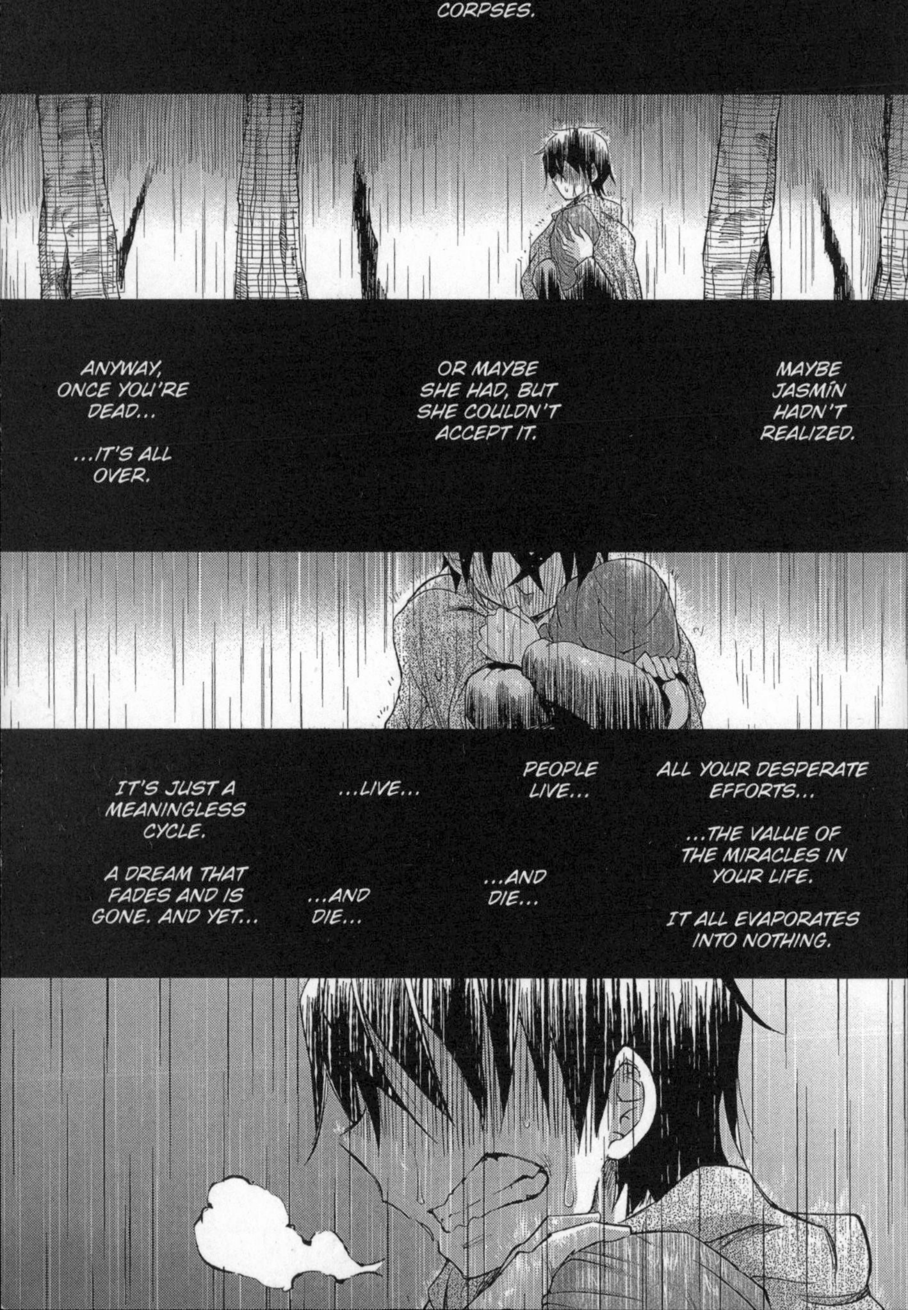
CORPSES.
MAYBE JASMÍN HADN'T REALIZED.
OR MAYBE SHE HAD, BUT SHE COULDN'T ACCEPT IT.
ANYWAY, ONCE YOU'RE DEAD...
...IT'S ALL OVER.
ALL YOUR DESPERATE EFFORTS...
...THE VALUE OF THE MIRACLES IN YOUR LIFE.
IT ALL EVAPORATES INTO NOTHING.
PEOPLE LIVE...
...AND DIE...
...LIVE...
...AND DIE...
IT'S JUST A MEANINGLESS CYCLE.
A DREAM THAT FADES AND IS GONE. AND YET...

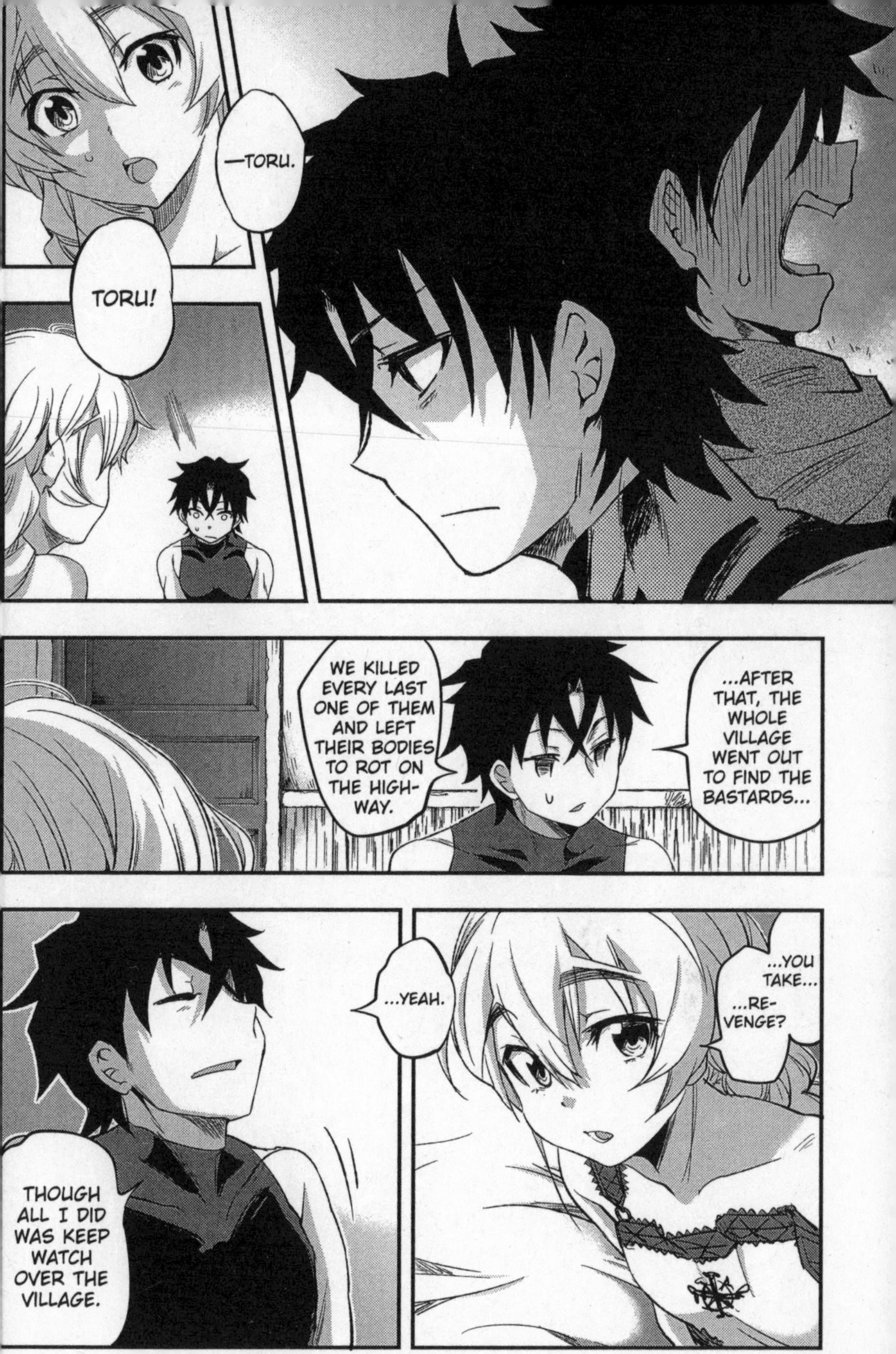
—TORU.
TORU!
...AFTER THAT, THE WHOLE VILLAGE WENT OUT TO FIND THE BASTARDS...
WE KILLED EVERY LAST ONE OF THEM AND LEFT THEIR BODIES TO ROT ON THE HIGH-WAY.
...YOU TAKE... ...RE-VENGE?
...YEAH.
THOUGH ALL I DID WAS KEEP WATCH OVER THE VILLAGE.

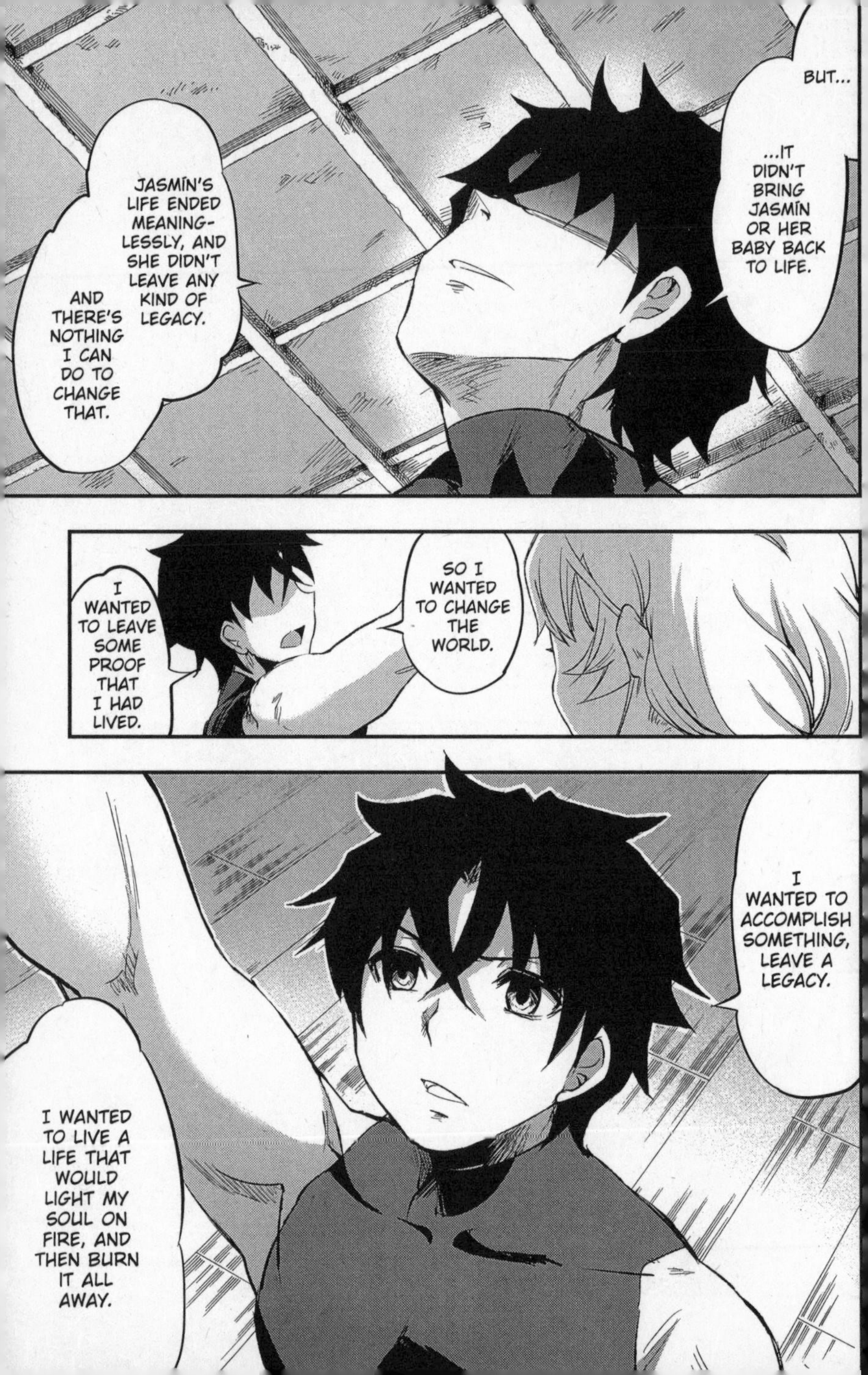
BUT...
...IT DIDN'T BRING JASMÍN OR HER BABY BACK TO LIFE.
JASMÍN'S LIFE ENDED MEANING-LESSLY, AND SHE DIDN'T LEAVE ANY KIND OF LEGACY.
AND THERE'S NOTHING I CAN DO TO CHANGE THAT.
SO I WANTED TO CHANGE THE WORLD.
I WANTED TO LEAVE SOME PROOF THAT I HAD LIVED.
I WANTED TO ACCOMPLISH SOMETHING, LEAVE A LEGACY.
I WANTED TO LIVE A LIFE THAT WOULD LIGHT MY SOUL ON FIRE, AND THEN BURN IT ALL AWAY.

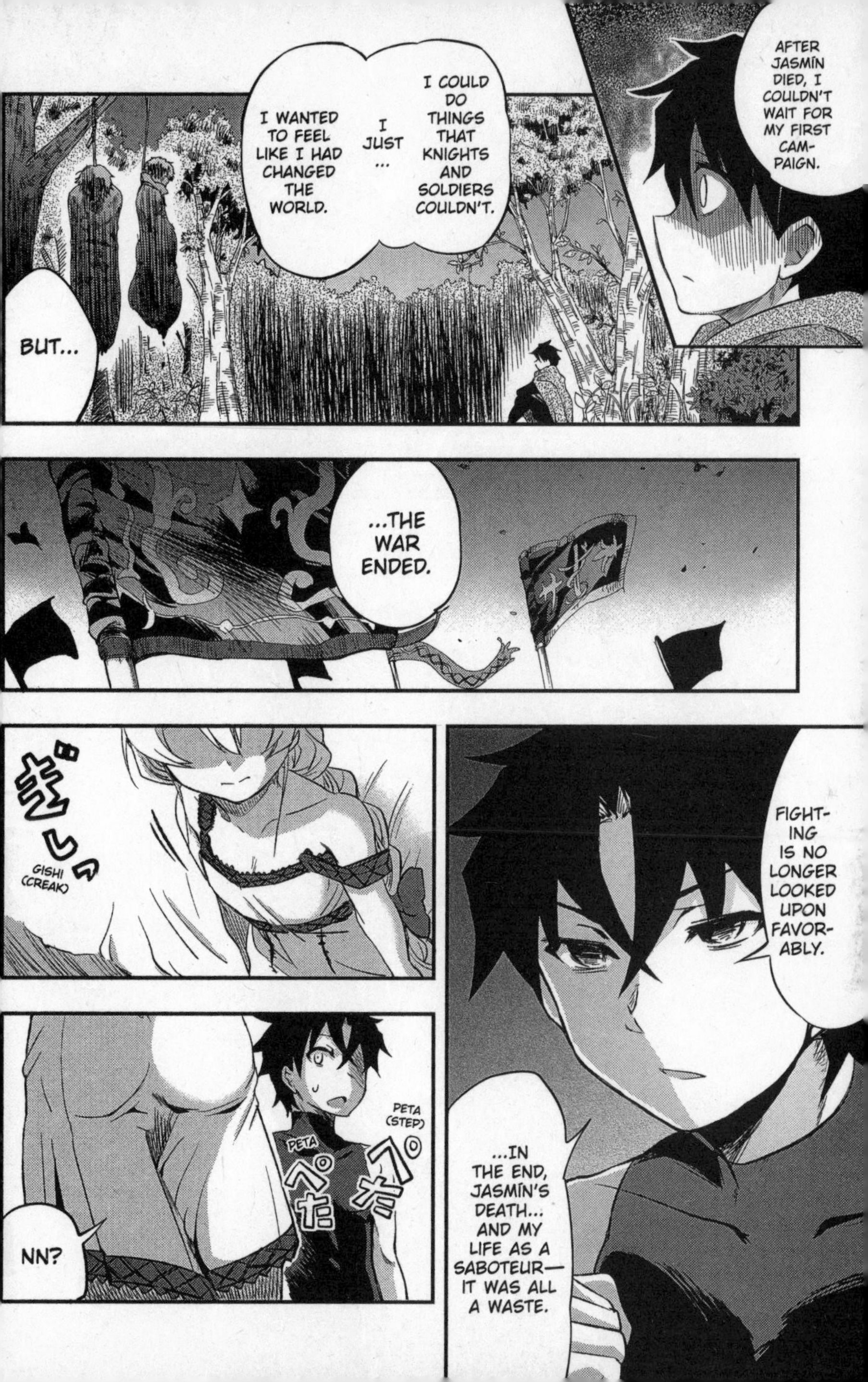
AFTER JASMÍN DIED, I COULDN'T WAIT FOR MY FIRST CAM-PAIGN.
I COULD DO THINGS THAT KNIGHTS AND SOLDIERS COULDN'T.
I JUST ...
I WANTED TO FEEL LIKE I HAD CHANGED THE WORLD.
BUT...
...THE WAR ENDED.
FIGHT-ING IS NO LONGER LOOKED UPON FAVOR-ABLY.
...IN THE END, JASMÍN'S DEATH... AND MY LIFE AS A SABOTEUR—IT WAS ALL A WASTE.
GISHI (CREAK)
PETA (STEP)
PETA
NN?

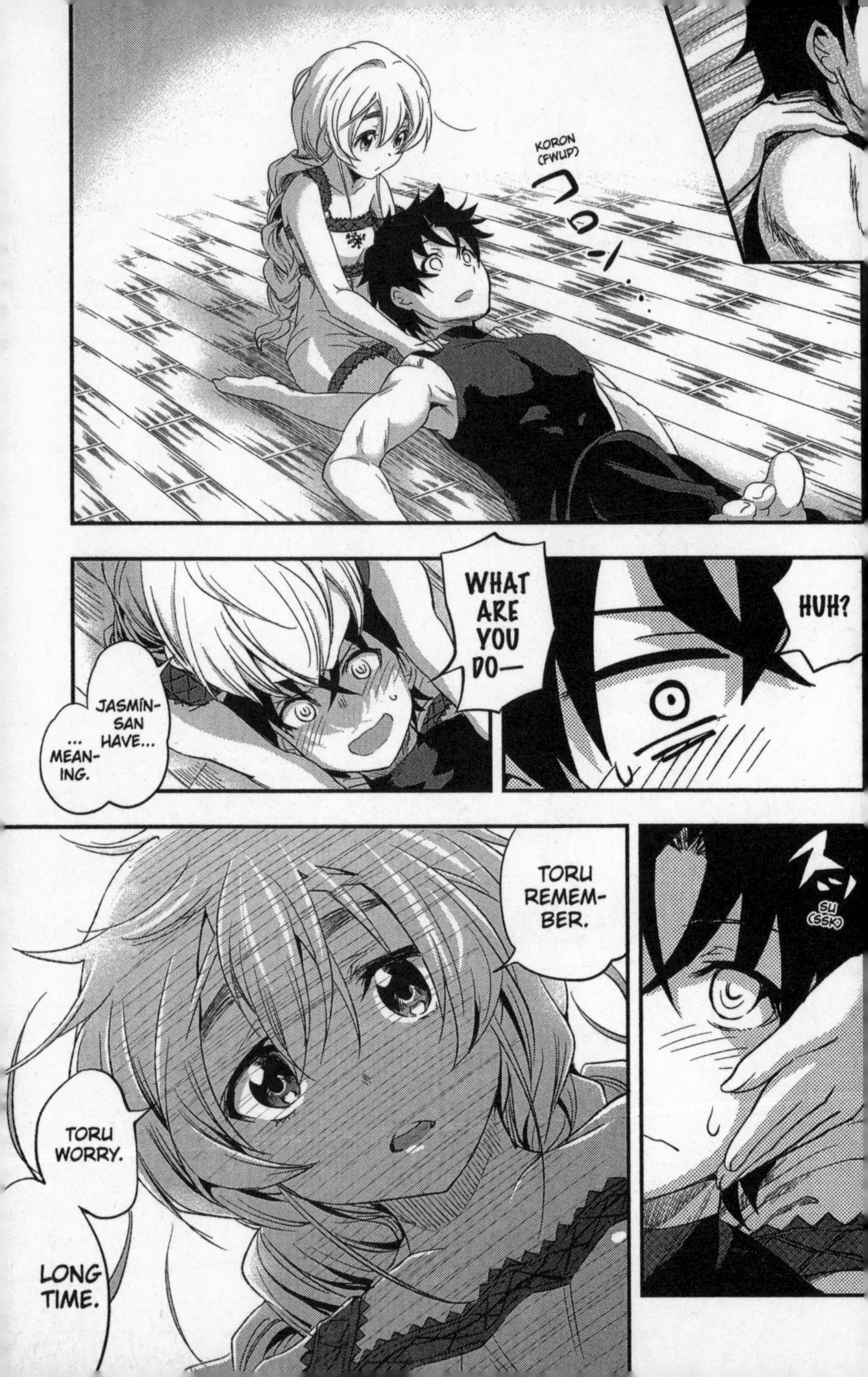
KORON (FWUP)
HUH?
WHAT ARE YOU DO—
JASMÍN-SAN HAVE...
... MEANING.
SU (SSK)
TORU REMEMBER.
TORU WORRY.
LONG TIME.

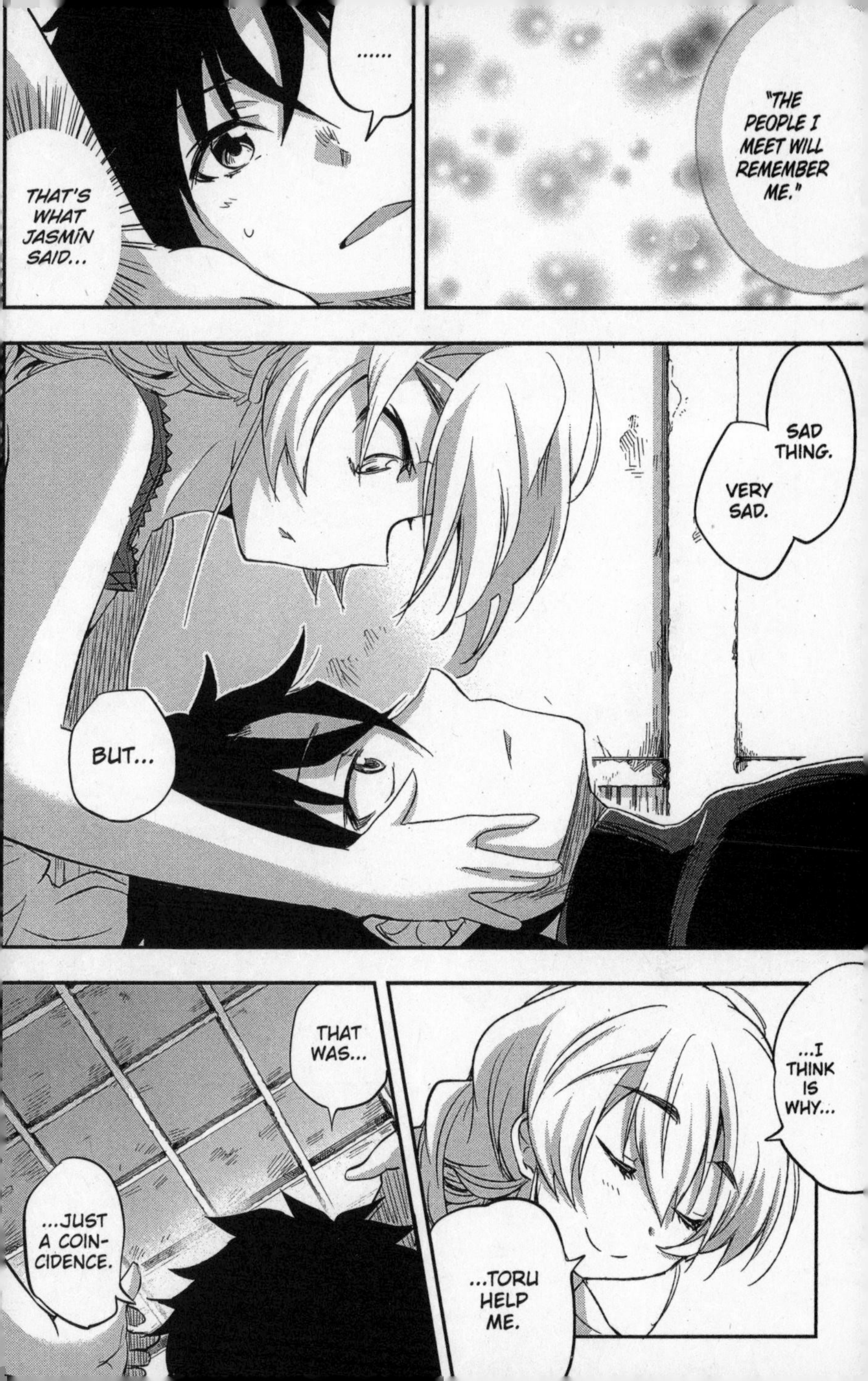
"THE PEOPLE I MEET WILL REMEMBER ME."
......
THAT'S WHAT JASMÍN SAID...
SAD THING.
VERY SAD.
BUT...
...I THINK IS WHY...
...TORU HELP ME.
THAT WAS...
...JUST A COINCIDENCE.

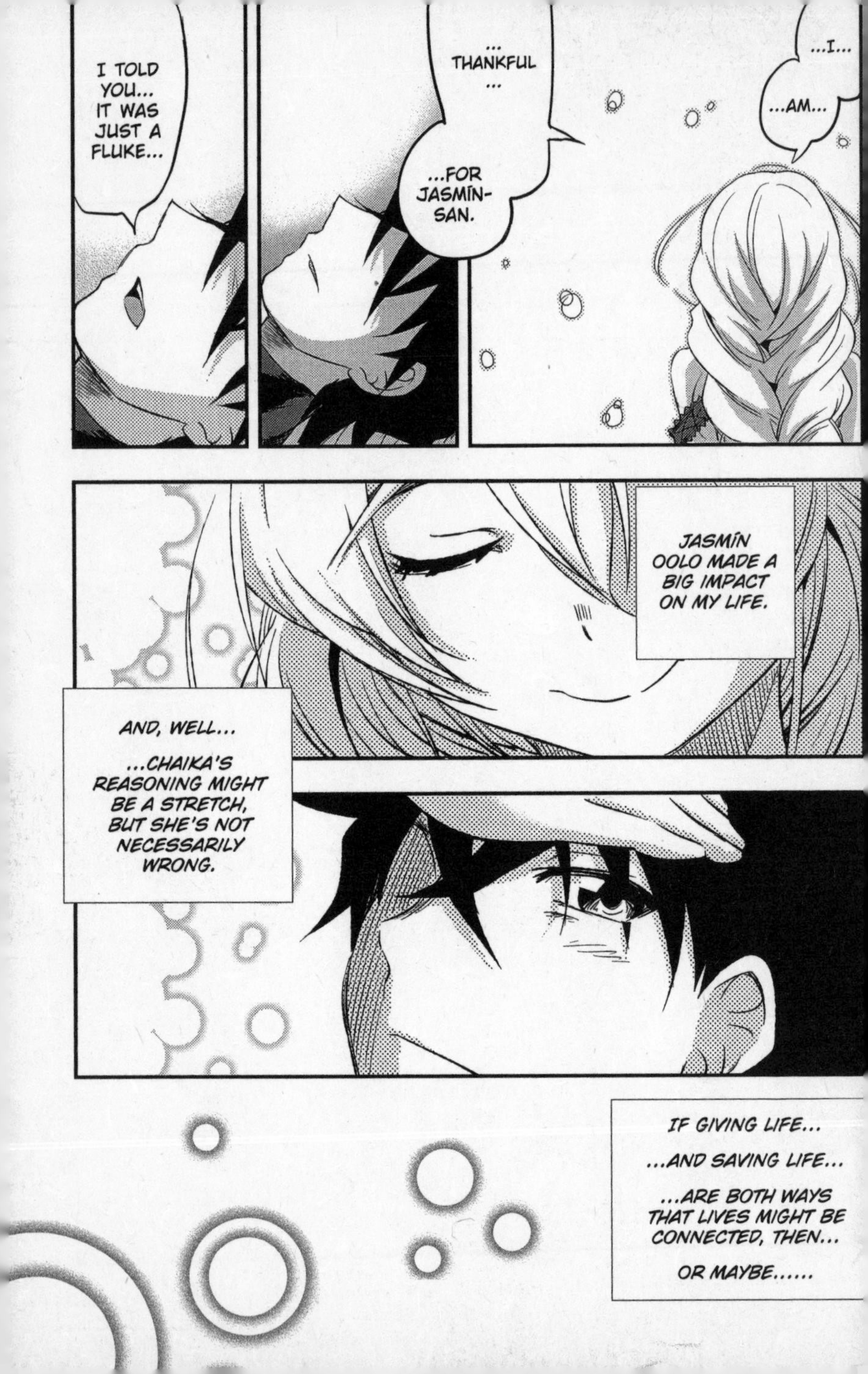
...I...
...AM...
...THANKFUL...
...FOR JASMÍN-SAN.
I TOLD YOU... IT WAS JUST A FLUKE...
JASMÍN OOLO MADE A BIG IMPACT ON MY LIFE.
AND, WELL...
...CHAIKA'S REASONING MIGHT BE A STRETCH, BUT SHE'S NOT NECESSARILY WRONG.
IF GIVING LIFE...
...AND SAVING LIFE...
...ARE BOTH WAYS THAT LIVES MIGHT BE CONNECTED, THEN...
OR MAYBE......

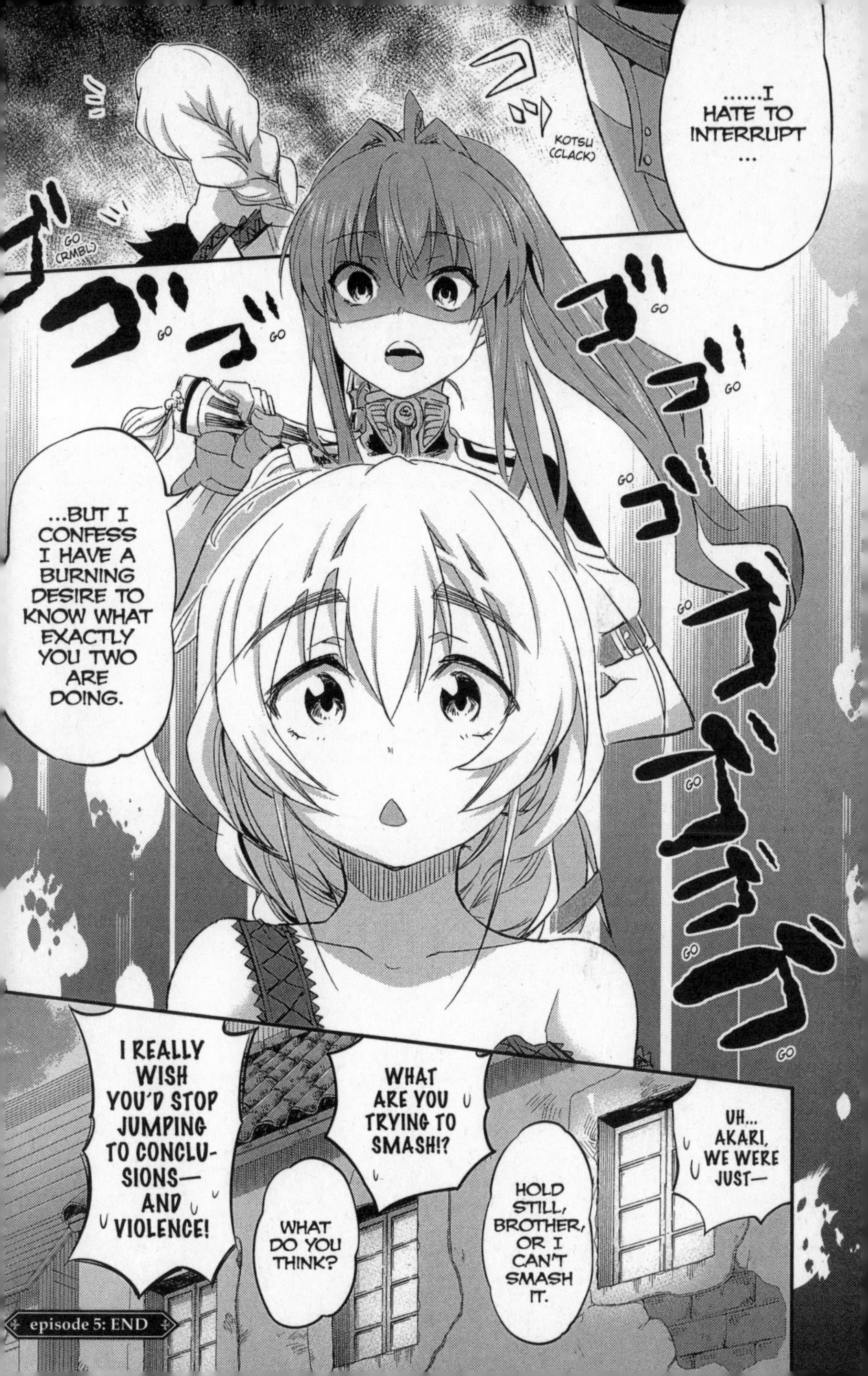
......I HATE TO INTERRUPT ...
KOTSU (CLACK)
GO (RMBL)
GO
GO
GO
GO
GO
GO
GO
GO
...BUT I CONFESS I HAVE A BURNING DESIRE TO KNOW WHAT EXACTLY YOU TWO ARE DOING.
GO
UH... AKARI, WE WERE JUST—
HOLD STILL, BROTHER, OR I CAN'T SMASH IT.
WHAT ARE YOU TRYING TO SMASH!?
WHAT DO YOU THINK?
I REALLY WISH YOU'D STOP JUMPING TO CONCLU-SIONS—AND VIOLENCE!
episode 5: END

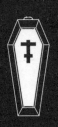

CHAIKA: THE COFFIN PRINCESS

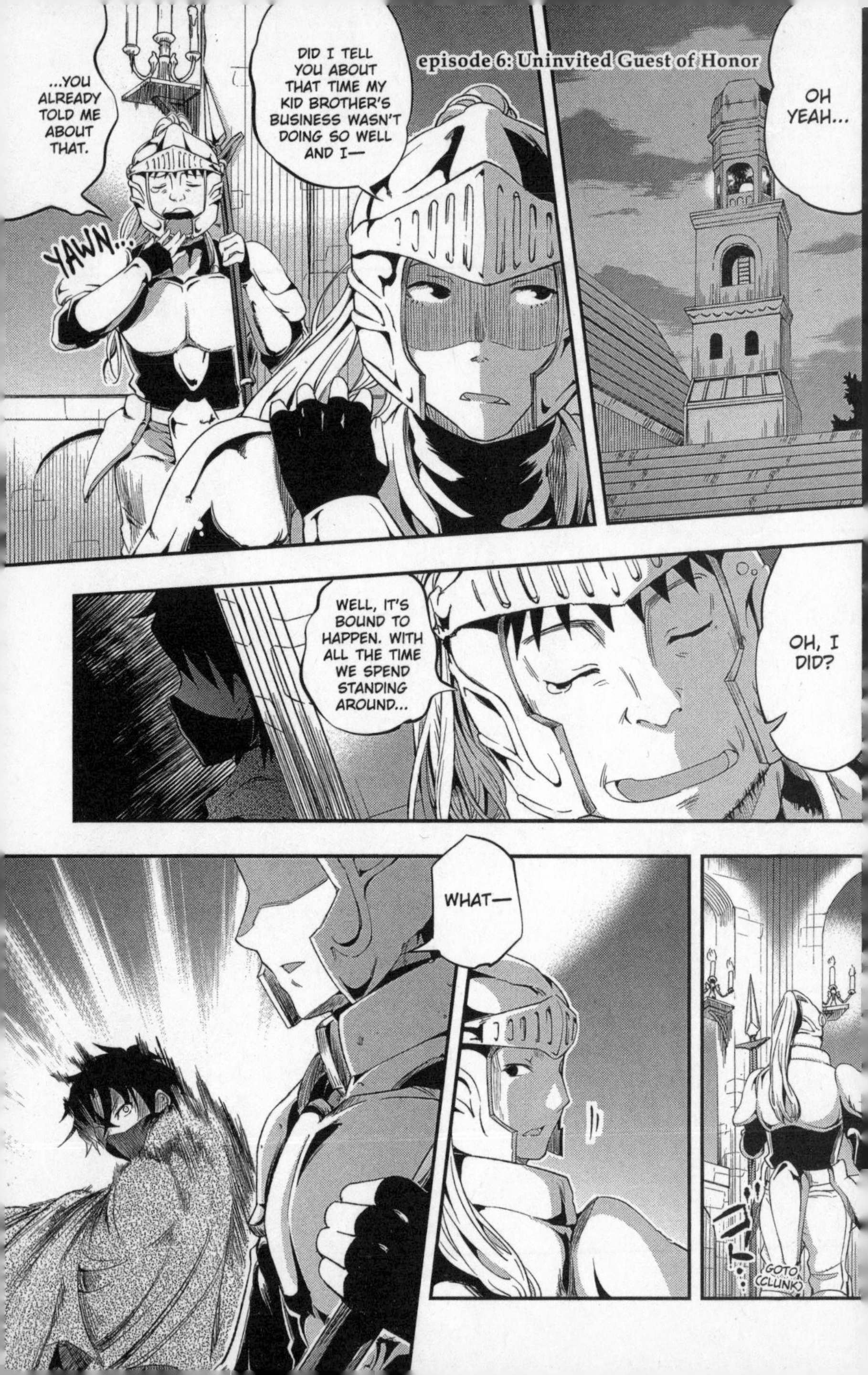
episode 6: Uninvited Guest of Honor
OH YEAH...
DID I TELL YOU ABOUT THAT TIME MY KID BROTHER'S BUSINESS WASN'T DOING SO WELL AND I—
...YOU ALREADY TOLD ME ABOUT THAT.
YAWN...
OH, I DID?
WELL, IT'S BOUND TO HAPPEN. WITH ALL THE TIME WE SPEND STANDING AROUND...
GOTO (CLINK)
WHAT—

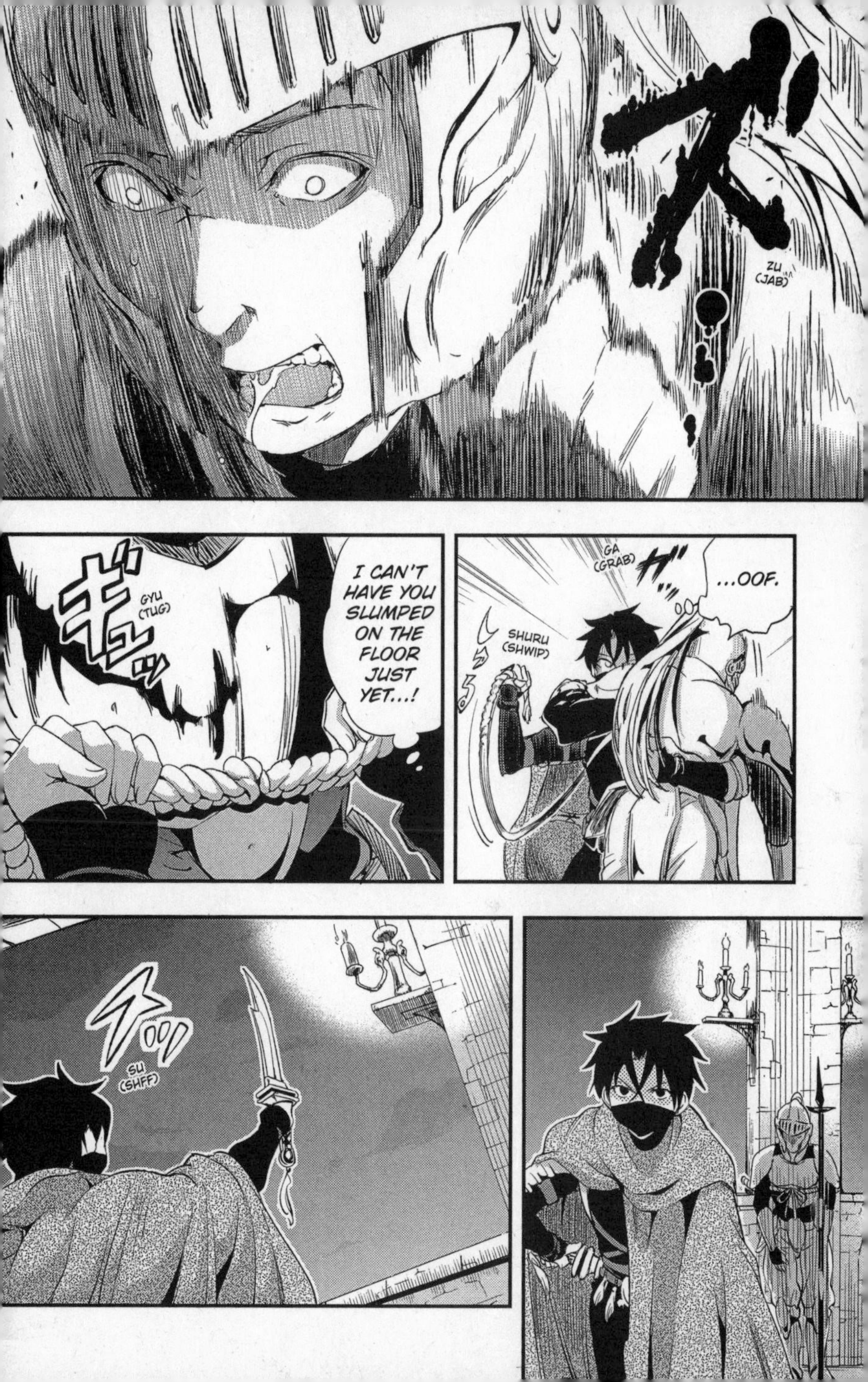
ZU (JAB)
GA (GRAB)
...OOF.
SHURU (SHWIP)
GYU (TUG)
I CAN'T HAVE YOU SLUMPED ON THE FLOOR JUST YET...!
SU (SHFF)

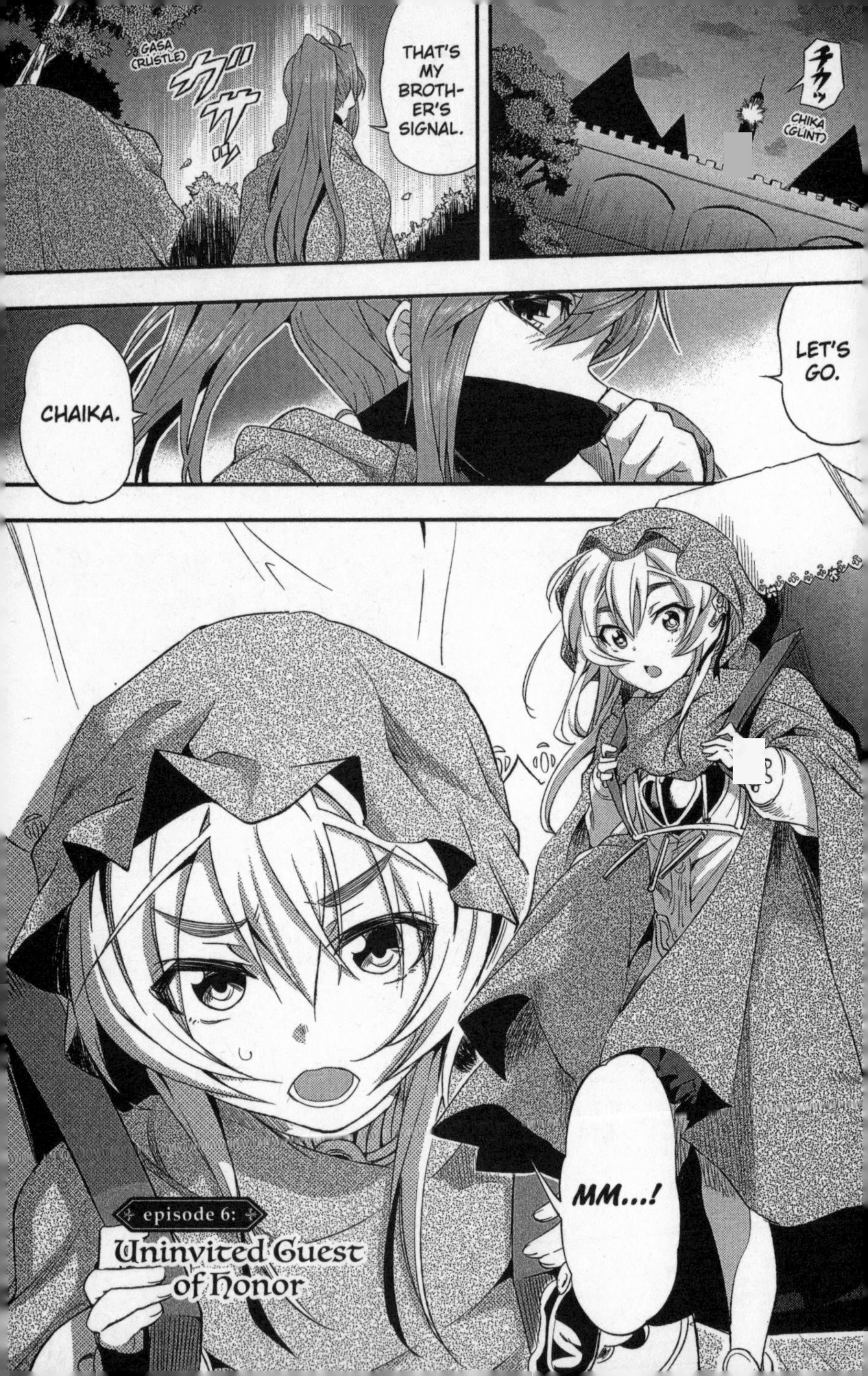

チカッ
CHIKA (GLINT)
ガサッ
GASA (RUSTLE)
THAT'S MY BROTHER'S SIGNAL.
LET'S GO.
CHAIKA.
MM...!
episode 6:
Uninvited Guest of Honor

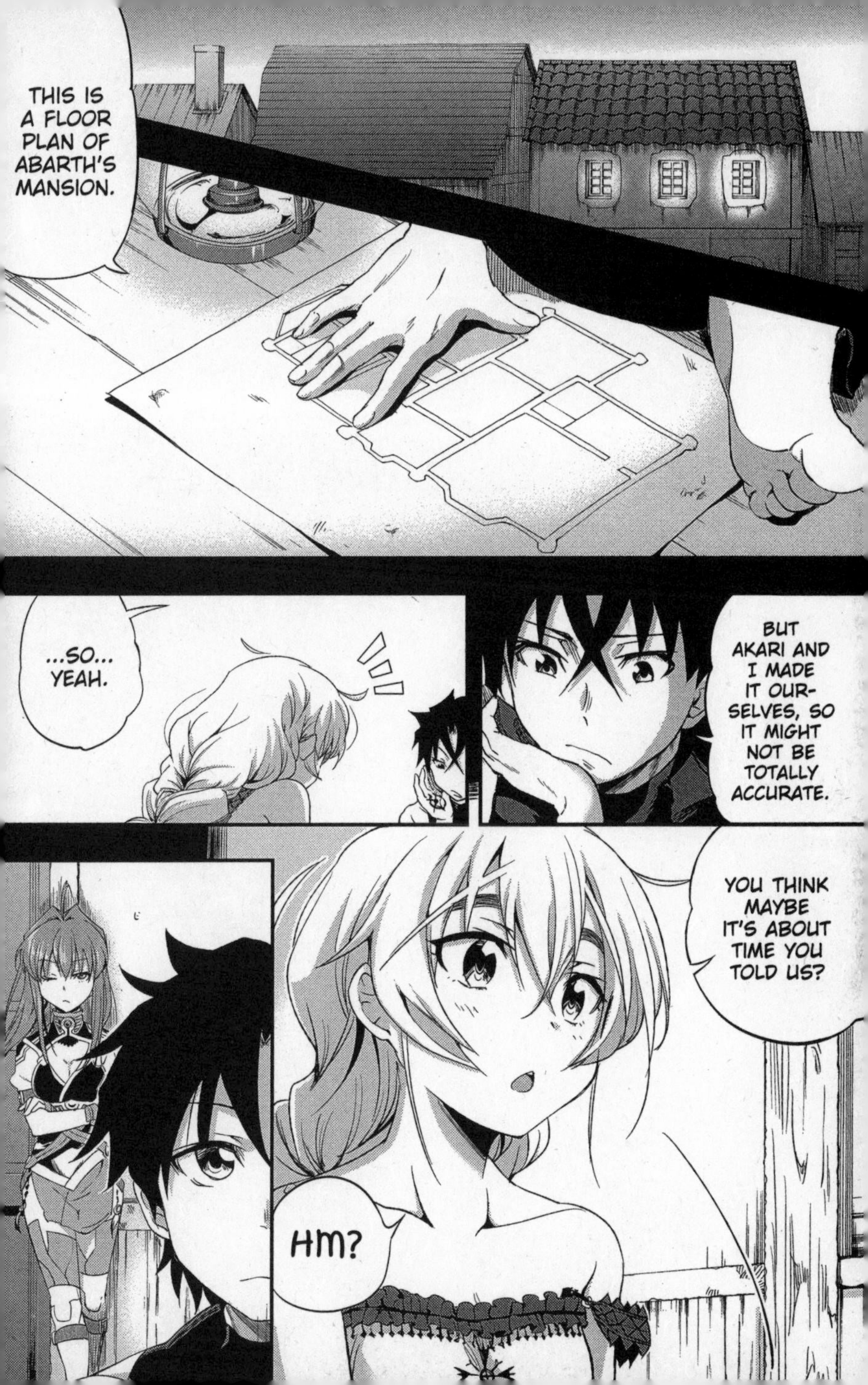
THIS IS A FLOOR PLAN OF ABARTH'S MANSION.
BUT AKARI AND I MADE IT OUR-SELVES, SO IT MIGHT NOT BE TOTALLY ACCURATE.
...SO... YEAH.
YOU THINK MAYBE IT'S ABOUT TIME YOU TOLD US?
HM?

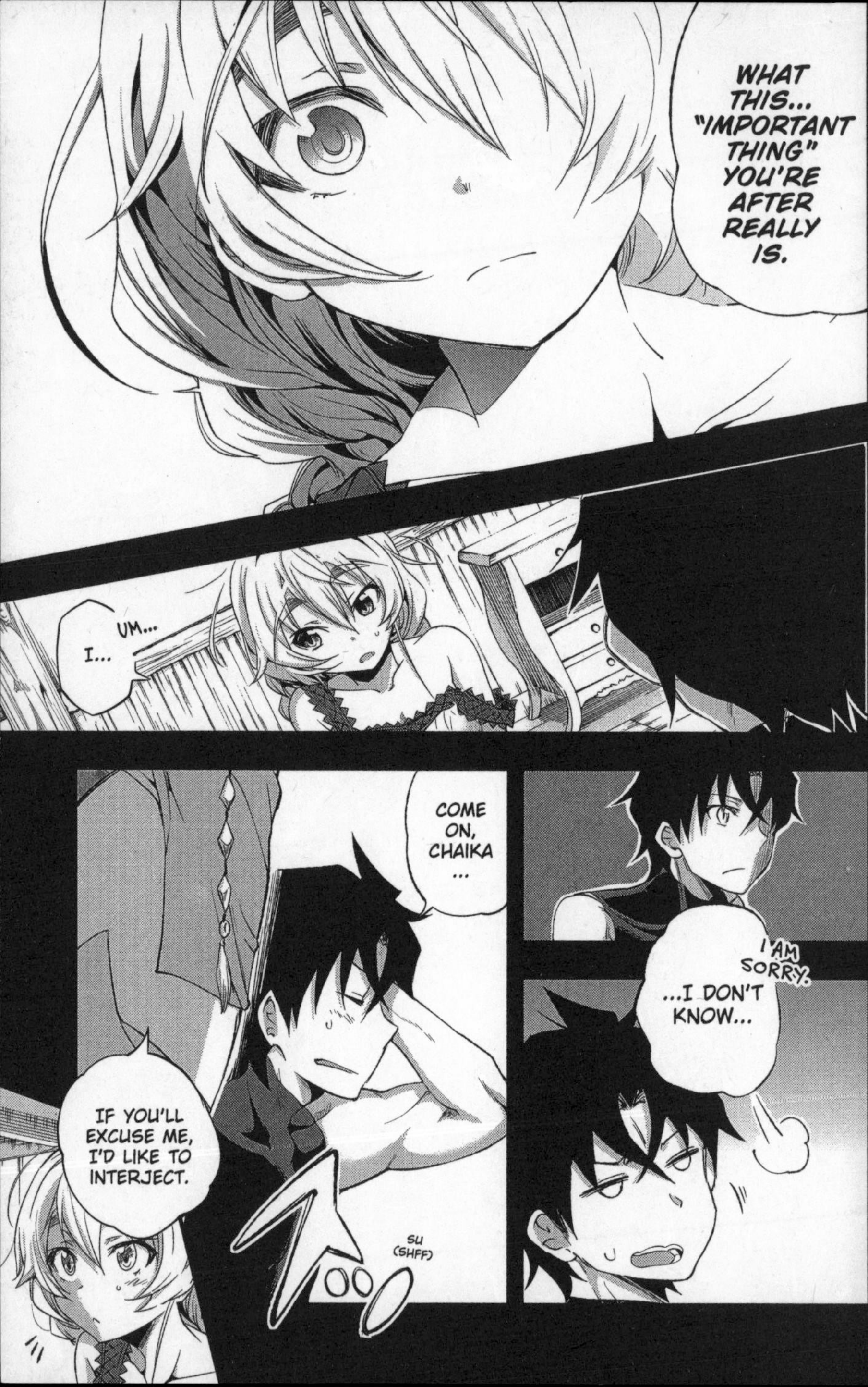
WHAT THIS... "IMPORTANT THING" YOU'RE AFTER REALLY IS.
UM... I...
I AM SORRY.
...I DON'T KNOW...
COME ON, CHAIKA ...
IF YOU'LL EXCUSE ME, I'D LIKE TO INTERJECT.
SU (SHFF)

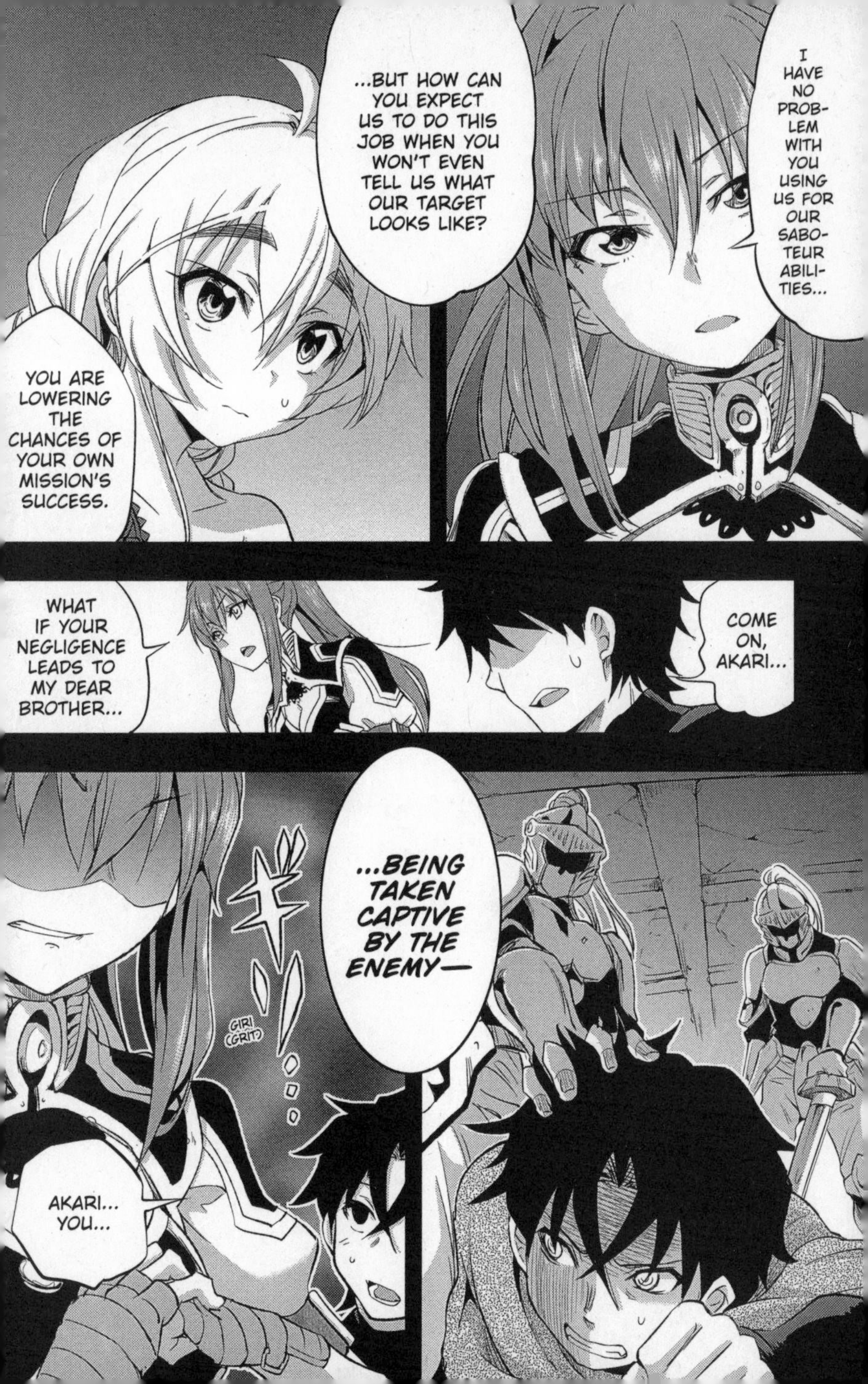
I HAVE NO PROBLEM WITH YOU USING US FOR OUR SABOTEUR ABILITIES...
...BUT HOW CAN YOU EXPECT US TO DO THIS JOB WHEN YOU WON'T EVEN TELL US WHAT OUR TARGET LOOKS LIKE?
YOU ARE LOWERING THE CHANCES OF YOUR OWN MISSION'S SUCCESS.
COME ON, AKARI...
WHAT IF YOUR NEGLIGENCE LEADS TO MY DEAR BROTHER...
...BEING TAKEN CAPTIVE BY THE ENEMY—
GIRI (GRIT)
AKARI... YOU...

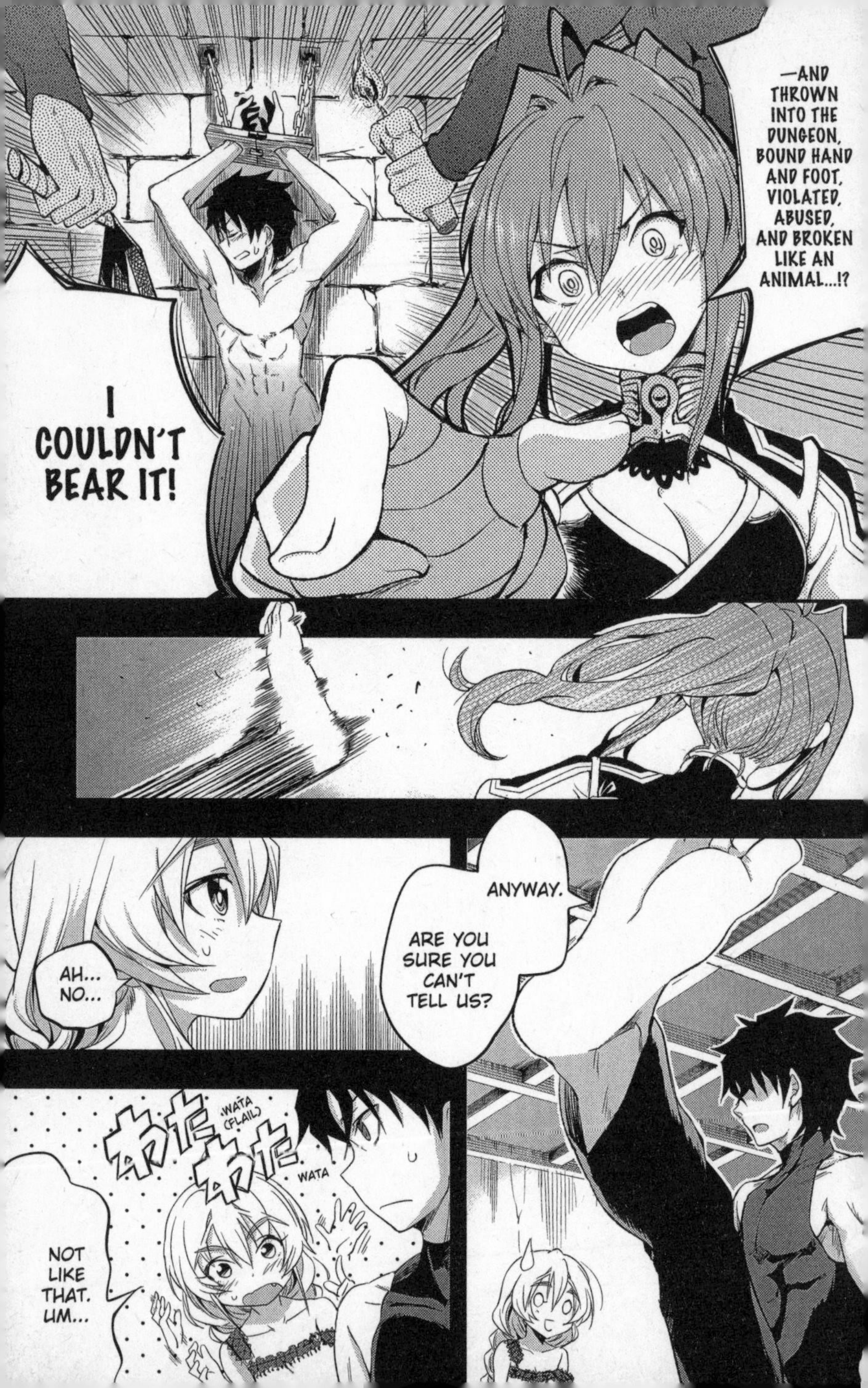
—AND THROWN INTO THE DUNGEON, BOUND HAND AND FOOT, VIOLATED, ABUSED, AND BROKEN LIKE AN ANIMAL...!?
I COULDN'T BEAR IT!
ANYWAY.
ARE YOU SURE YOU CAN'T TELL US?
AH... NO...
わた
WATA (FLAIL)
わた
WATA
NOT LIKE THAT. UM...

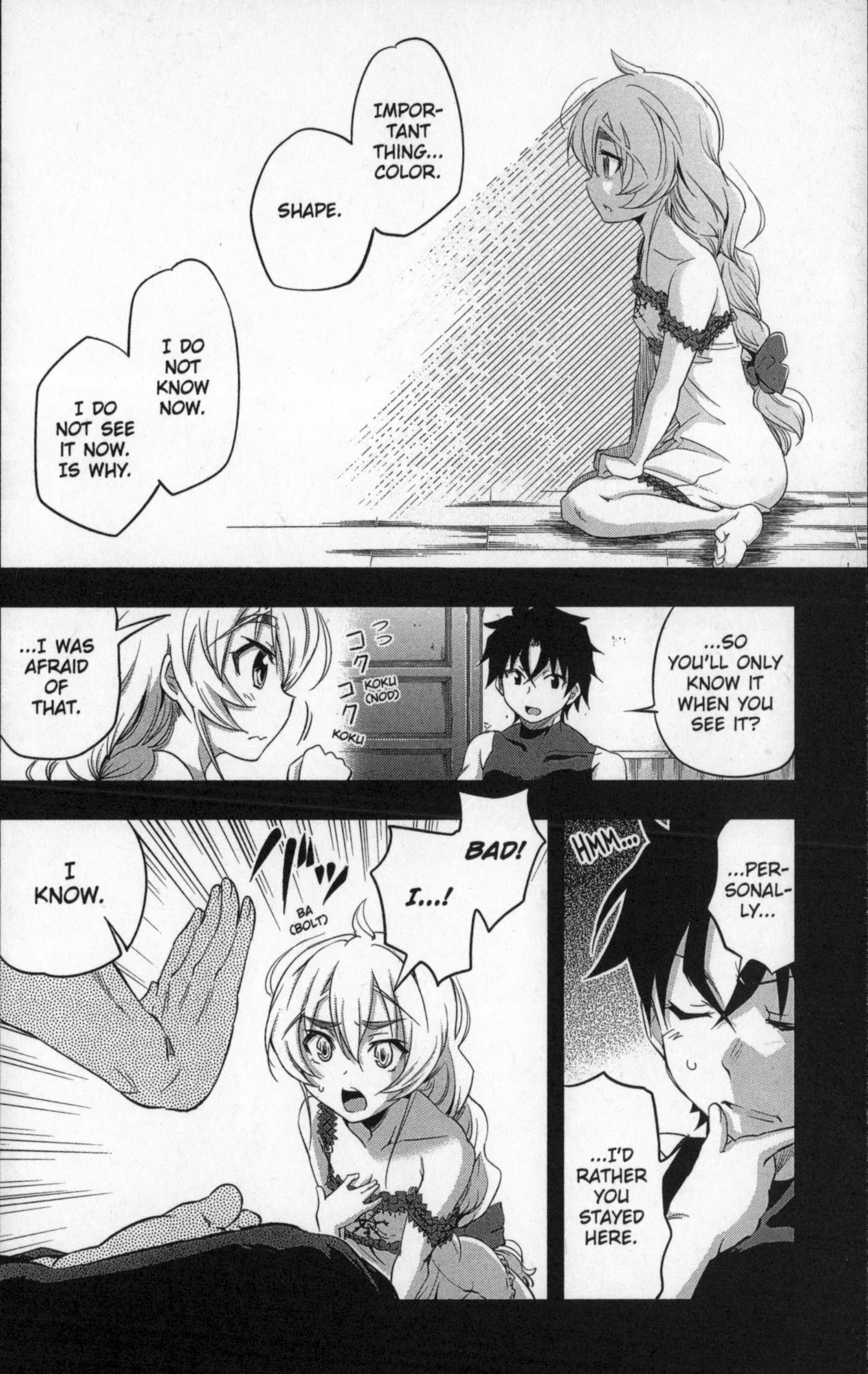
IMPORTANT THING... COLOR.
SHAPE.
I DO NOT KNOW NOW.
I DO NOT SEE IT NOW. IS WHY.
...SO YOU'LL ONLY KNOW IT WHEN YOU SEE IT?
KOKU (NOD)
KOKU
...I WAS AFRAID OF THAT.
HMM...
...PERSONALLY...
...I'D RATHER YOU STAYED HERE.
BAD!
I...!
BA (BOLT)
I KNOW.

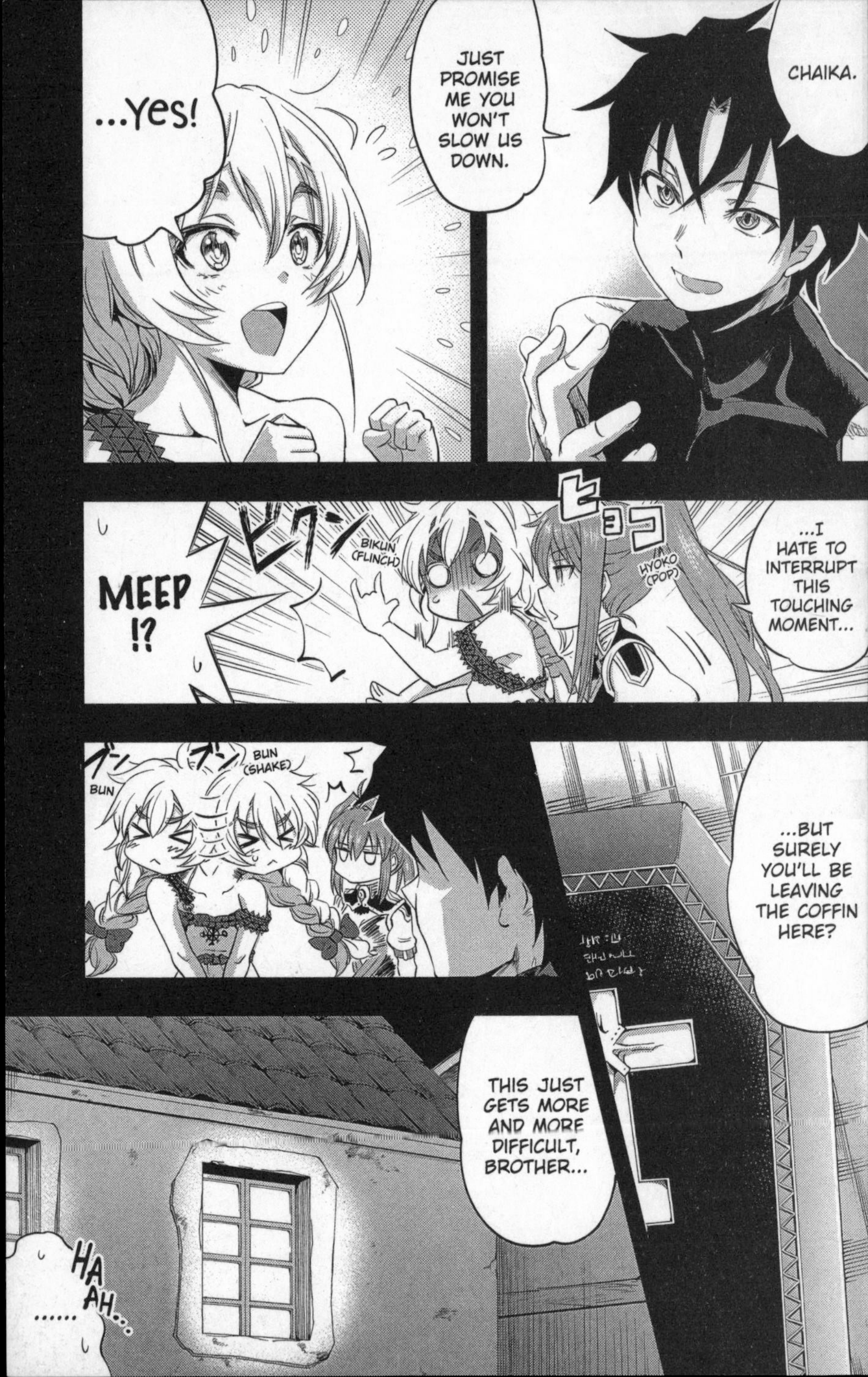
CHAIKA.
JUST PROMISE ME YOU WON'T SLOW US DOWN.
...Yes!
...I HATE TO INTERRUPT THIS TOUCHING MOMENT...
HYOKO (POP)
BIKUN (FLINCH)
MEEP !?
...BUT SURELY YOU'LL BE LEAVING THE COFFIN HERE?
BUN (SHAKE)
BUN
THIS JUST GETS MORE AND MORE DIFFICULT, BROTHER...
HAAAH...
......

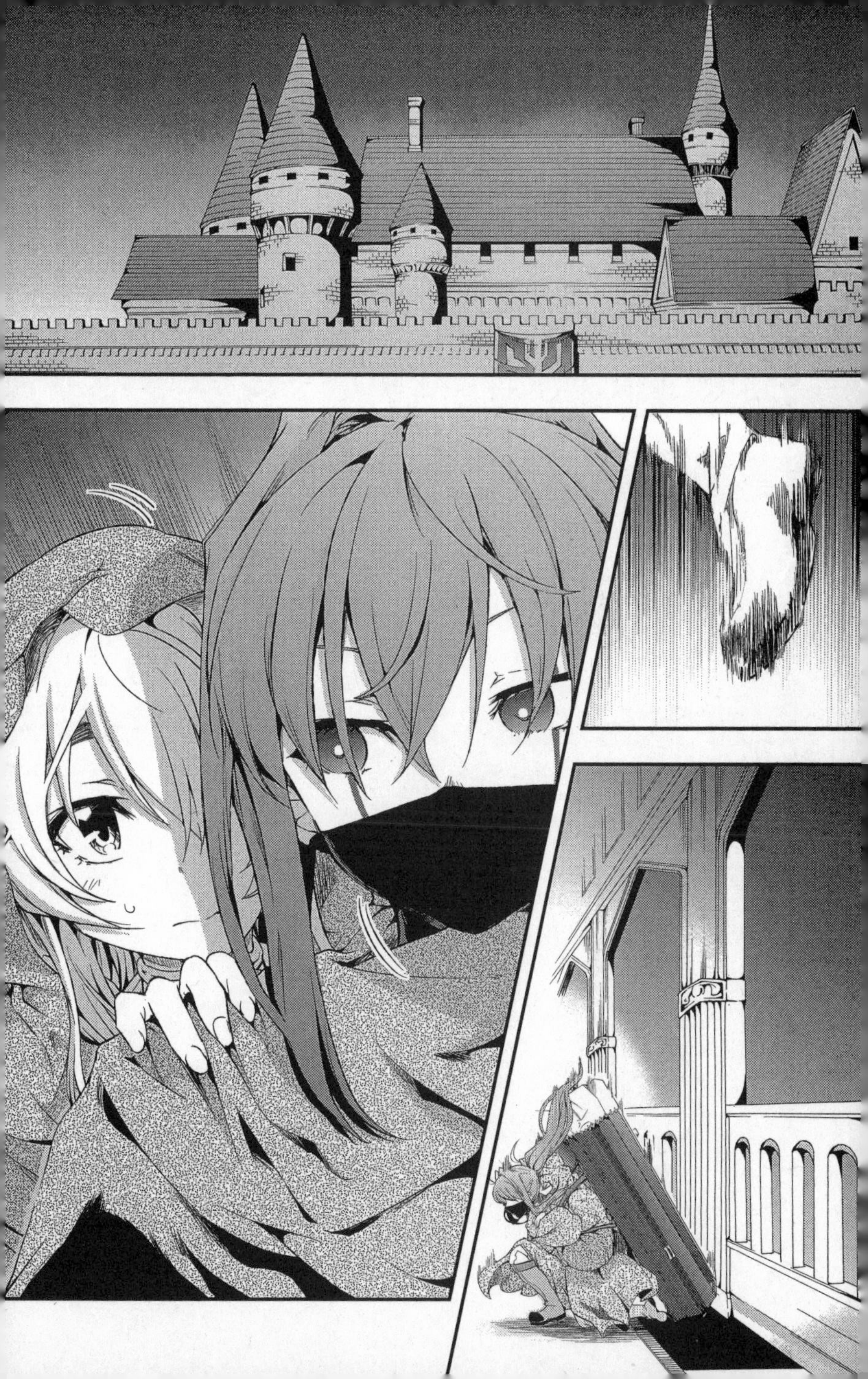

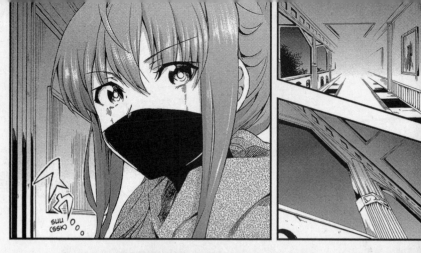

SUU
(SSK)

...IT'S AWFULLY QUIET.

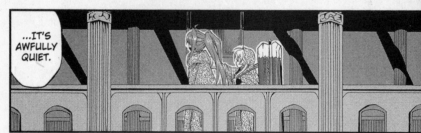

I CAST SPELL. SHORT TIME BUT WORKS.

"THE SUCKER."

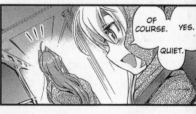

OF COURSE. YES. QUIET.

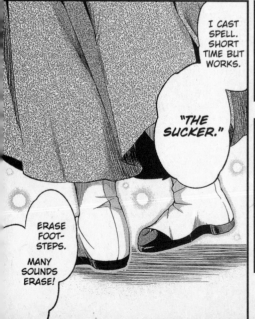

ERASE FOOT-STEPS.

MANY SOUNDS ERASE!

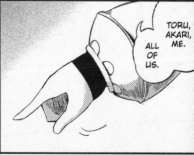

TORU, AKARI, ME.

ALL OF US.

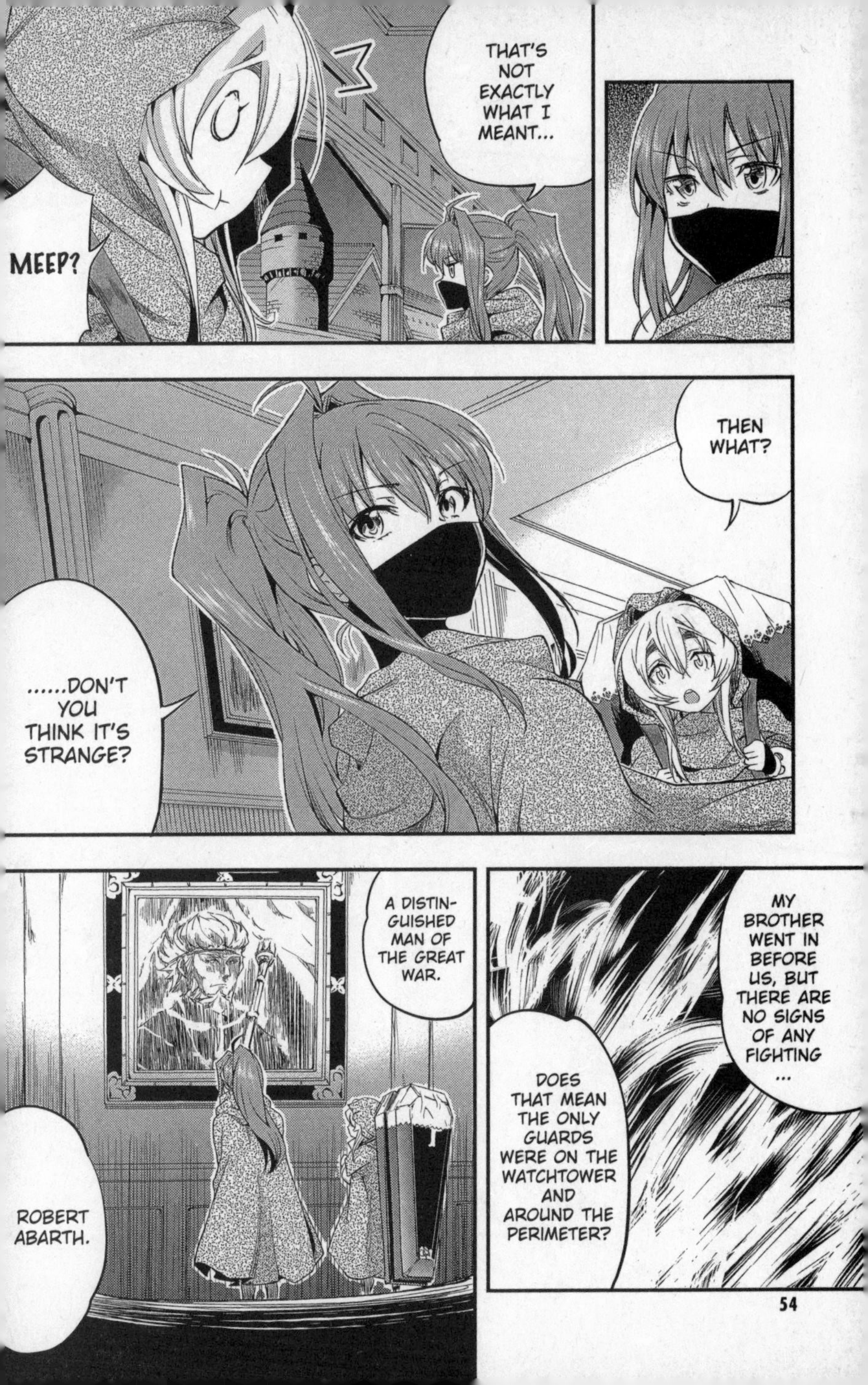
THAT'S NOT EXACTLY WHAT I MEANT...
MEEP?
THEN WHAT?
......DON'T YOU THINK IT'S STRANGE?
MY BROTHER WENT IN BEFORE US, BUT THERE ARE NO SIGNS OF ANY FIGHTING ...
DOES THAT MEAN THE ONLY GUARDS WERE ON THE WATCHTOWER AND AROUND THE PERIMETER?
A DISTIN-GUISHED MAN OF THE GREAT WAR.
ROBERT ABARTH.

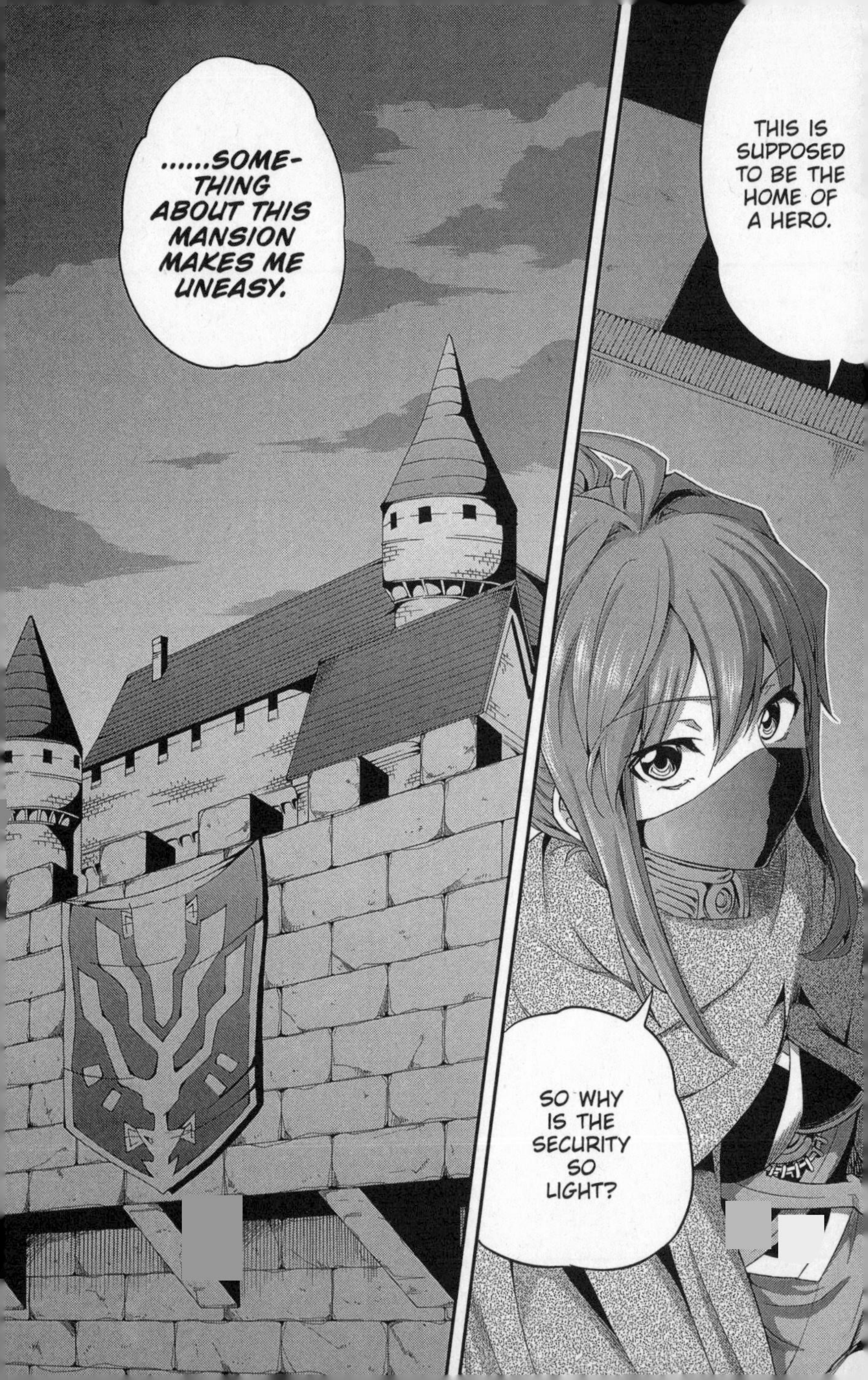
THIS IS SUPPOSED TO BE THE HOME OF A HERO.
SO WHY IS THE SECURITY SO LIGHT?
......SOME-THING ABOUT THIS MANSION MAKES ME UNEASY.

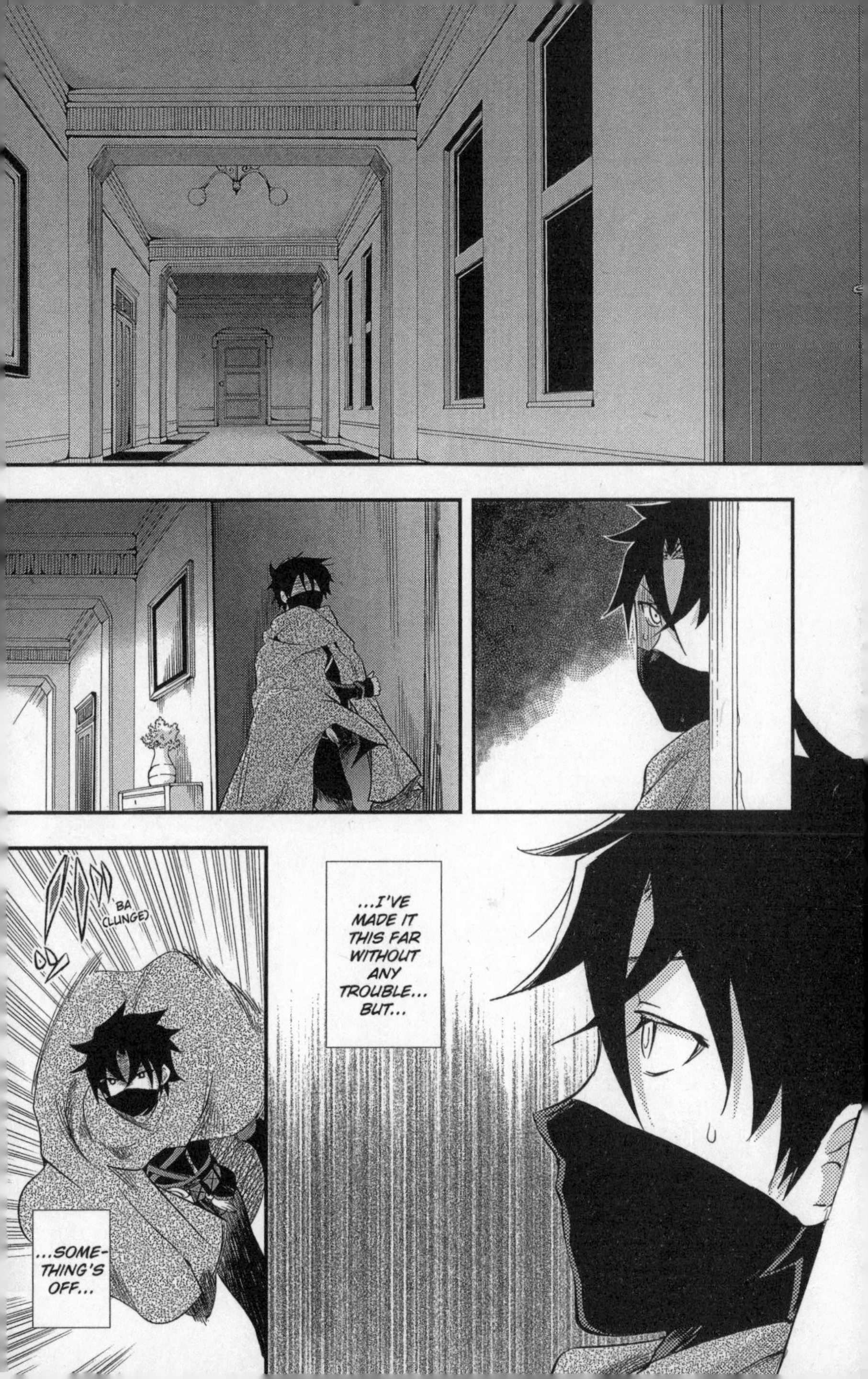
...I'VE MADE IT THIS FAR WITHOUT ANY TROUBLE... BUT...
BA (LUNGE)
...SOME-THING'S OFF...

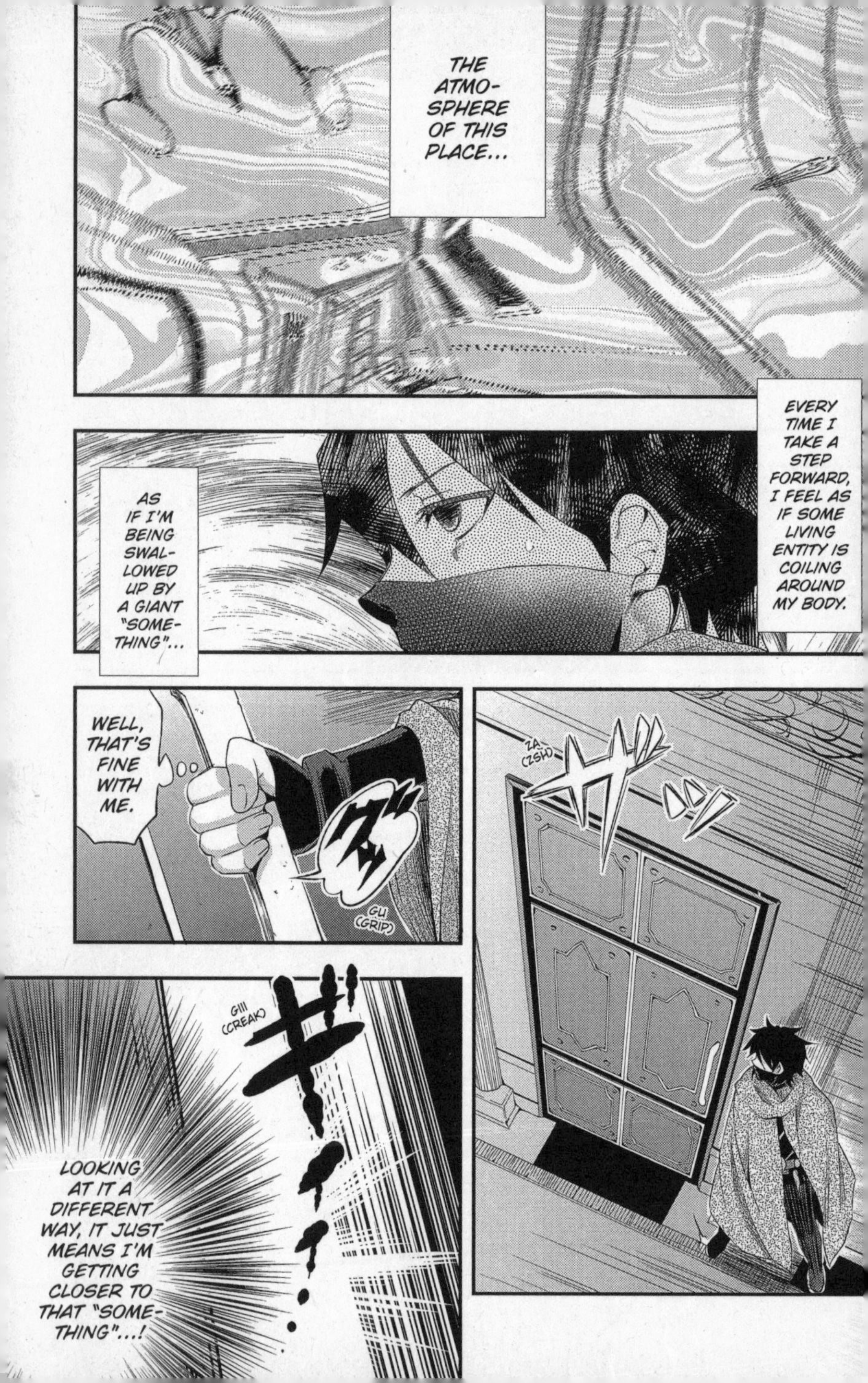
THE ATMOSPHERE OF THIS PLACE...
EVERY TIME I TAKE A STEP FORWARD, I FEEL AS IF SOME LIVING ENTITY IS COILING AROUND MY BODY.
AS IF I'M BEING SWALLOWED UP BY A GIANT "SOMETHING"...
ZA (ZSH)
WELL, THAT'S FINE WITH ME.
GU (GRIP)
GIII (CREAK)
LOOKING AT IT A DIFFERENT WAY, IT JUST MEANS I'M GETTING CLOSER TO THAT "SOMETHING"...!

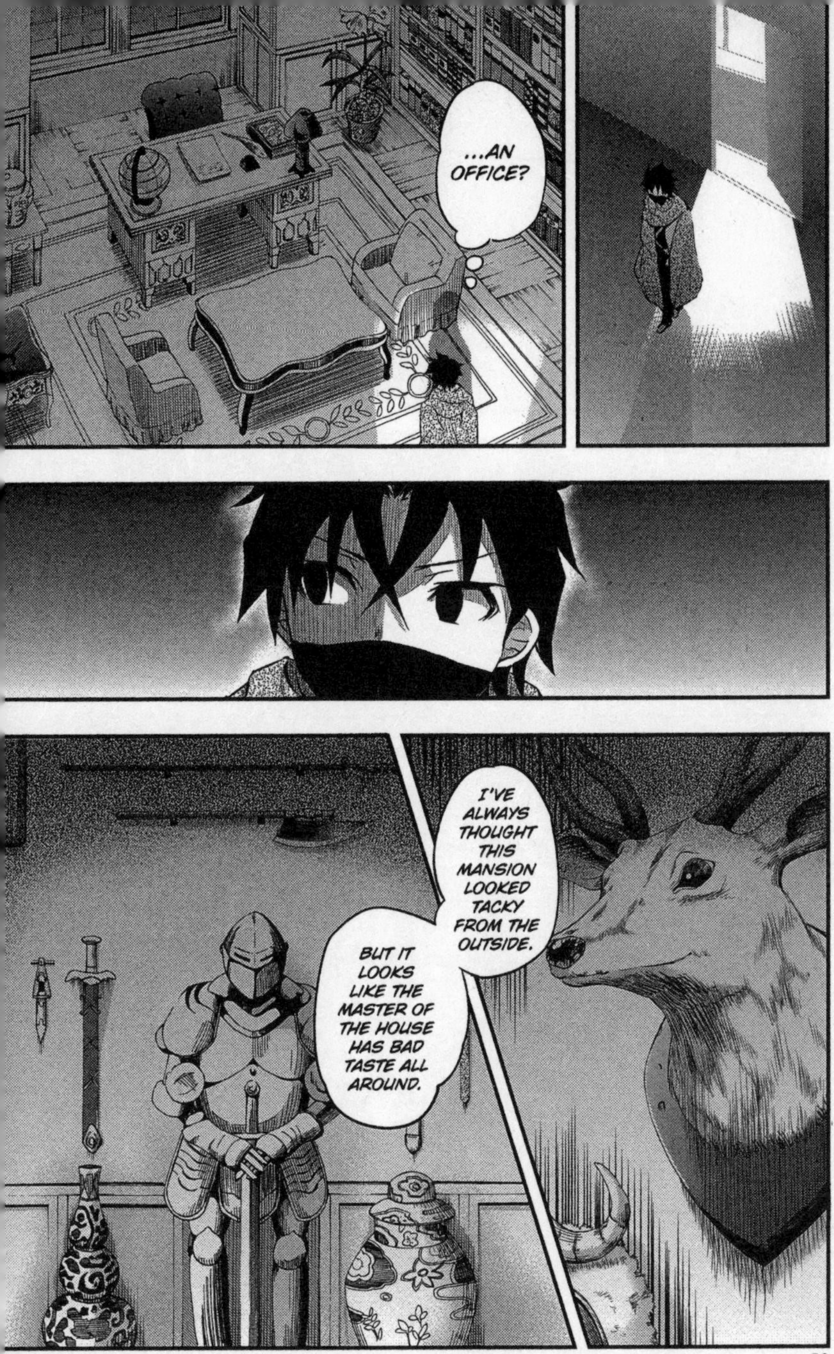
...AN OFFICE?
I'VE ALWAYS THOUGHT THIS MANSION LOOKED TACKY FROM THE OUTSIDE.
BUT IT LOOKS LIKE THE MASTER OF THE HOUSE HAS BAD TASTE ALL AROUND.

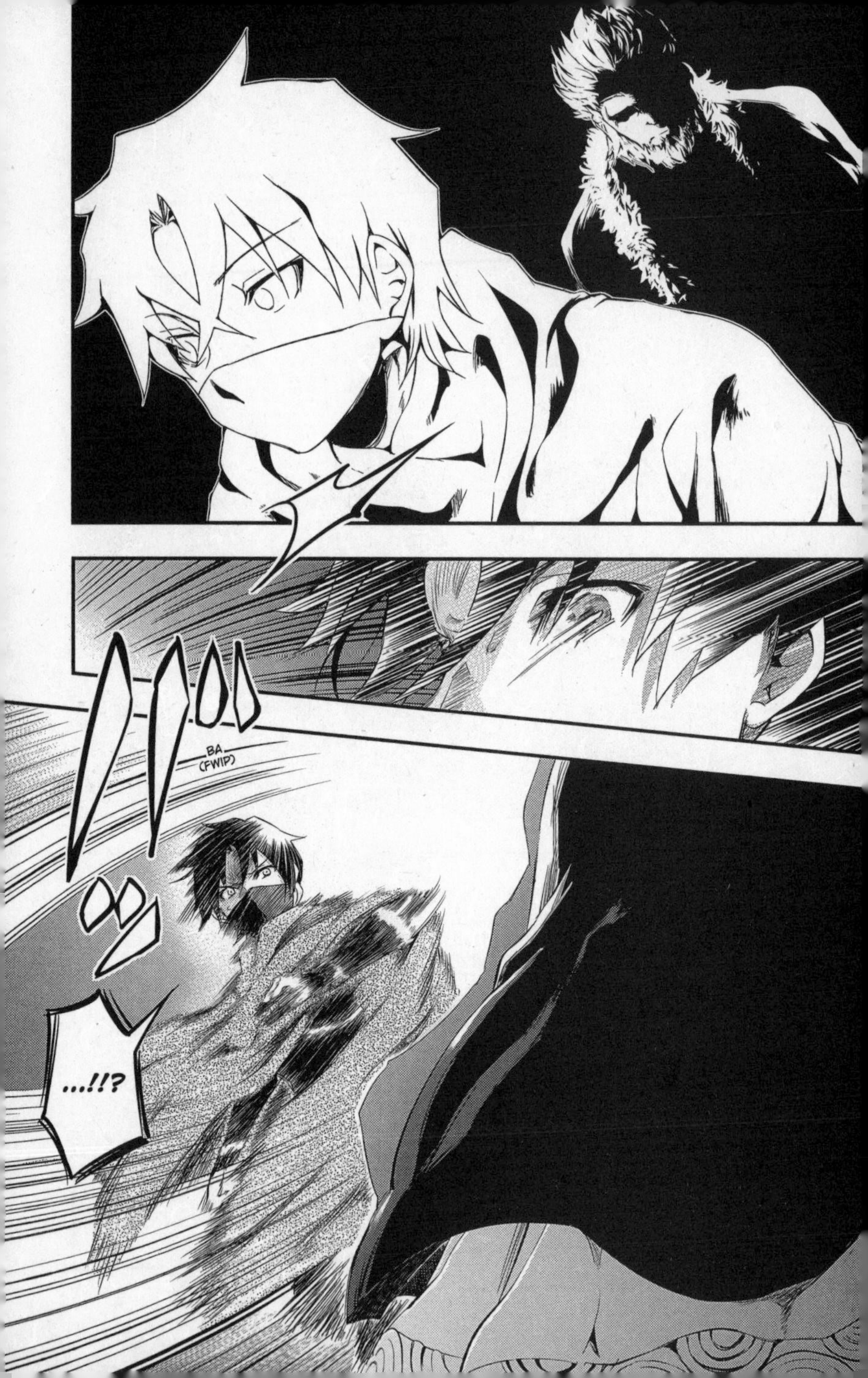
BA
(FWIP)
...!!?

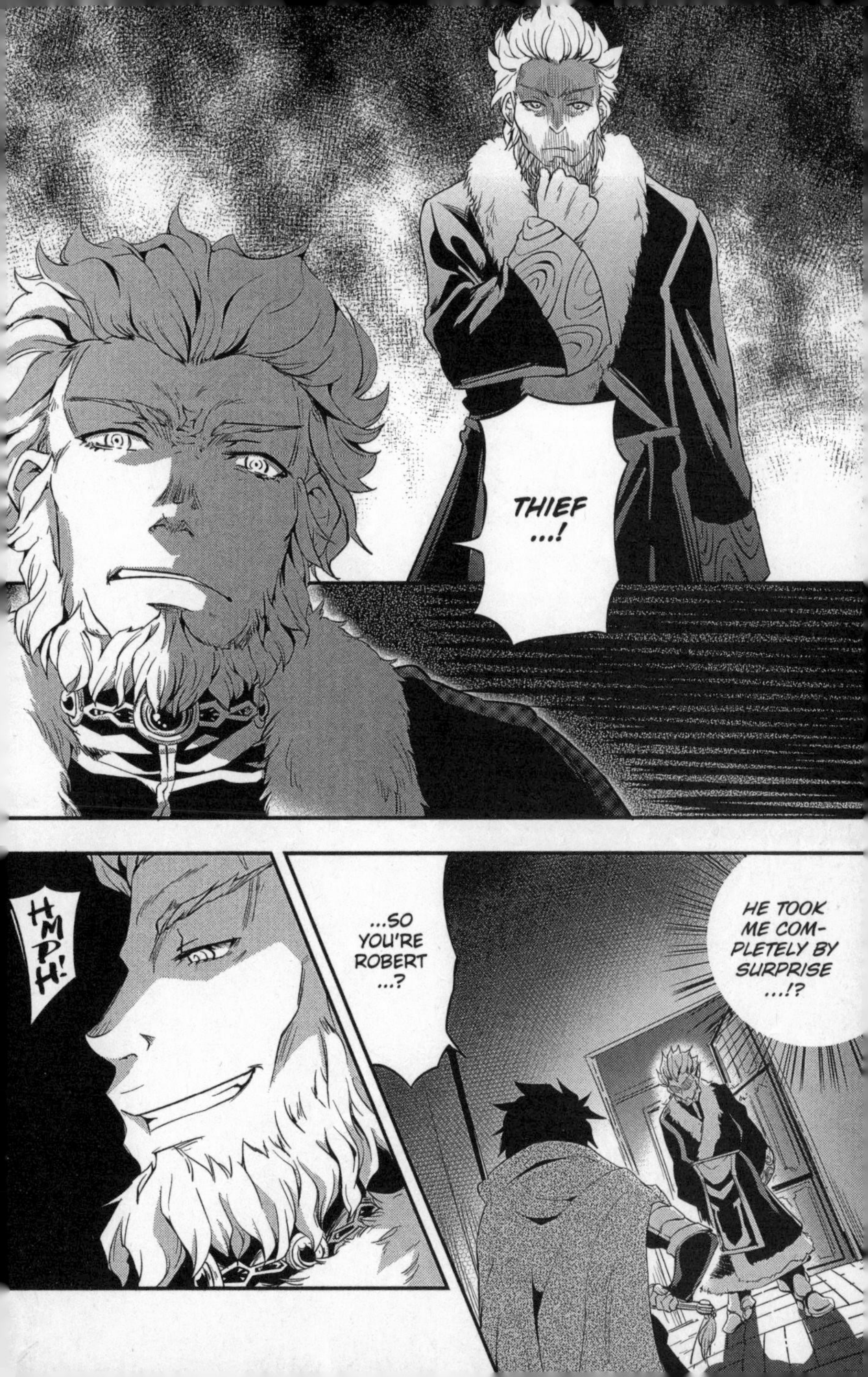
THIEF ...!
HE TOOK ME COMPLETELY BY SURPRISE ...!?
...SO YOU'RE ROBERT ...?
HMPH!

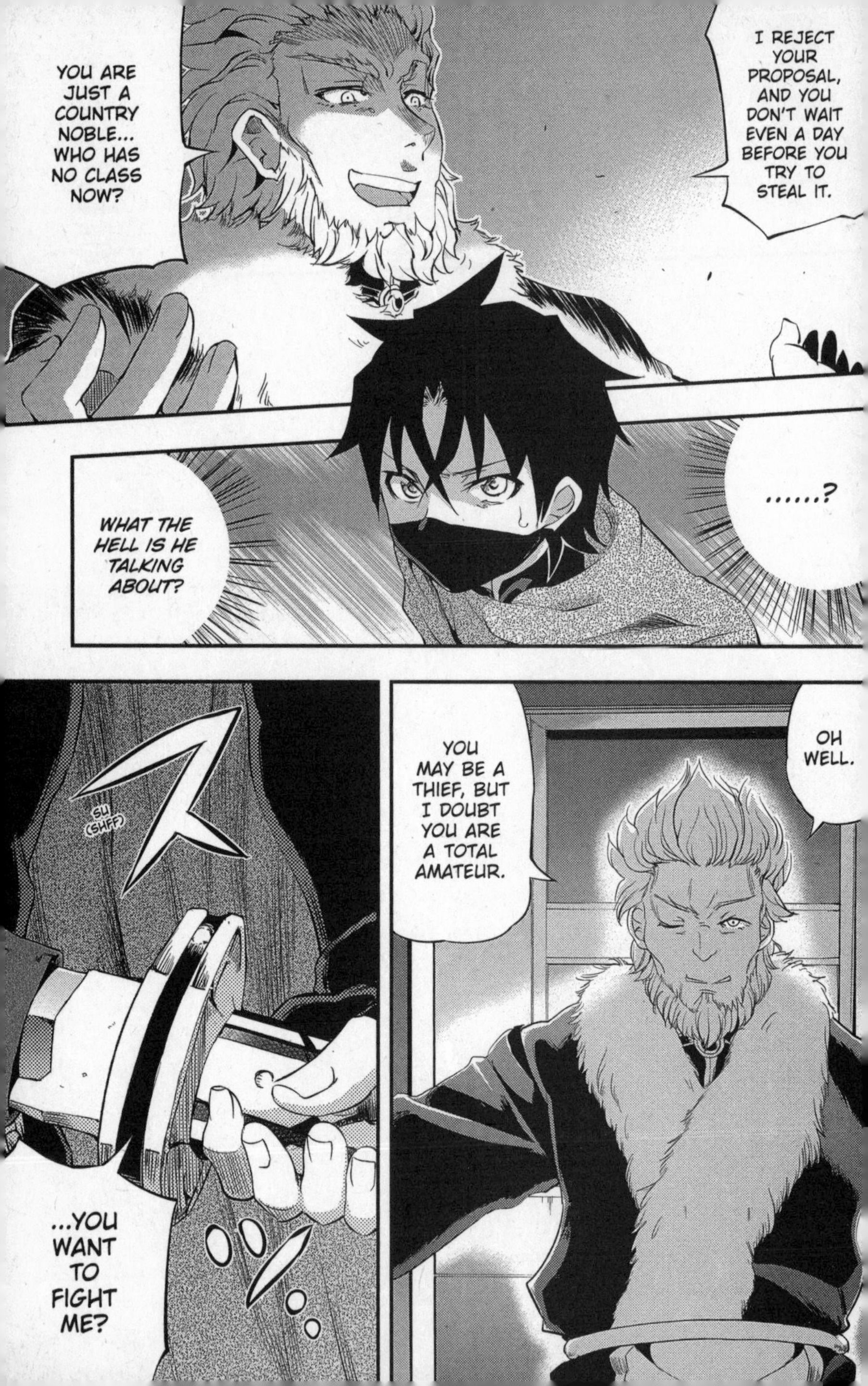
I REJECT YOUR PROPOSAL, AND YOU DON'T WAIT EVEN A DAY BEFORE YOU TRY TO STEAL IT.
YOU ARE JUST A COUNTRY NOBLE... WHO HAS NO CLASS NOW?
......?
WHAT THE HELL IS HE TALKING ABOUT?
OH WELL.
YOU MAY BE A THIEF, BUT I DOUBT YOU ARE A TOTAL AMATEUR.
SU (SHFF)
...YOU WANT TO FIGHT ME?

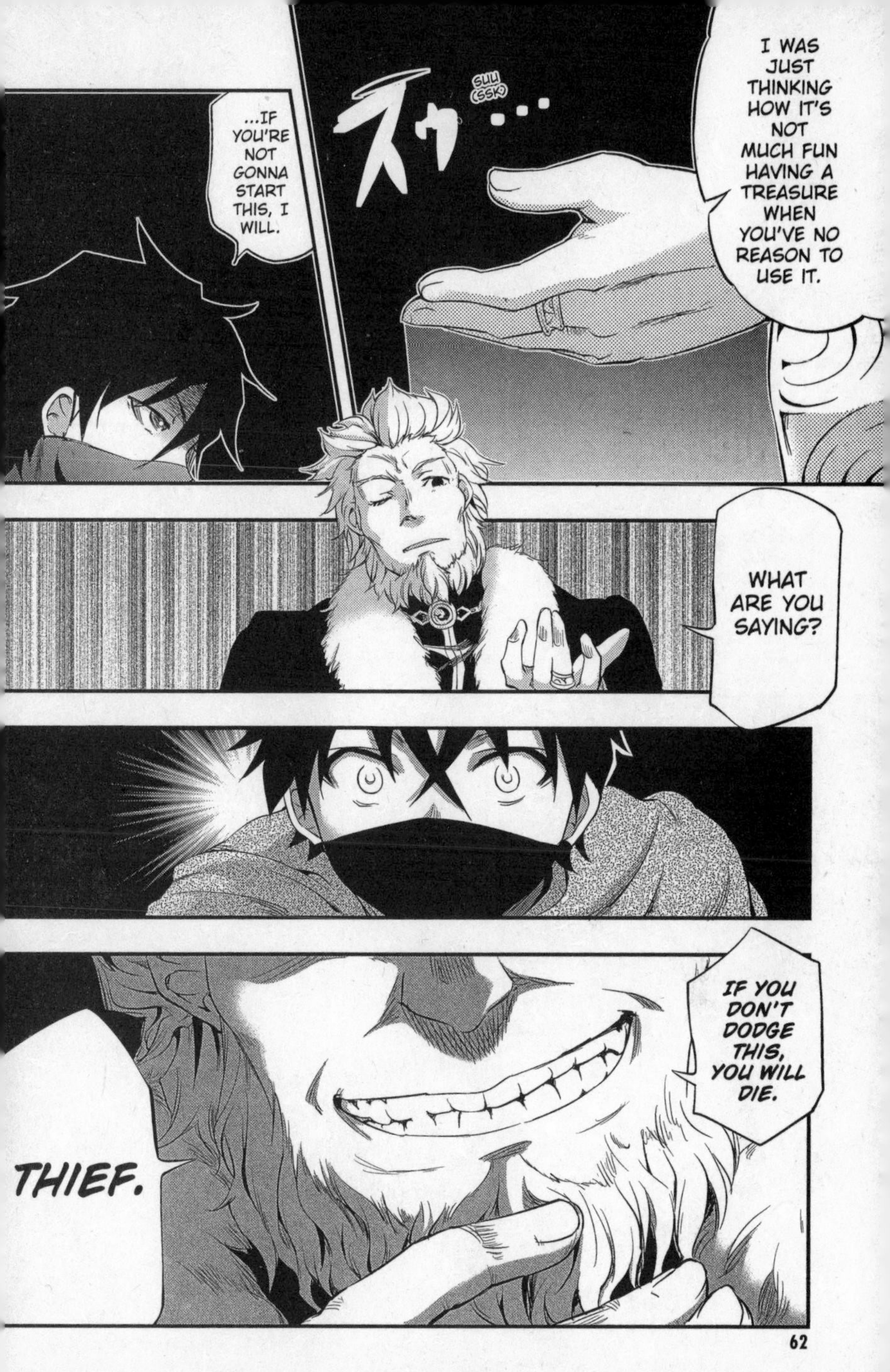
I WAS JUST THINKING HOW IT'S NOT MUCH FUN HAVING A TREASURE WHEN YOU'VE NO REASON TO USE IT.
スゥ…
SUU (SSK)
...IF YOU'RE NOT GONNA START THIS, I WILL.
WHAT ARE YOU SAYING?
IF YOU DON'T DODGE THIS, YOU WILL DIE.
THIEF.

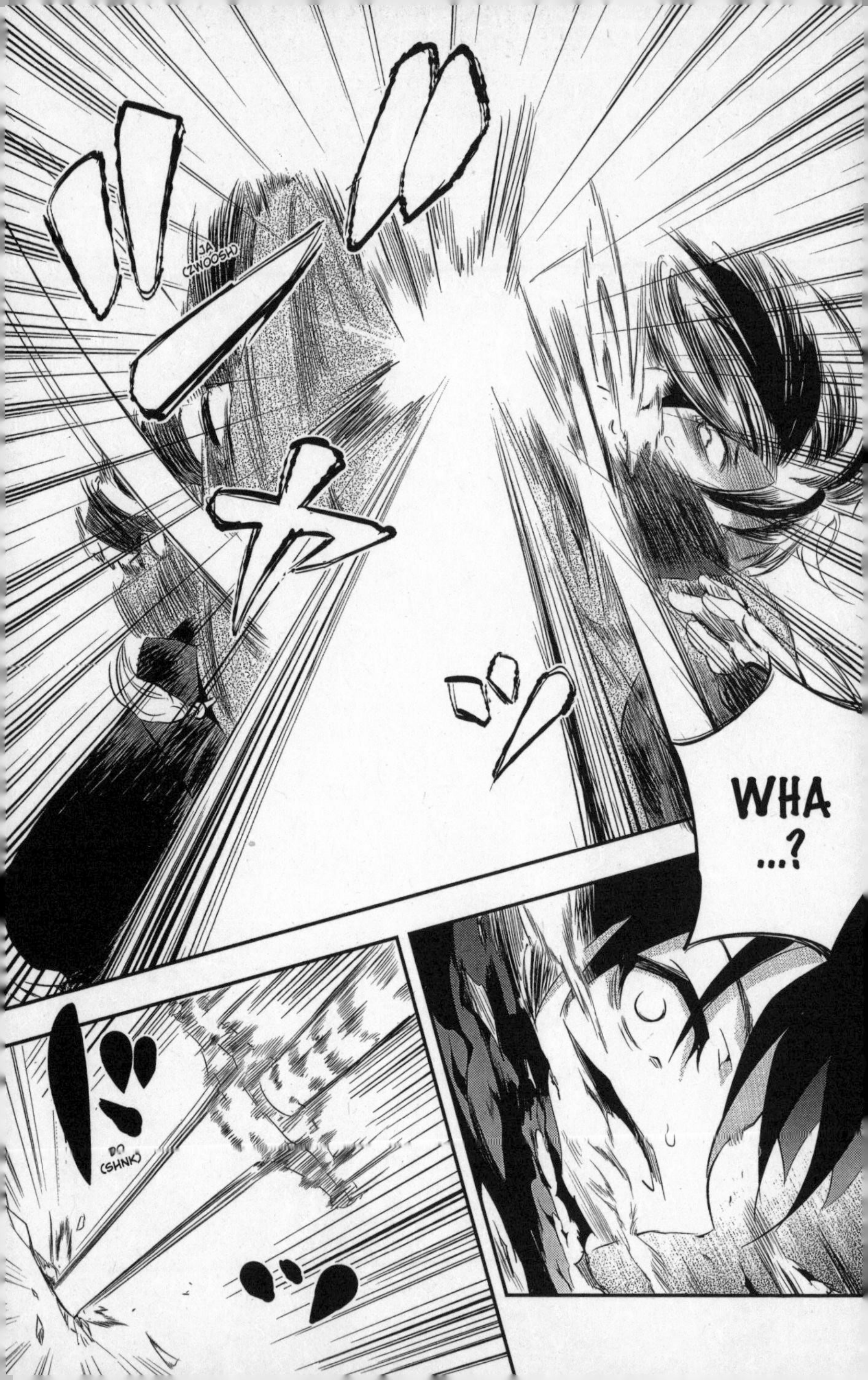
JA (ZWOOSH)
WHA ...?
DO (SHNK)

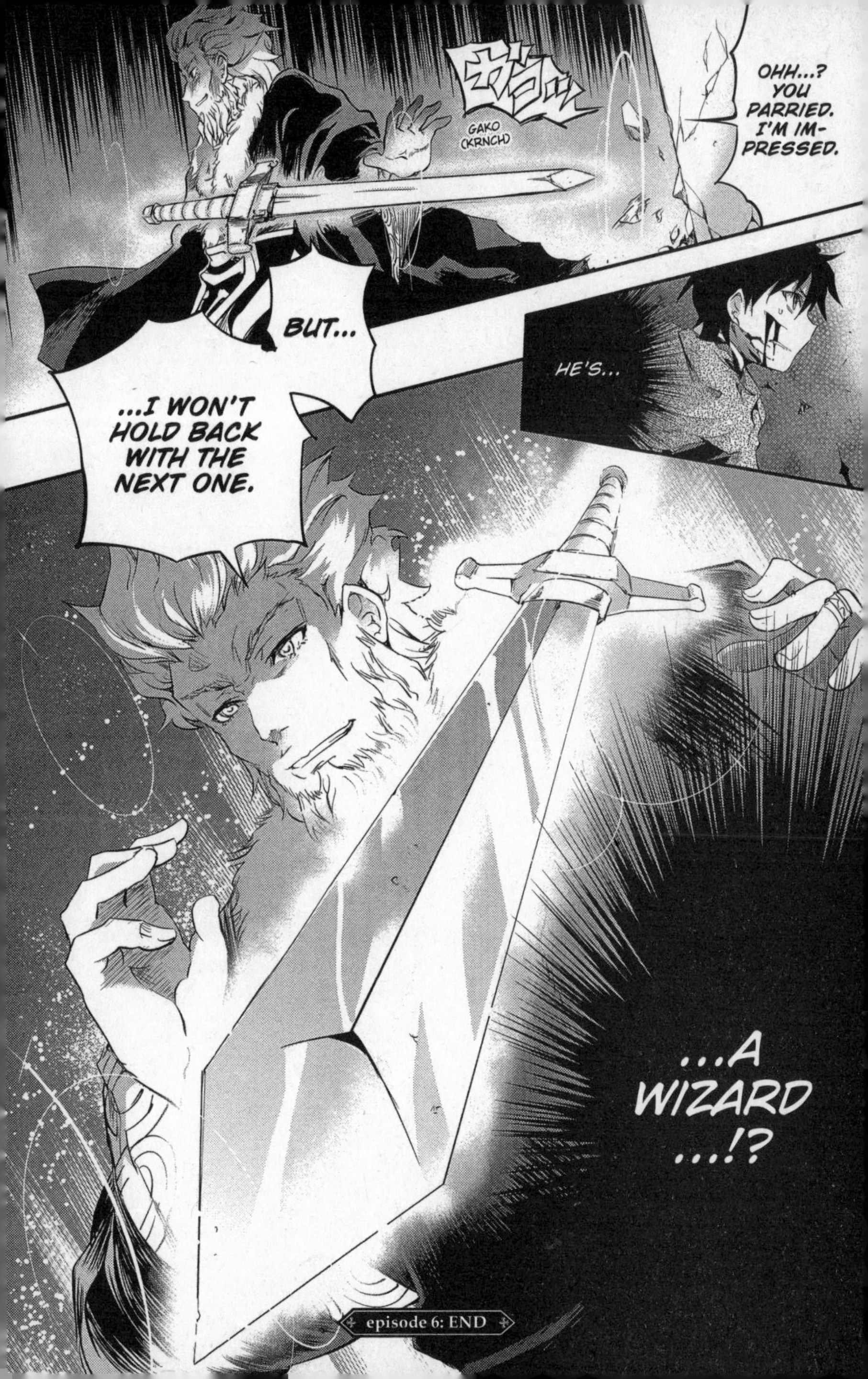
OHH...? YOU PARRIED. I'M IM-PRESSED.
GAKO (KRNCH)
BUT...
HE'S...
...I WON'T HOLD BACK WITH THE NEXT ONE.
...A WIZARD ...!?
episode 6: END

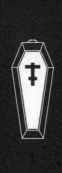

CHAIKA: THE
COFFIN PRINCESS

episode 7: Chance Encounter with the Past

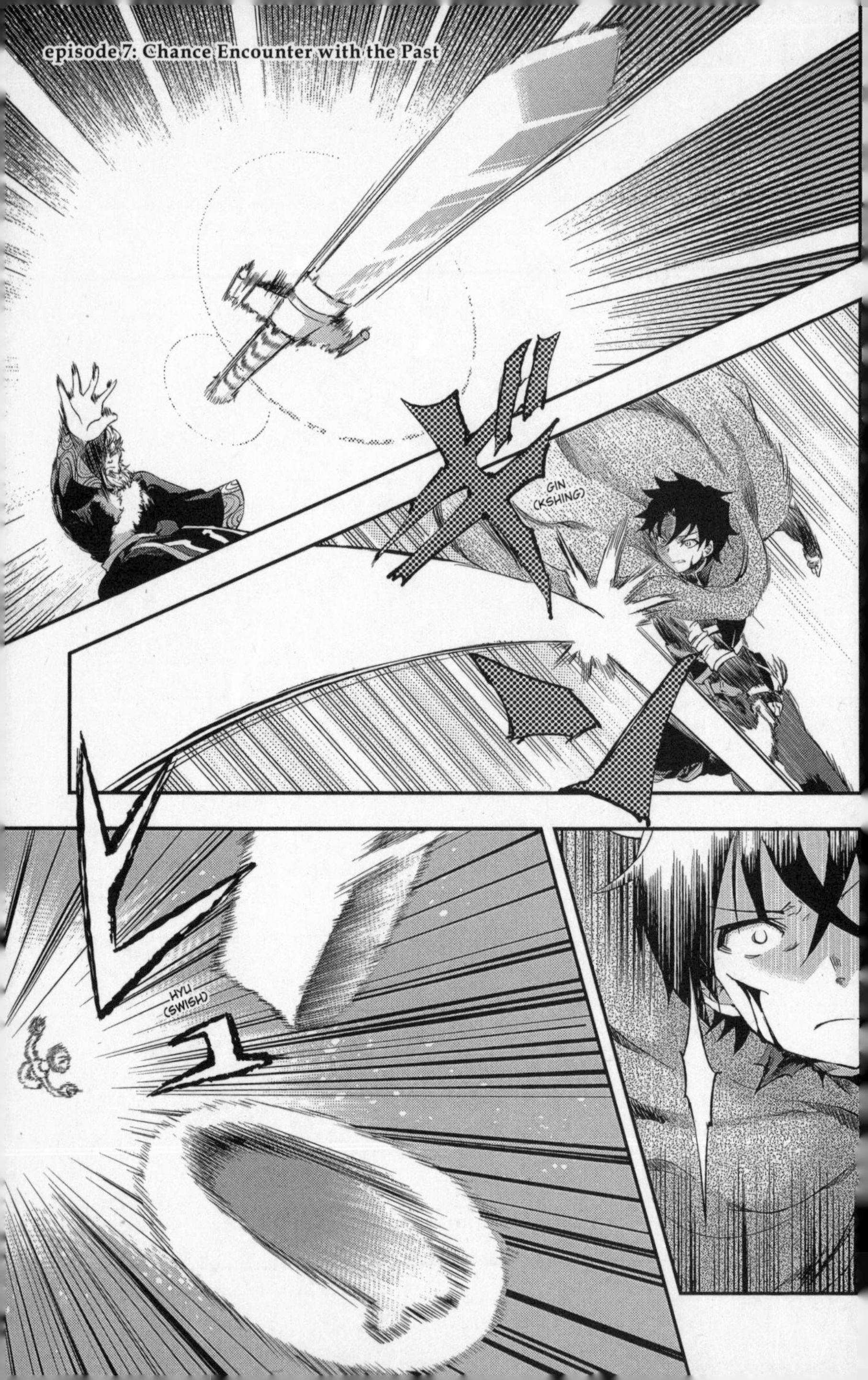
GIN
(KSHING)
HYU
(SWISH)

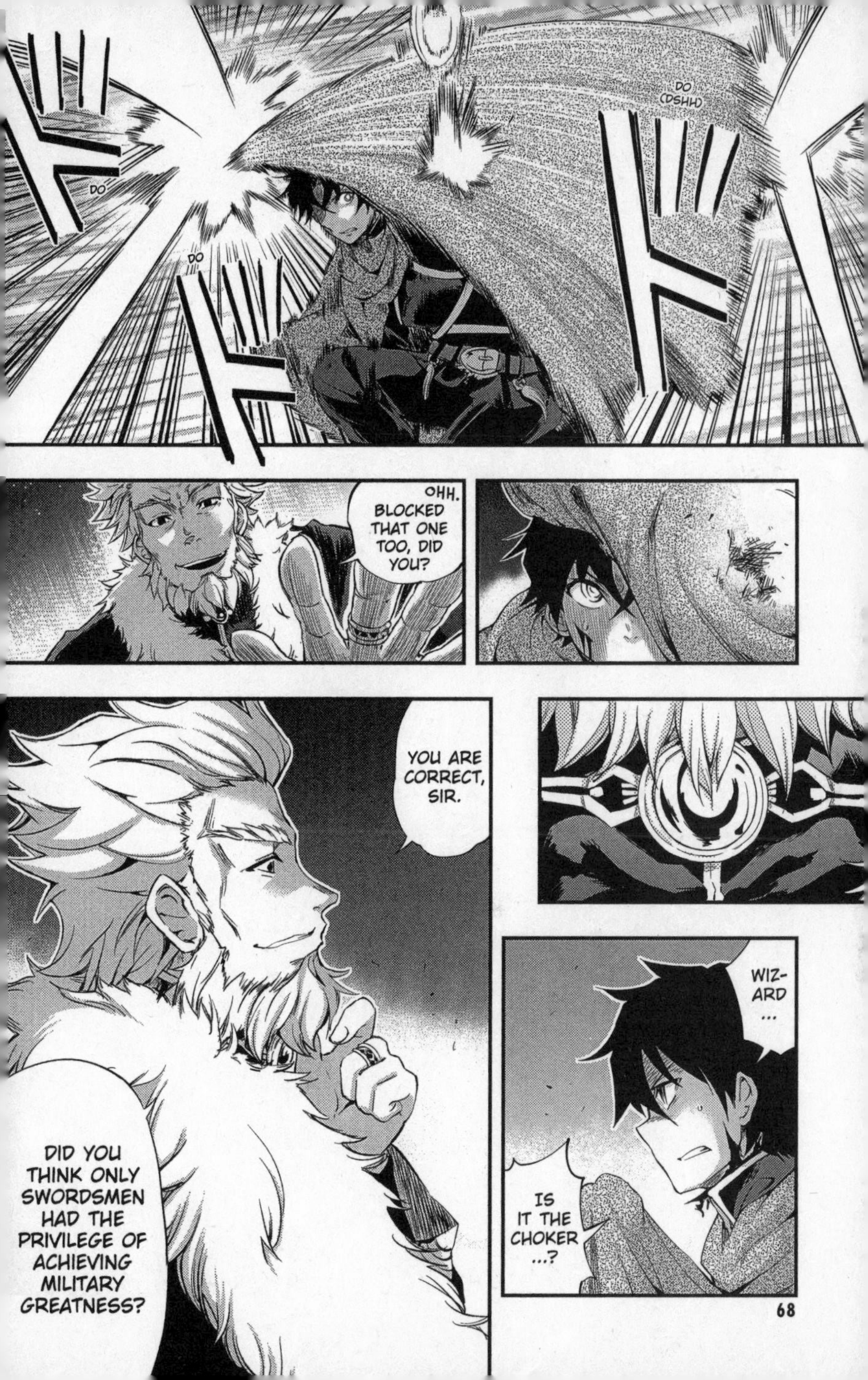
DO
(DSHH)
DO
DO
OHH. BLOCKED THAT ONE TOO, DID YOU?
WIZ-ARD ...
IS IT THE CHOKER ...?
YOU ARE CORRECT, SIR.
DID YOU THINK ONLY SWORDSMEN HAD THE PRIVILEGE OF ACHIEVING MILITARY GREATNESS?

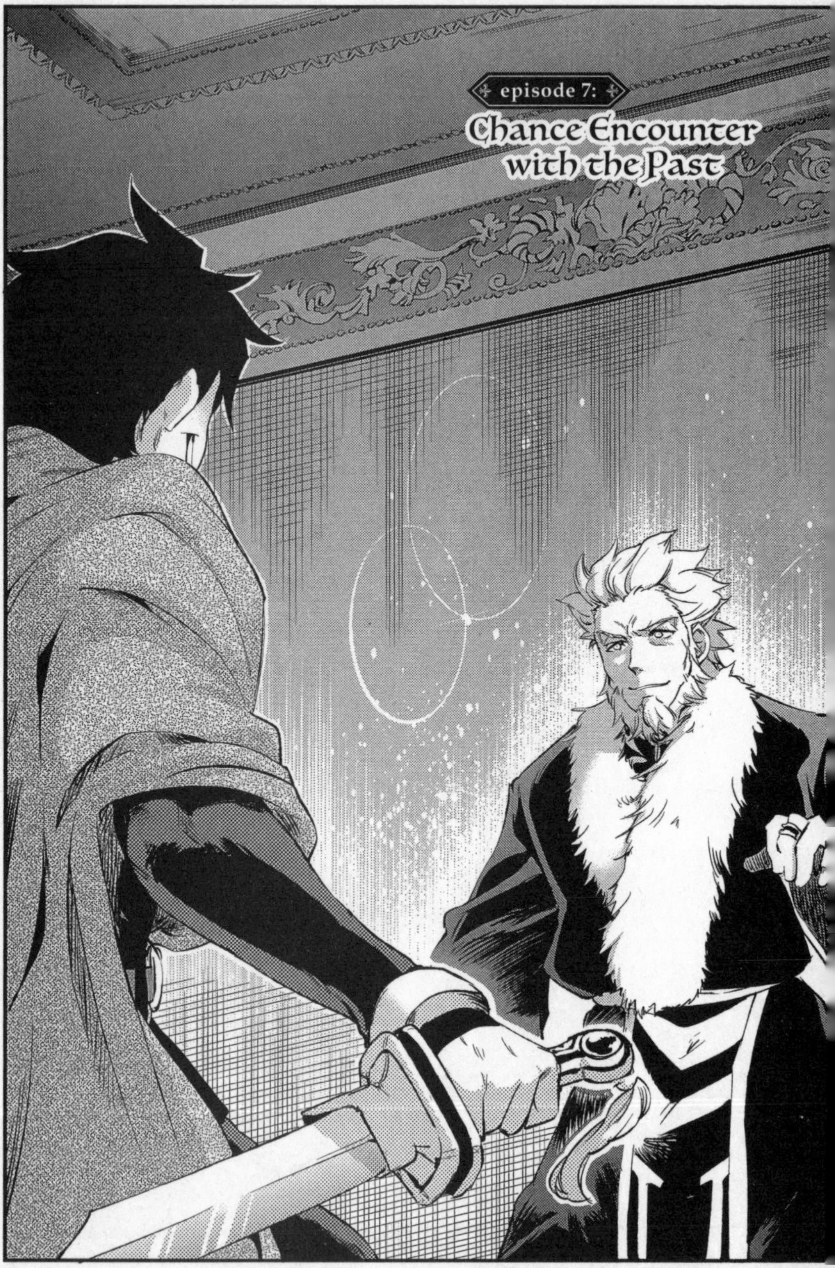
episode 7:
Chance Encounter with the Past

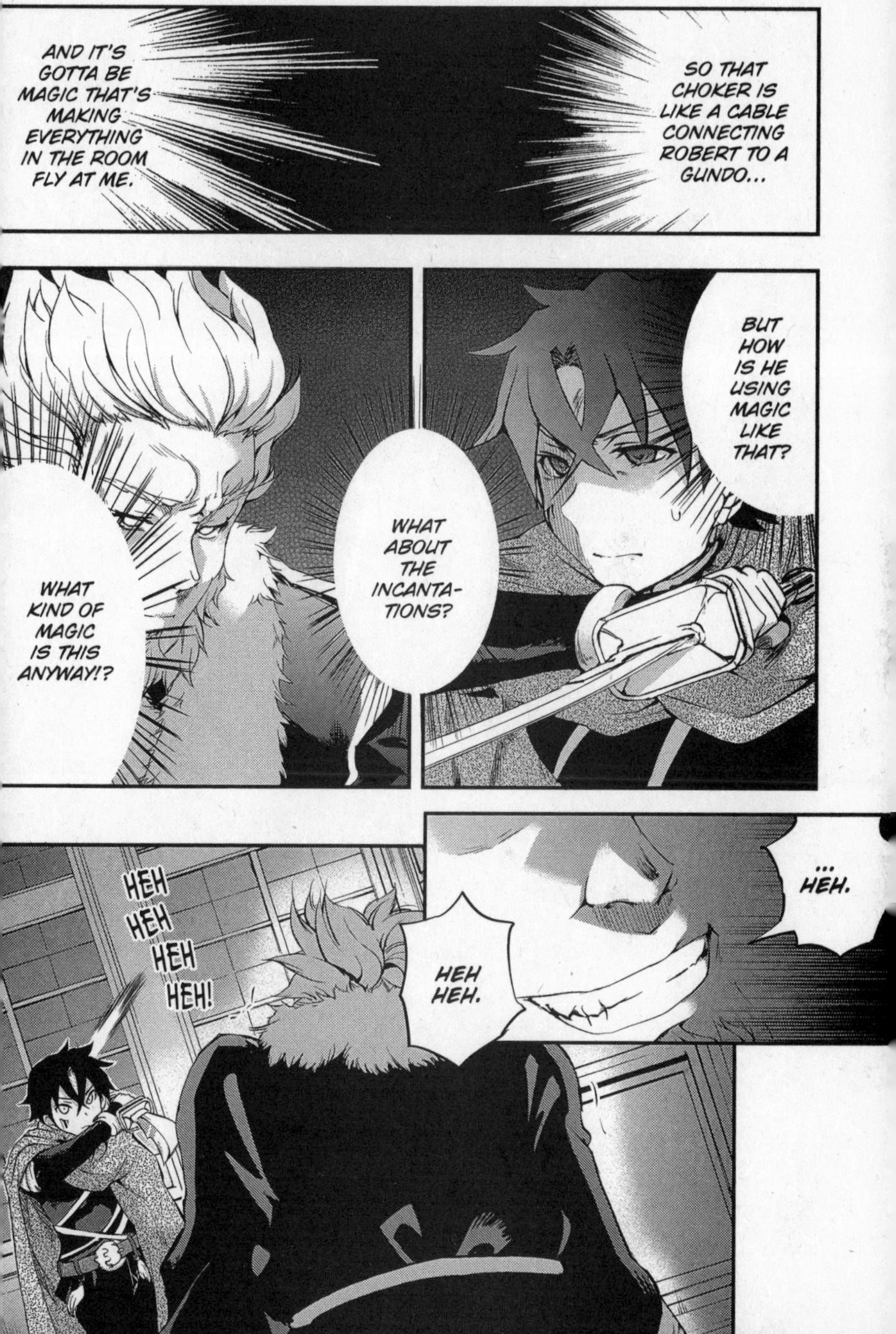
SO THAT CHOKER IS LIKE A CABLE CONNECTING ROBERT TO A GUNDO...
AND IT'S GOTTA BE MAGIC THAT'S MAKING EVERYTHING IN THE ROOM FLY AT ME.
BUT HOW IS HE USING MAGIC LIKE THAT?
WHAT ABOUT THE INCANTA-TIONS?
WHAT KIND OF MAGIC IS THIS ANYWAY!?
...HEH.
HEH HEH.
HEH HEH HEH HEH!

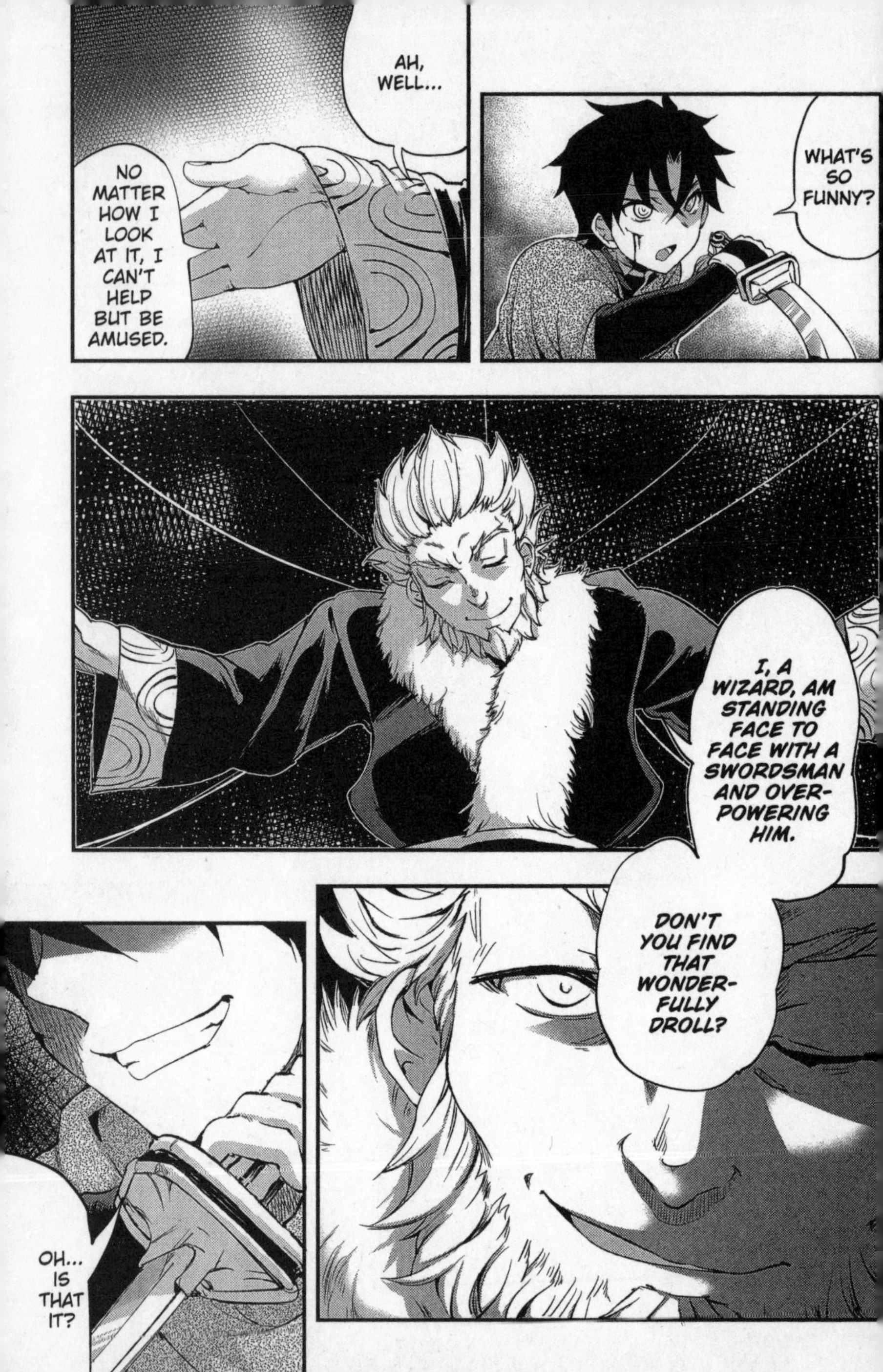
WHAT'S SO FUNNY?
AH, WELL...
NO MATTER HOW I LOOK AT IT, I CAN'T HELP BUT BE AMUSED.
I, A WIZARD, AM STANDING FACE TO FACE WITH A SWORDSMAN AND OVER-POWERING HIM.
DON'T YOU FIND THAT WONDER-FULLY DROLL?
OH... IS THAT IT?

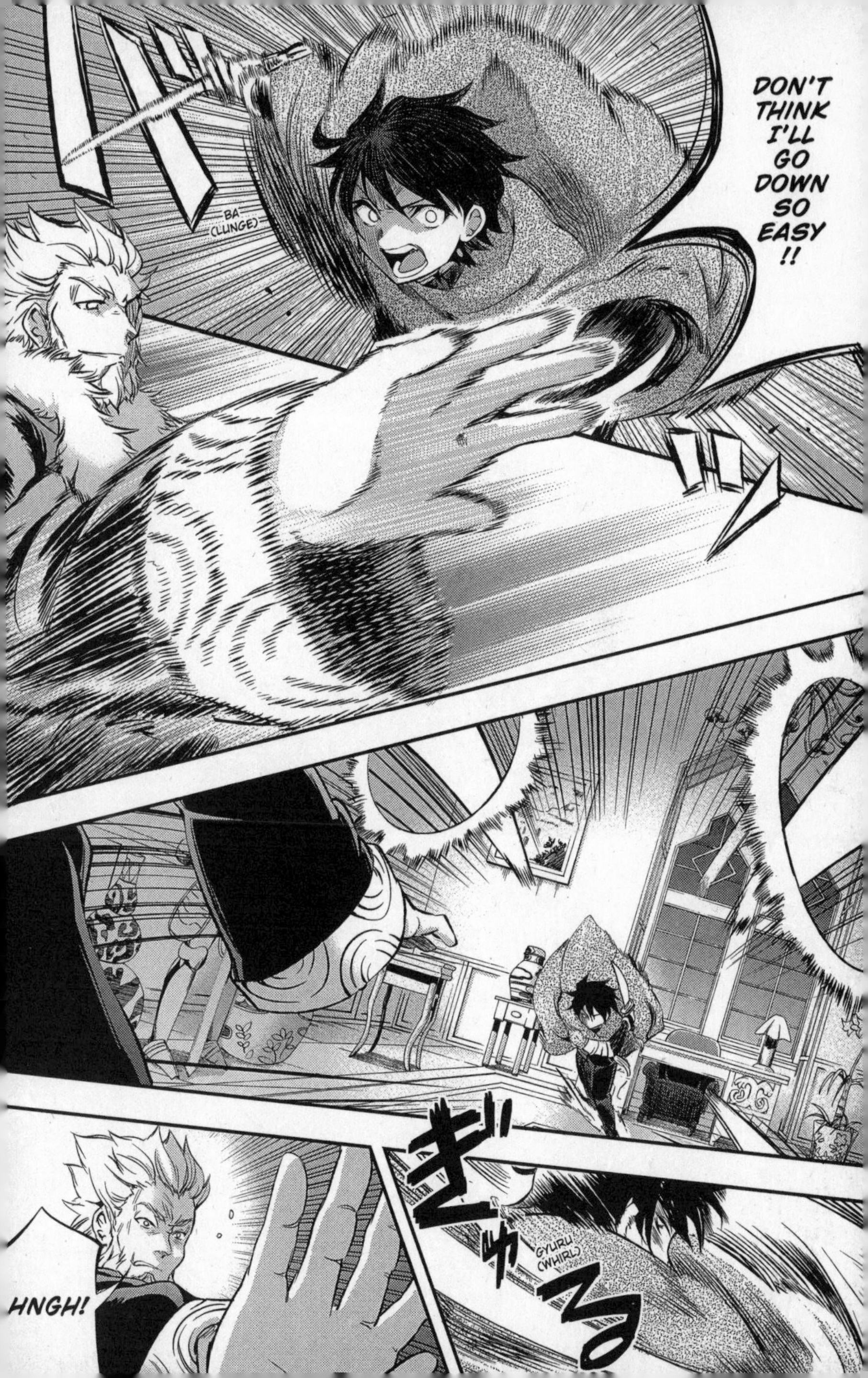
DON'T THINK I'LL GO DOWN SO EASY!!
BA (LUNGE)
GYURU (WHIRL)
HNGH!

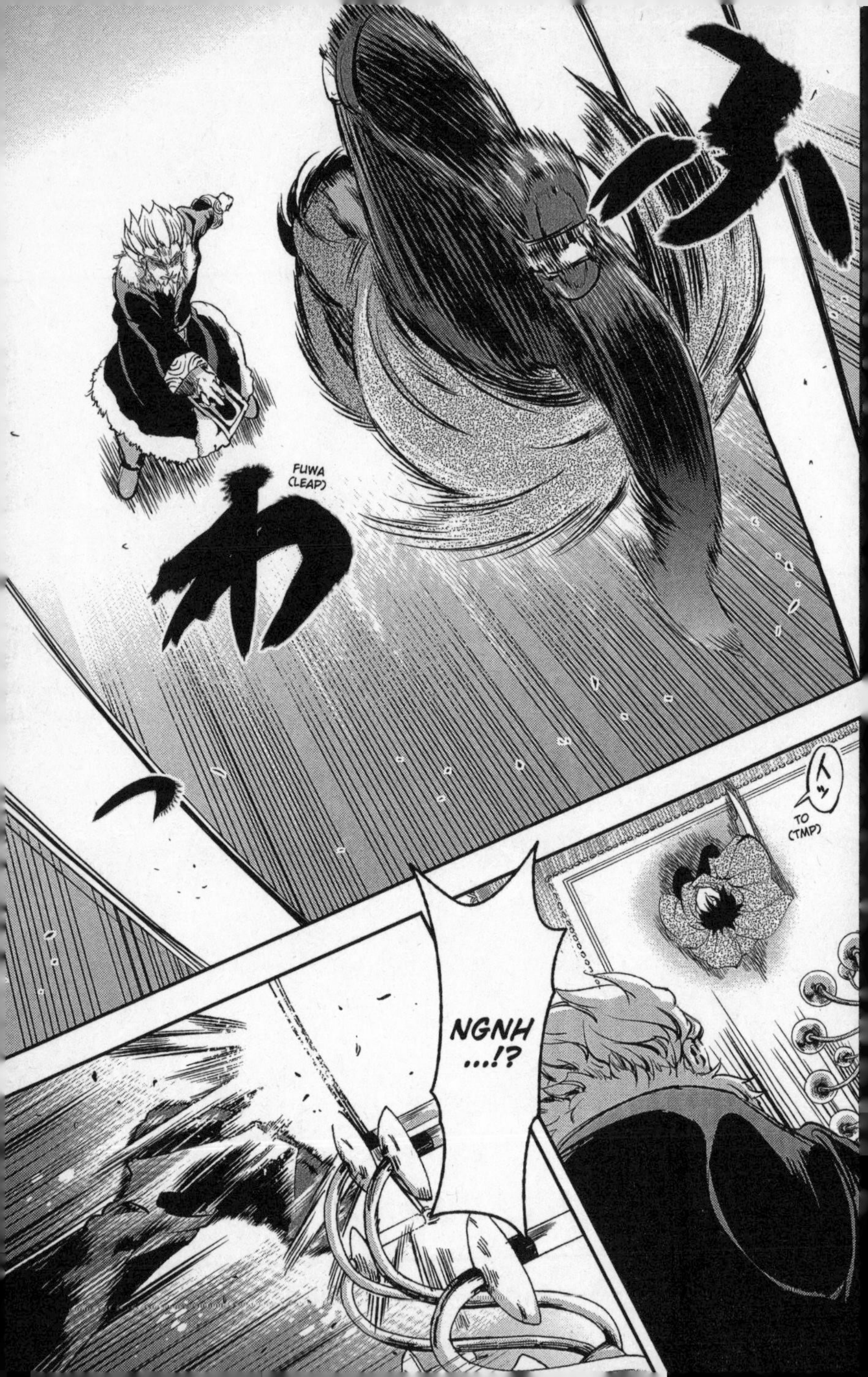
FUWA
(LEAP)
TO
(TMP)
NGNH
...!?

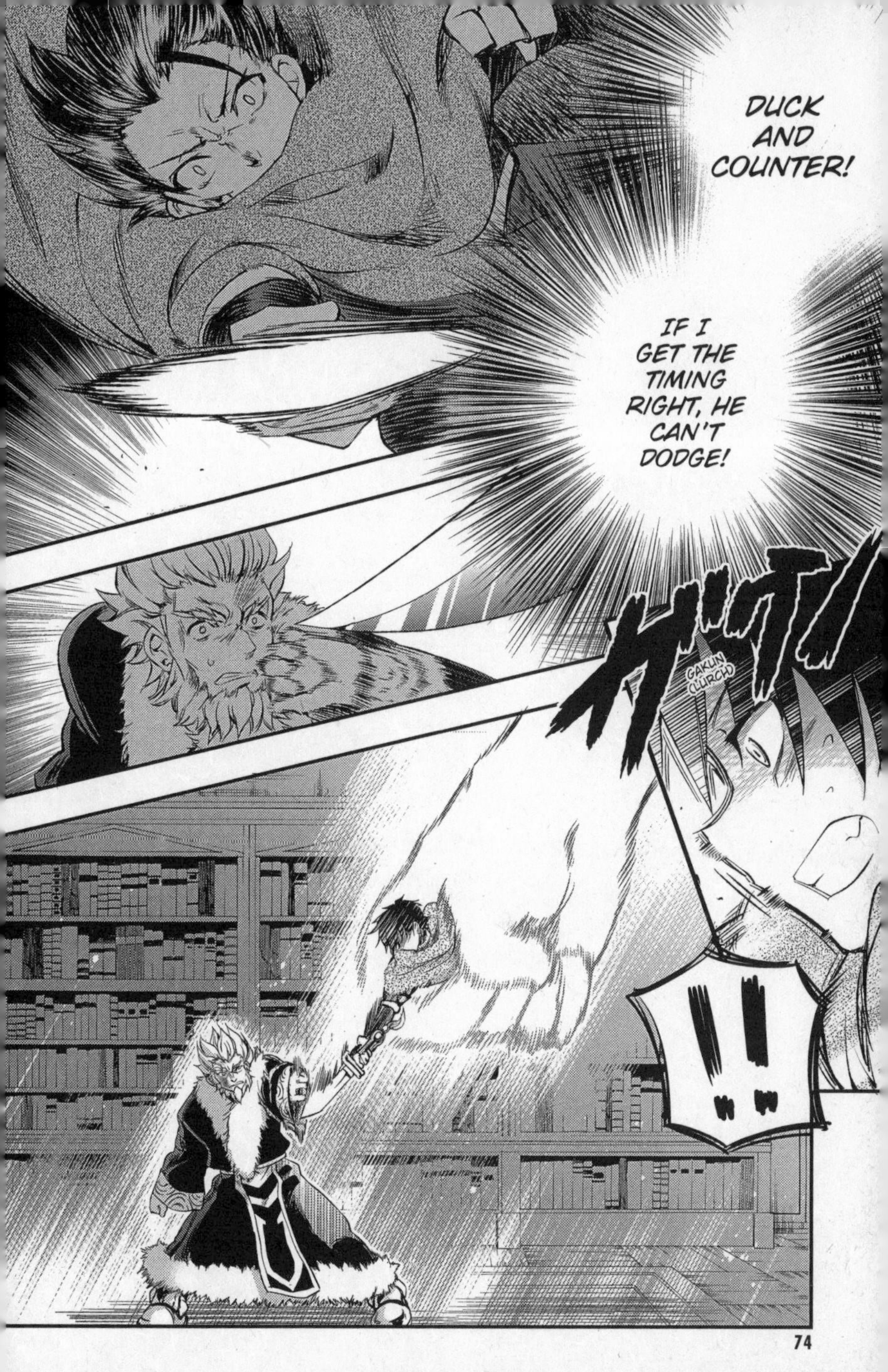
DUCK AND COUNTER!
IF I GET THE TIMING RIGHT, HE CAN'T DODGE!
GAKUN (LURCH)
!!

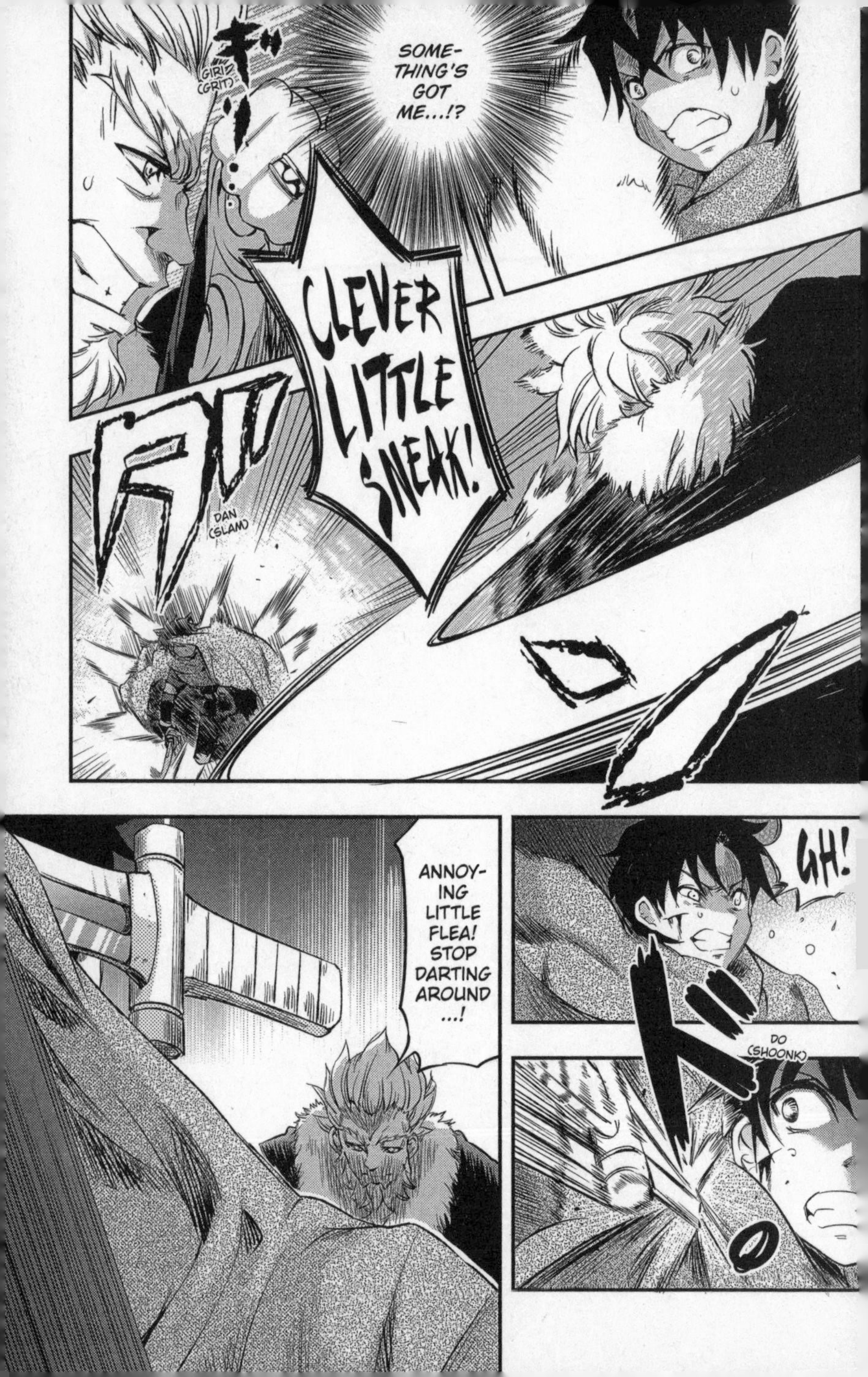
SOME-THING'S GOT ME...!?
GIRI (GRIT)
CLEVER LITTLE SNEAK!
DAN (SLAM)
GH!
DO (SHOONK)
ANNOY-ING LITTLE FLEA! STOP DARTING AROUND ...!

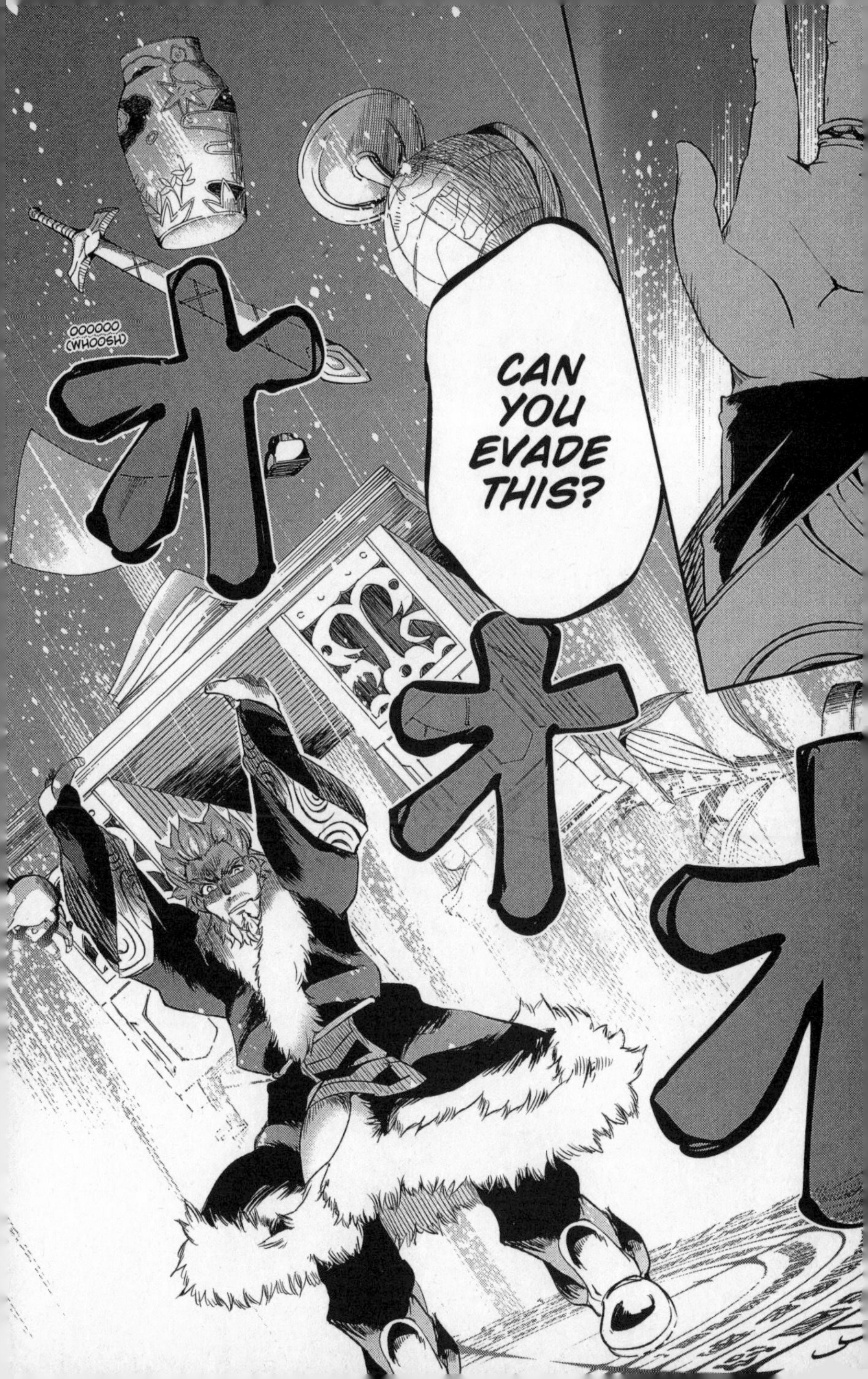
CAN YOU EVADE THIS?
OOOOOO (WHOOSH)

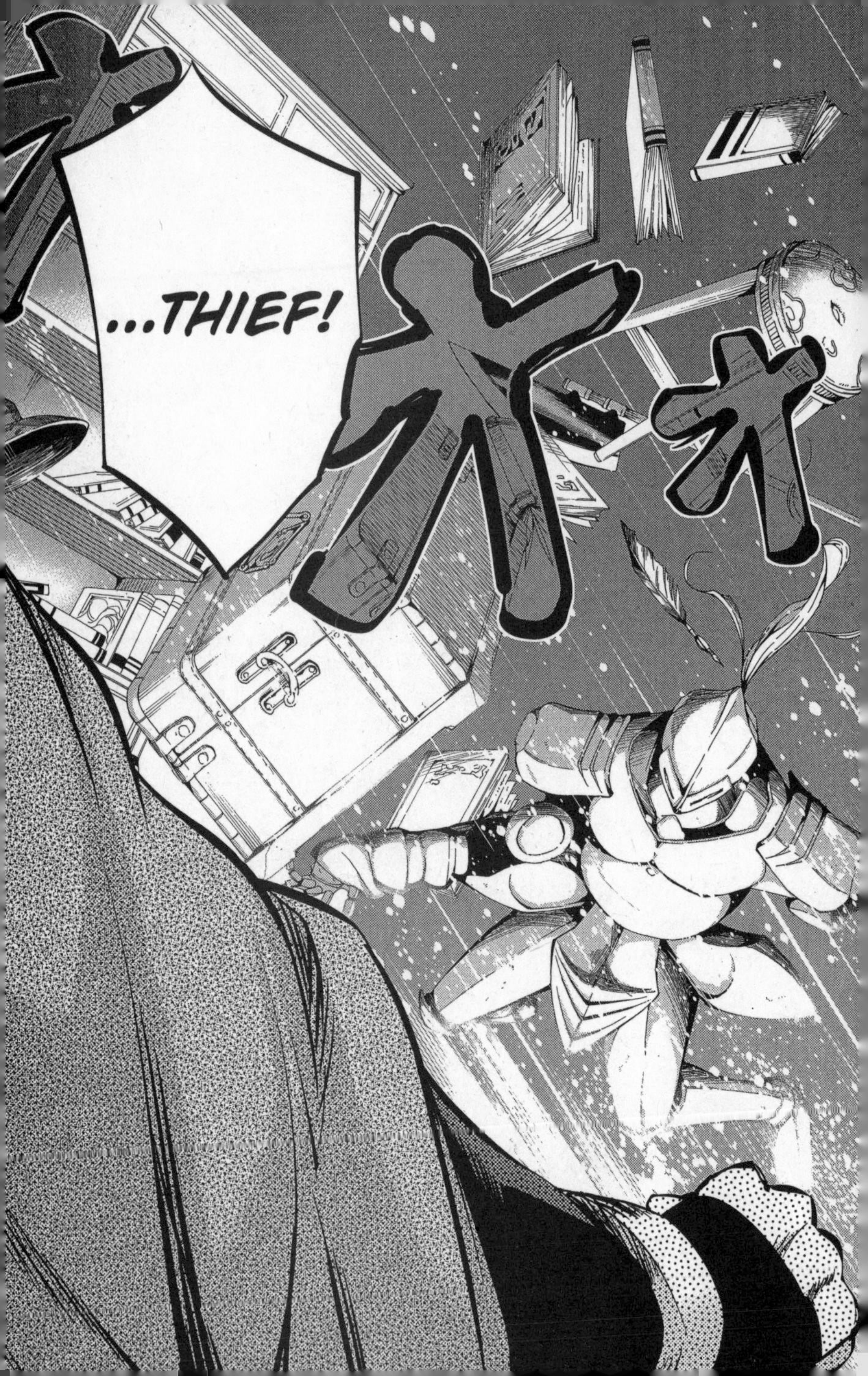
...THIEF!

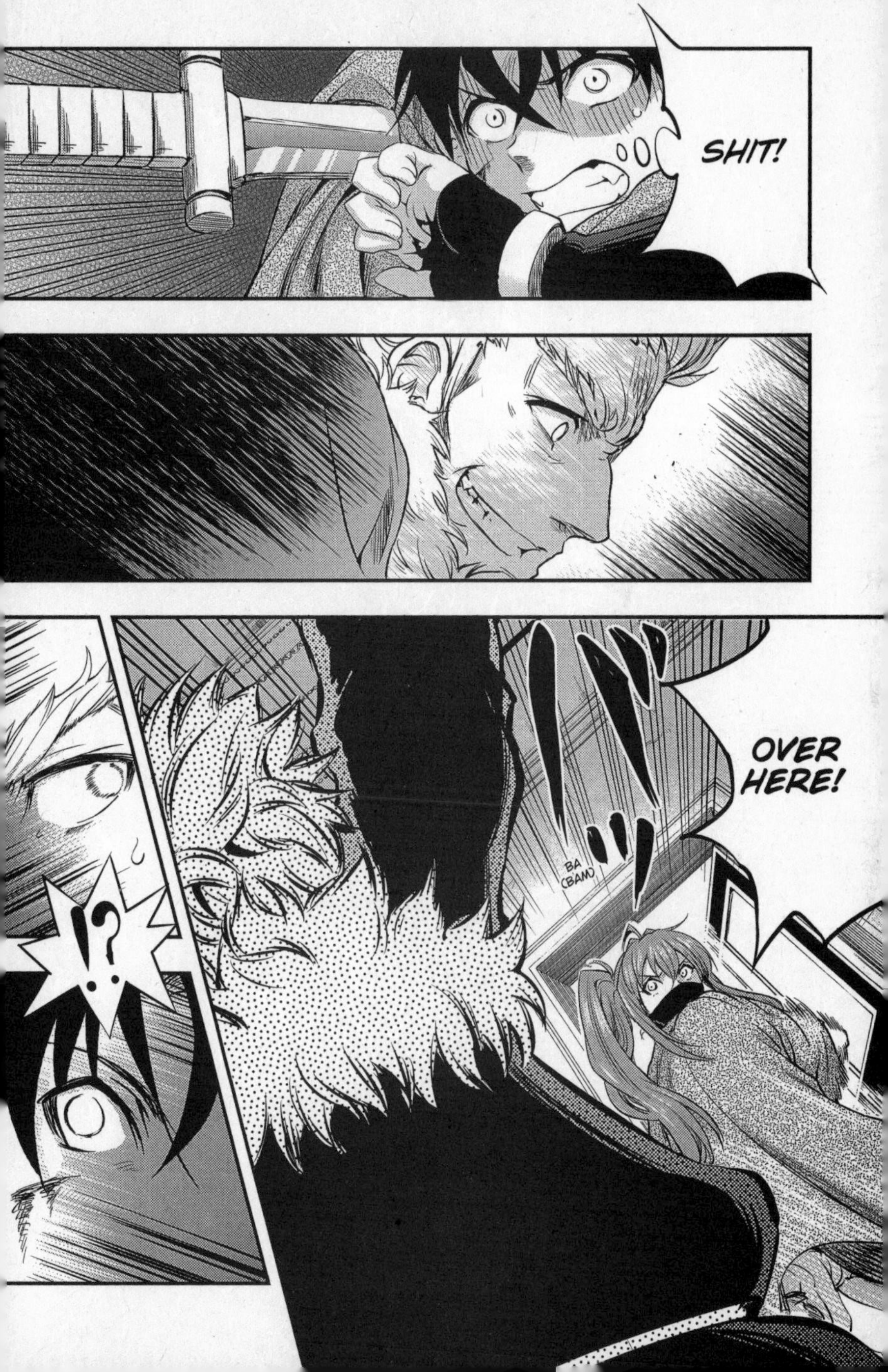
SHIT!
OVER HERE!
BA (BAM)
!?

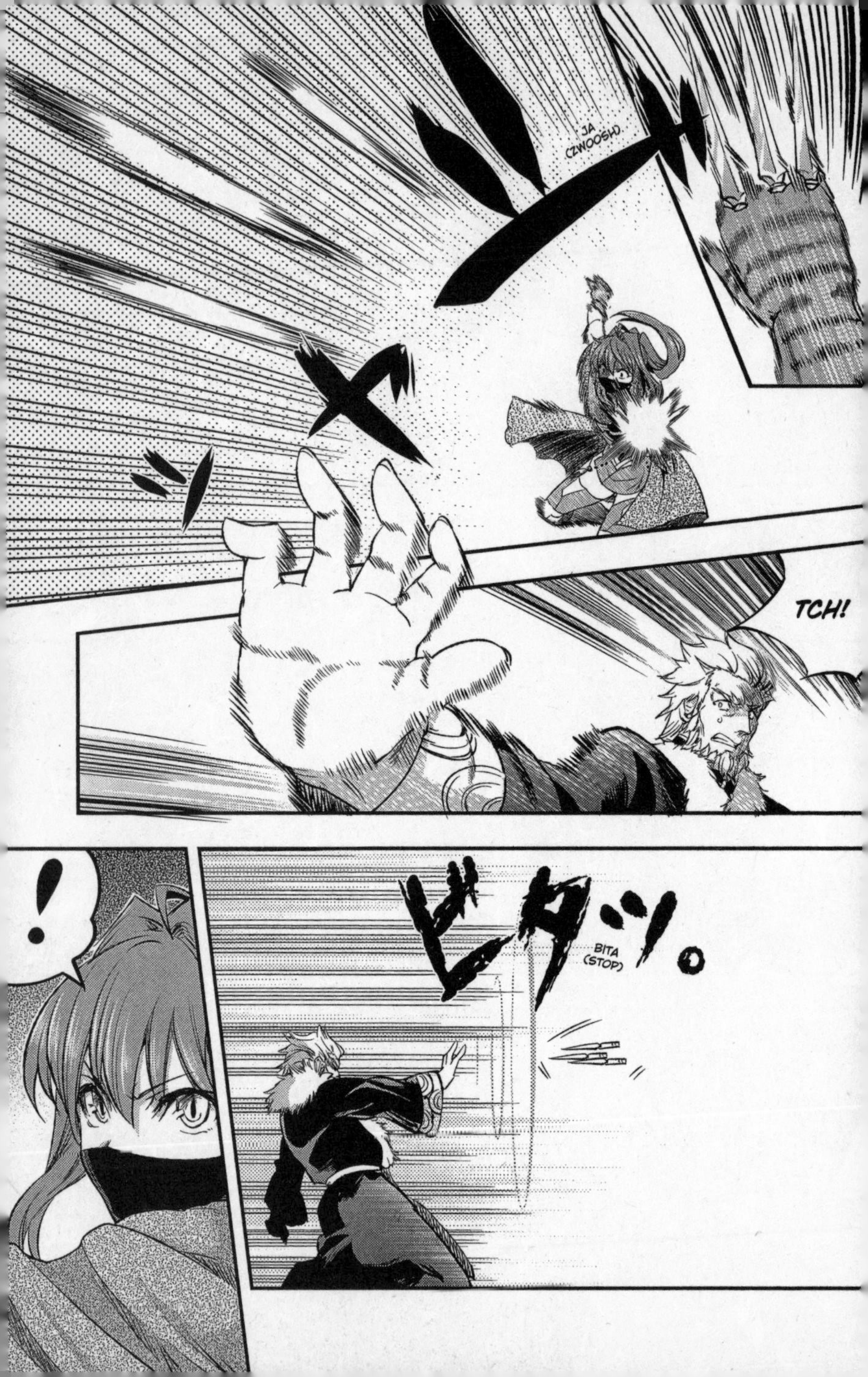
JA (ZWOOSH)
TCH!
BITA (STOP)
!

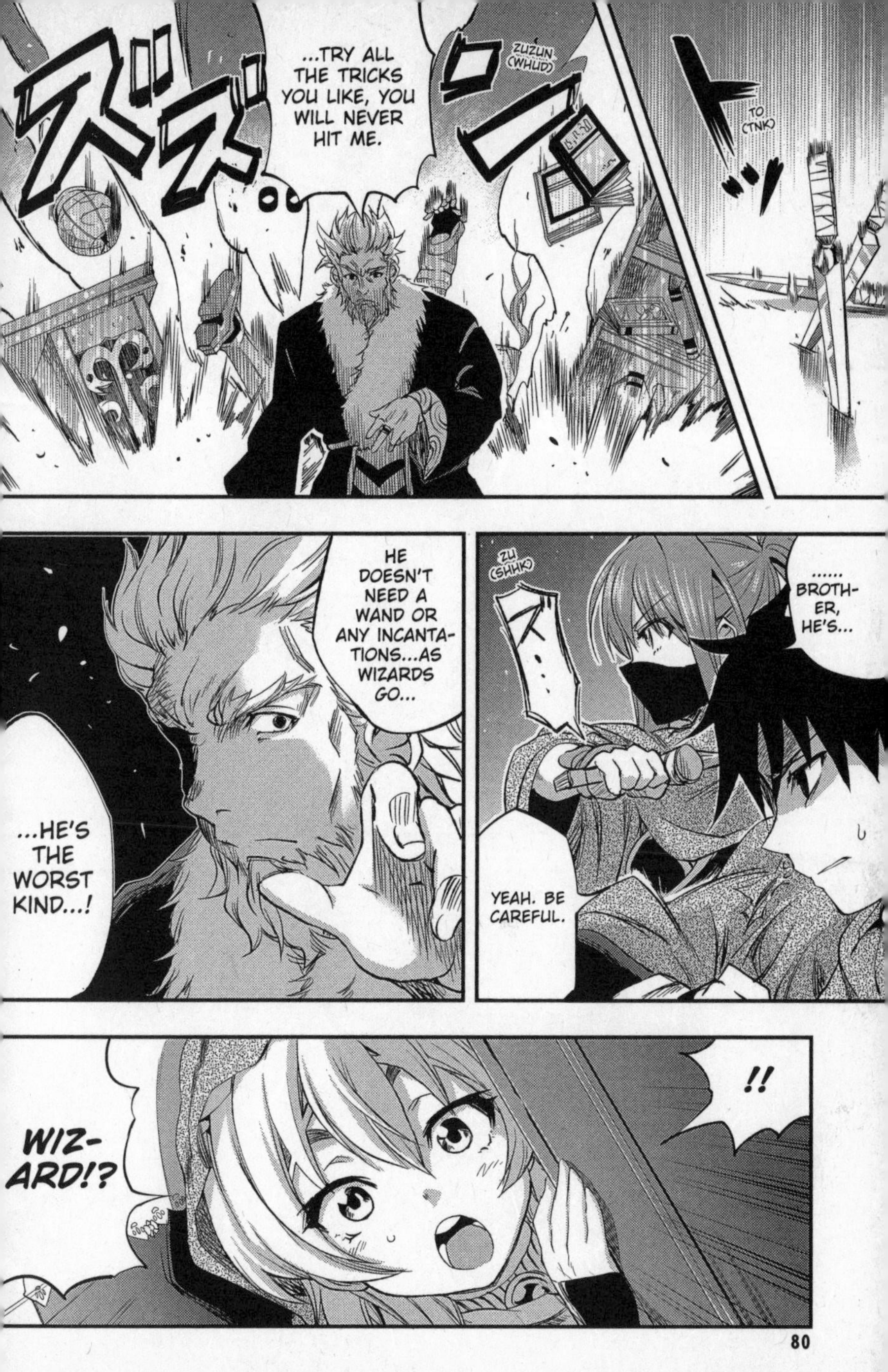
TO (TNK)
ZUZUN (WHUD)
...TRY ALL THE TRICKS YOU LIKE, YOU WILL NEVER HIT ME.
ZU (SHHK)
...... BROTHER, HE'S...
YEAH. BE CAREFUL.
HE DOESN'T NEED A WAND OR ANY INCANTATIONS...AS WIZARDS GO...
...HE'S THE WORST KIND...!
!!
WIZARD!?

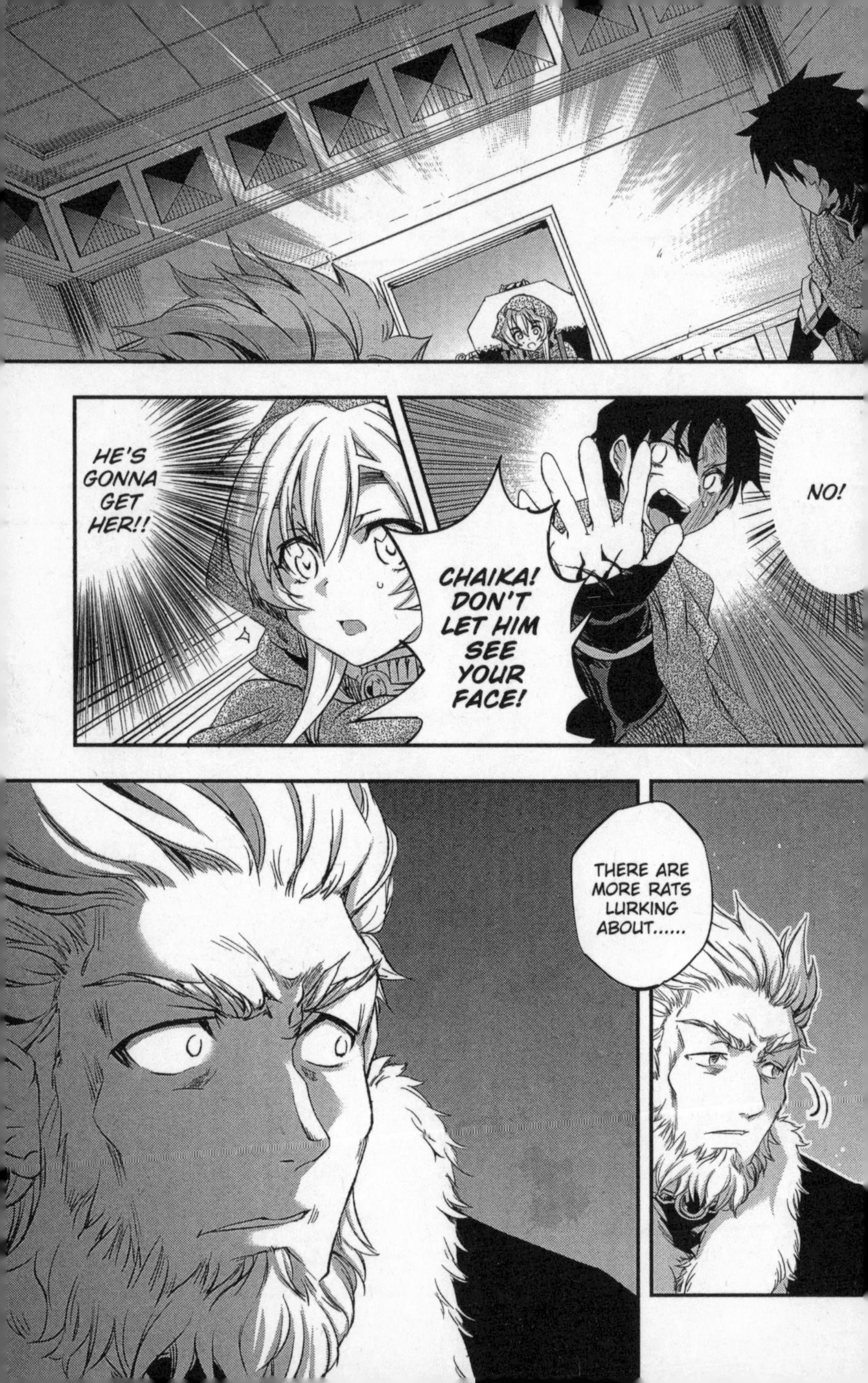
NO!
CHAIKA! DON'T LET HIM SEE YOUR FACE!
HE'S GONNA GET HER!!
THERE ARE MORE RATS LURKING ABOUT......

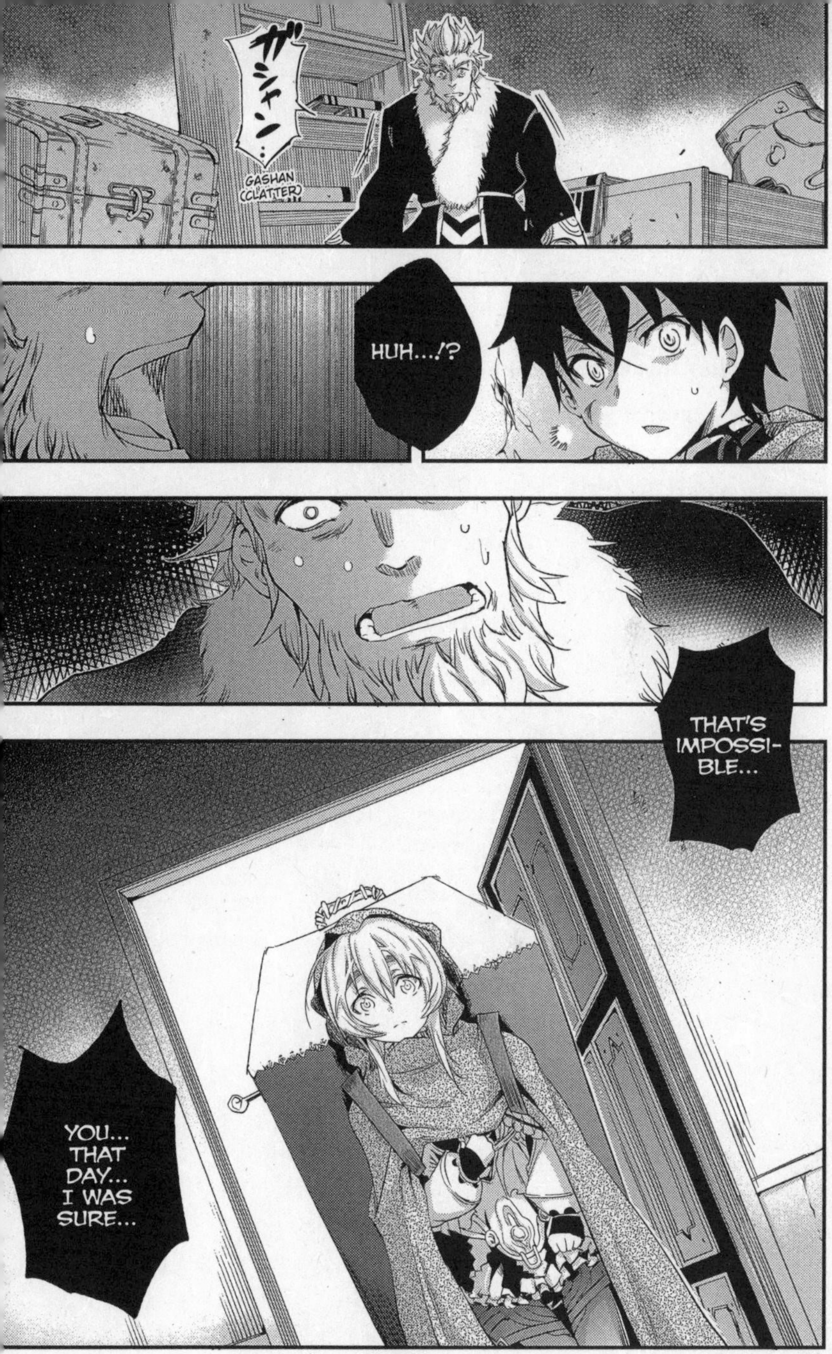
ガシャン…
GASHAN (CLATTER)
HUH...!?
THAT'S IMPOSSI-BLE...
YOU... THAT DAY... I WAS SURE...

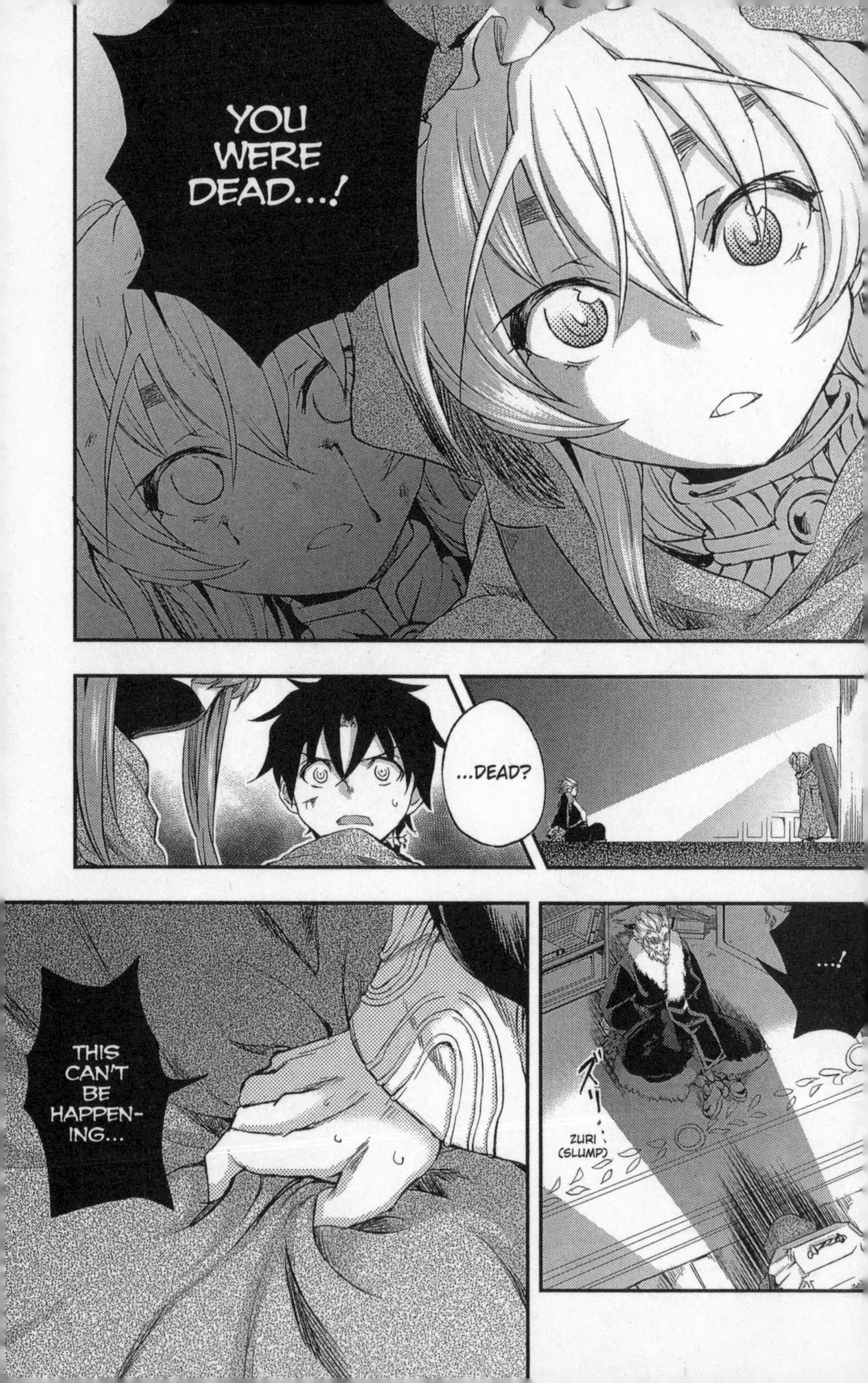
YOU WERE DEAD...!
...DEAD?
...!
ZURI (SLUMP)
THIS CAN'T BE HAPPEN-ING...

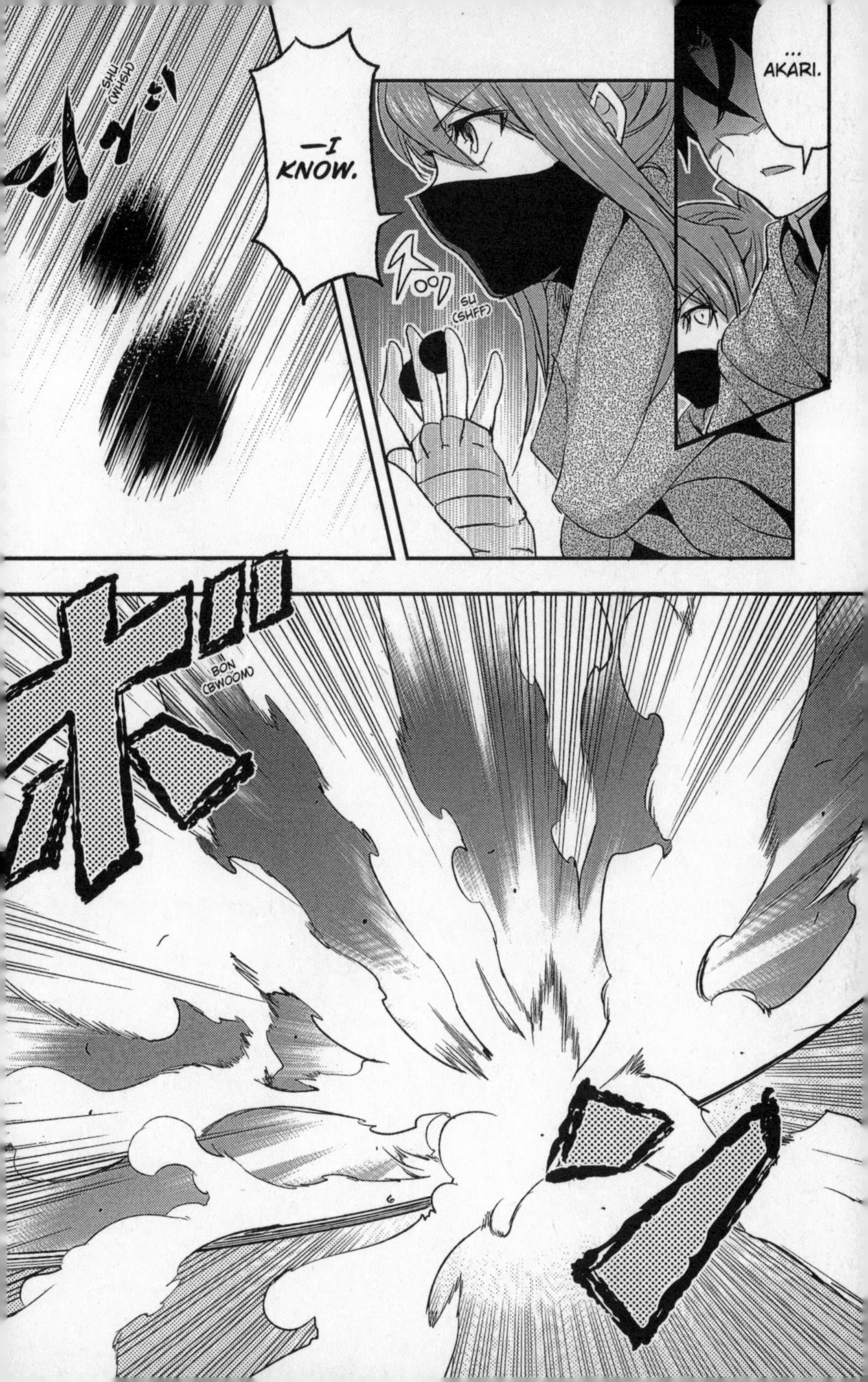
...AKARI.
—I KNOW.
SU (SHFF)
SHU (WHSH)
BON (BWOOM)

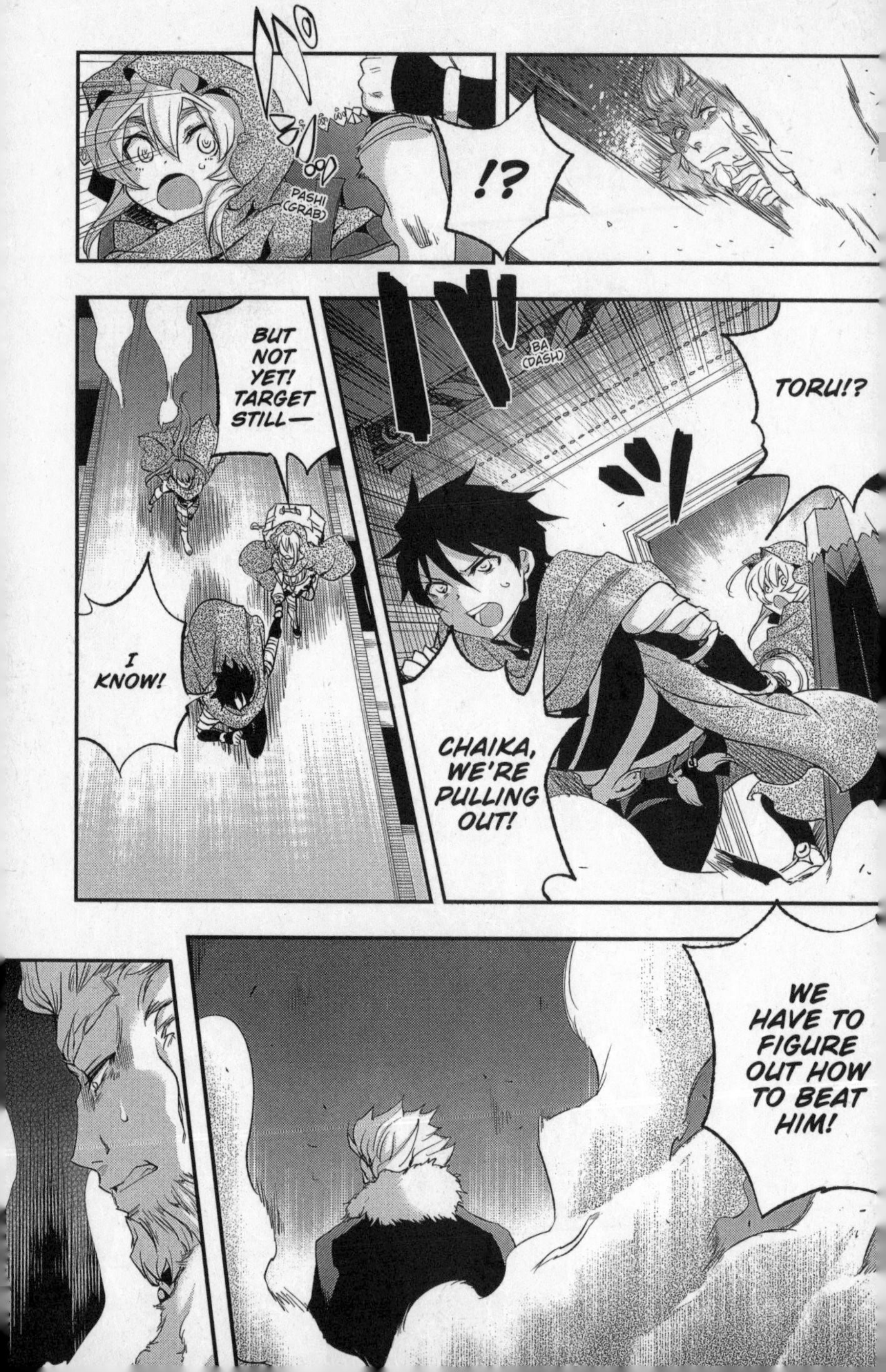
!?
PASHI (GRAB)
TORU!?
BA (DASH)
CHAIKA, WE'RE PULLING OUT!
BUT NOT YET! TARGET STILL—
I KNOW!
WE HAVE TO FIGURE OUT HOW TO BEAT HIM!

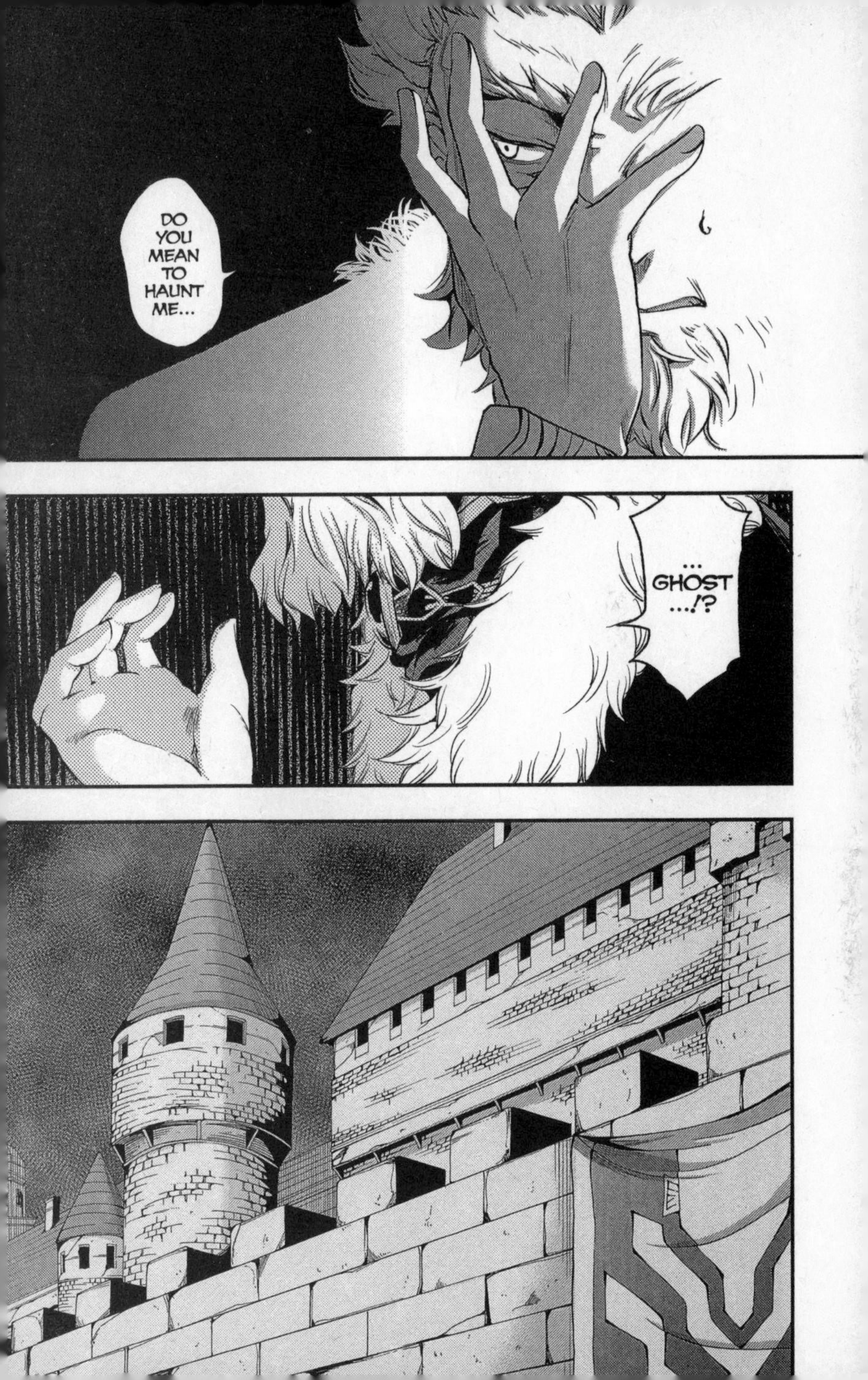
DO YOU MEAN TO HAUNT ME...
...GHOST ...!?

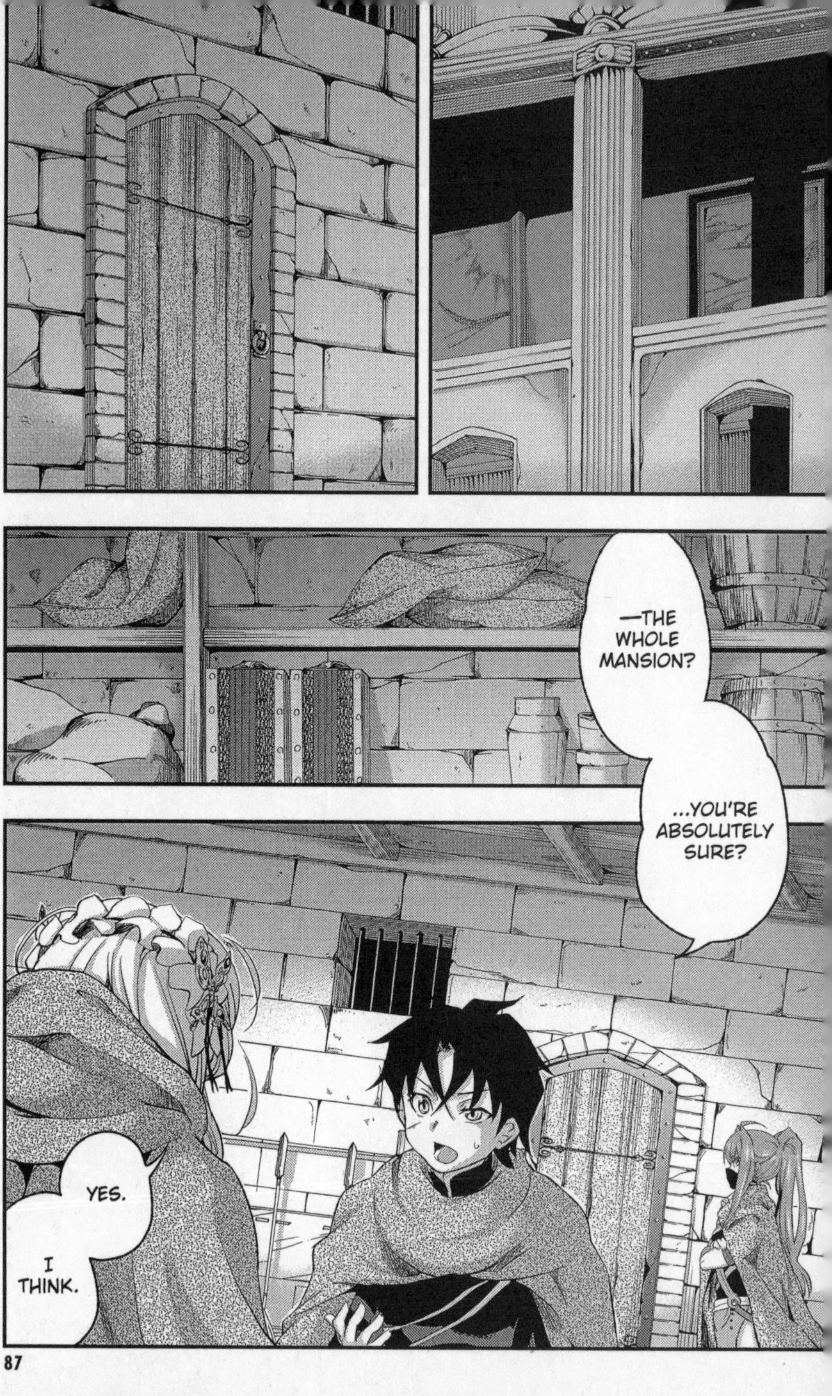
—THE WHOLE MANSION?
...YOU'RE ABSOLUTELY SURE?
YES.
I THINK.

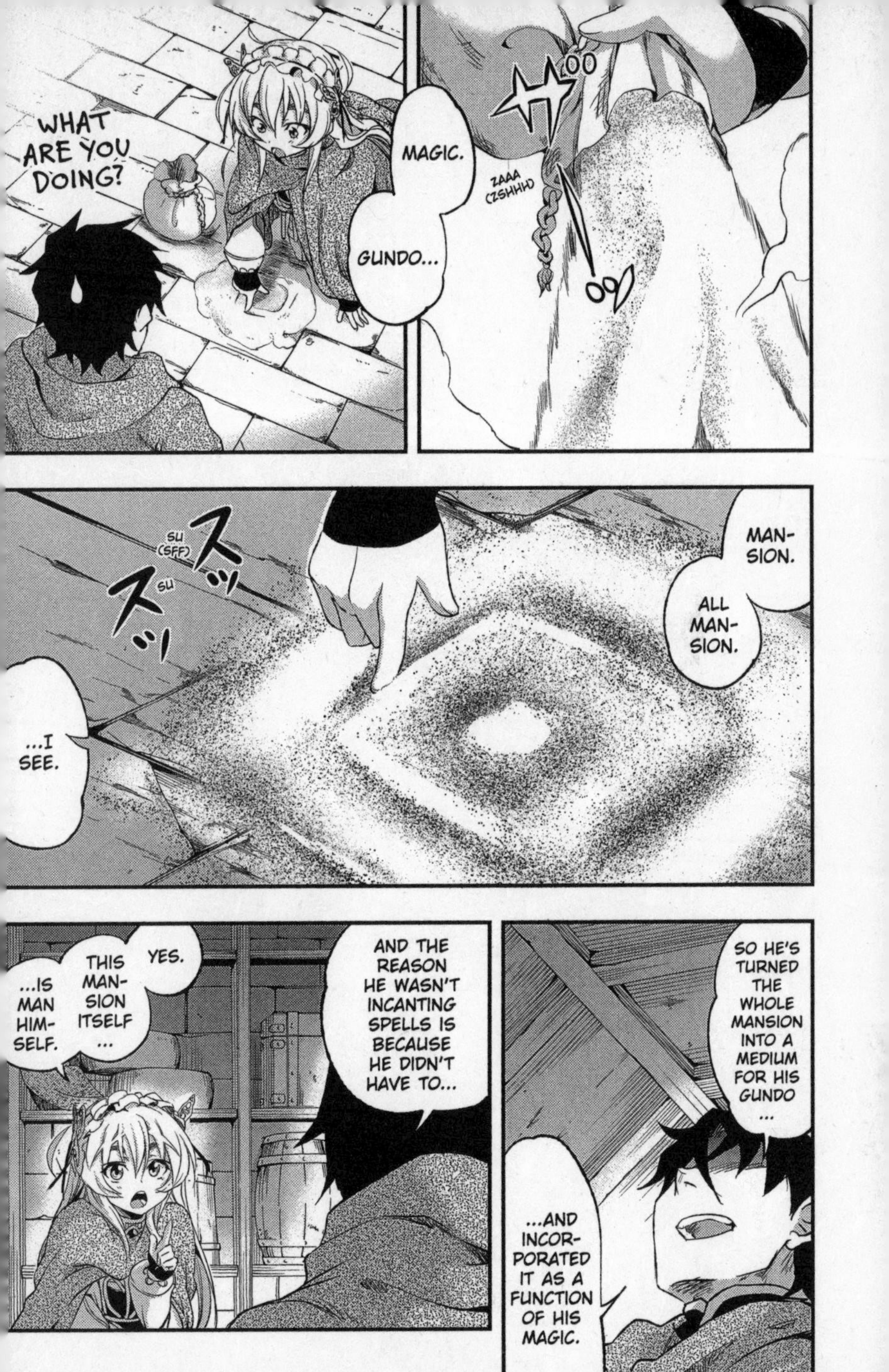
ZAAA (ZSHHH)
WHAT ARE YOU DOING?
MAGIC.
GUNDO...
MANSION.
ALL MANSION.
SU (SFF)
SU
...I SEE.
SO HE'S TURNED THE WHOLE MANSION INTO A MEDIUM FOR HIS GUNDO ...
...AND INCORPORATED IT AS A FUNCTION OF HIS MAGIC.
AND THE REASON HE WASN'T INCANTING SPELLS IS BECAUSE HE DIDN'T HAVE TO...
YES.
THIS MANSION ITSELF ...
...IS MAN HIMSELF.

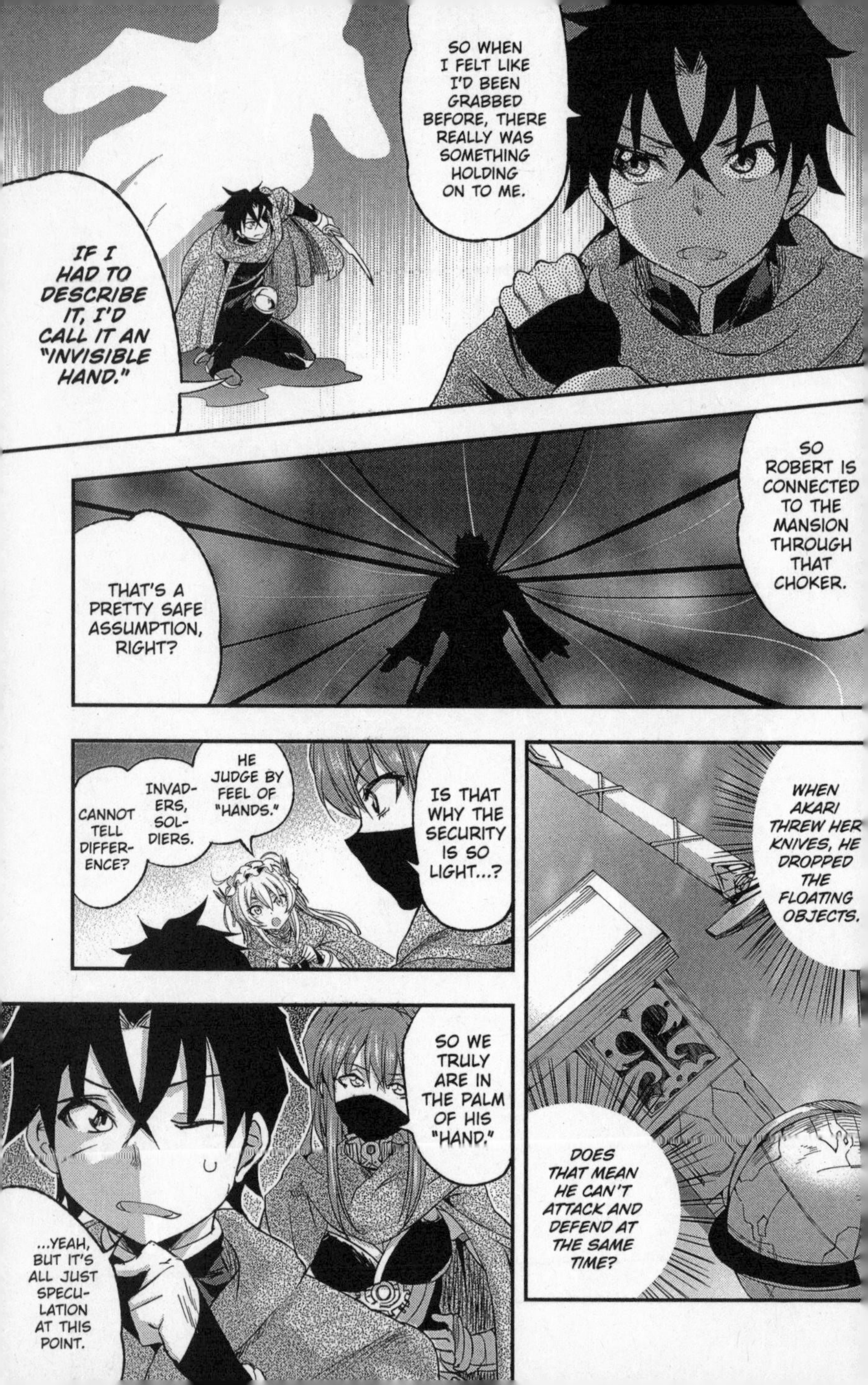
SO WHEN I FELT LIKE I'D BEEN GRABBED BEFORE, THERE REALLY WAS SOMETHING HOLDING ON TO ME.
IF I HAD TO DESCRIBE IT, I'D CALL IT AN "INVISIBLE HAND."
SO ROBERT IS CONNECTED TO THE MANSION THROUGH THAT CHOKER.
THAT'S A PRETTY SAFE ASSUMPTION, RIGHT?
WHEN AKARI THREW HER KNIVES, HE DROPPED THE FLOATING OBJECTS.
DOES THAT MEAN HE CAN'T ATTACK AND DEFEND AT THE SAME TIME?
IS THAT WHY THE SECURITY IS SO LIGHT...?
HE JUDGE BY FEEL OF "HANDS."
INVADERS, SOLDIERS.
CANNOT TELL DIFFERENCE?
SO WE TRULY ARE IN THE PALM OF HIS "HAND."
...YEAH, BUT IT'S ALL JUST SPECULATION AT THIS POINT.

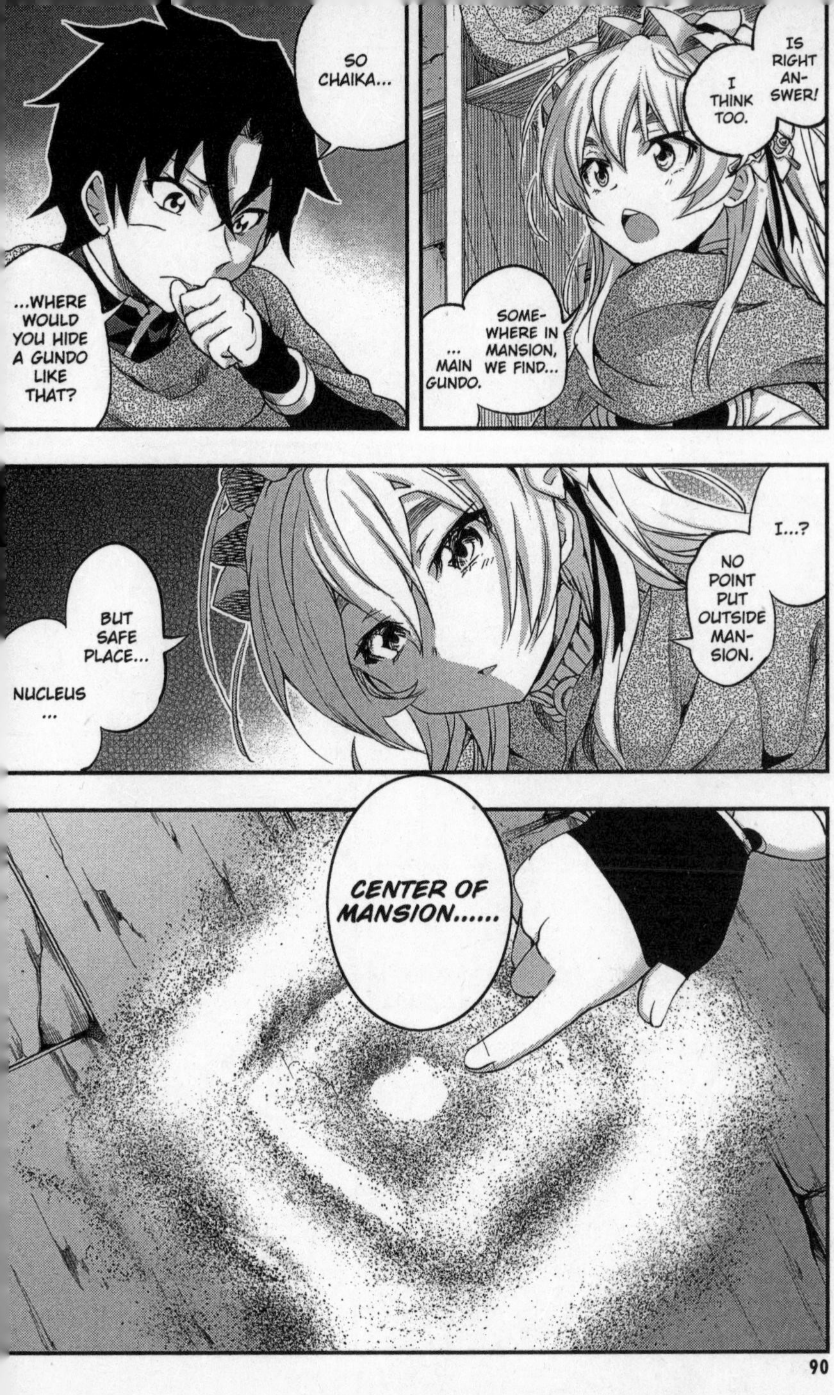
I THINK TOO.
IS RIGHT ANSWER!
SOMEWHERE IN MANSION, WE FIND...
... MAIN GUNDO.
SO CHAIKA...
...WHERE WOULD YOU HIDE A GUNDO LIKE THAT?
I...?
NO POINT PUT OUTSIDE MANSION.
BUT SAFE PLACE...
NUCLEUS ...
CENTER OF MANSION......

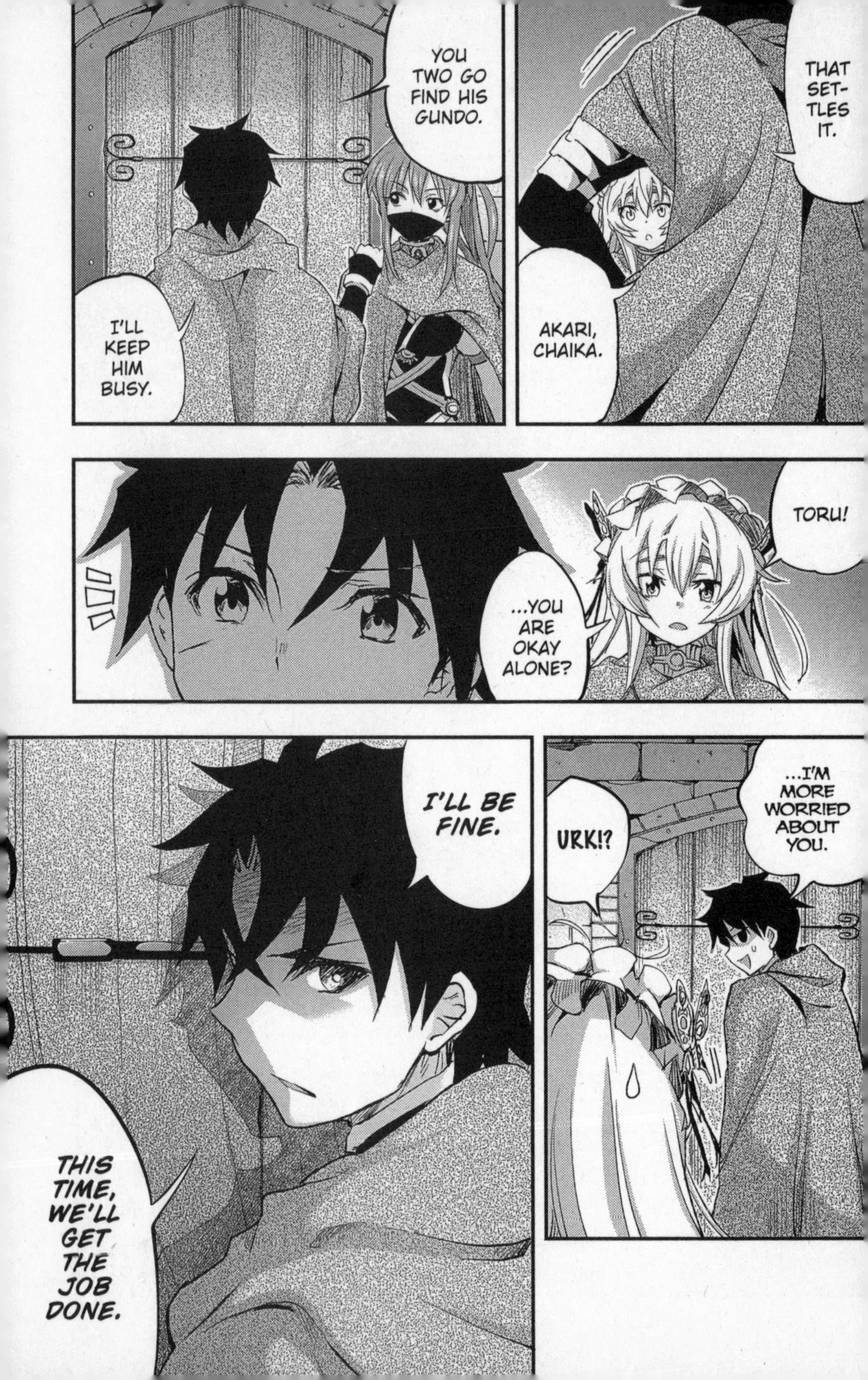
THAT SET-TLES IT.
AKARI, CHAIKA.
YOU TWO GO FIND HIS GUNDO.
I'LL KEEP HIM BUSY.
TORU!
...YOU ARE OKAY ALONE?
...I'M MORE WORRIED ABOUT YOU.
URK!?
I'LL BE FINE.
THIS TIME, WE'LL GET THE JOB DONE.

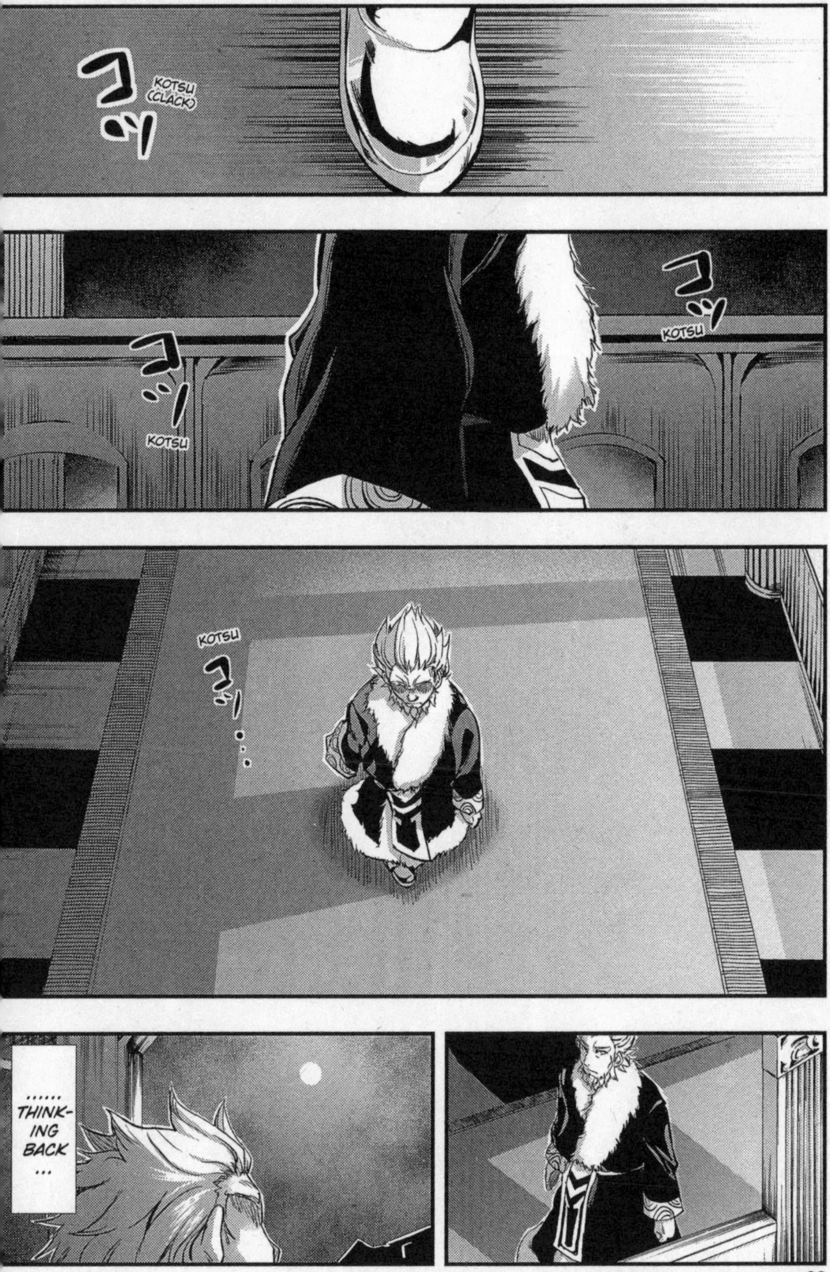
KOTSU (CLACK)
KOTSU
KOTSU
KOTSU
...
...... THINK- ING BACK ...

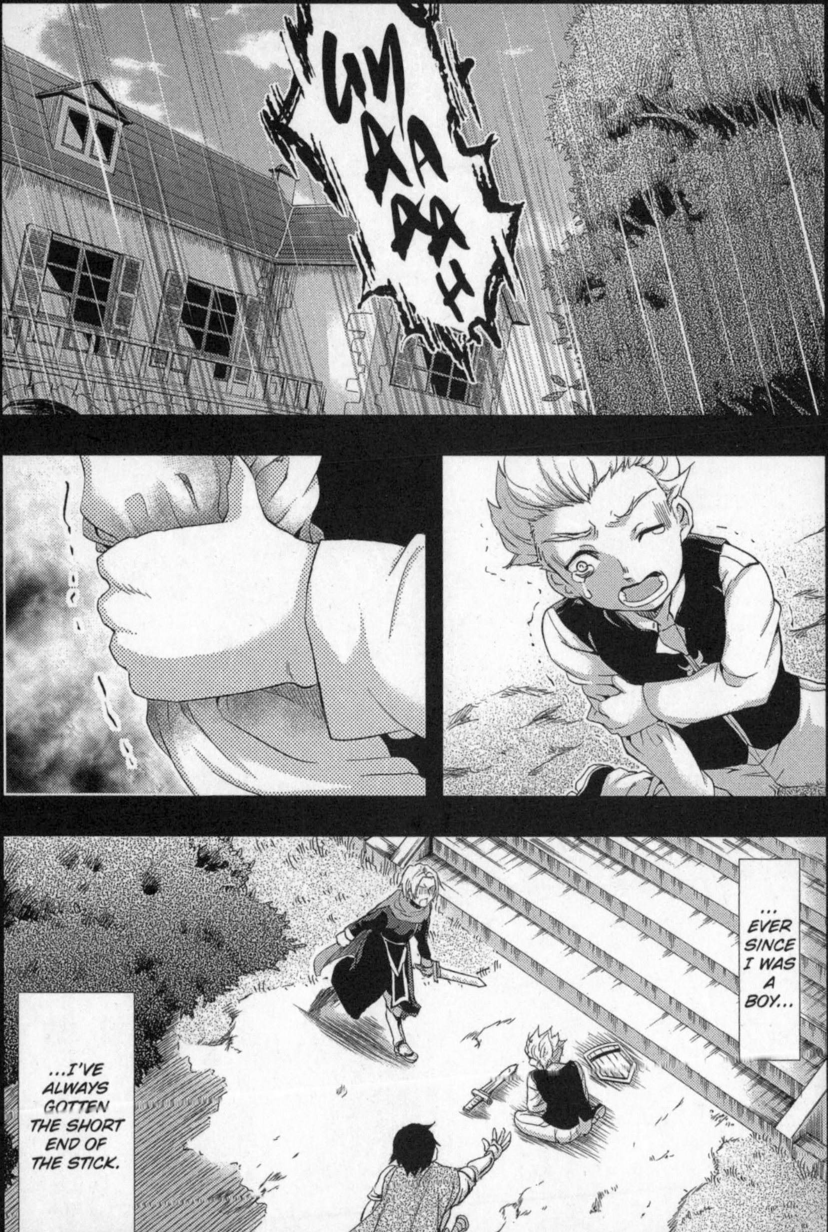
UWAAAAH
...EVER SINCE I WAS A BOY...
...I'VE ALWAYS GOTTEN THE SHORT END OF THE STICK.

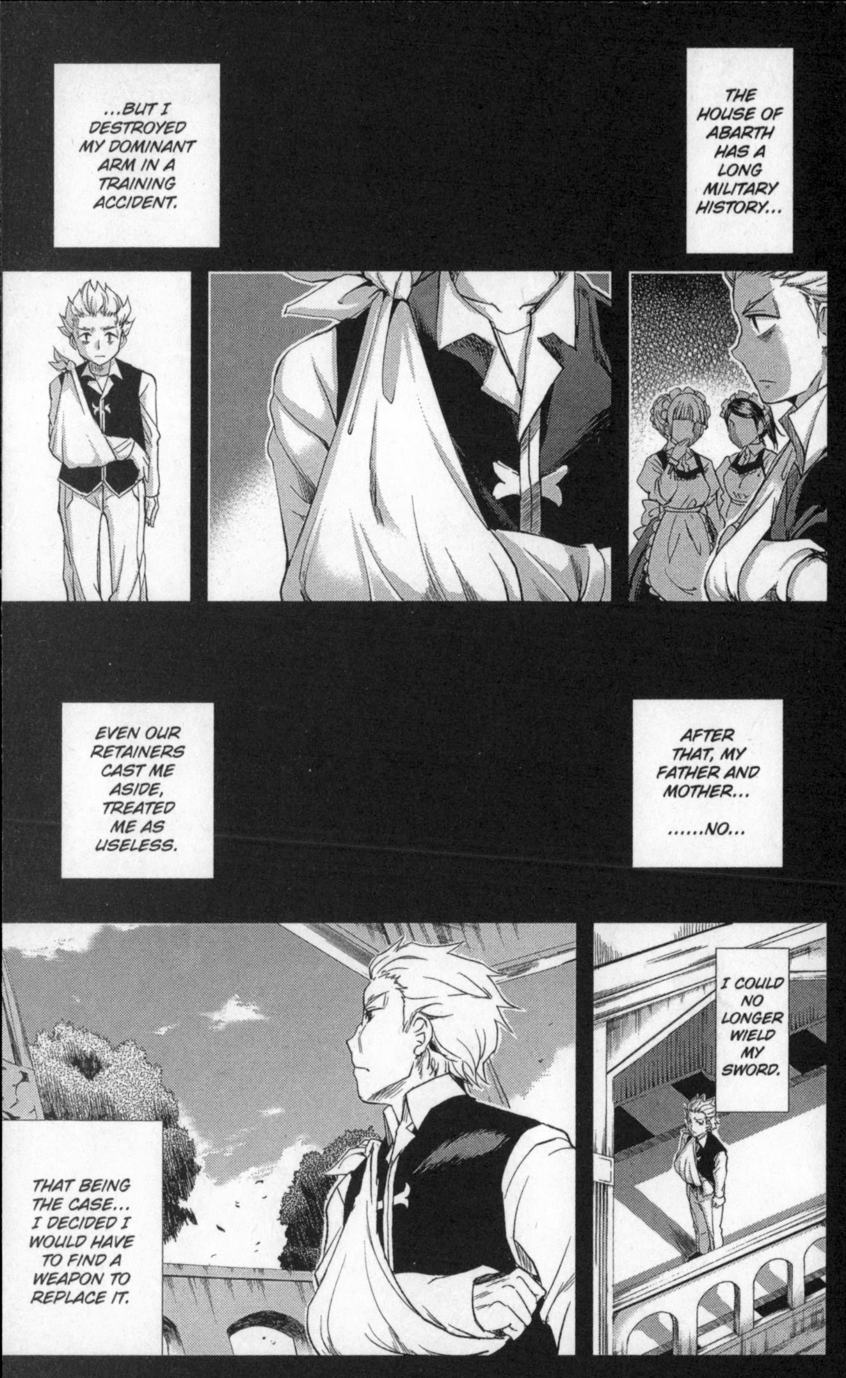
THE HOUSE OF ABARTH HAS A LONG MILITARY HISTORY...
...BUT I DESTROYED MY DOMINANT ARM IN A TRAINING ACCIDENT.
AFTER THAT, MY FATHER AND MOTHER...
......NO...
EVEN OUR RETAINERS CAST ME ASIDE, TREATED ME AS USELESS.
I COULD NO LONGER WIELD MY SWORD.
THAT BEING THE CASE... I DECIDED I WOULD HAVE TO FIND A WEAPON TO REPLACE IT.

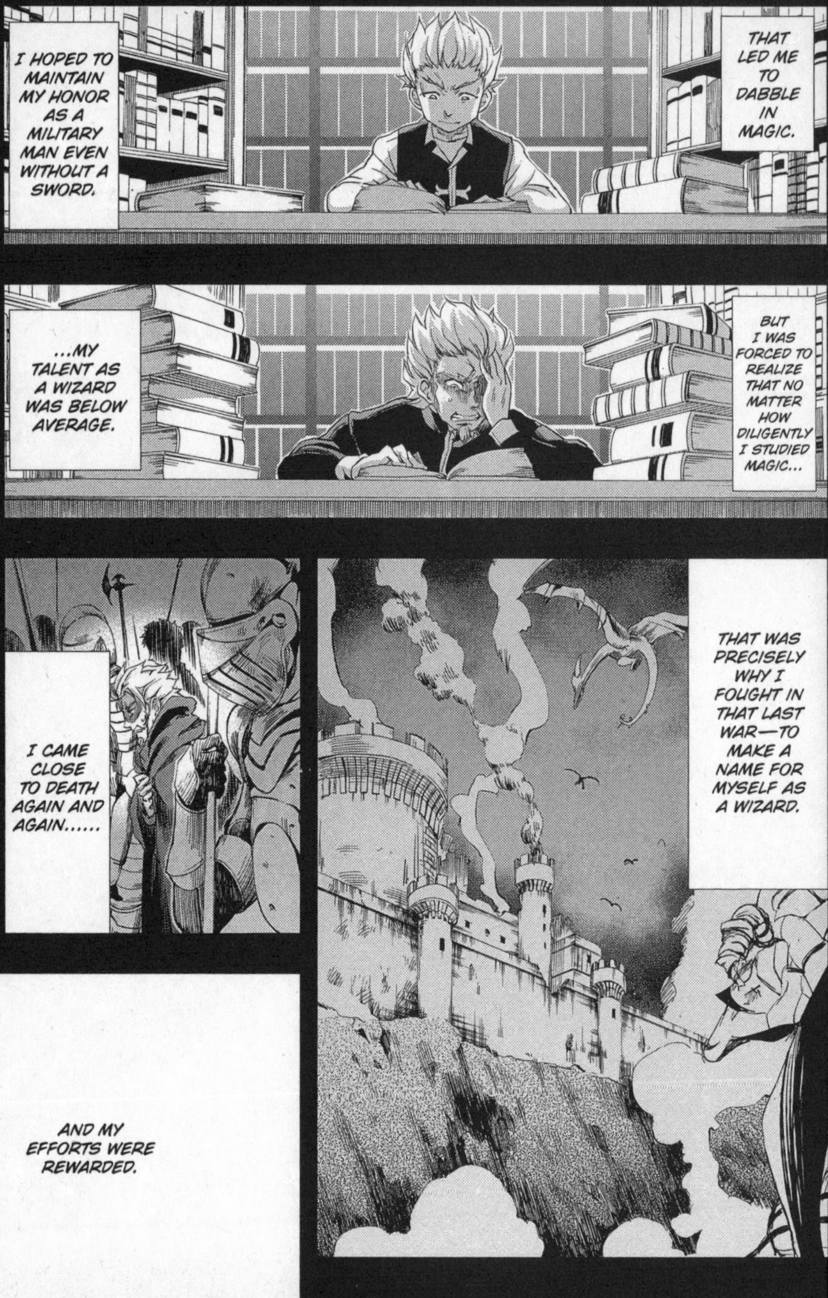
THAT LED ME TO DABBLE IN MAGIC.
I HOPED TO MAINTAIN MY HONOR AS A MILITARY MAN EVEN WITHOUT A SWORD.
BUT I WAS FORCED TO REALIZE THAT NO MATTER HOW DILIGENTLY I STUDIED MAGIC...
...MY TALENT AS A WIZARD WAS BELOW AVERAGE.
THAT WAS PRECISELY WHY I FOUGHT IN THAT LAST WAR—TO MAKE A NAME FOR MYSELF AS A WIZARD.
I CAME CLOSE TO DEATH AGAIN AND AGAIN......
AND MY EFFORTS WERE REWARDED.

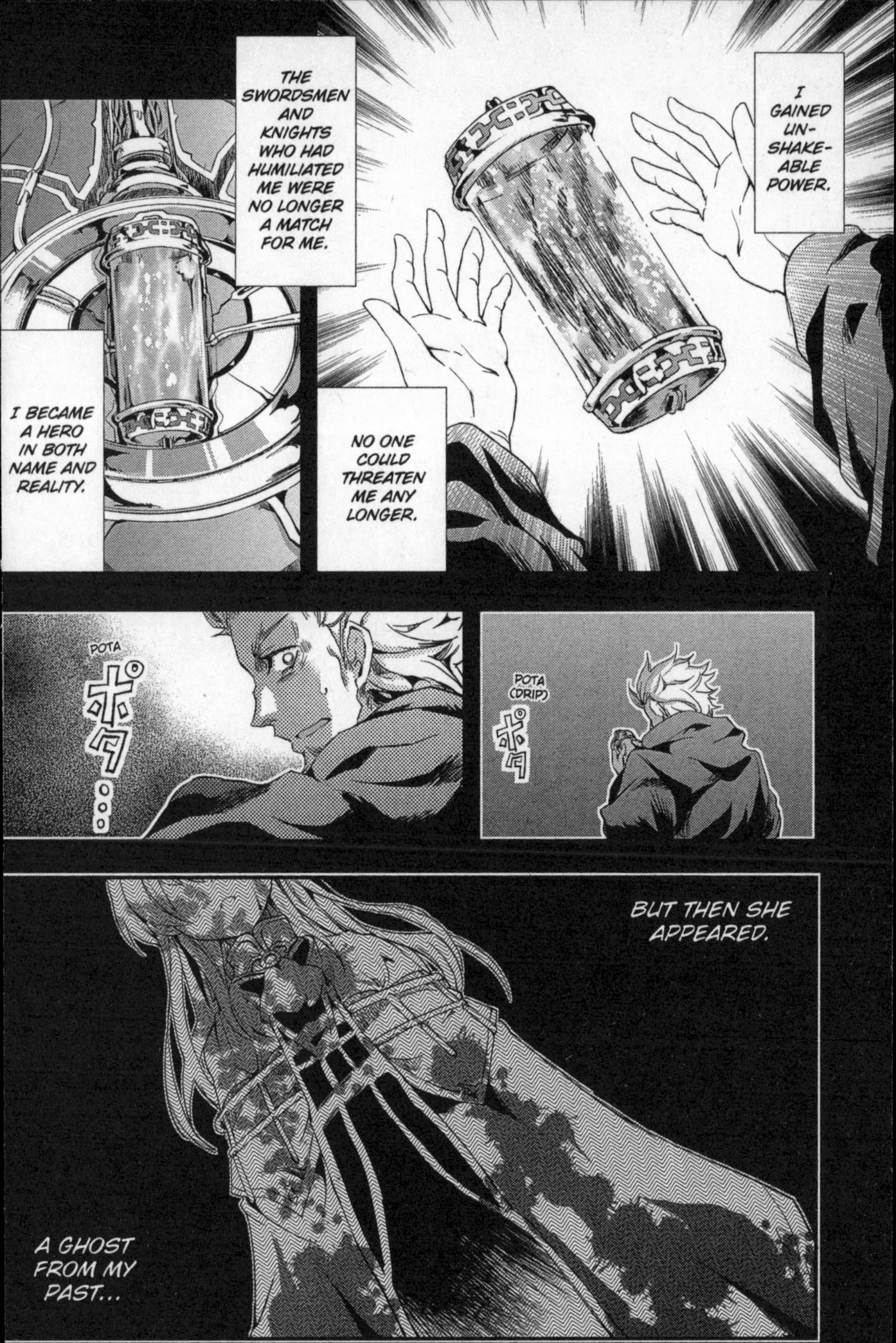
I GAINED UN-SHAKE-ABLE POWER.
THE SWORDSMEN AND KNIGHTS WHO HAD HUMILIATED ME WERE NO LONGER A MATCH FOR ME.
NO ONE COULD THREATEN ME ANY LONGER.
I BECAME A HERO IN BOTH NAME AND REALITY.
POTA (DRIP)
ポタ
POTA
ポタ…
BUT THEN SHE APPEARED.
A GHOST FROM MY PAST...

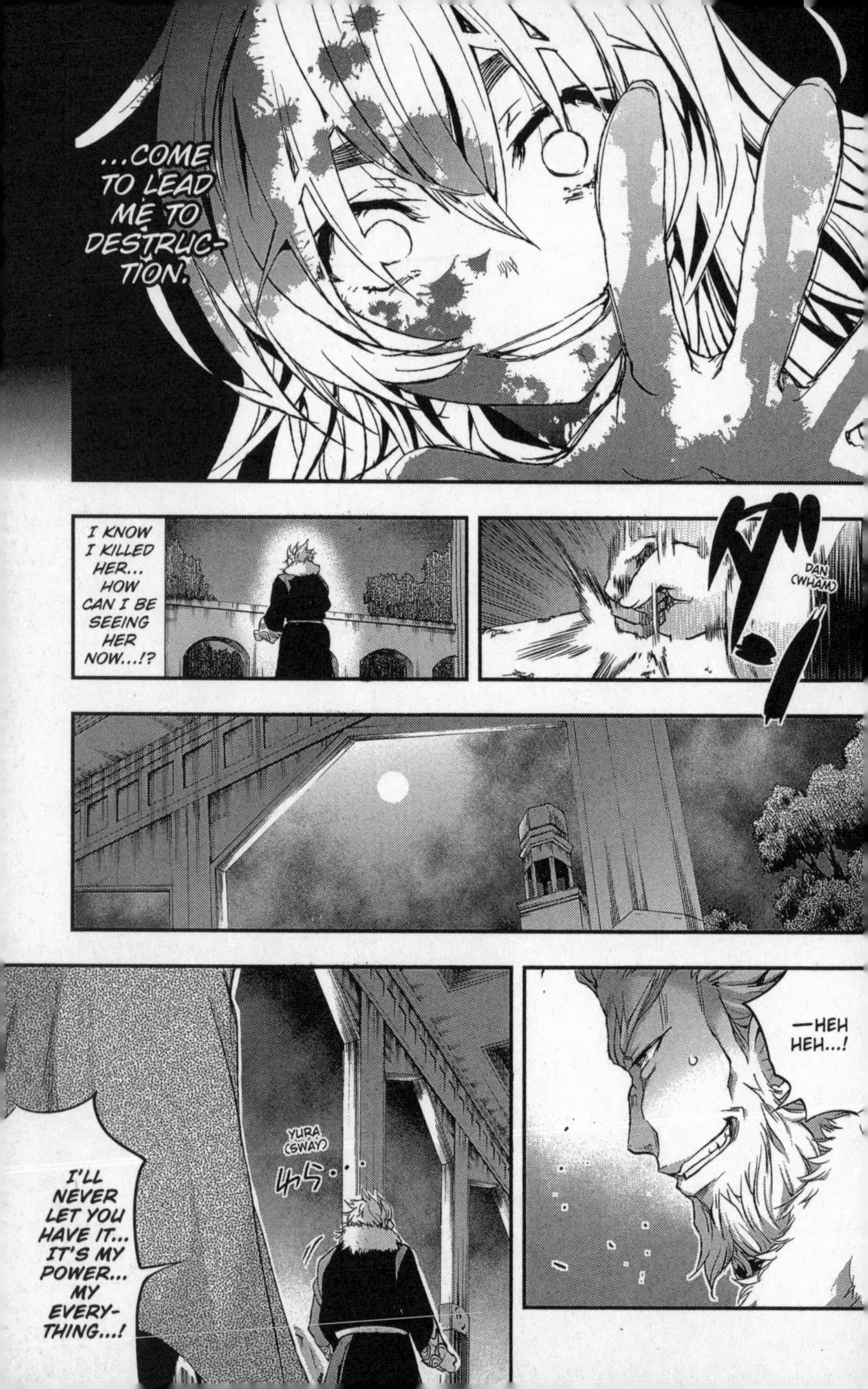
...COME TO LEAD ME TO DESTRUC-TION.
DAN (WHAM)
I KNOW I KILLED HER... HOW CAN I BE SEEING HER NOW...!?
—HEH HEH...!
YURA (SWAY)
I'LL NEVER LET YOU HAVE IT... IT'S MY POWER... MY EVERY-THING...!

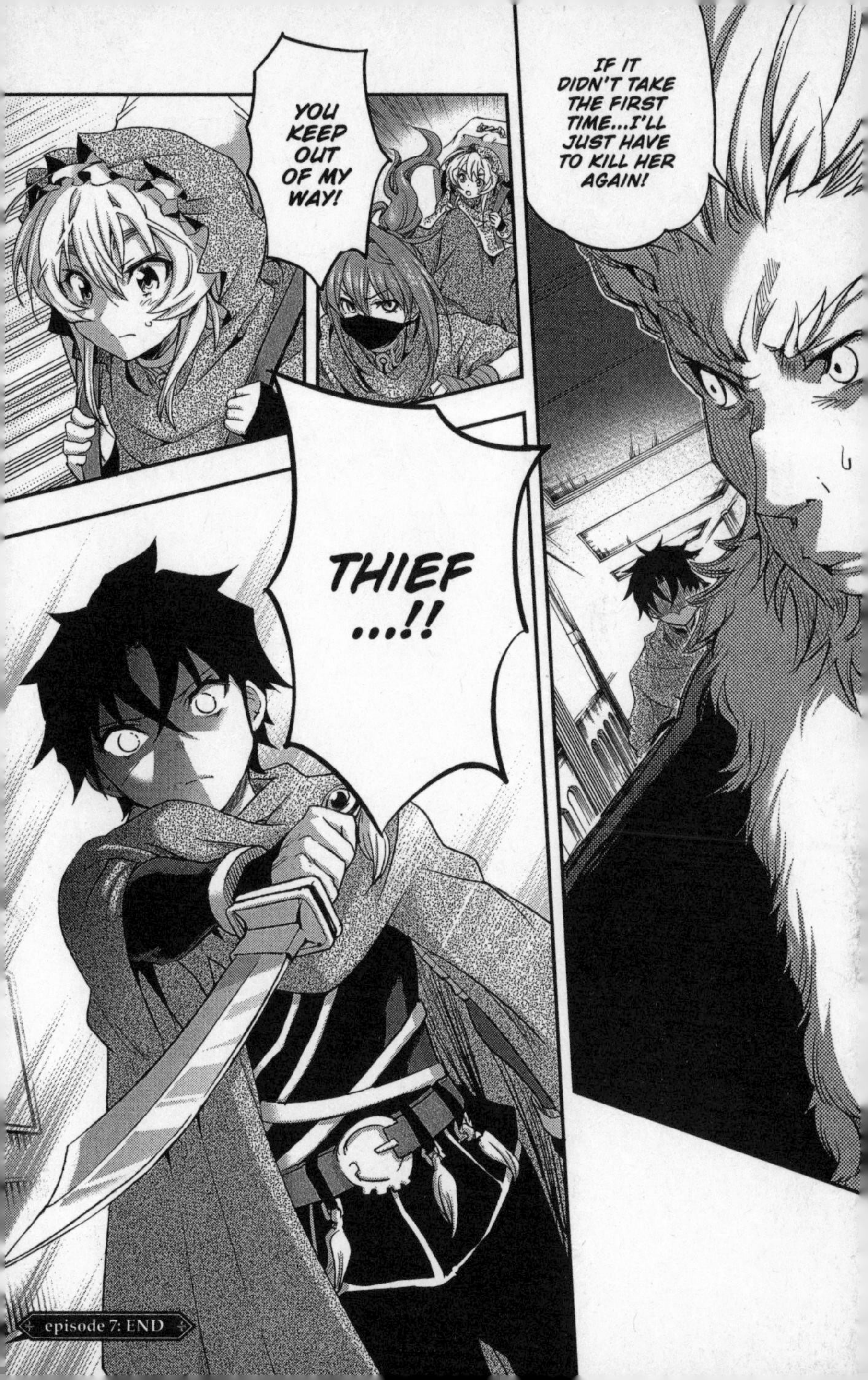
IF IT DIDN'T TAKE THE FIRST TIME...I'LL JUST HAVE TO KILL HER AGAIN!
YOU KEEP OUT OF MY WAY!
THIEF ...!!
episode 7: END

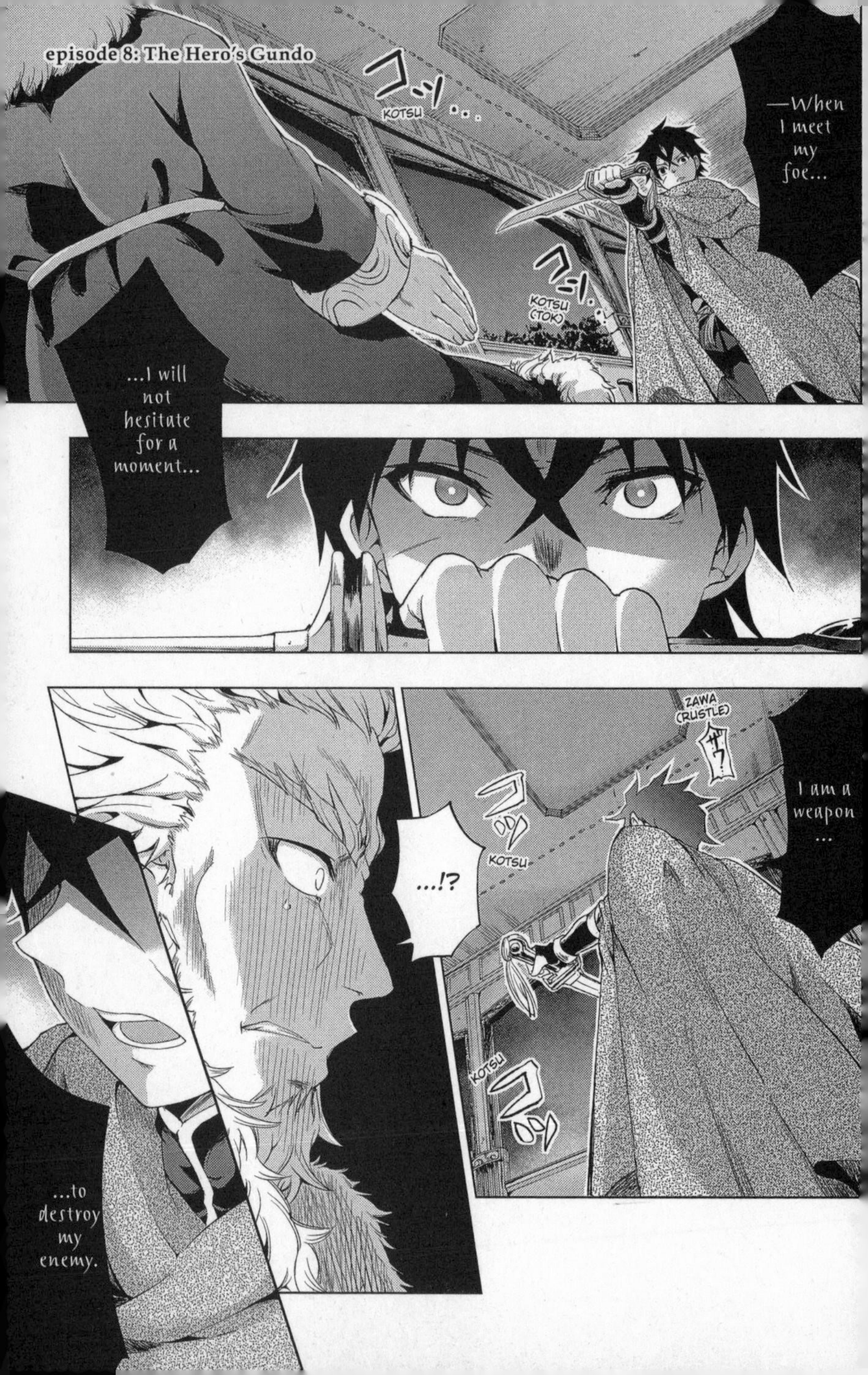
episode 8: The Hero's Gundo
—When I meet my foe...
KOTSU
KOTSU (TOK)
...I will not hesitate for a moment...
ZAWA (RUSTLE)
I am a weapon ...
KOTSU
KOTSU
...!?
...to destroy my enemy.

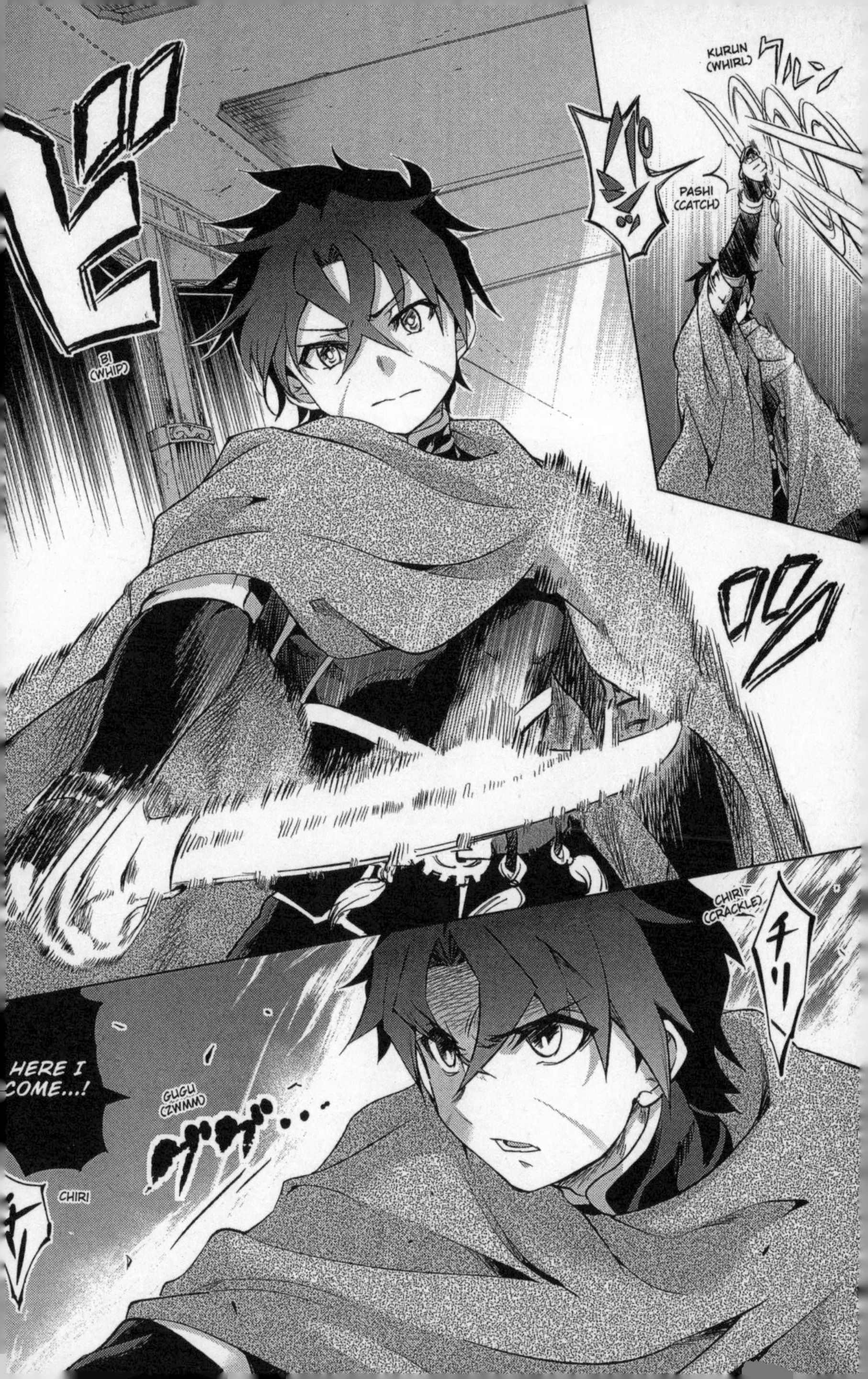
KURUN (WHIRL)
PASHI (CATCH)
BI (WHIP)
CHIRI (CRACKLE)
チリ
HERE I COME...!
GUGU (ZWMM)
CHIRI

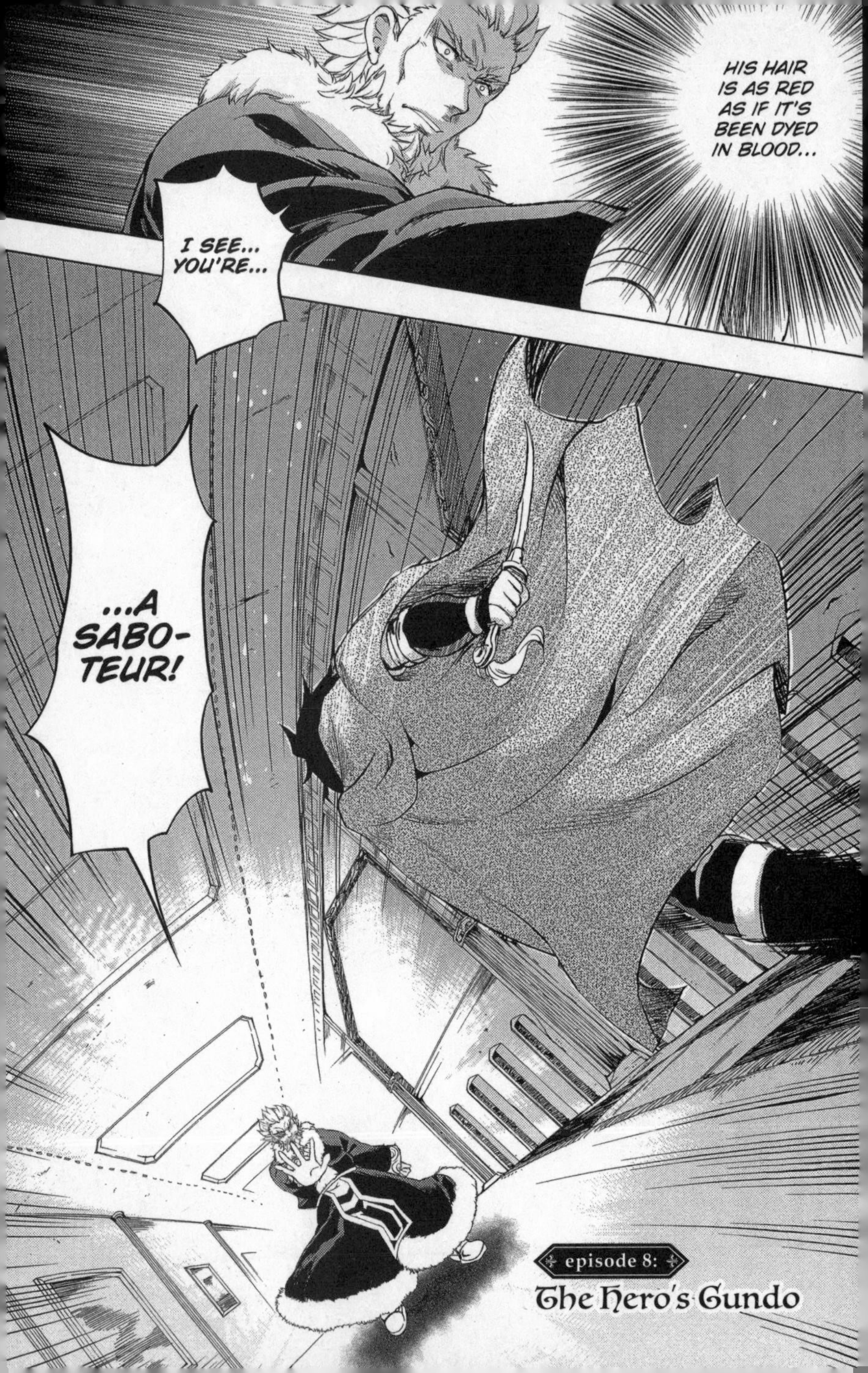
HIS HAIR IS AS RED AS IF IT'S BEEN DYED IN BLOOD...
I SEE... YOU'RE...
...A SABO-TEUR!
episode 8:
The Hero's Gundo

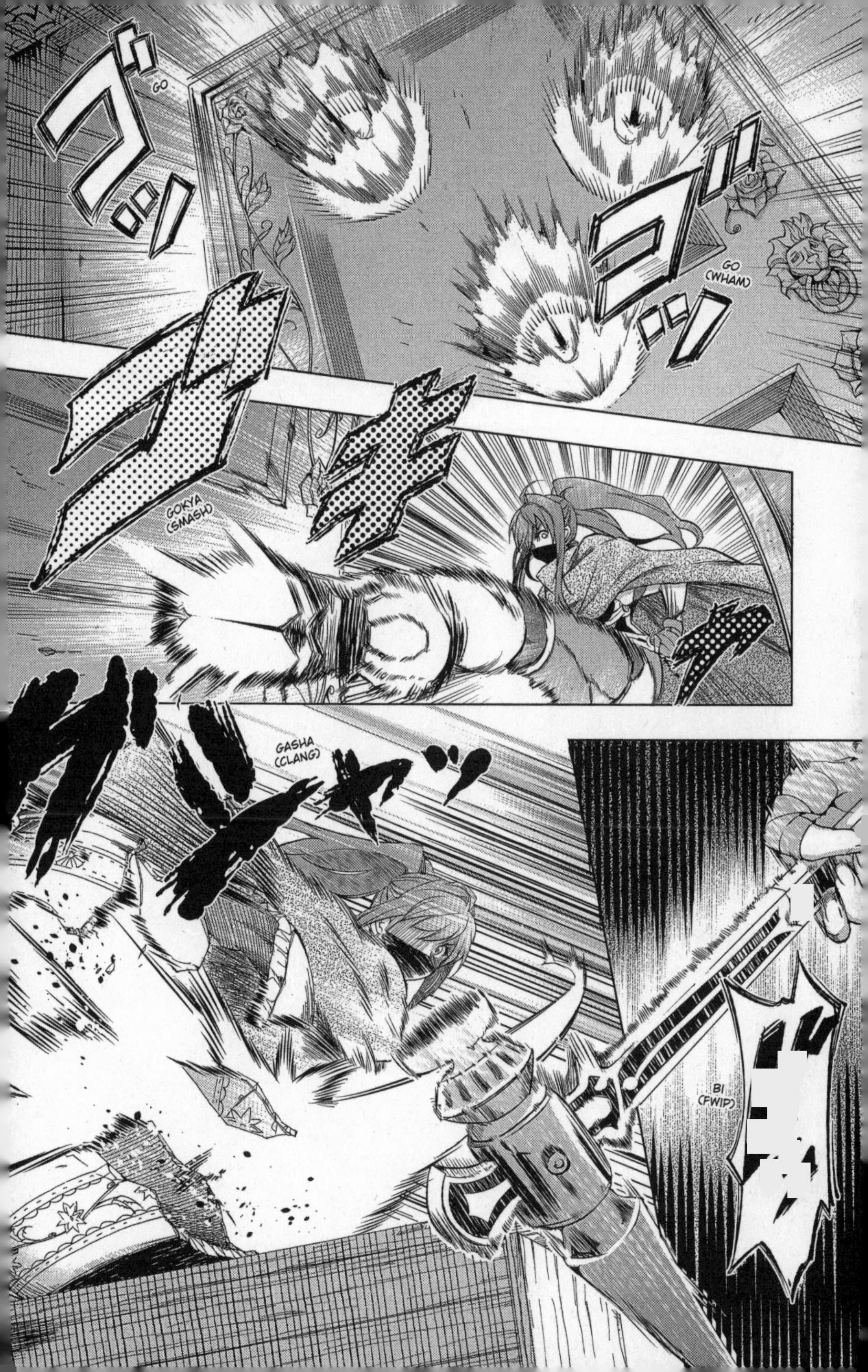
GO (WHAM)
GO
GOKYA (SMASH)
BI (FWIP)
GASHA (CLANG)

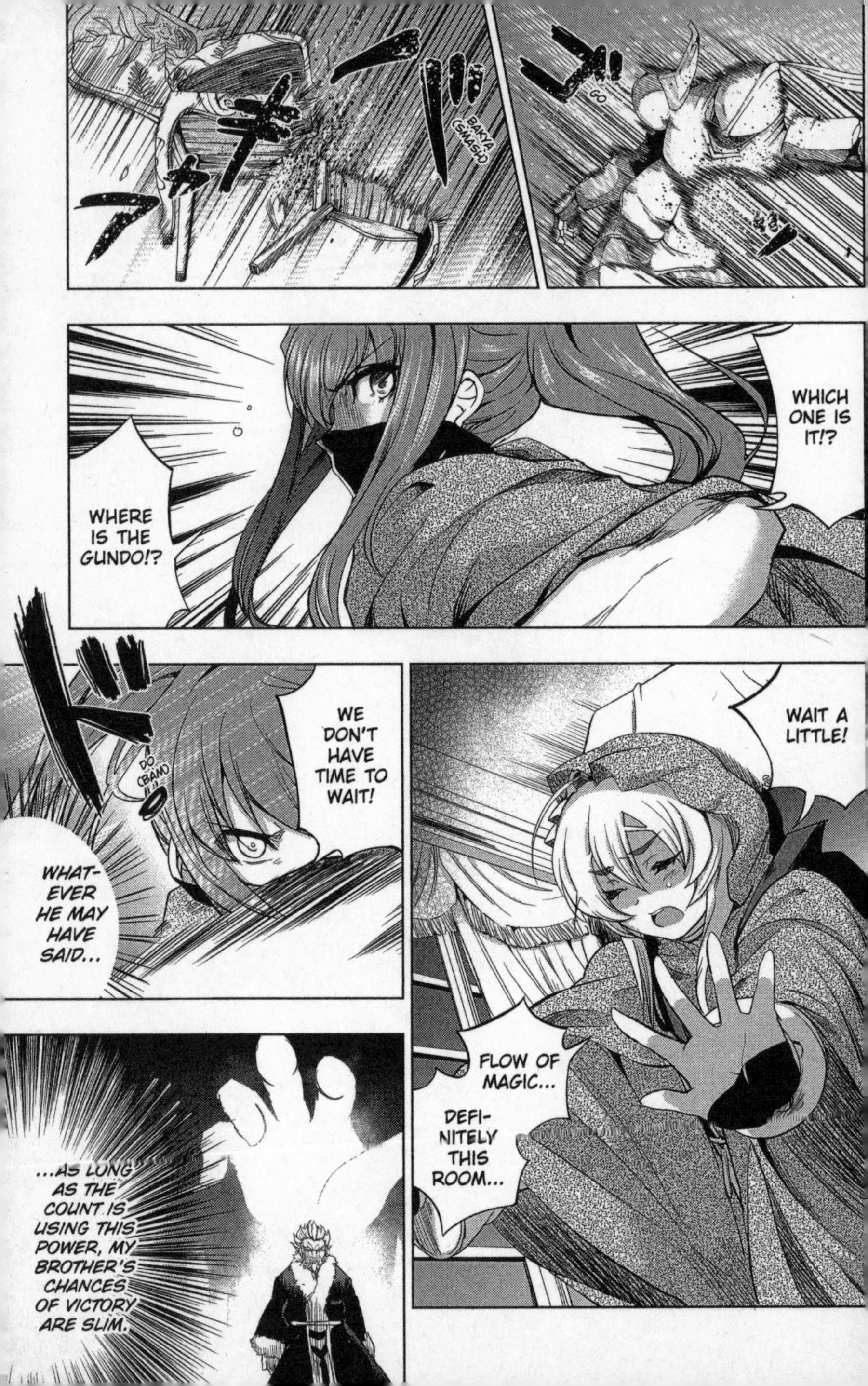
GO
BAKYA (SMASH)
WHICH ONE IS IT!?
WHERE IS THE GUNDO!?
WAIT A LITTLE!
FLOW OF MAGIC...
DEFI-NITELY THIS ROOM...
WE DON'T HAVE TIME TO WAIT!
DO (BAM)
WHAT-EVER HE MAY HAVE SAID...
...AS LONG AS THE COUNT IS USING THIS POWER, MY BROTHER'S CHANCES OF VICTORY ARE SLIM.

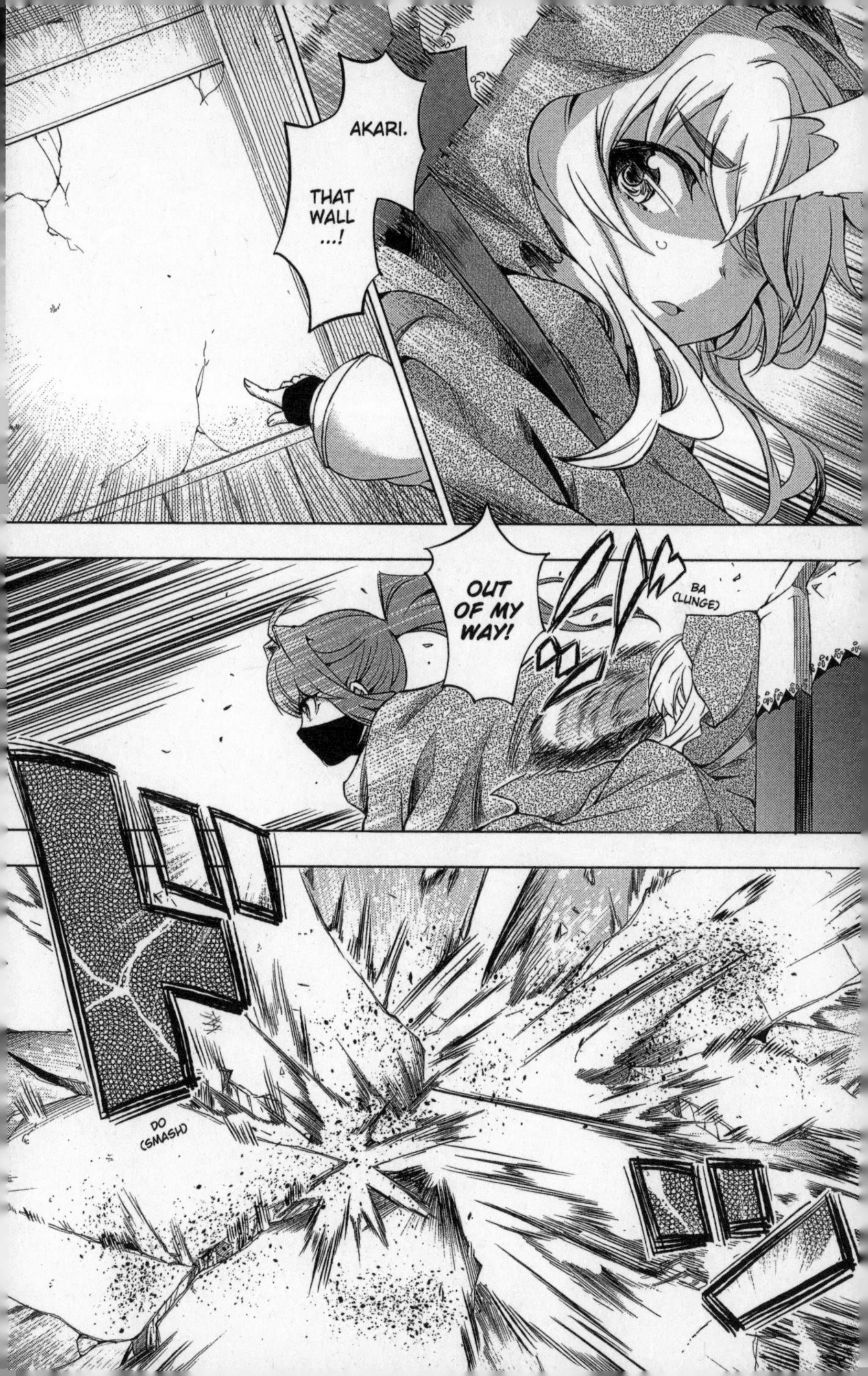
AKARI.
THAT WALL ...!
BA (LUNGE)
OUT OF MY WAY!
DO (SMASH)

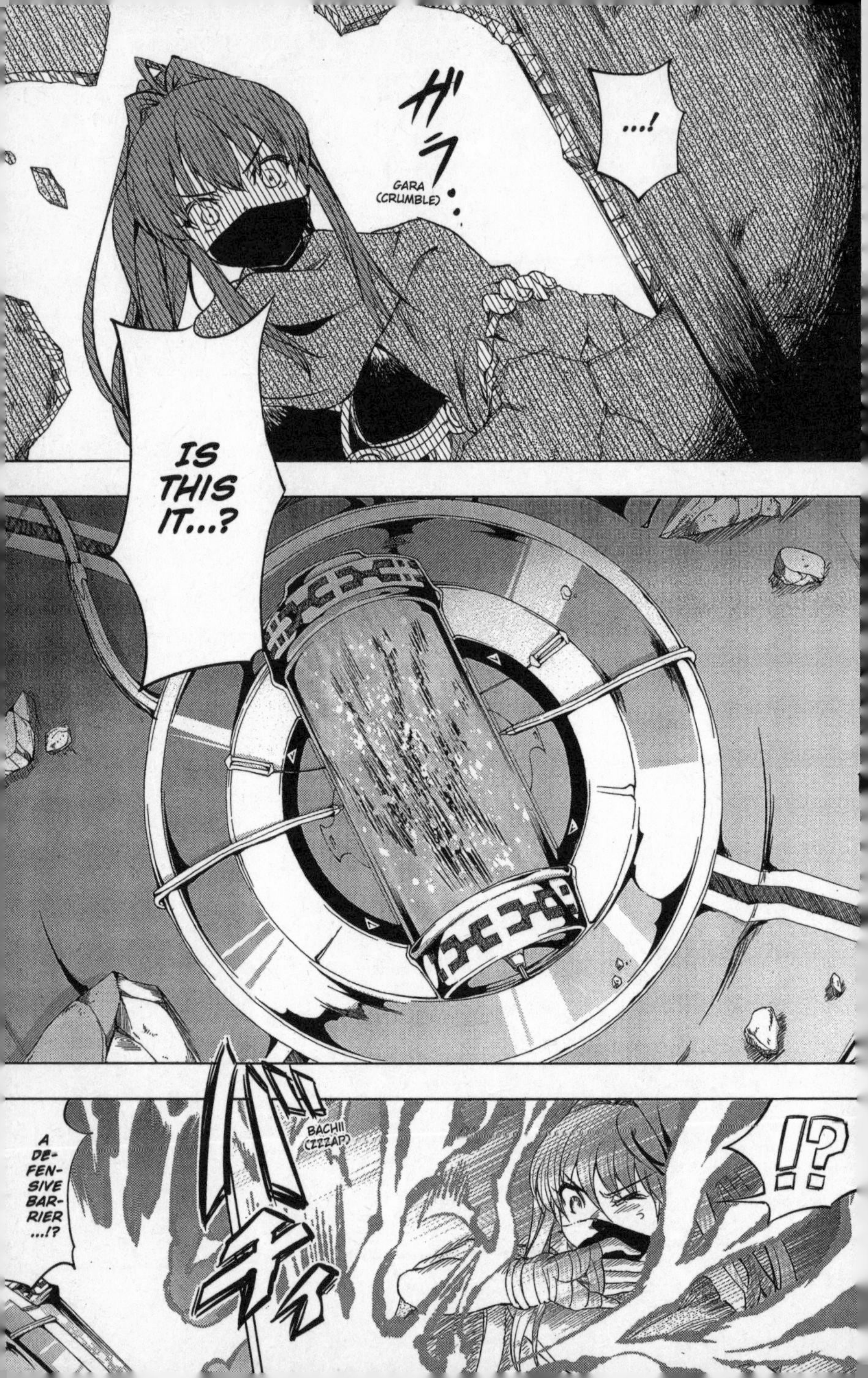
...!
ガラ
GARA (CRUMBLE)
IS THIS IT...?
!?
BACHII (ZZZAP)
A DEFENSIVE BARRIER ...!?

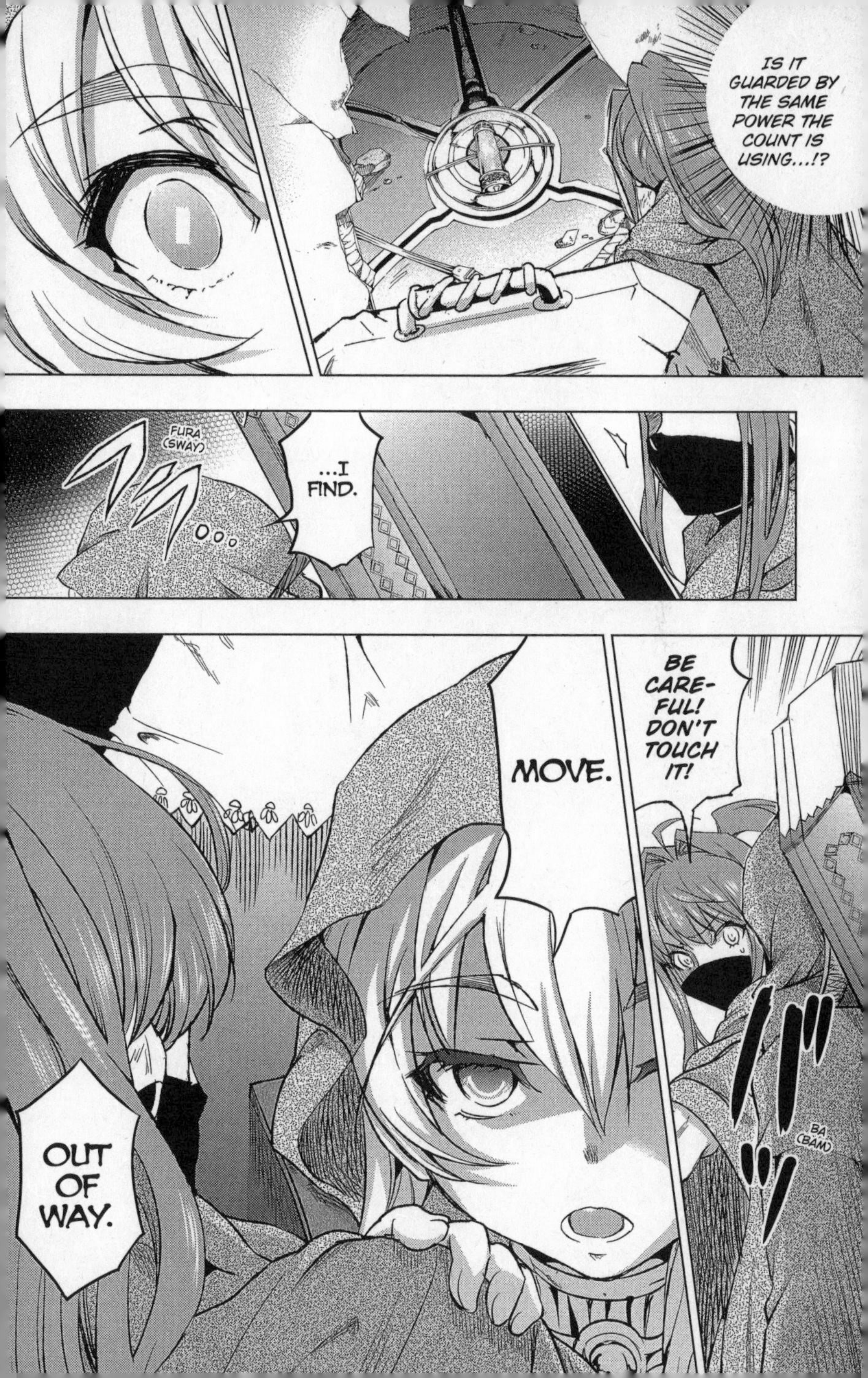
IS IT GUARDED BY THE SAME POWER THE COUNT IS USING...!?
...I FIND.
FURA (SWAY)
BE CAREFUL! DON'T TOUCH IT!
MOVE.
BA (BAM)
OUT OF WAY.

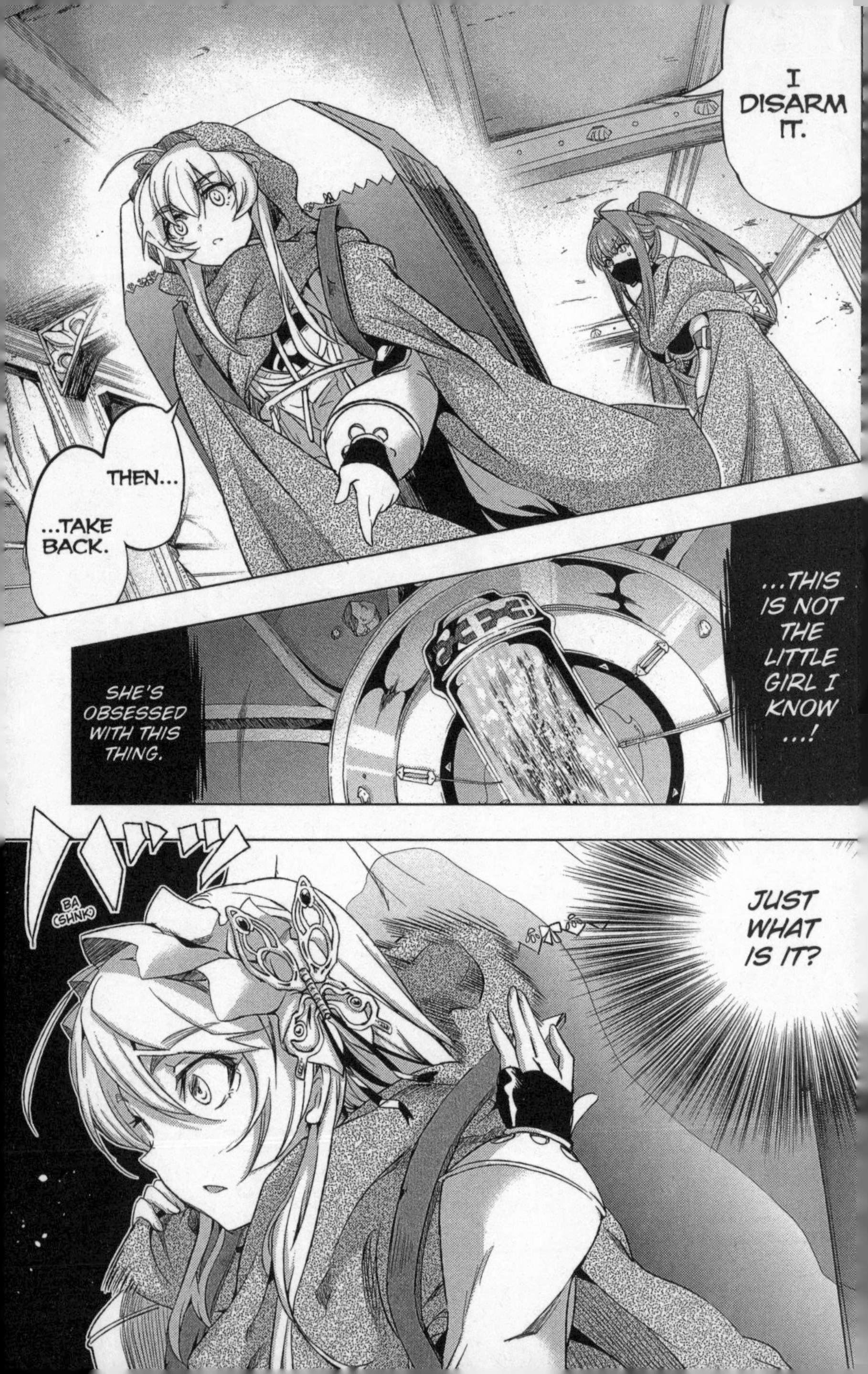
I DISARM IT.
THEN...
...TAKE BACK.
...THIS IS NOT THE LITTLE GIRL I KNOW...!
SHE'S OBSESSED WITH THIS THING.
JUST WHAT IS IT?
BA (SHNK)

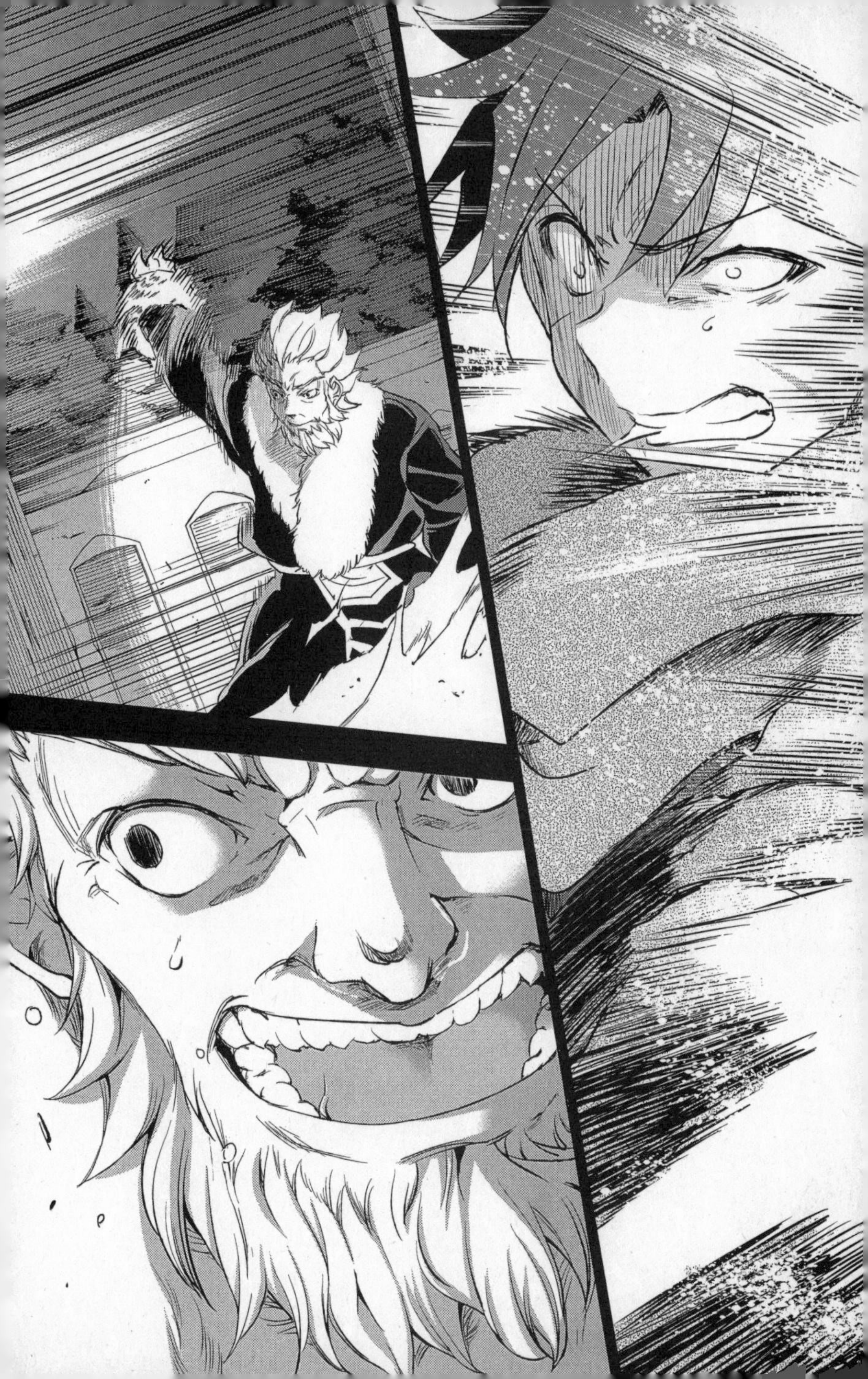

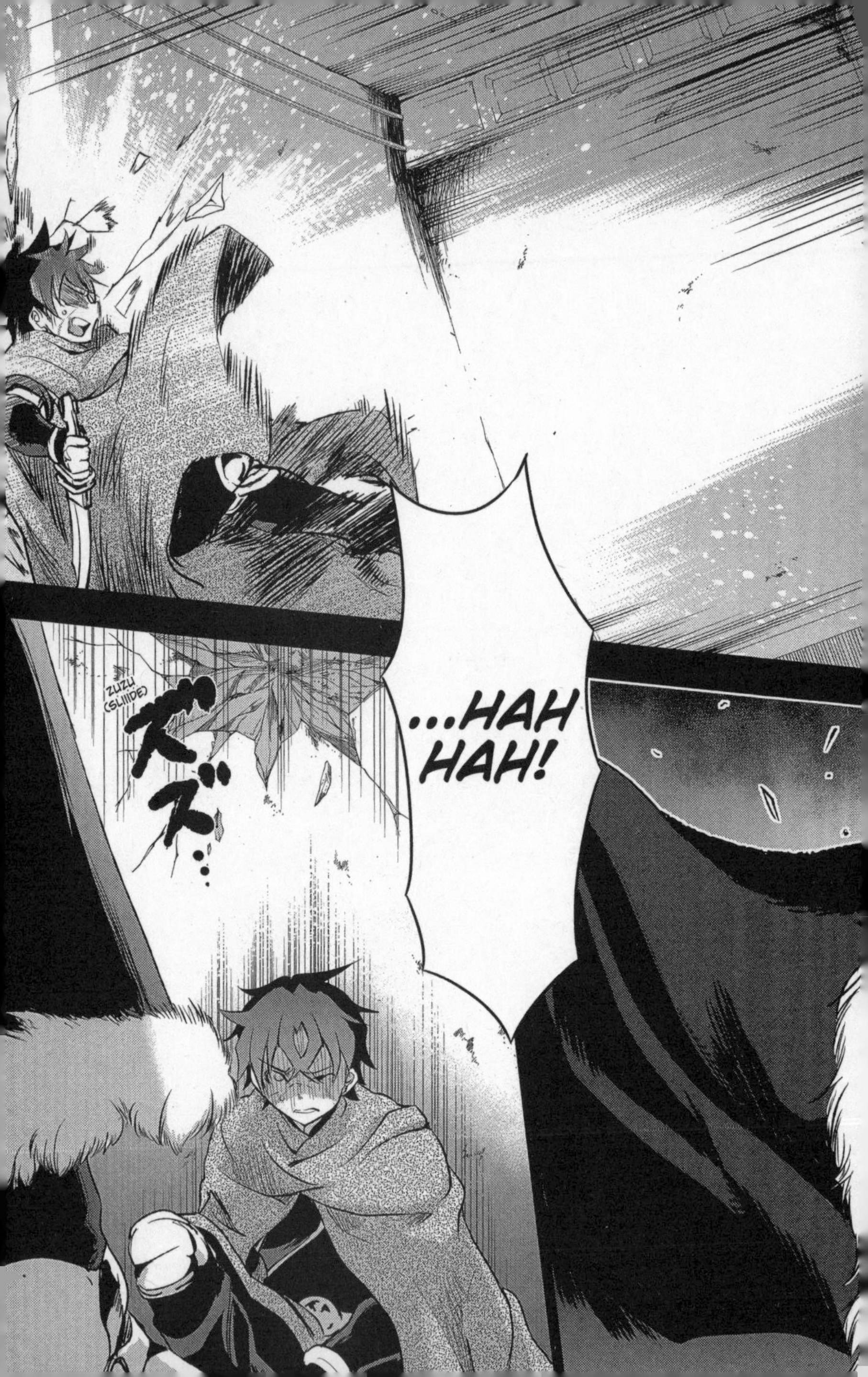
...HAH HAH!
ズズ…
ZUZU (SLIIIDE)

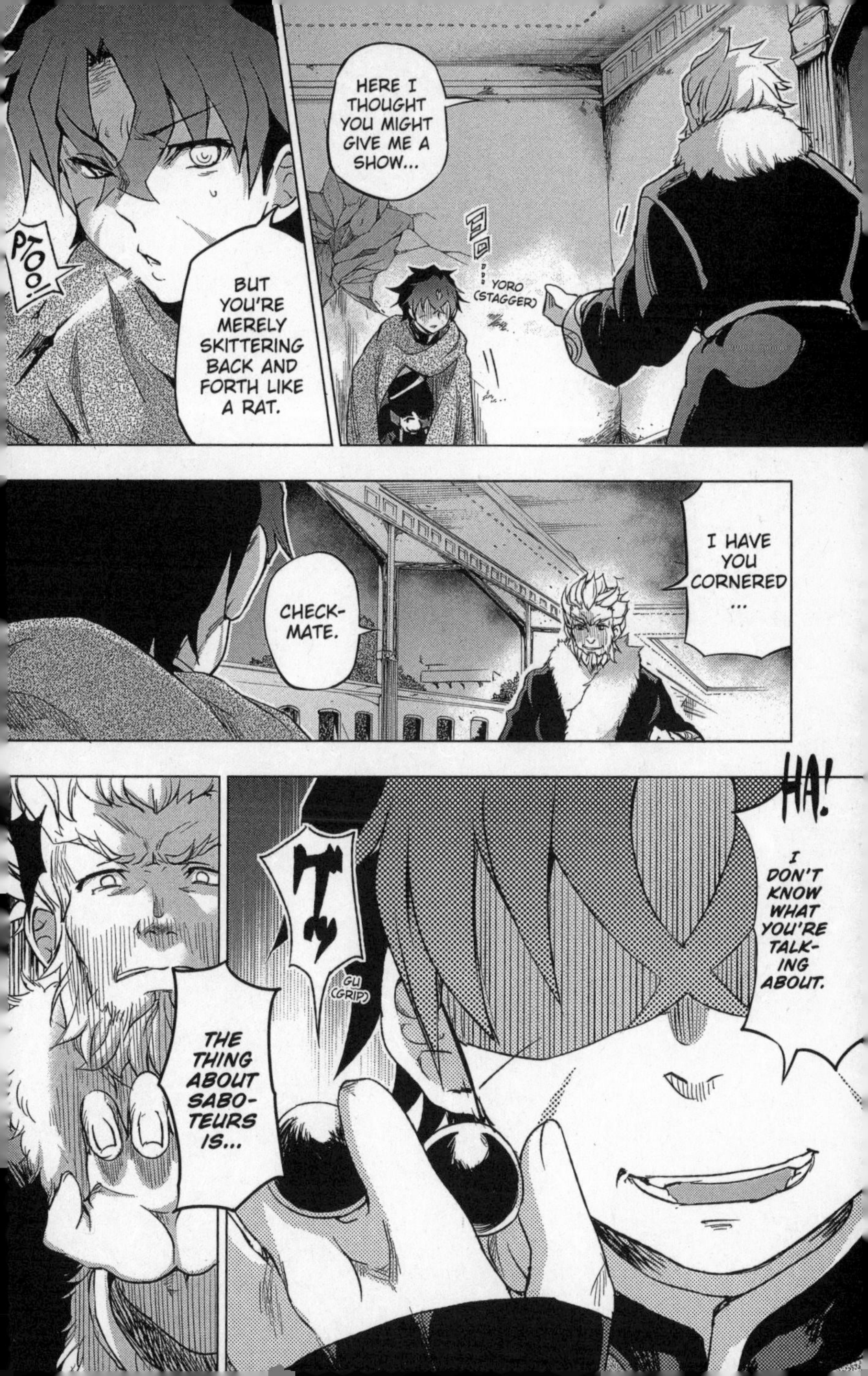
HERE I THOUGHT YOU MIGHT GIVE ME A SHOW...
YORO (STAGGER)
BUT YOU'RE MERELY SKITTERING BACK AND FORTH LIKE A RAT.
PTOO!
I HAVE YOU CORNERED...
CHECK-MATE.
HA!
I DON'T KNOW WHAT YOU'RE TALK-ING ABOUT.
GU (GRIP)
THE THING ABOUT SABO-TEURS IS...

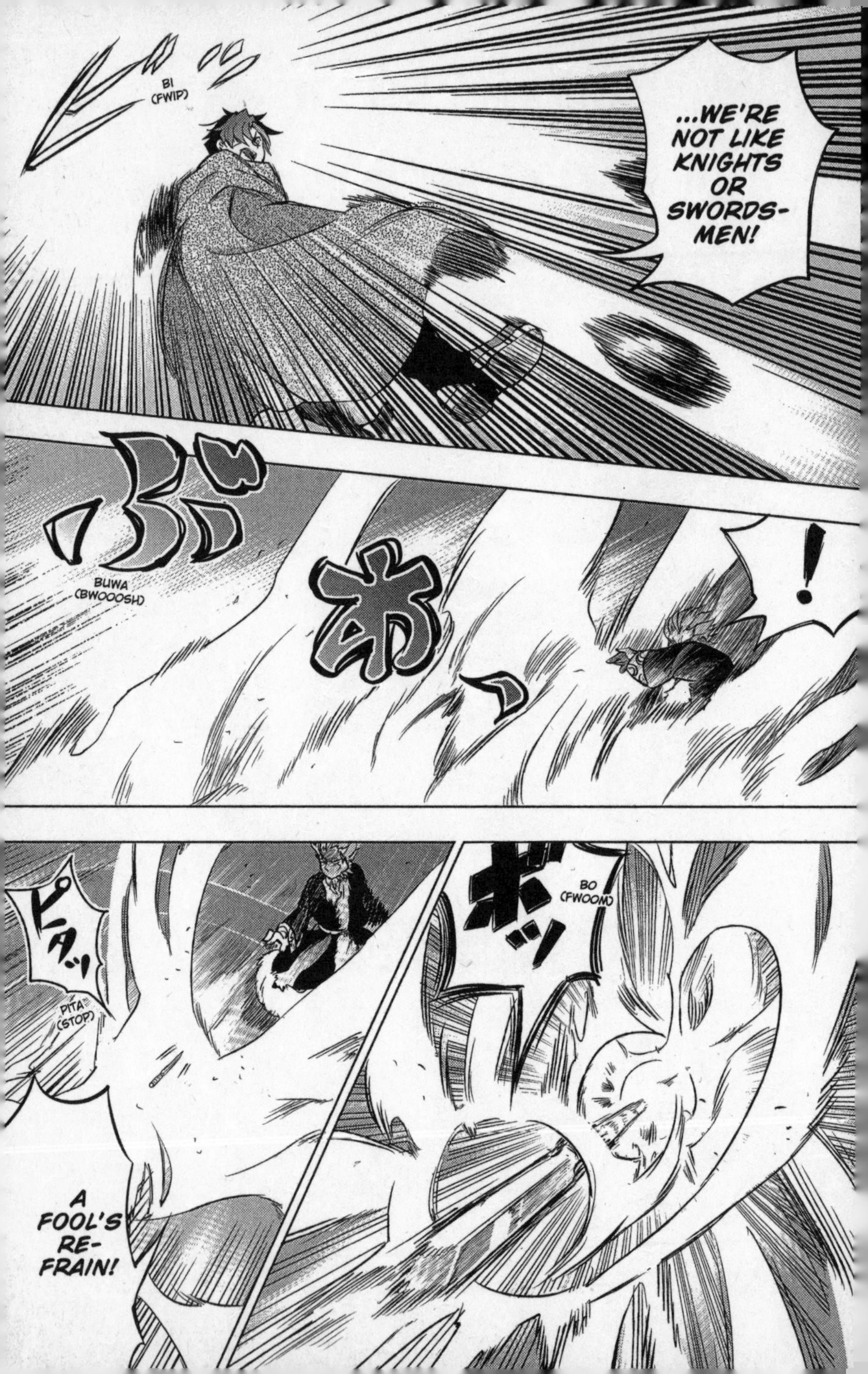
...WE'RE NOT LIKE KNIGHTS OR SWORDS-MEN!
BI (FWIP)
!
BUWA (BWOOOSH)
BO (FWOOM)
PITA (STOP)
A FOOL'S RE-FRAIN!

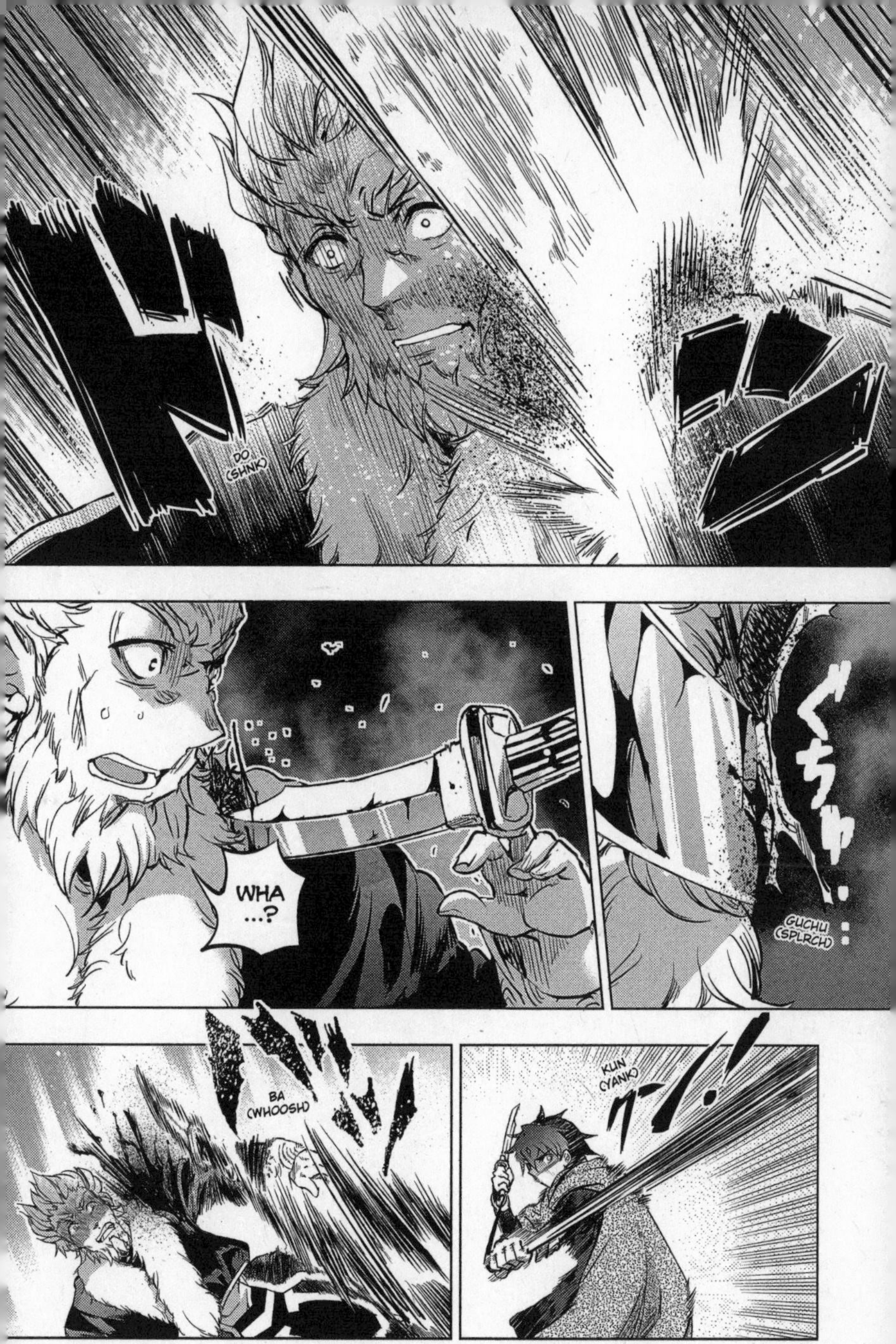
DO (SHNK)
ぐちゅ…
GUCHU (SPLRCH)
WHA ...?
KUN (YANK)
BA (WHOOSH)

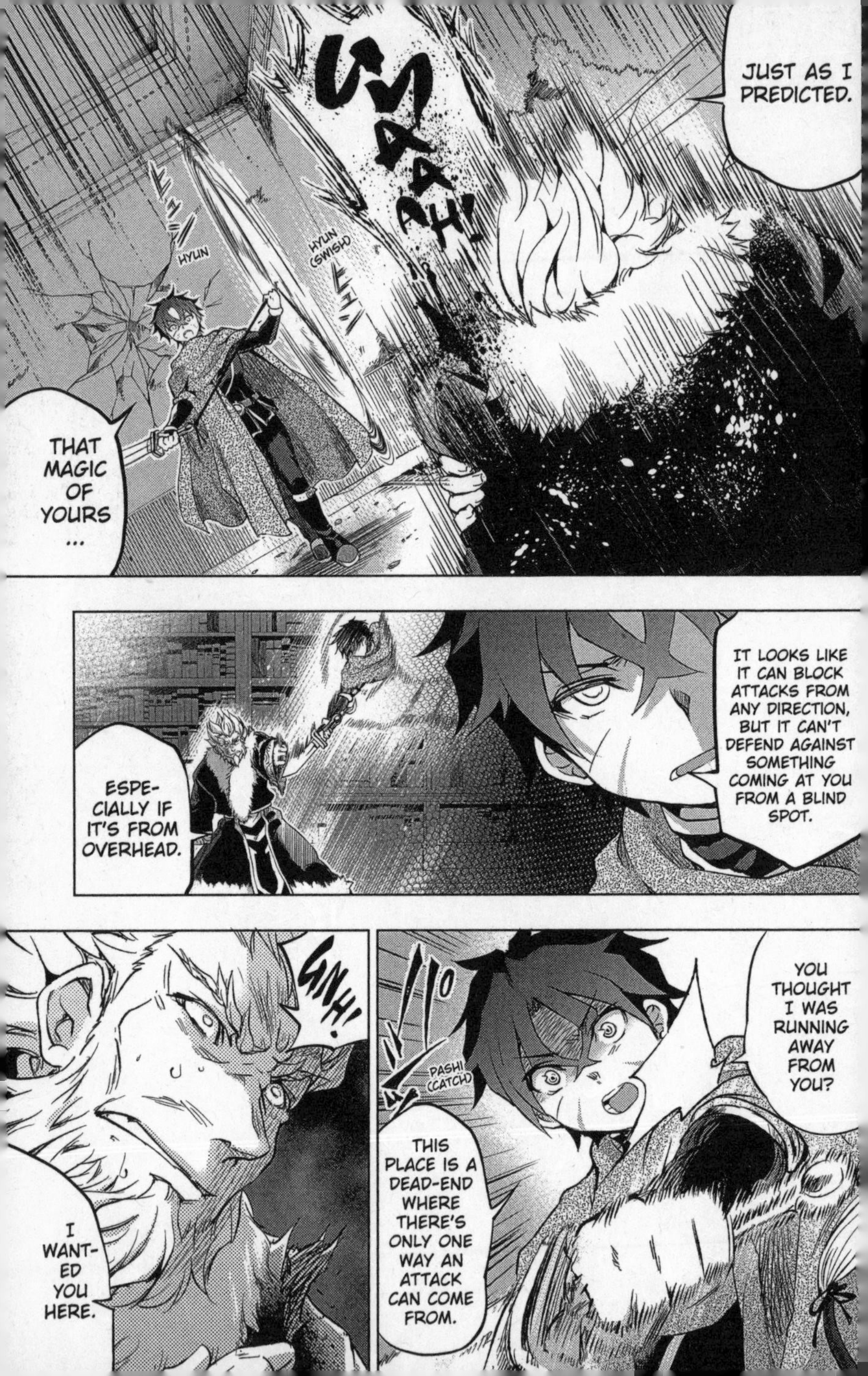
JUST AS I PREDICTED.
UWAAAH!
HYUN (SWISH)
HYUN
THAT MAGIC OF YOURS ...
IT LOOKS LIKE IT CAN BLOCK ATTACKS FROM ANY DIRECTION, BUT IT CAN'T DEFEND AGAINST SOMETHING COMING AT YOU FROM A BLIND SPOT.
ESPE-CIALLY IF IT'S FROM OVERHEAD.
YOU THOUGHT I WAS RUNNING AWAY FROM YOU?
PASHI (CATCH)
THIS PLACE IS A DEAD-END WHERE THERE'S ONLY ONE WAY AN ATTACK CAN COME FROM.
GNH!
I WANT-ED YOU HERE.

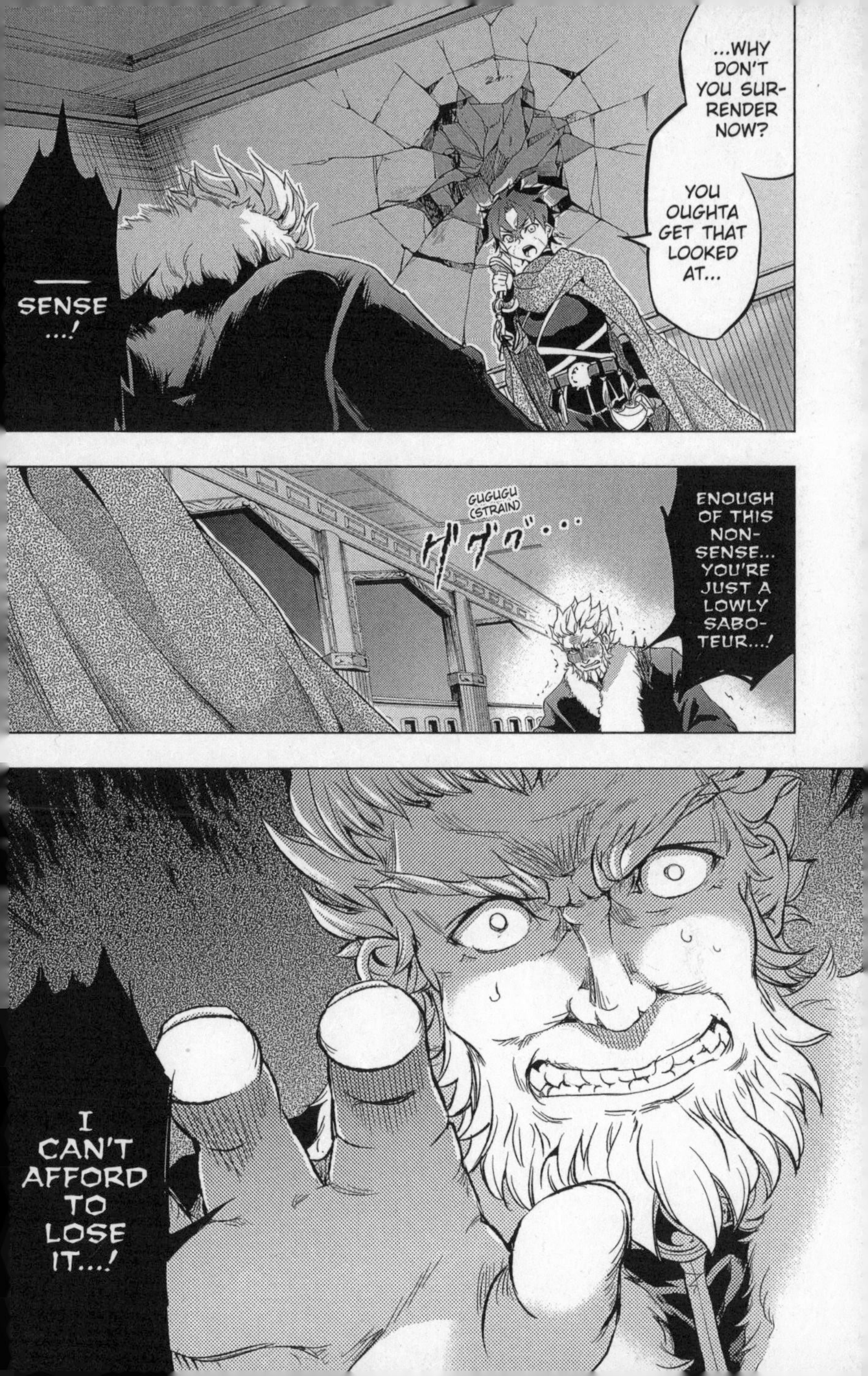
...WHY DON'T YOU SUR-RENDER NOW?
YOU OUGHTA GET THAT LOOKED AT...
—SENSE ...!
ENOUGH OF THIS NON-SENSE... YOU'RE JUST A LOWLY SABO-TEUR...!
GUGUGU (STRAIN)
I CAN'T AFFORD TO LOSE IT...!

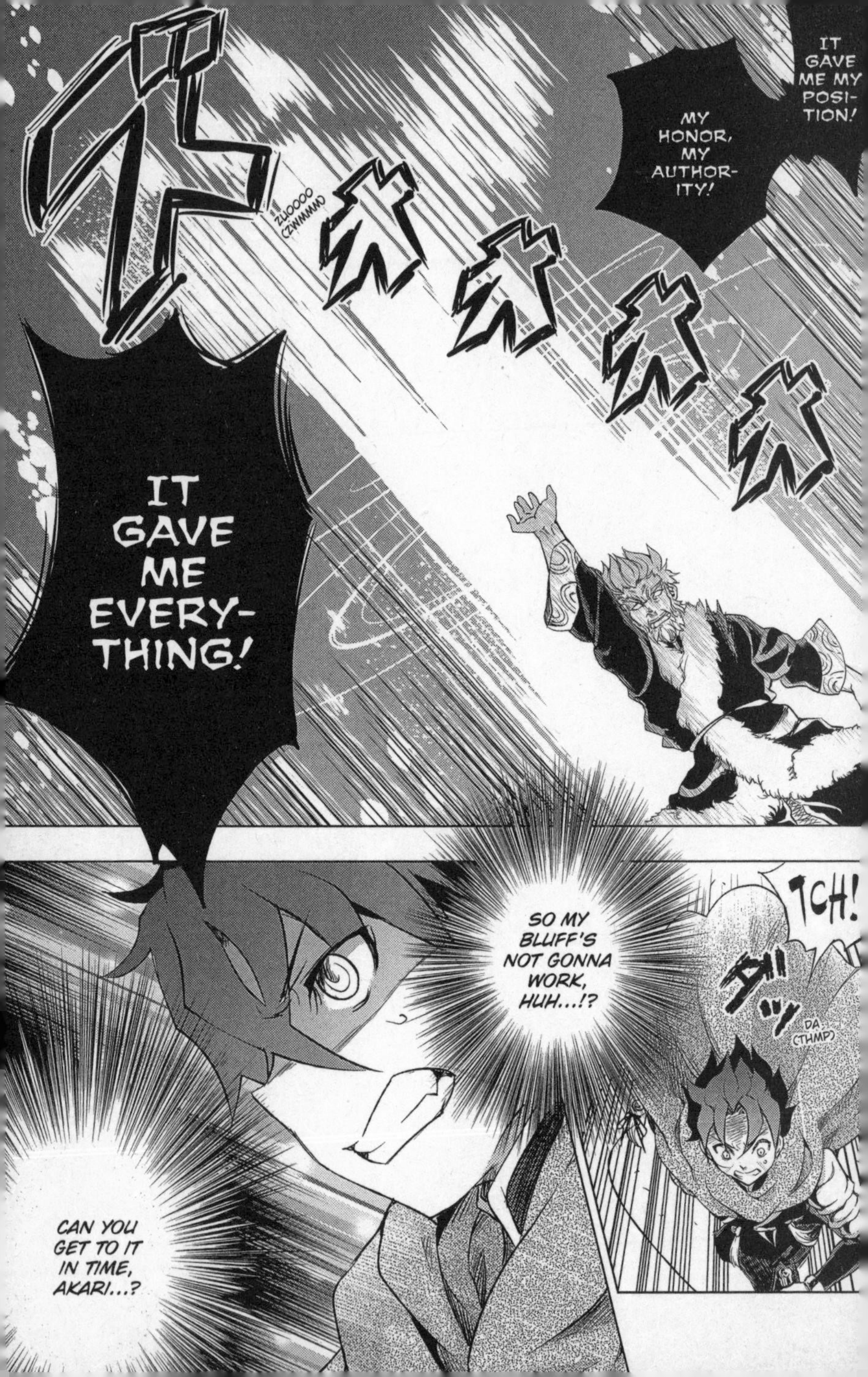
IT GAVE ME MY POSI- TION!
MY HONOR, MY AUTHOR- ITY!
ZUOOOO (ZWMMM)
IT GAVE ME EVERY- THING!
TCH!
DA (THMP)
SO MY BLUFF'S NOT GONNA WORK, HUH...!?
CAN YOU GET TO IT IN TIME, AKARI...?

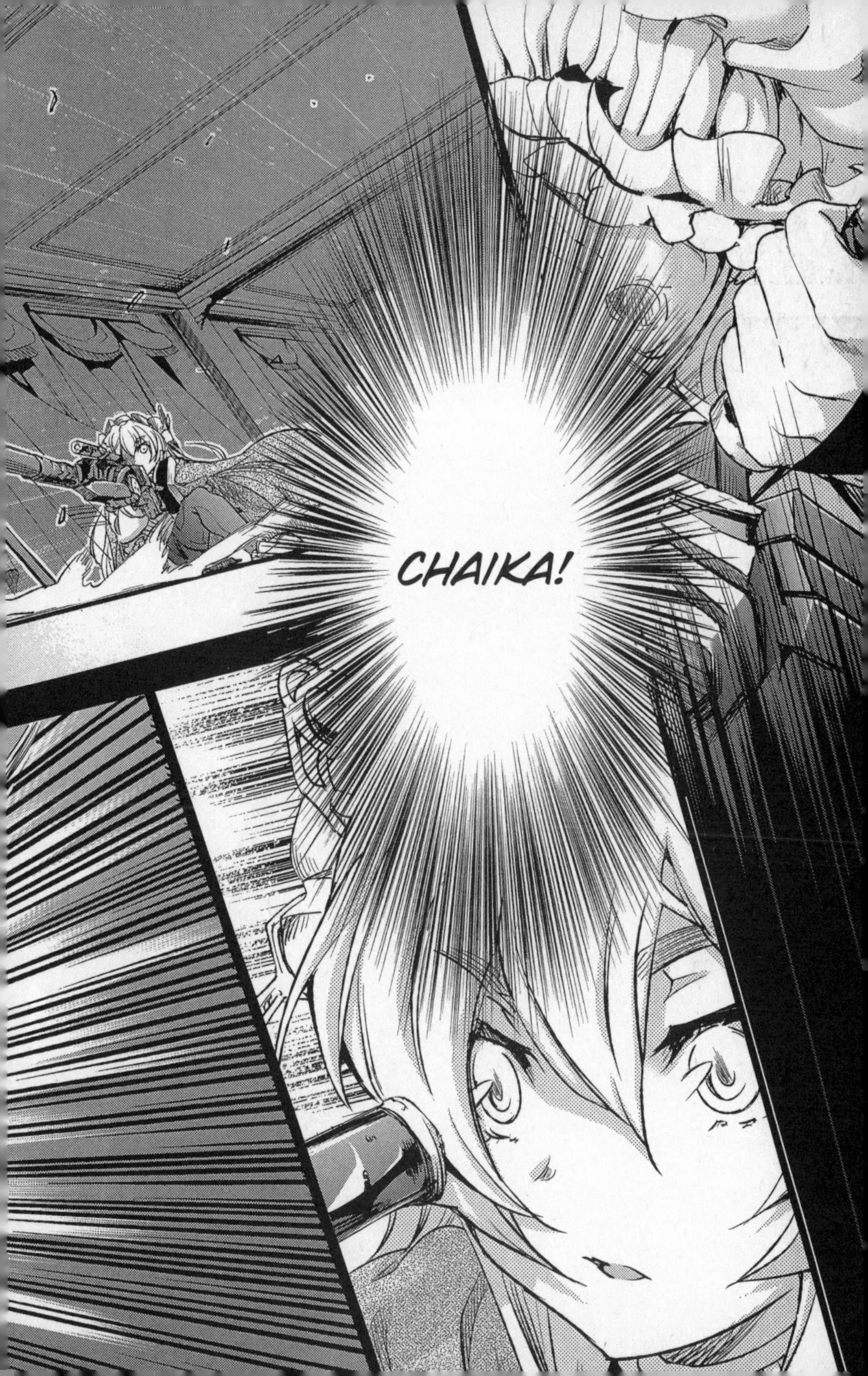
CHAIKA!

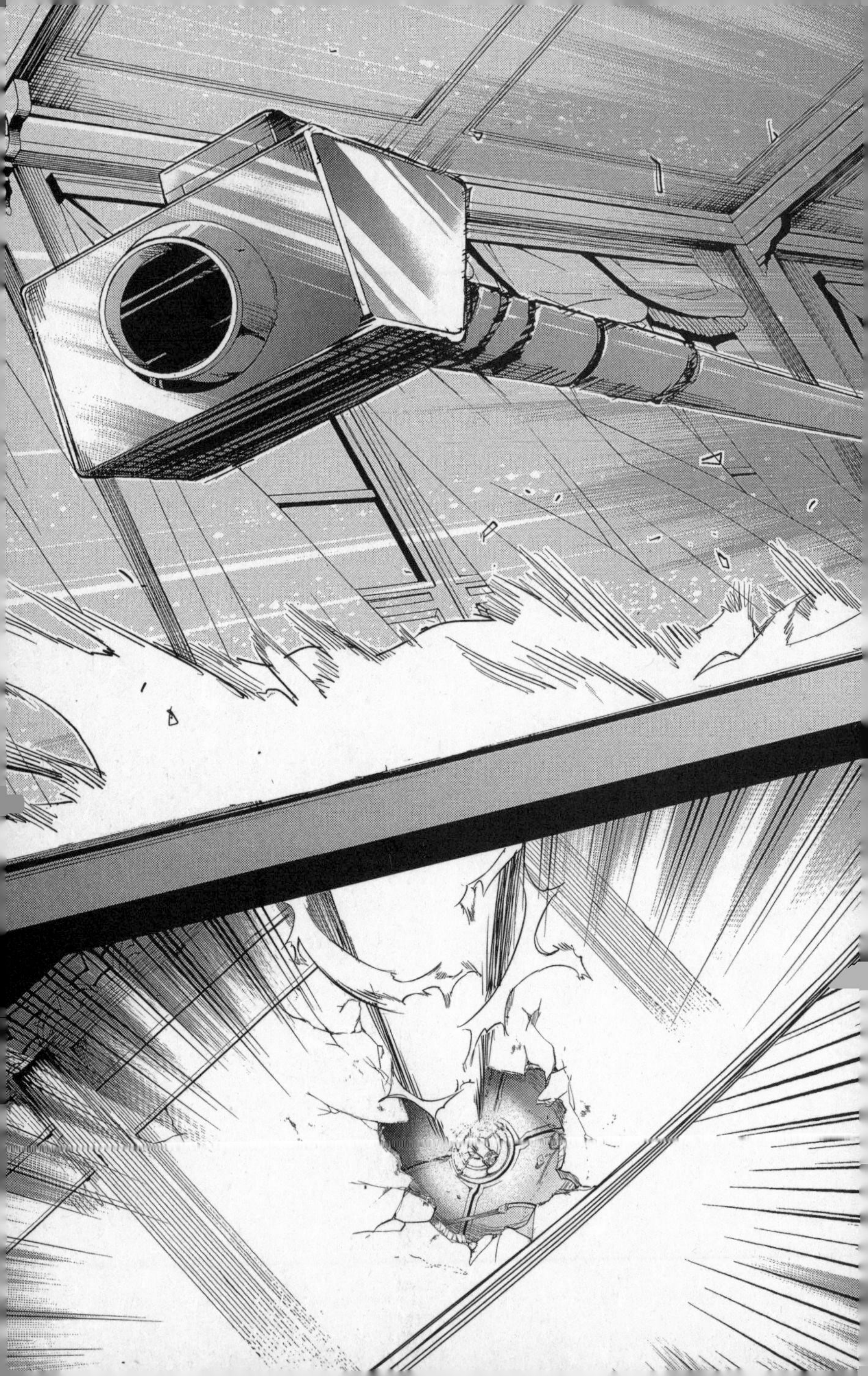

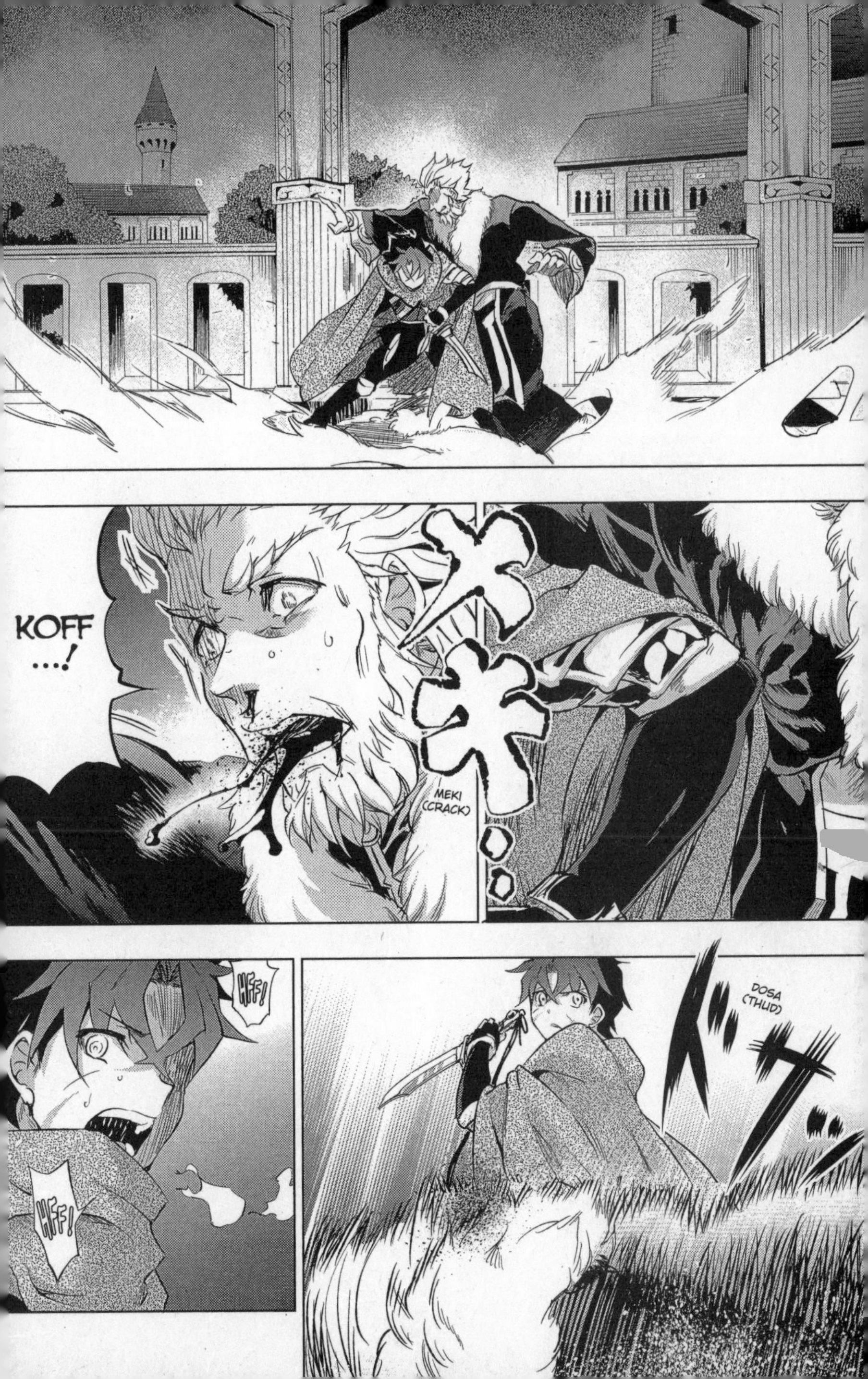
MEKI
(CRACK)
KOFF
...!
DOSA
(THUD)
HFF!
HFF!

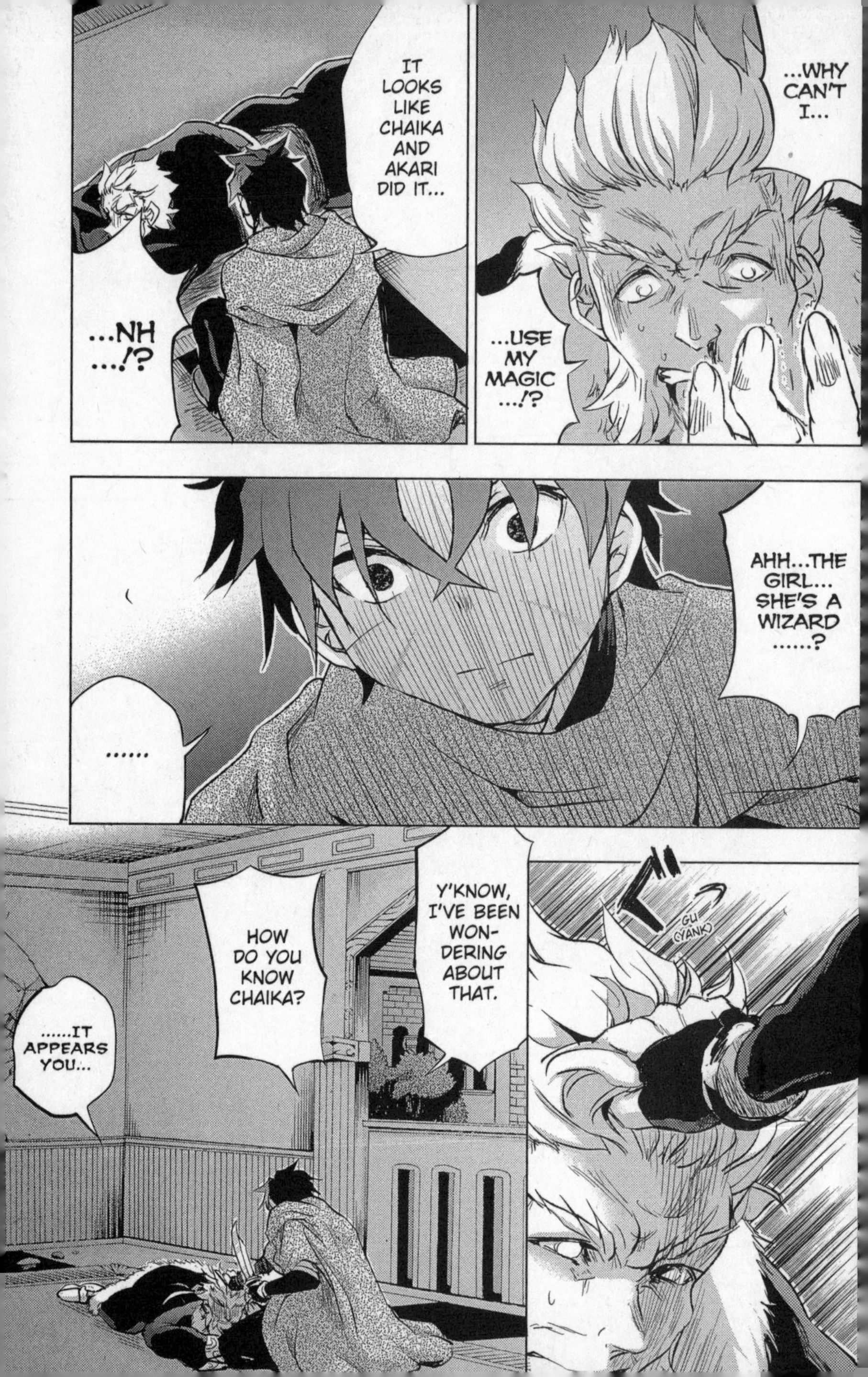
...WHY CAN'T I...
...USE MY MAGIC ...!?
IT LOOKS LIKE CHAIKA AND AKARI DID IT...
...NH ...!?
AHH...THE GIRL... SHE'S A WIZARD ......?
......
GU (YANK)
Y'KNOW, I'VE BEEN WON-DERING ABOUT THAT.
HOW DO YOU KNOW CHAIKA?
......IT APPEARS YOU...

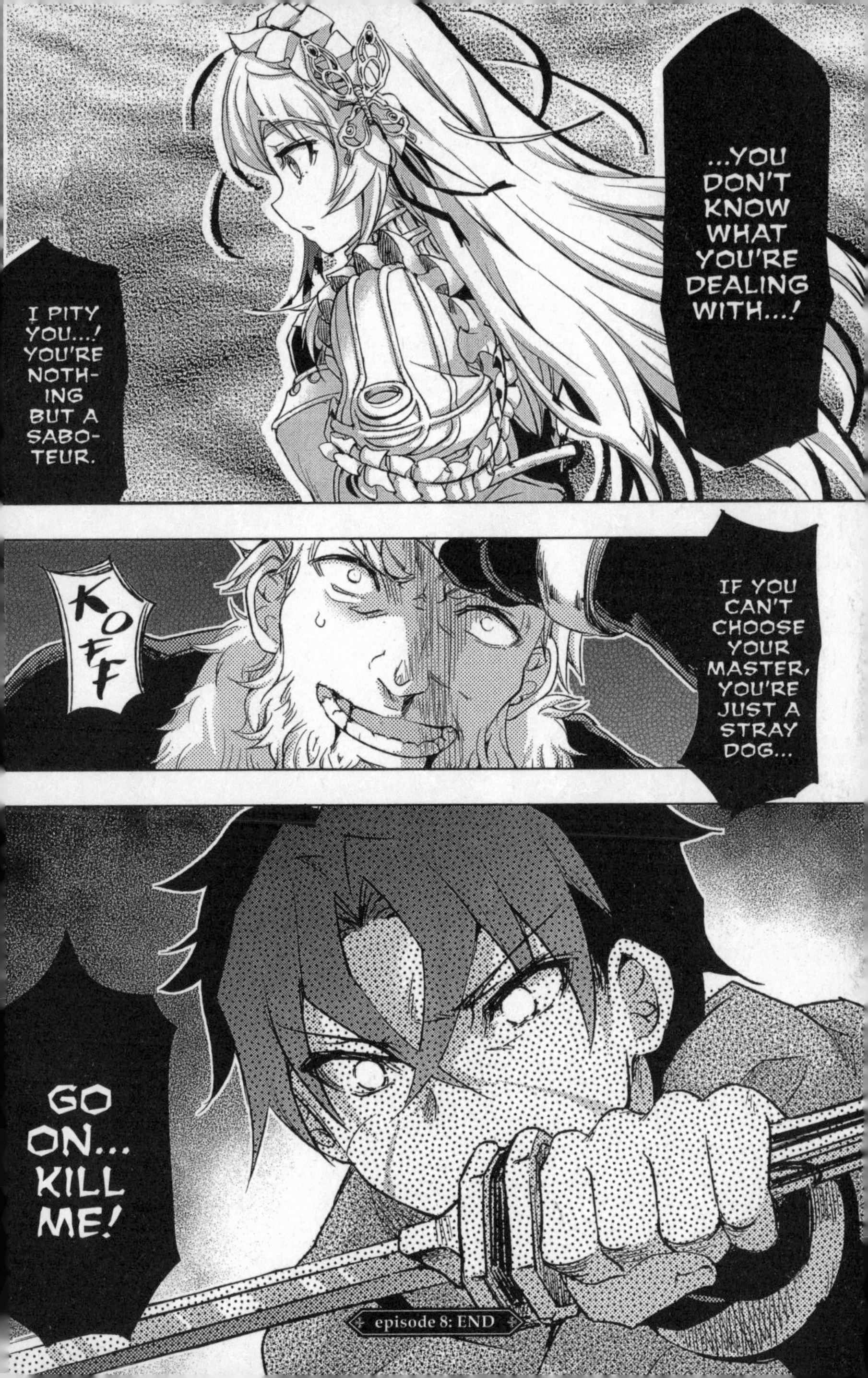
...YOU DON'T KNOW WHAT YOU'RE DEALING WITH...!
I PITY YOU...! YOU'RE NOTHING BUT A SABOTEUR.
IF YOU CAN'T CHOOSE YOUR MASTER, YOU'RE JUST A STRAY DOG...
KOFF
GO ON... KILL ME!
episode 8: END

episode 9: Rejection and...

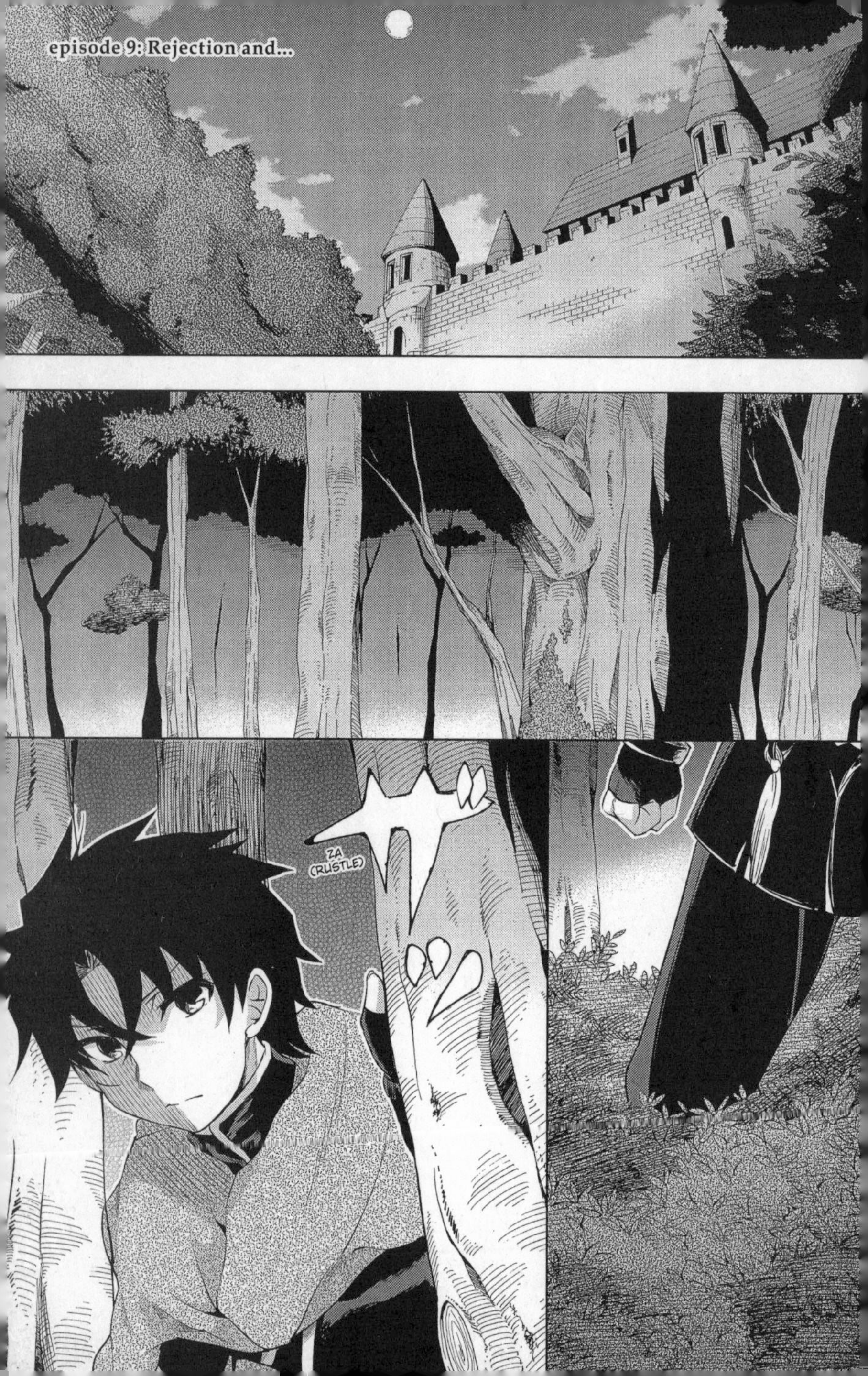
ZA
(RUSTLE)

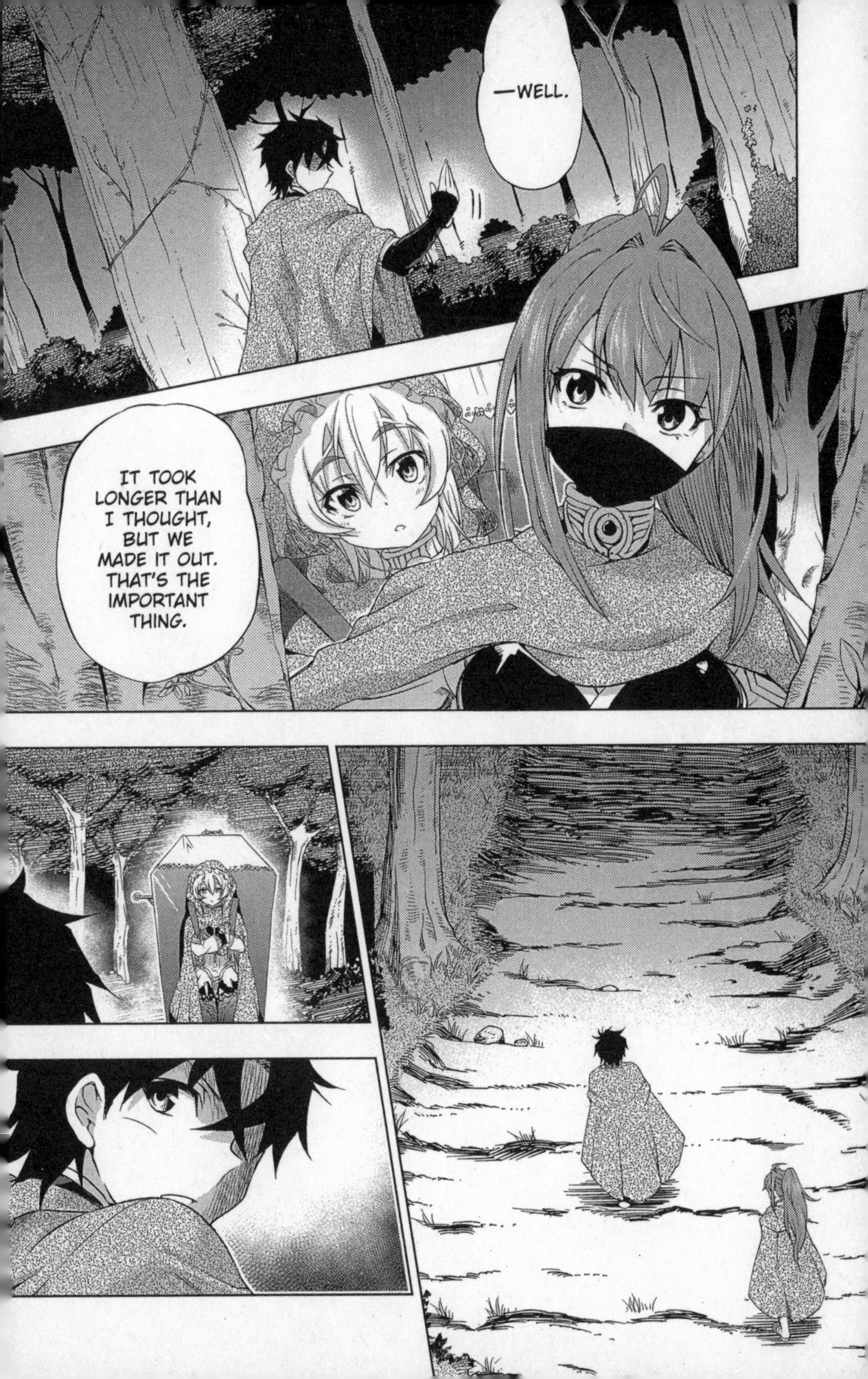
—WELL.
IT TOOK LONGER THAN I THOUGHT, BUT WE MADE IT OUT. THAT'S THE IMPORTANT THING.

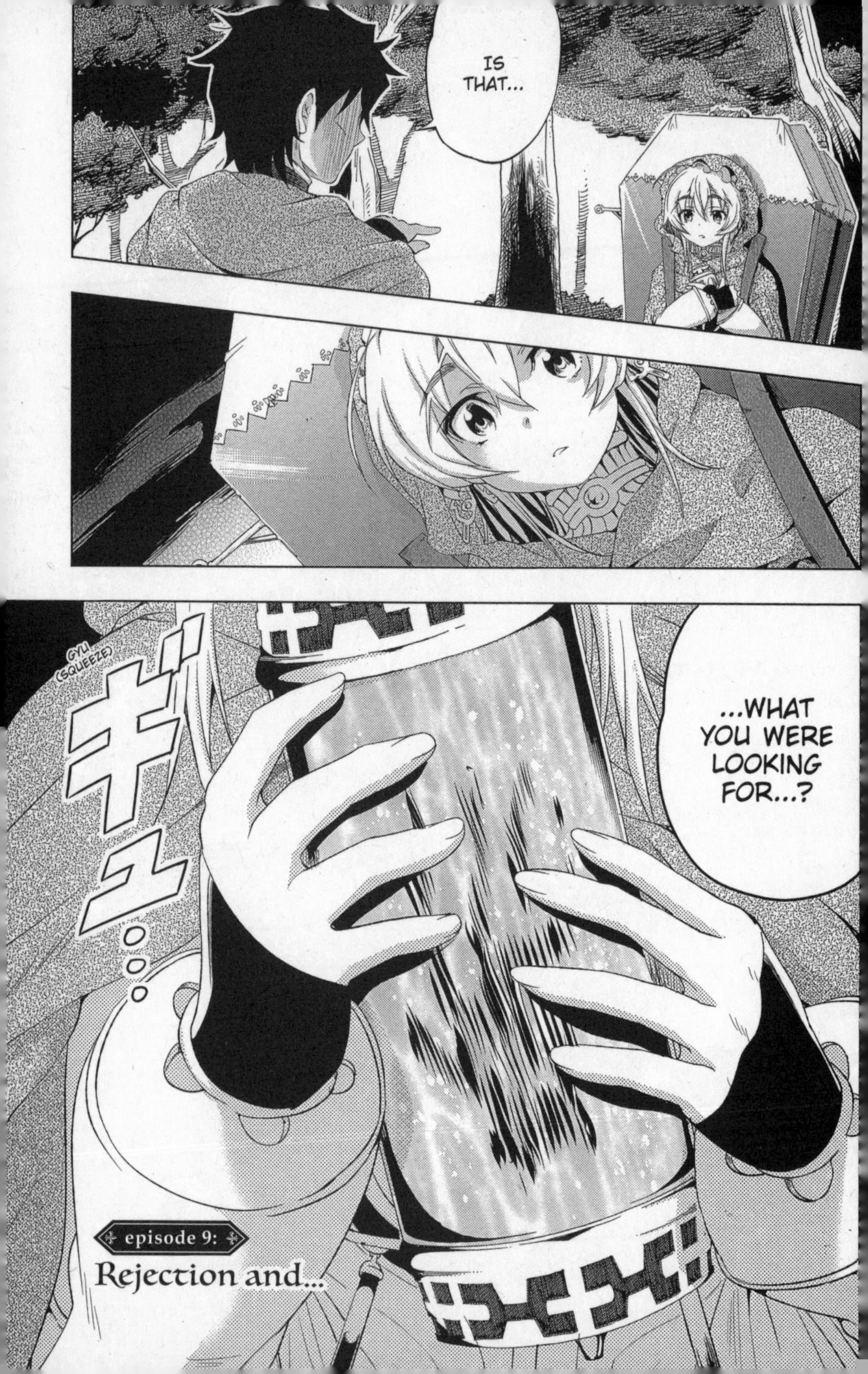
IS THAT...
...WHAT YOU WERE LOOKING FOR...?
ギュ
GYU (SQUEEZE)
episode 9:
Rejection and...

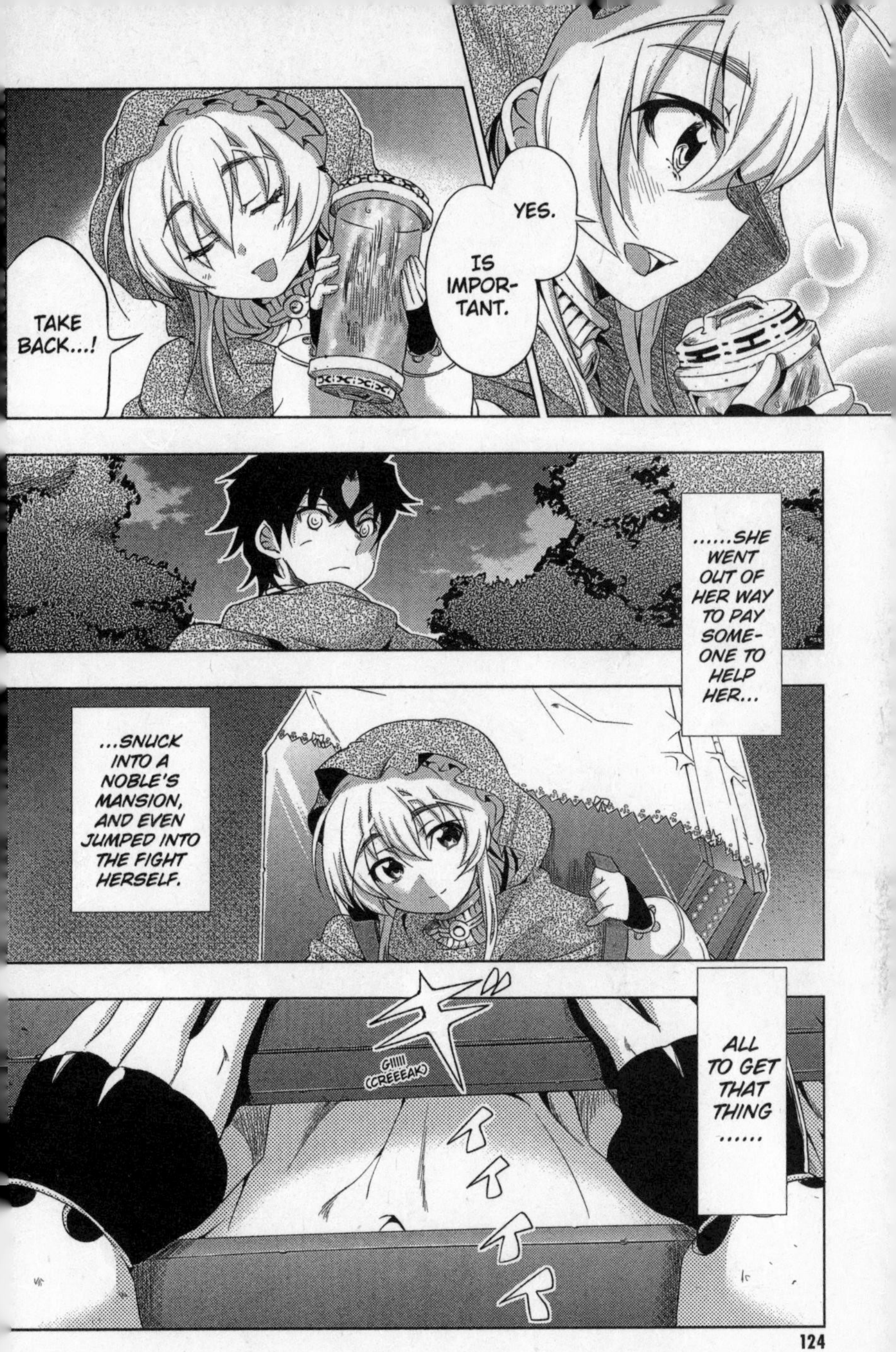
YES.
IS IMPOR-TANT.
TAKE BACK...!
......SHE WENT OUT OF HER WAY TO PAY SOME-ONE TO HELP HER...
...SNUCK INTO A NOBLE'S MANSION, AND EVEN JUMPED INTO THE FIGHT HERSELF.
ALL TO GET THAT THING ......
GIIII (CREEEAK)

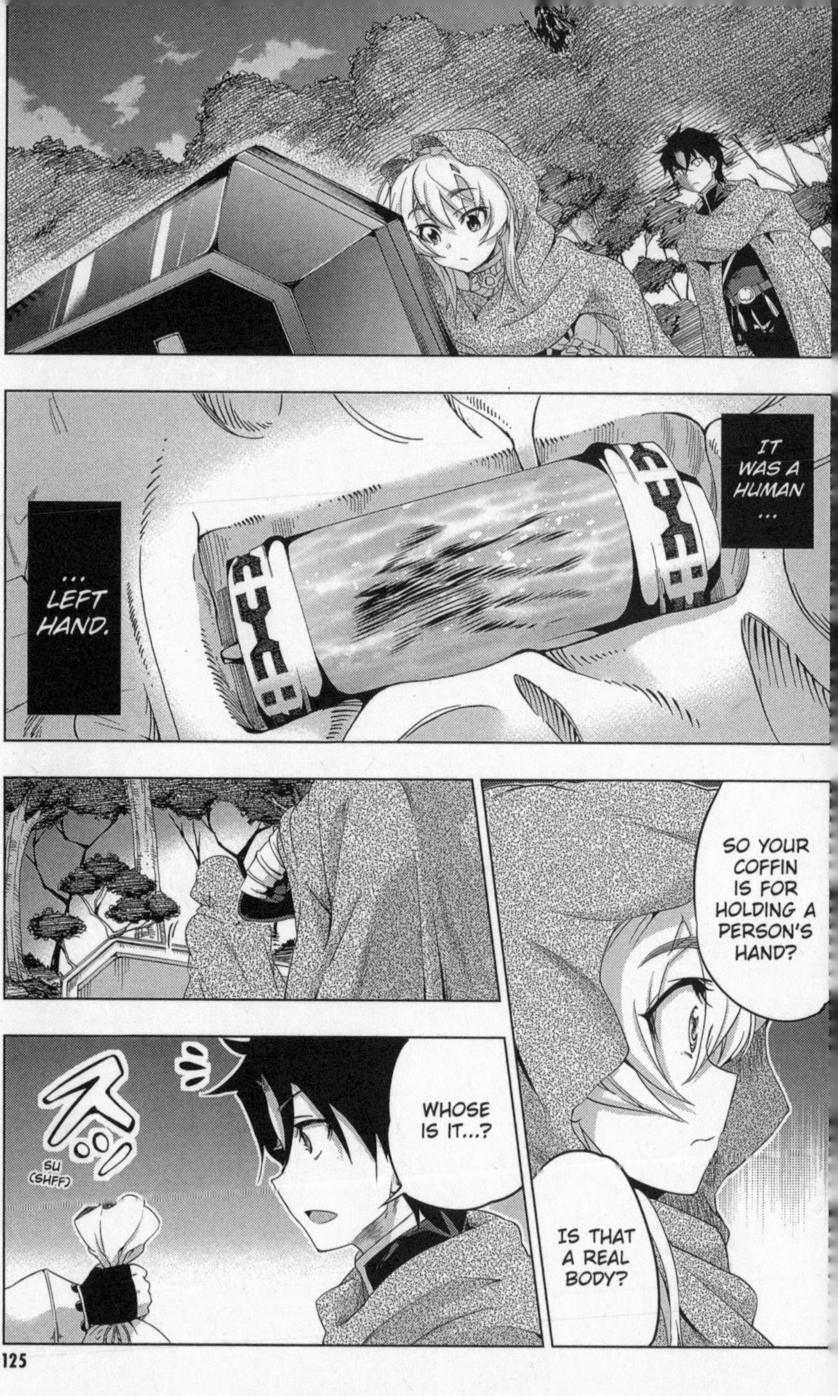
IT WAS A HUMAN ...
... LEFT HAND.
SO YOUR COFFIN IS FOR HOLDING A PERSON'S HAND?
IS THAT A REAL BODY?
WHOSE IS IT...?
SU (SHFF)

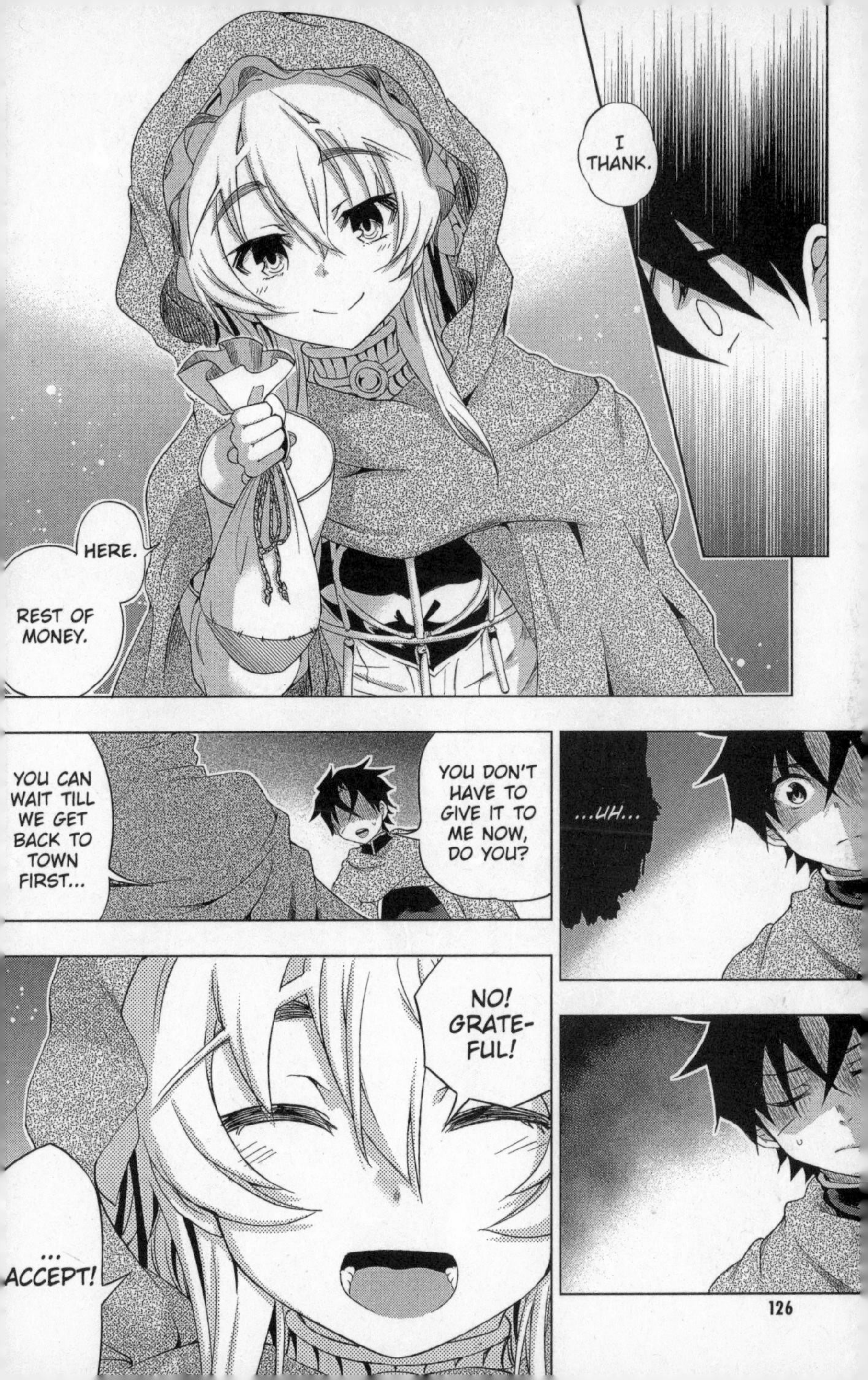
I THANK.
HERE.
REST OF MONEY.
...UH...
YOU DON'T HAVE TO GIVE IT TO ME NOW, DO YOU?
YOU CAN WAIT TILL WE GET BACK TO TOWN FIRST...
NO! GRATE-FUL!
...ACCEPT!

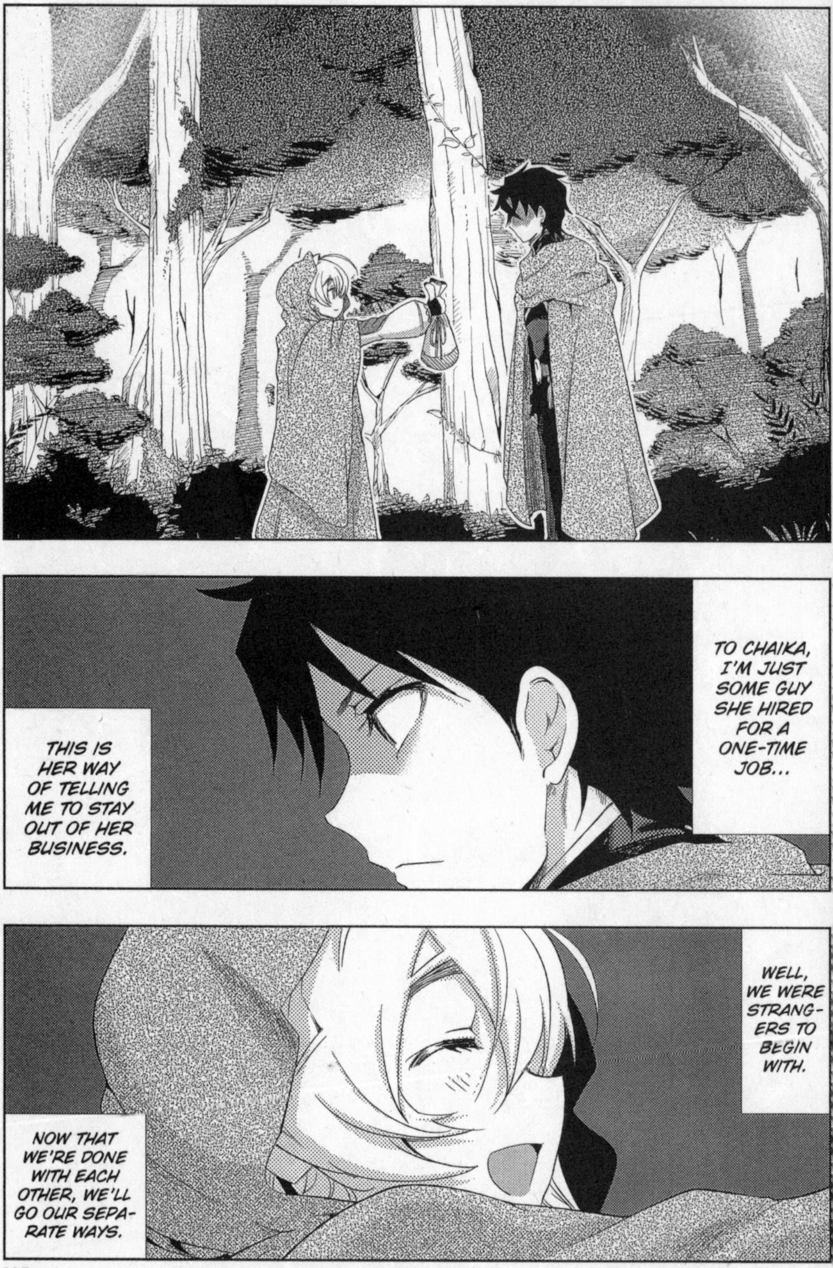
TO CHAIKA, I'M JUST SOME GUY SHE HIRED FOR A ONE-TIME JOB...
THIS IS HER WAY OF TELLING ME TO STAY OUT OF HER BUSINESS.
WELL, WE WERE STRANGERS TO BEGIN WITH.
NOW THAT WE'RE DONE WITH EACH OTHER, WE'LL GO OUR SEPARATE WAYS.

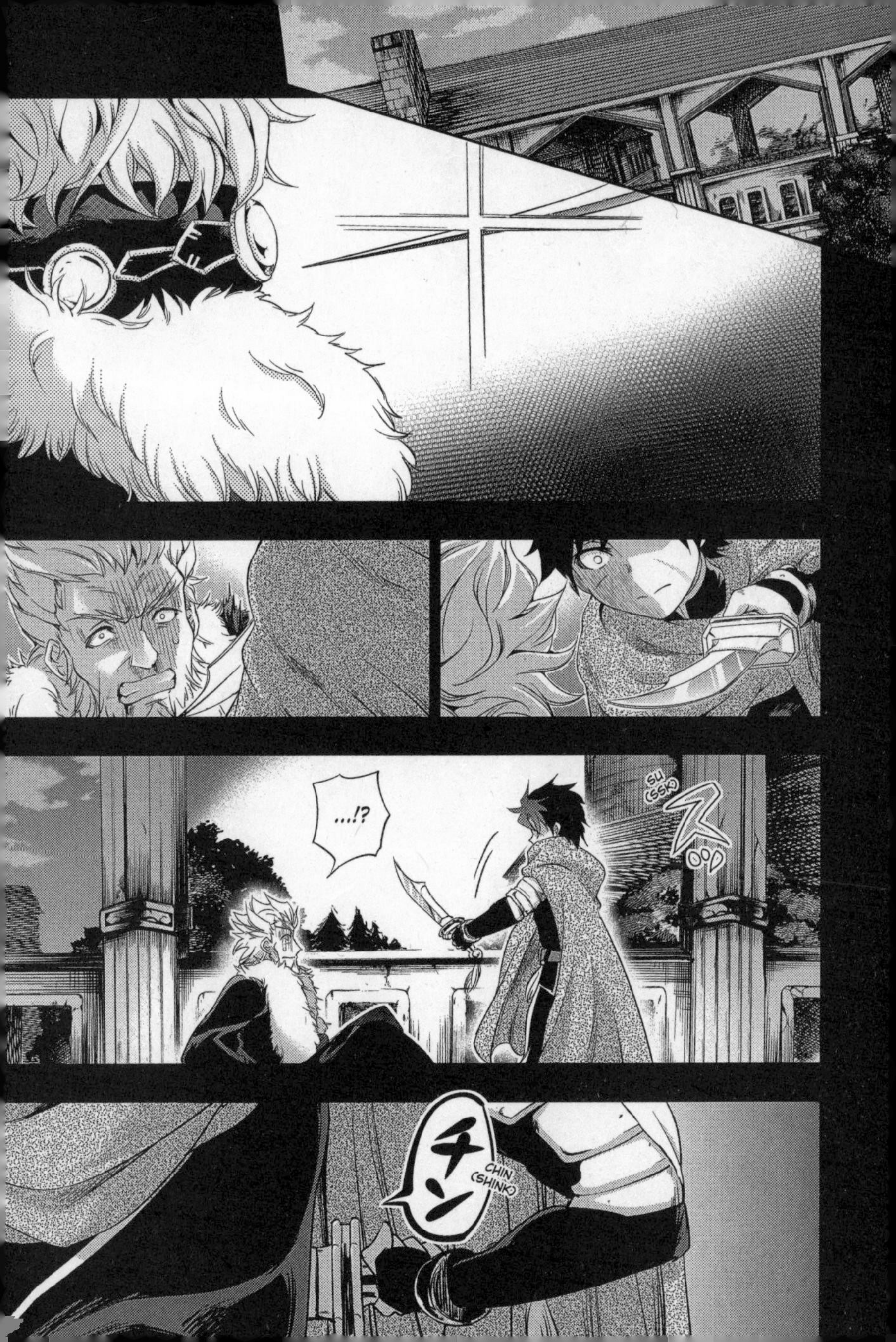
SU (SSK)
ス
ZOOP
...!?
チン
CHIN (SHINK)

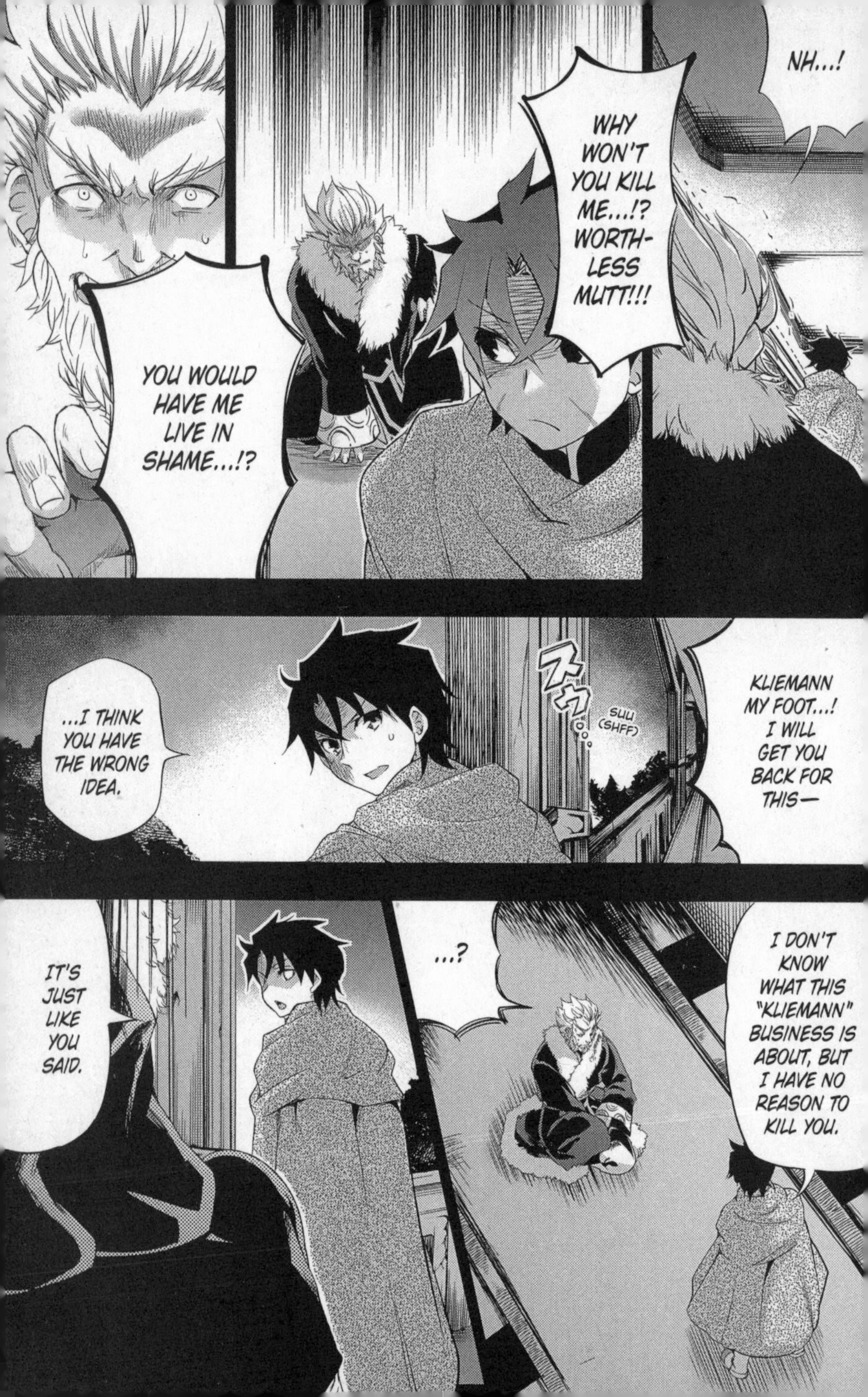
NH...!
WHY WON'T YOU KILL ME...!? WORTHLESS MUTT!!!
YOU WOULD HAVE ME LIVE IN SHAME...!?
KLIEMANN MY FOOT...! I WILL GET YOU BACK FOR THIS—
スゥ
SUU (SHFF)
...I THINK YOU HAVE THE WRONG IDEA.
I DON'T KNOW WHAT THIS "KLIEMANN" BUSINESS IS ABOUT, BUT I HAVE NO REASON TO KILL YOU.
...?
IT'S JUST LIKE YOU SAID.

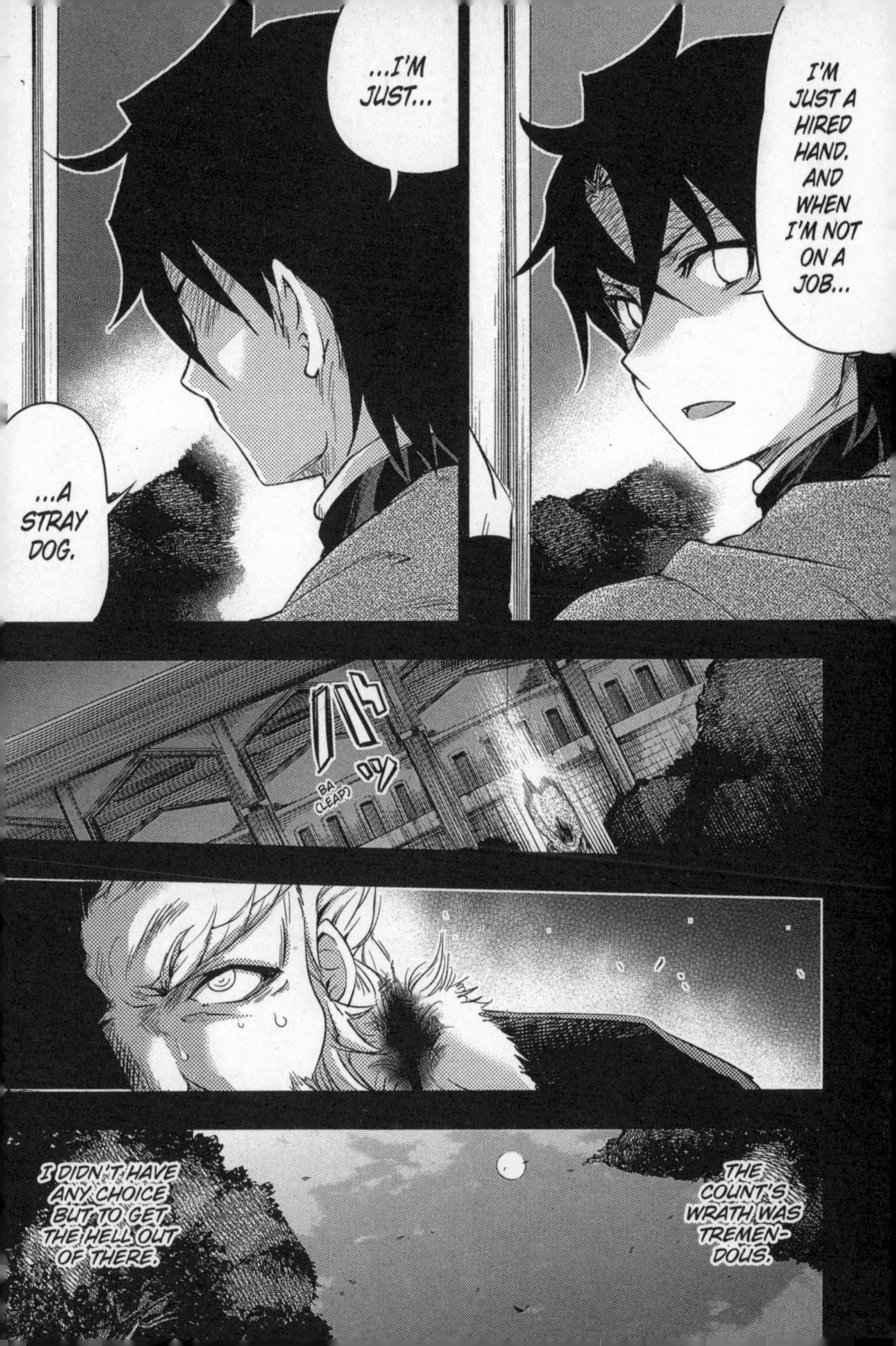
I'M JUST A HIRED HAND. AND WHEN I'M NOT ON A JOB...
...I'M JUST...
...A STRAY DOG.
BA (LEAP)
THE COUNT'S WRATH WAS TREMEN-DOUS.
I DIDN'T HAVE ANY CHOICE BUT TO GET THE HELL OUT OF THERE.

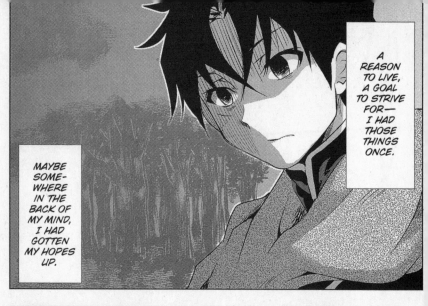

A REASON TO LIVE, A GOAL TO STRIVE FOR— I HAD THOSE THINGS ONCE.

MAYBE SOMEWHERE IN THE BACK OF MY MIND, I HAD GOTTEN MY HOPES UP.

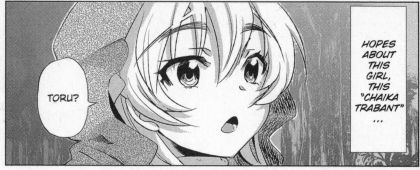

TORU?

HOPES ABOUT THIS GIRL, THIS "CHAIKA TRABANT"...

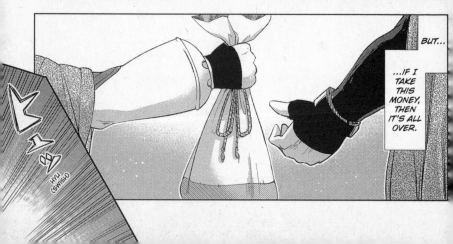

BUT...

...IF I TAKE THIS MONEY, THEN IT'S ALL OVER.

HYU (SWISH)

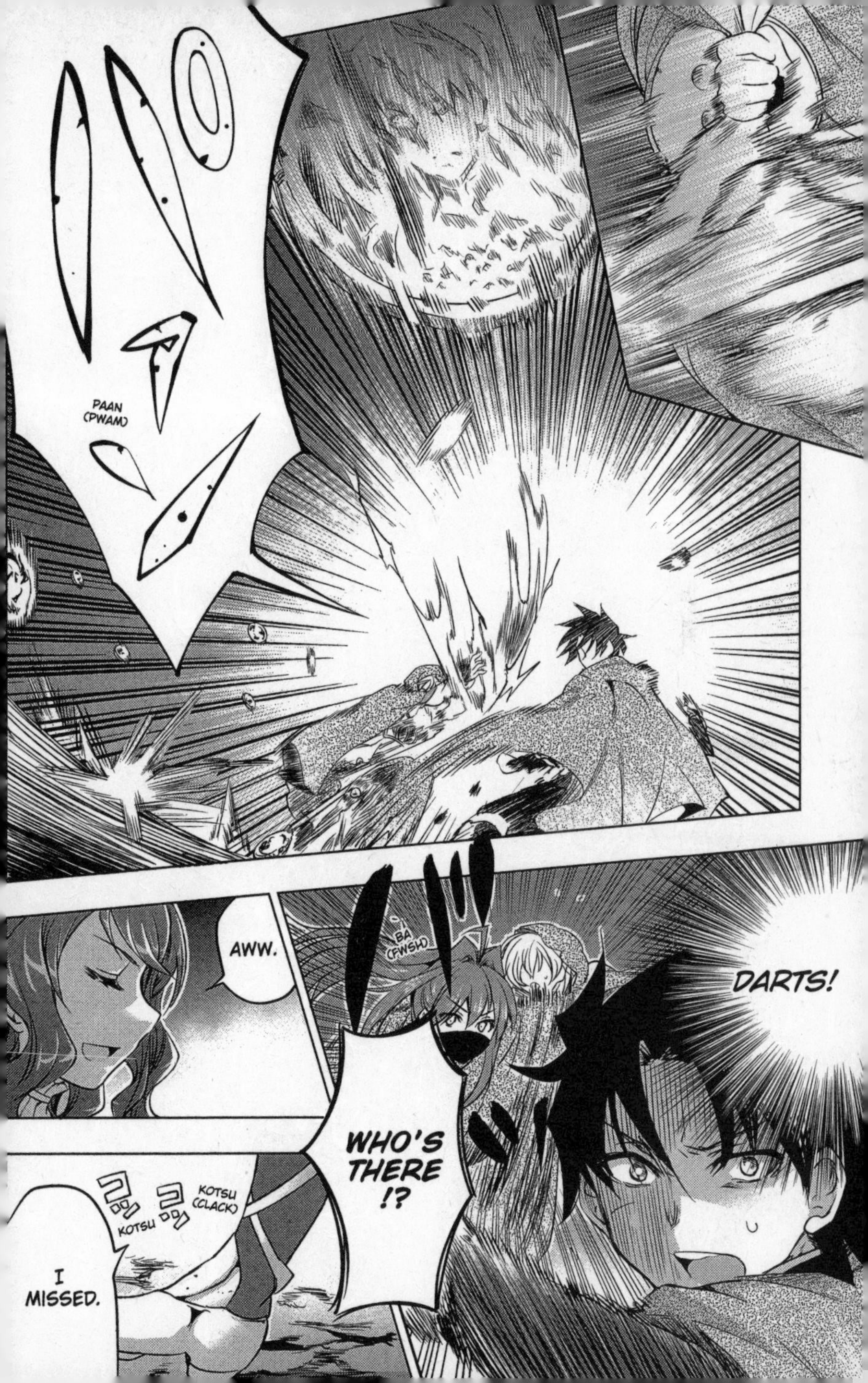
PAAN
(PWAM)
DARTS!
BA
(FWSH)
WHO'S THERE!?
AWW.
KOTSU
(CLACK)
KOTSU
I MISSED.

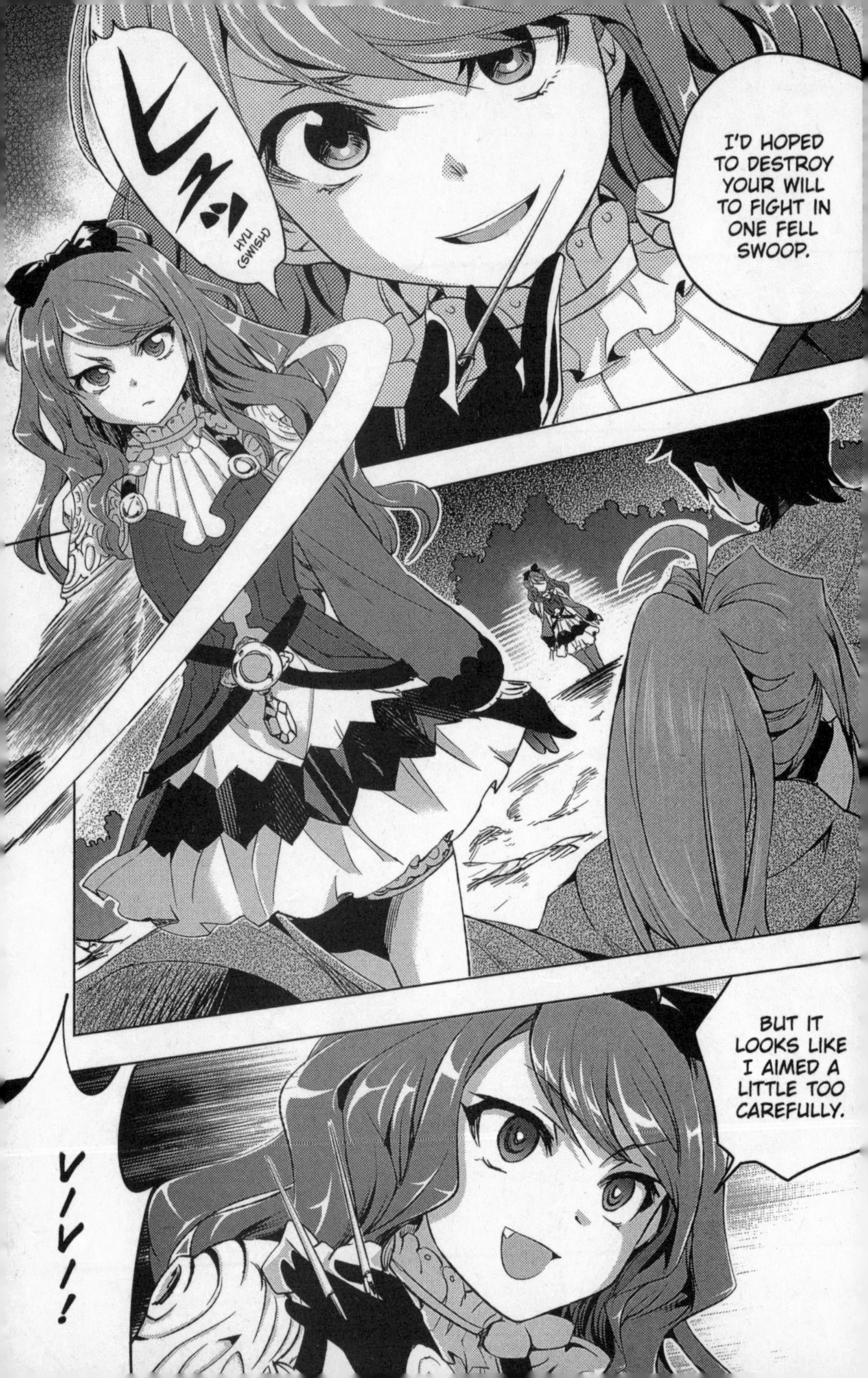
I'D HOPED TO DESTROY YOUR WILL TO FIGHT IN ONE FELL SWOOP.
HYU (SWISH)
BUT IT LOOKS LIKE I AIMED A LITTLE TOO CAREFULLY.

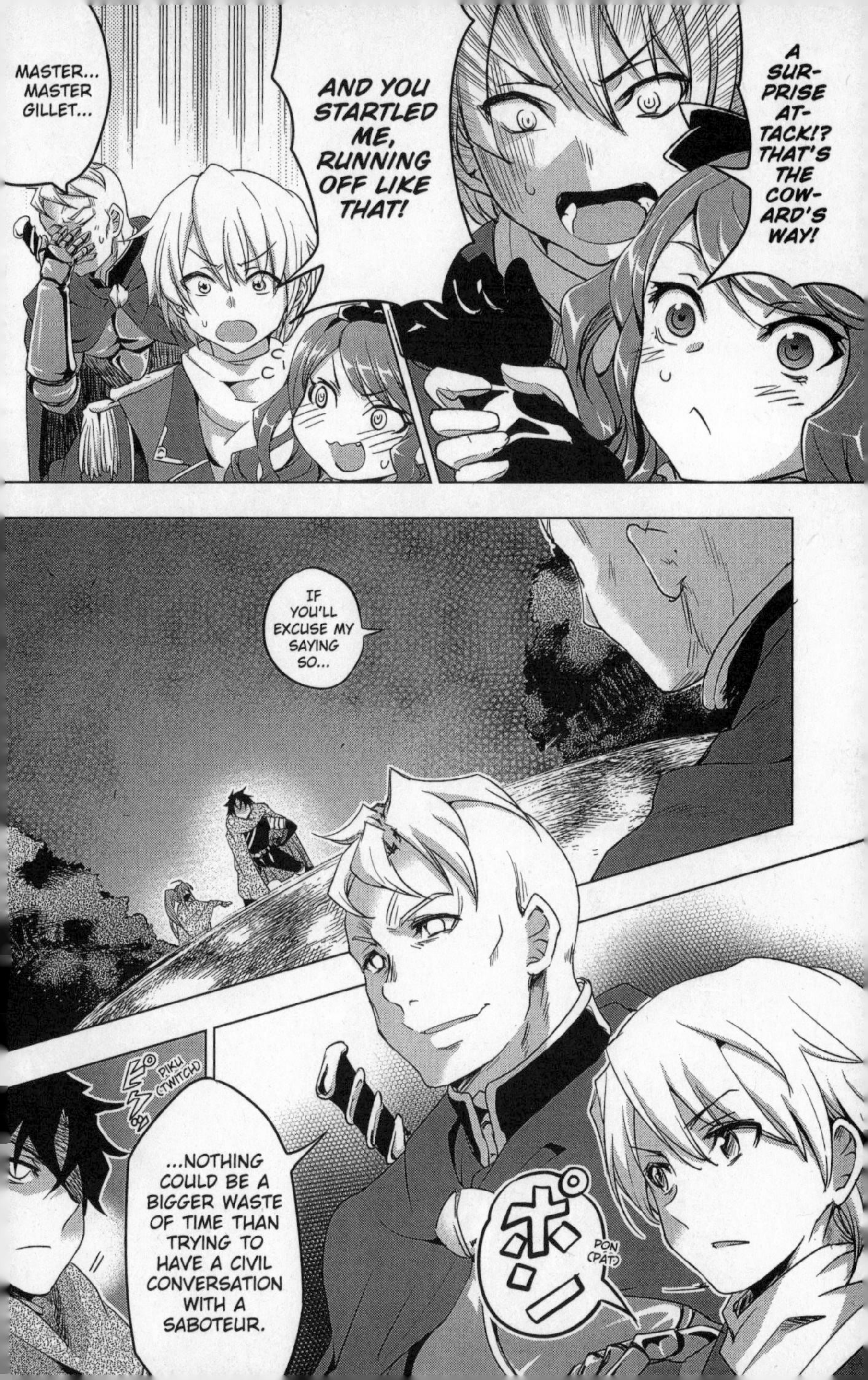
A SURPRISE ATTACK!? THAT'S THE COWARD'S WAY!
AND YOU STARTLED ME, RUNNING OFF LIKE THAT!
MASTER... MASTER GILLET...
IF YOU'LL EXCUSE MY SAYING SO...
ポン
PON (PAT)
PIKU (TWITCH)
...NOTHING COULD BE A BIGGER WASTE OF TIME THAN TRYING TO HAVE A CIVIL CONVERSATION WITH A SABOTEUR.

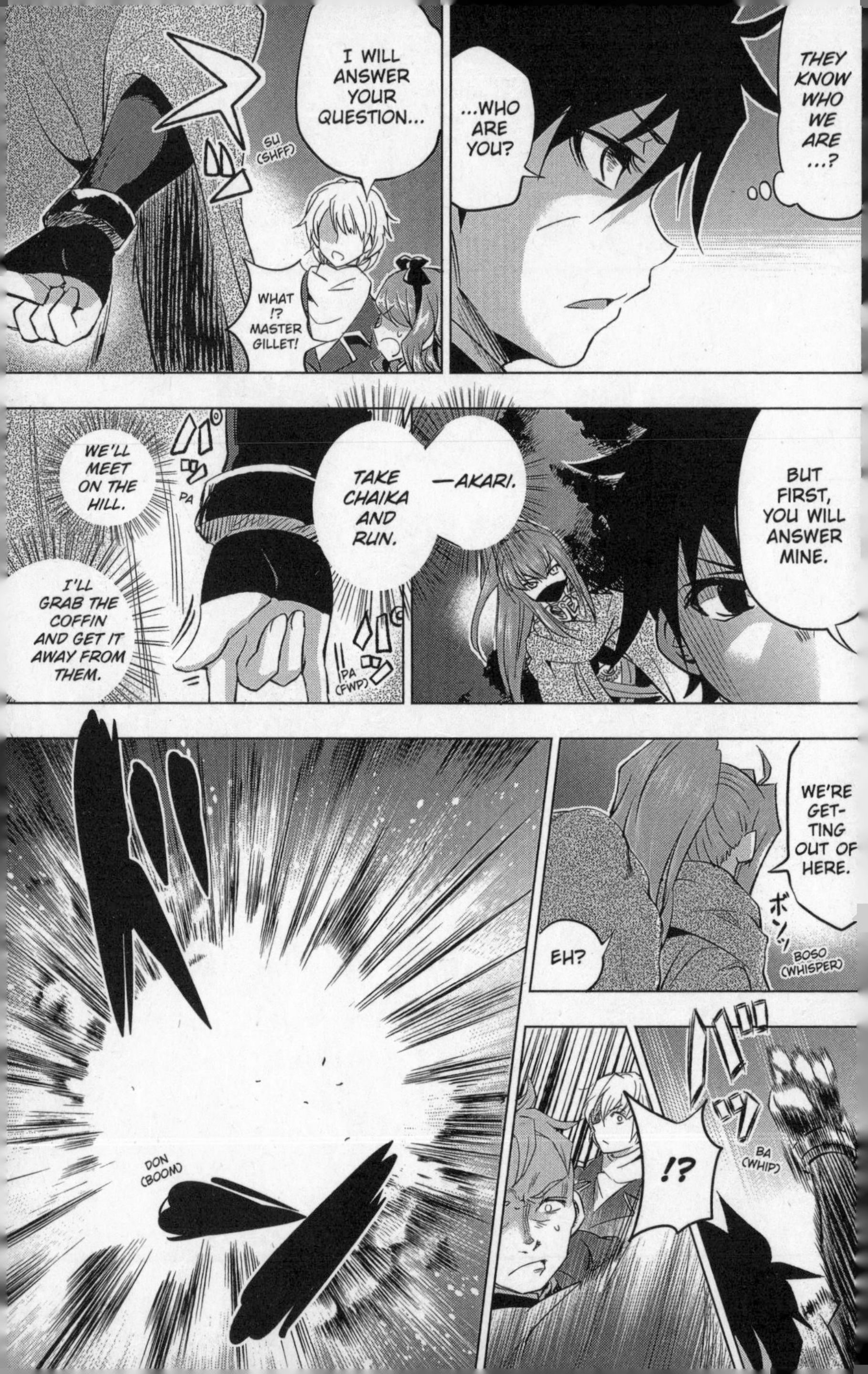
THEY KNOW WHO WE ARE ...?
...WHO ARE YOU?
I WILL ANSWER YOUR QUESTION...
SU (SHFF)
WHAT !? MASTER GILLET!
BUT FIRST, YOU WILL ANSWER MINE.
—AKARI.
TAKE CHAIKA AND RUN.
PA
WE'LL MEET ON THE HILL.
I'LL GRAB THE COFFIN AND GET IT AWAY FROM THEM.
PA (FWP)
WE'RE GET-TING OUT OF HERE.
ボソッ
BOSO (WHISPER)
EH?
BA (WHIP)
!?
DON (BOOM)

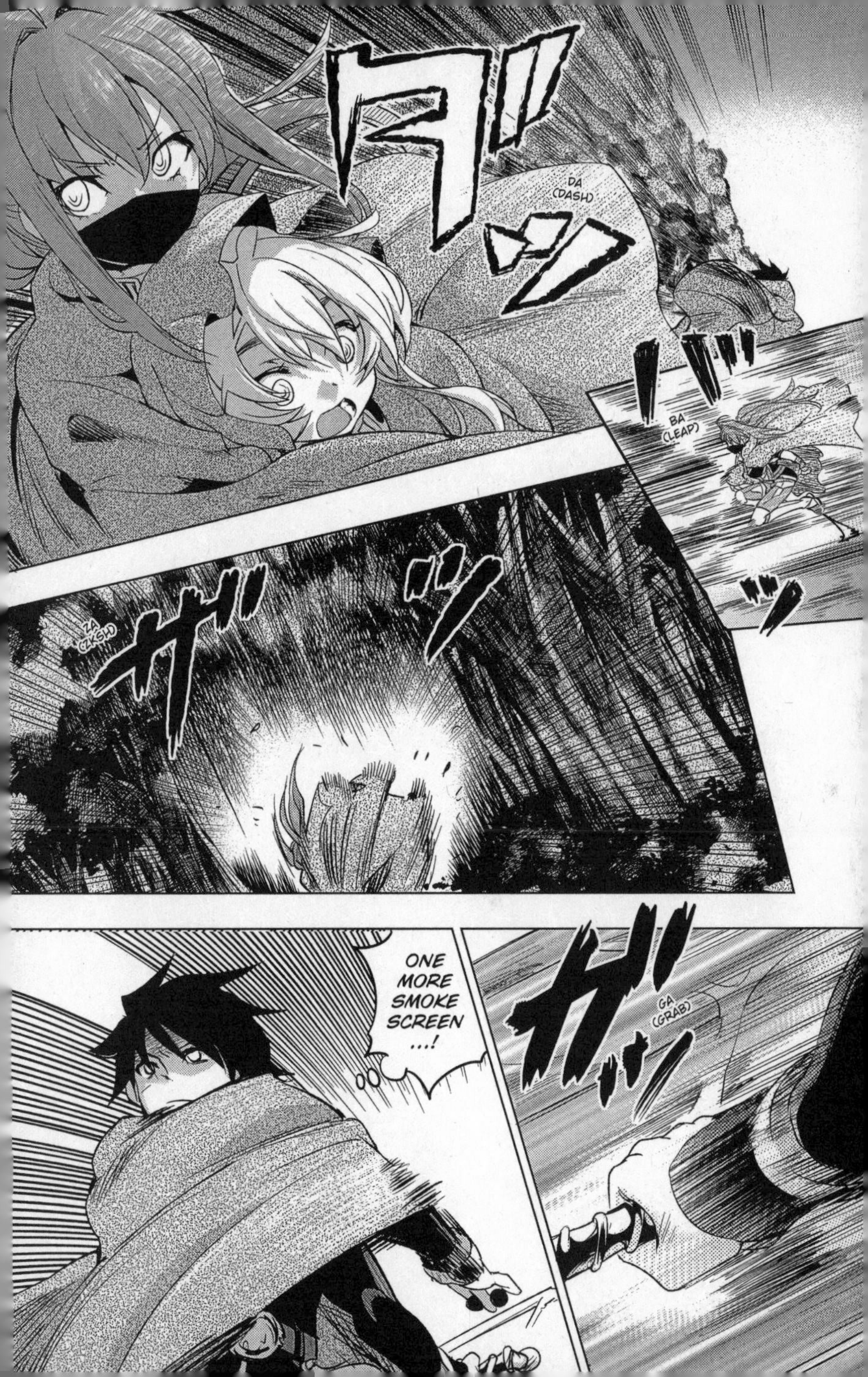
DA (DASH)
BA (LEAP)
ZA (ZKSH)
GA (GRAB)
ONE MORE SMOKE SCREEN ...!

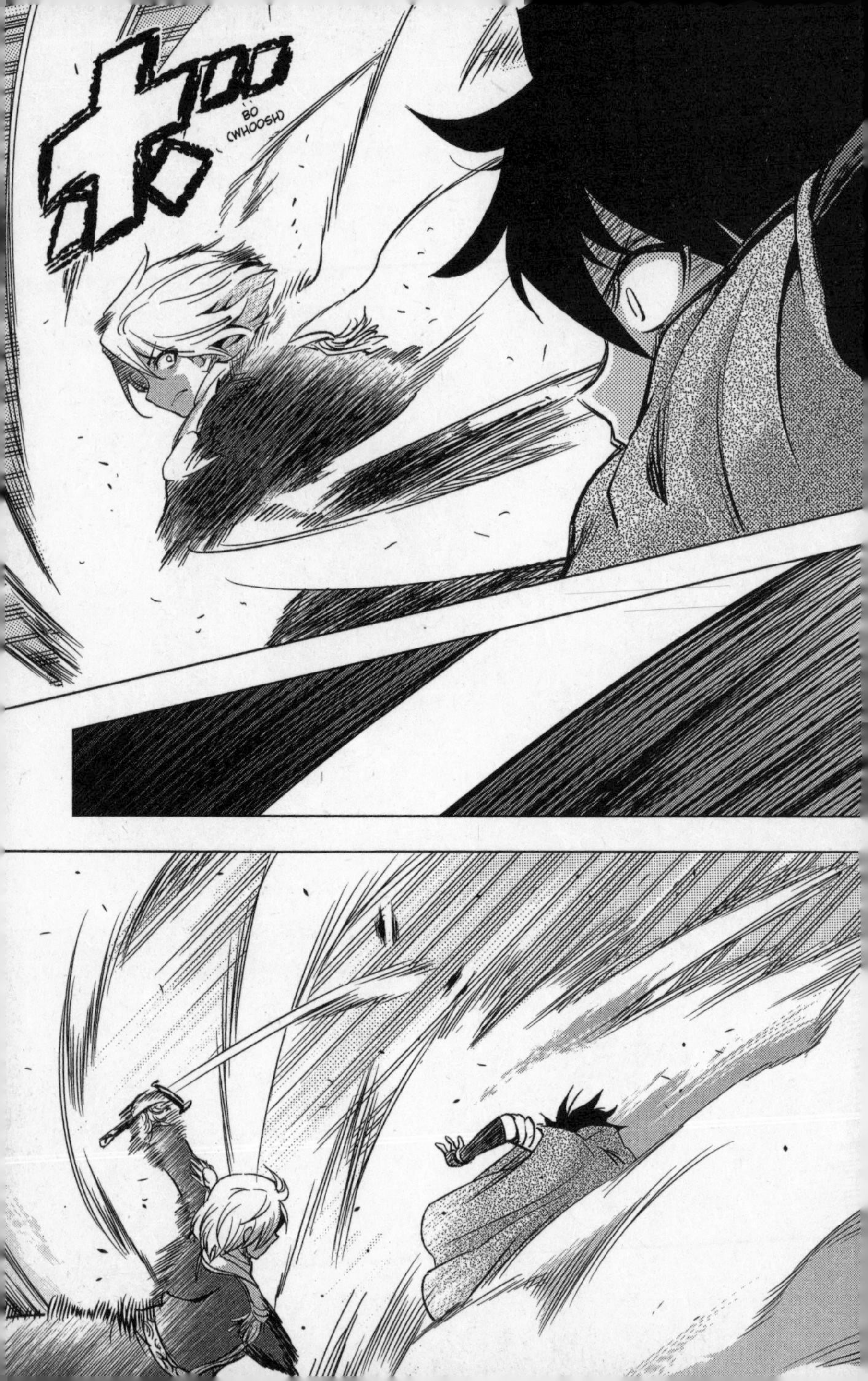
BO
(WHOOSH)

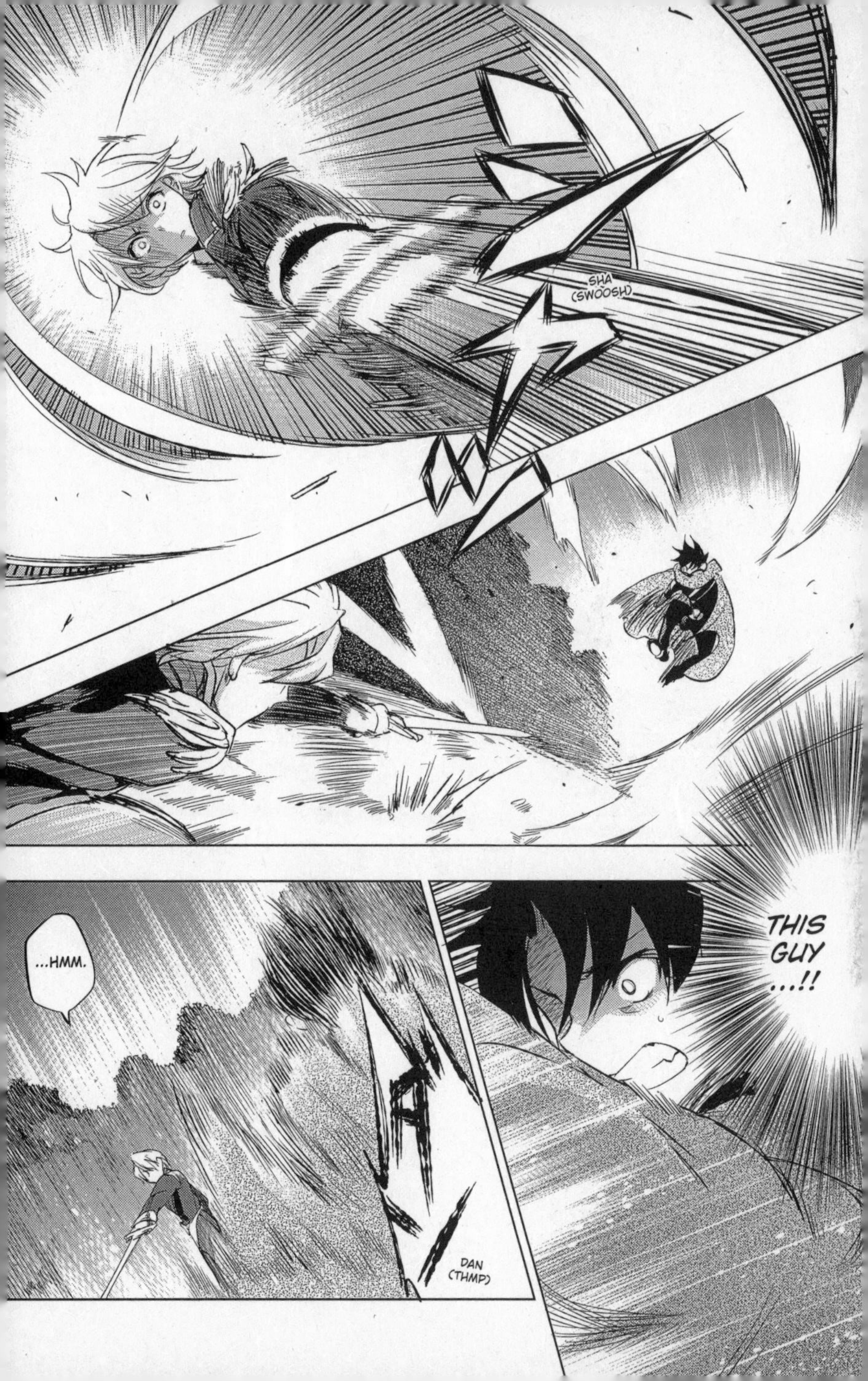
SHA
(SWOOSH)
THIS GUY ...!!
...HMM.
DAN
(THMP)

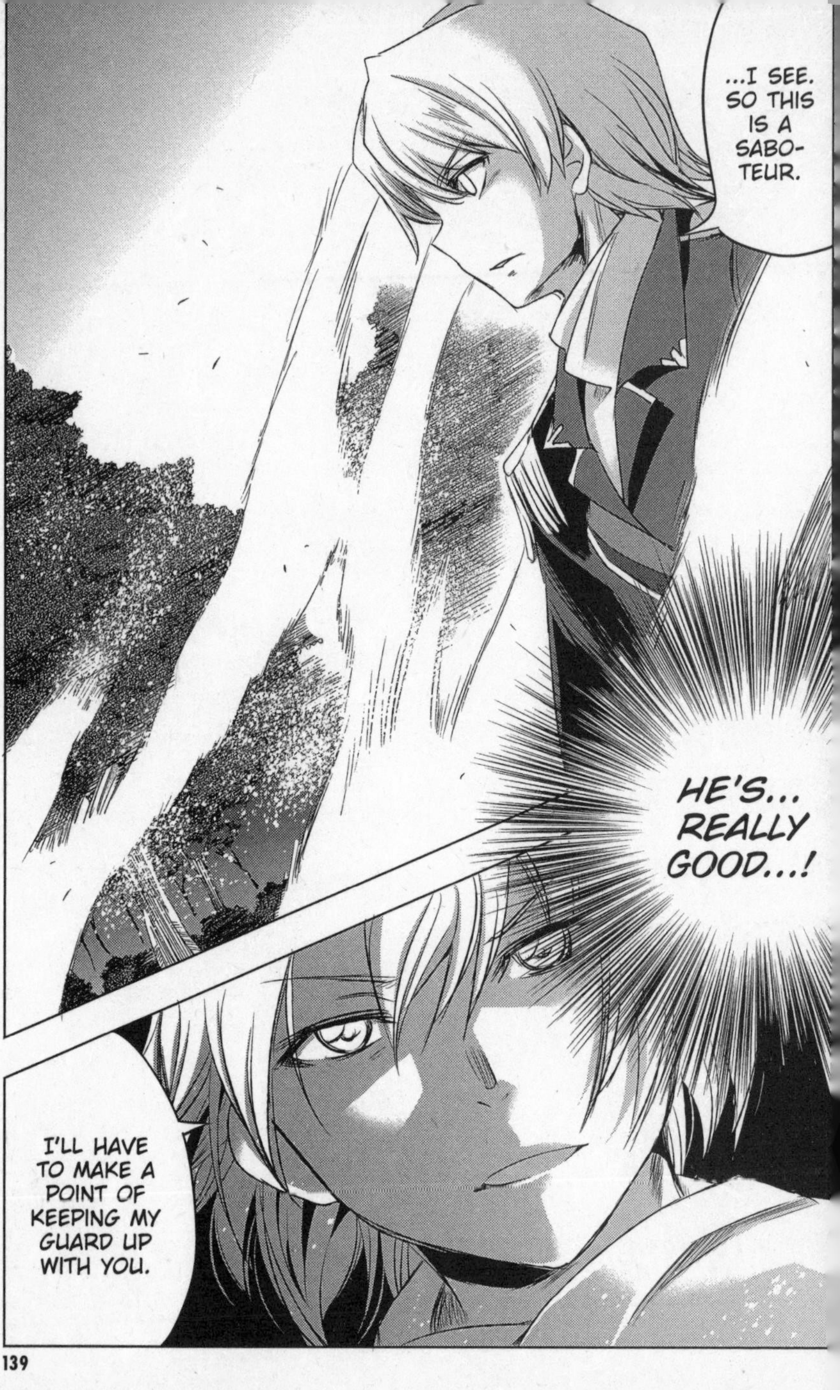
...I SEE. SO THIS IS A SABOTEUR.
HE'S... REALLY GOOD...!
I'LL HAVE TO MAKE A POINT OF KEEPING MY GUARD UP WITH YOU.

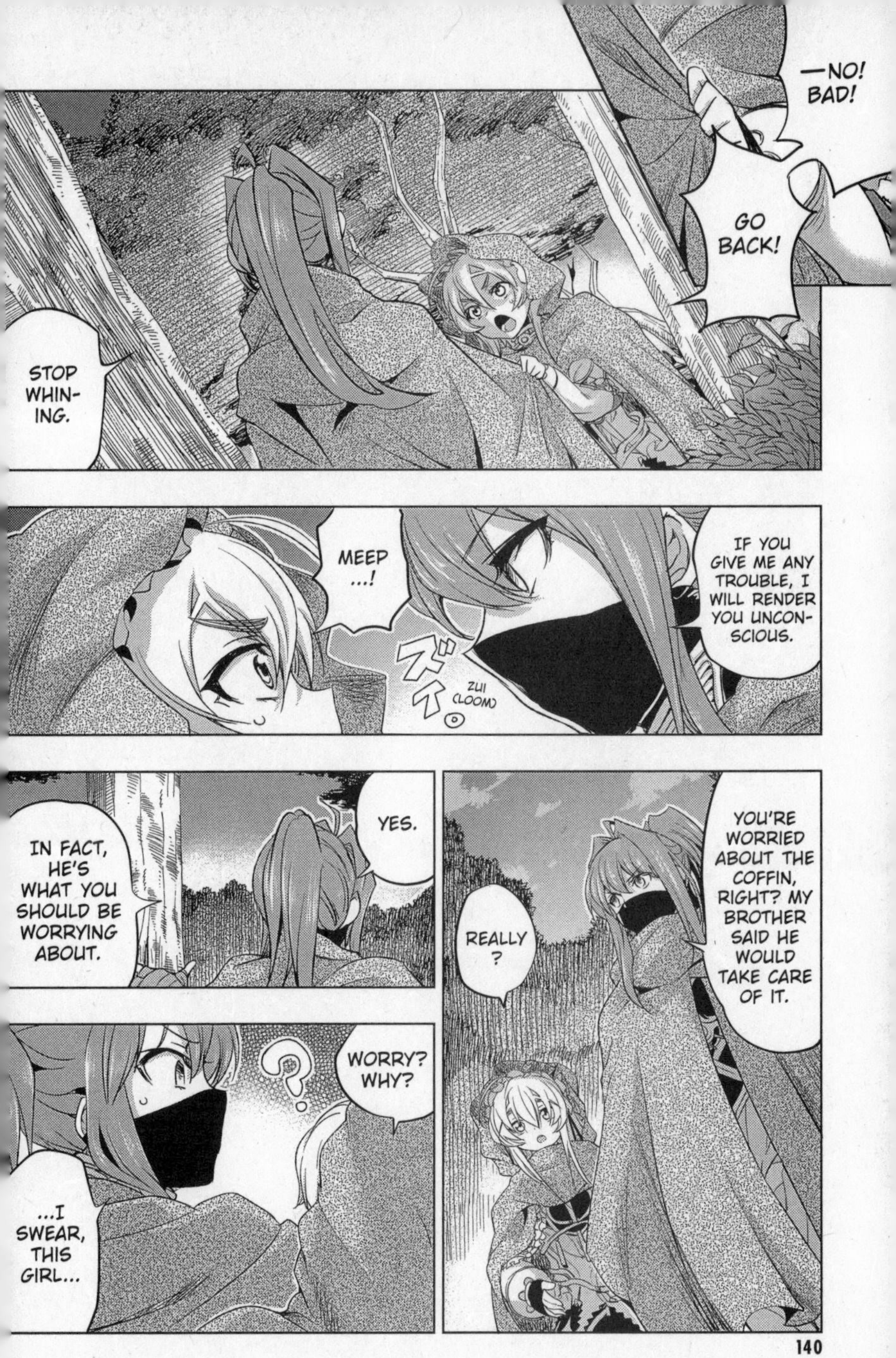
—NO! BAD!
GO BACK!
STOP WHINING.
IF YOU GIVE ME ANY TROUBLE, I WILL RENDER YOU UNCONSCIOUS.
MEEP ...!
ズイ
ZUI (LOOM)
YOU'RE WORRIED ABOUT THE COFFIN, RIGHT? MY BROTHER SAID HE WOULD TAKE CARE OF IT.
REALLY?
YES.
IN FACT, HE'S WHAT YOU SHOULD BE WORRYING ABOUT.
WORRY? WHY?
...I SWEAR, THIS GIRL...

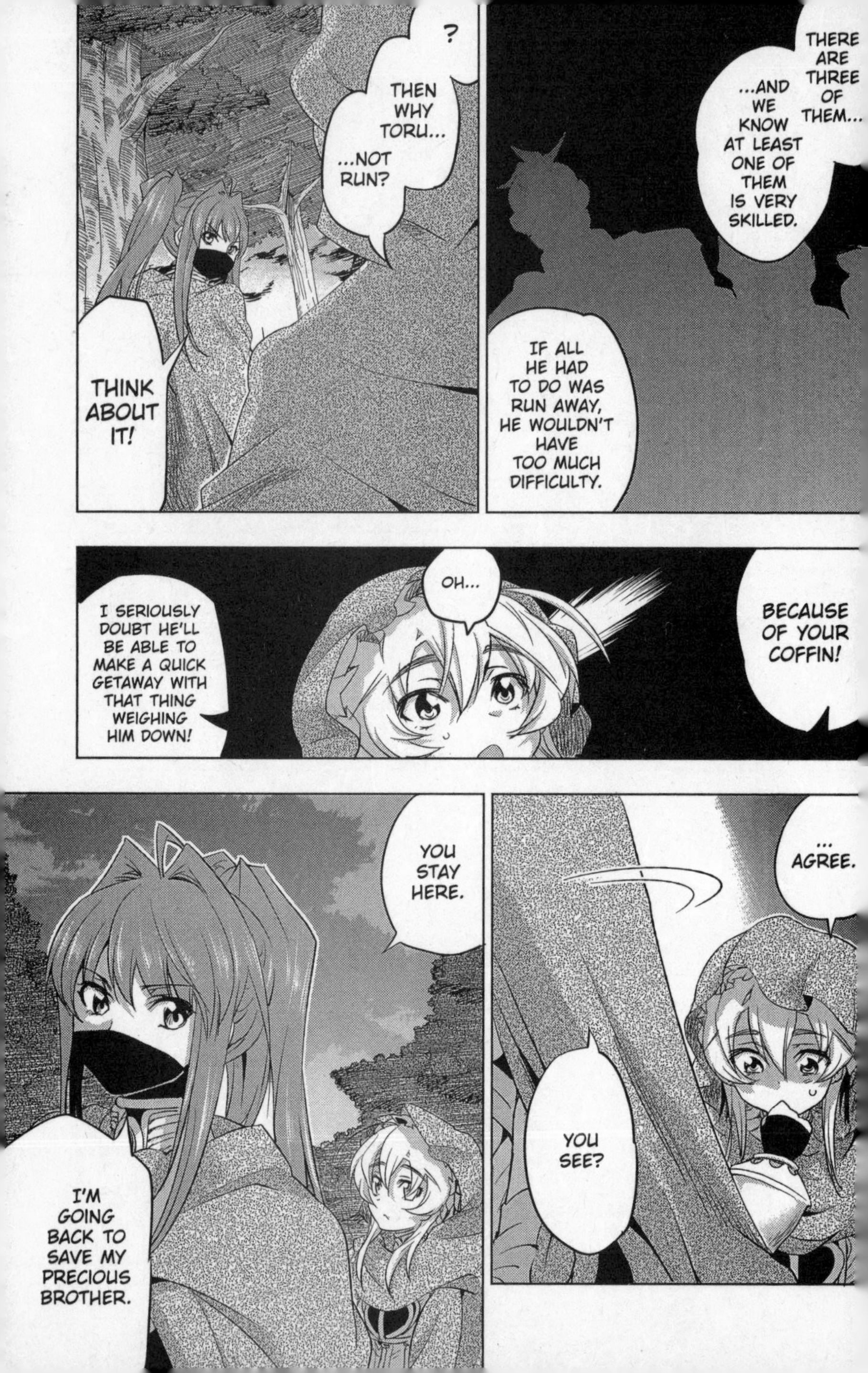

THERE ARE THREE OF THEM...
...AND WE KNOW AT LEAST ONE OF THEM IS VERY SKILLED.
IF ALL HE HAD TO DO WAS RUN AWAY, HE WOULDN'T HAVE TOO MUCH DIFFICULTY.
?
THEN WHY TORU...
...NOT RUN?
THINK ABOUT IT!
BECAUSE OF YOUR COFFIN!
OH...
I SERIOUSLY DOUBT HE'LL BE ABLE TO MAKE A QUICK GETAWAY WITH THAT THING WEIGHING HIM DOWN!
... AGREE.
YOU SEE?
YOU STAY HERE.
I'M GOING BACK TO SAVE MY PRECIOUS BROTHER.

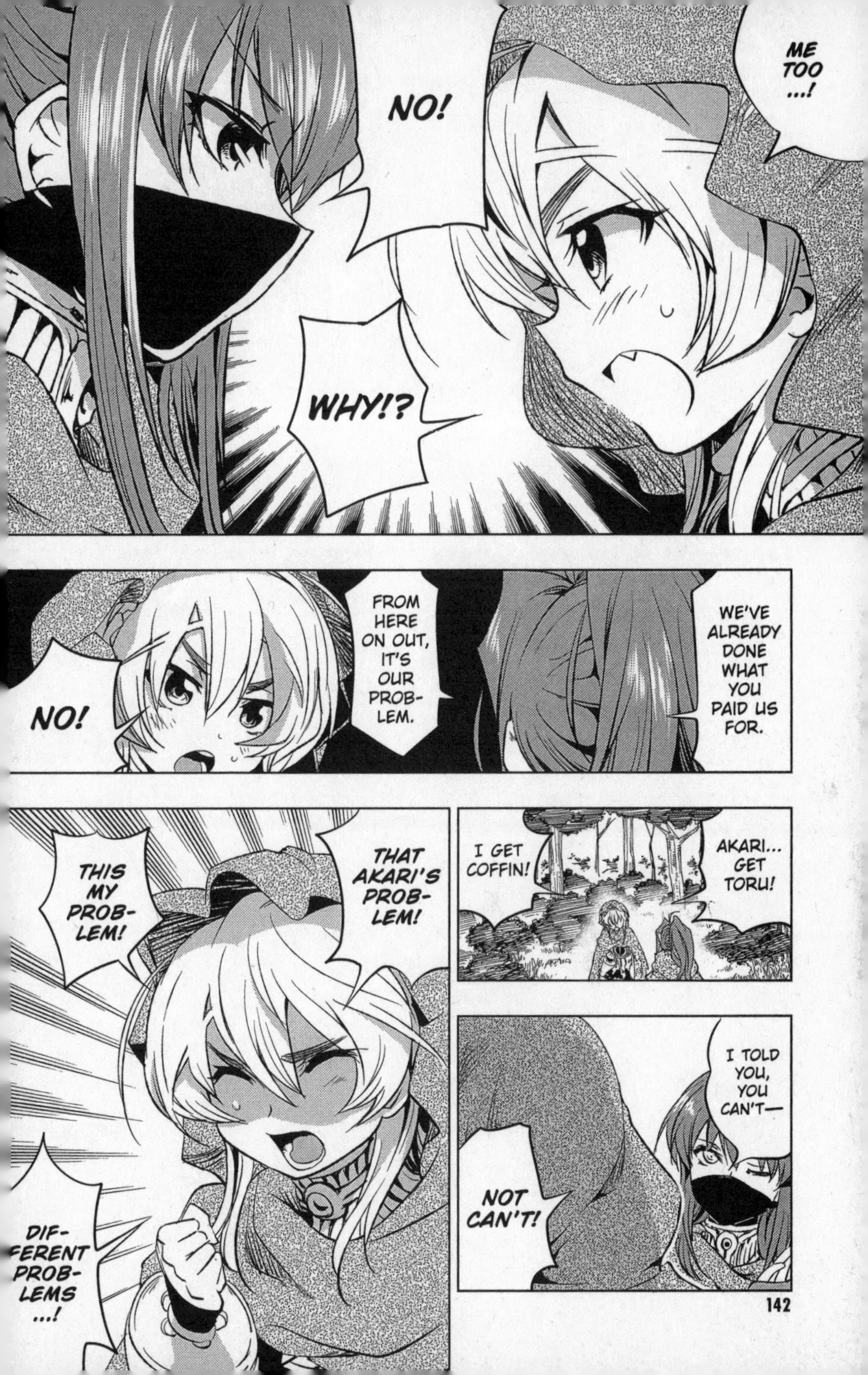
ME TOO ...!
NO!
WHY!?
WE'VE ALREADY DONE WHAT YOU PAID US FOR.
FROM HERE ON OUT, IT'S OUR PROB-LEM.
NO!
AKARI... GET TORU!
I GET COFFIN!
I TOLD YOU, YOU CAN'T—
NOT CAN'T!
THAT AKARI'S PROB-LEM!
THIS MY PROB-LEM!
DIF-FERENT PROB-LEMS ...!

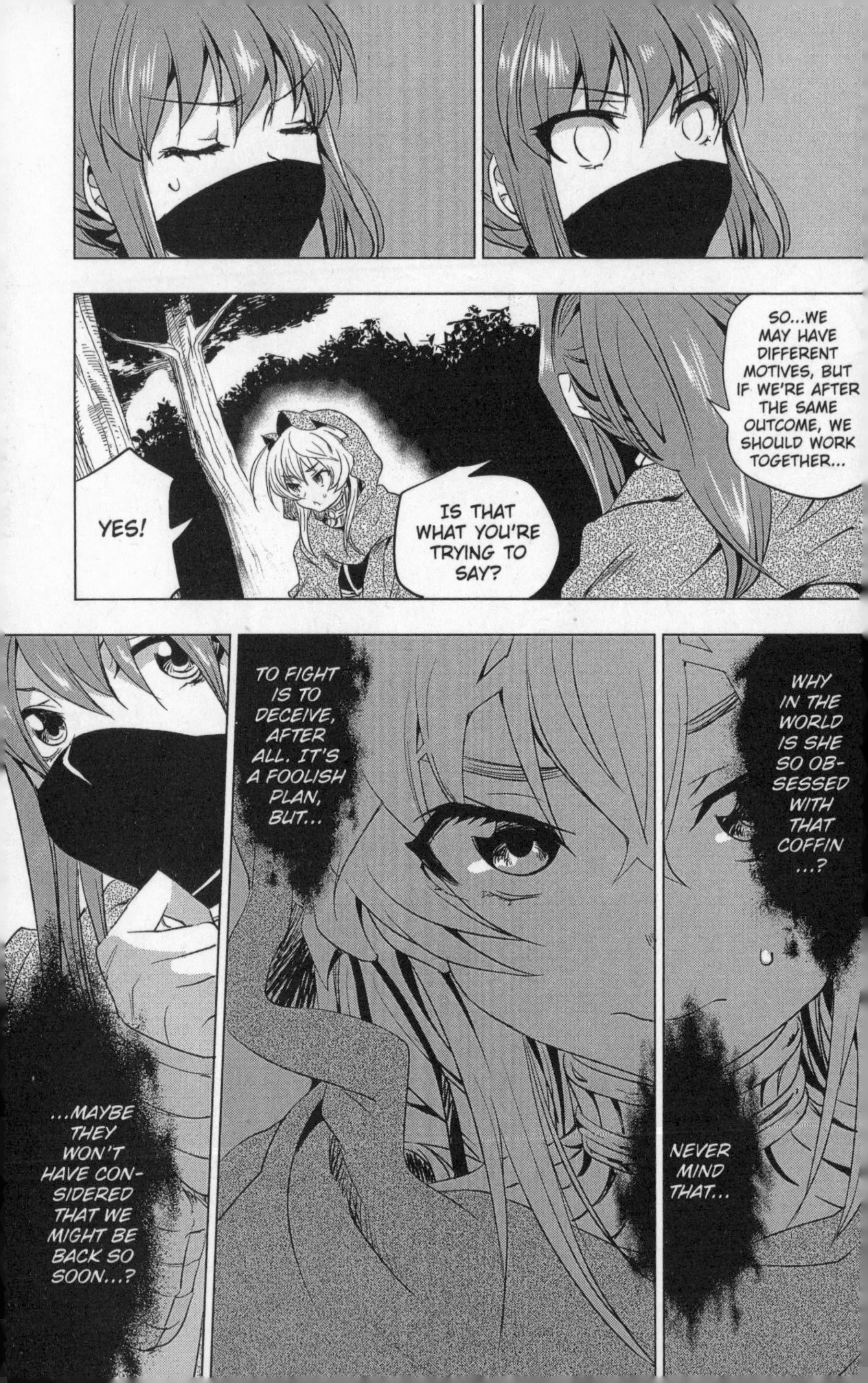
SO...WE MAY HAVE DIFFERENT MOTIVES, BUT IF WE'RE AFTER THE SAME OUTCOME, WE SHOULD WORK TOGETHER...
IS THAT WHAT YOU'RE TRYING TO SAY?
YES!
WHY IN THE WORLD IS SHE SO OB-SESSED WITH THAT COFFIN ...?
NEVER MIND THAT...
TO FIGHT IS TO DECEIVE, AFTER ALL. IT'S A FOOLISH PLAN, BUT...
...MAYBE THEY WON'T HAVE CON-SIDERED THAT WE MIGHT BE BACK SO SOON...?

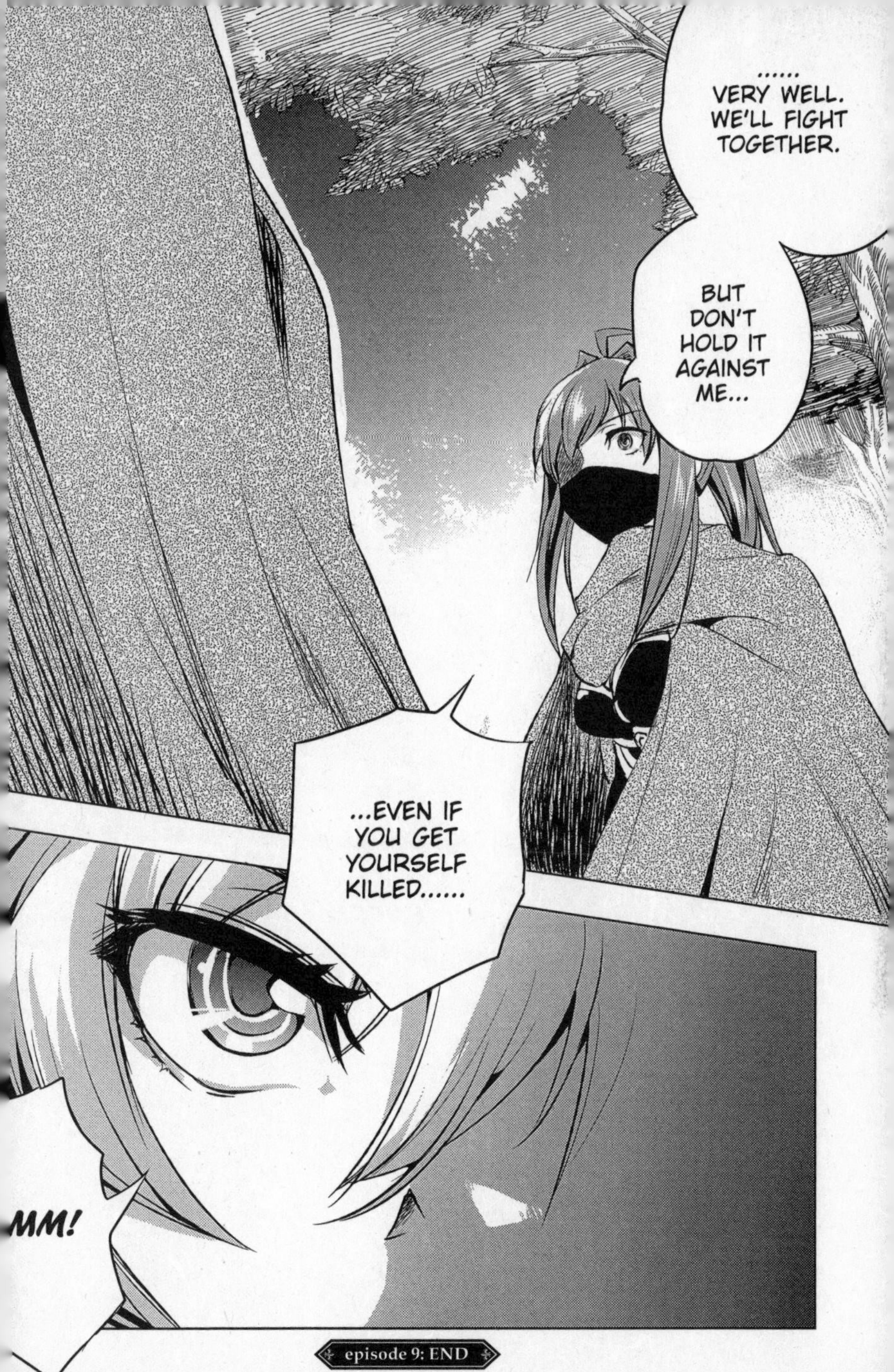

...... VERY WELL. WE'LL FIGHT TOGETHER.
BUT DON'T HOLD IT AGAINST ME...
...EVEN IF YOU GET YOURSELF KILLED......
MM!

episode 9: END

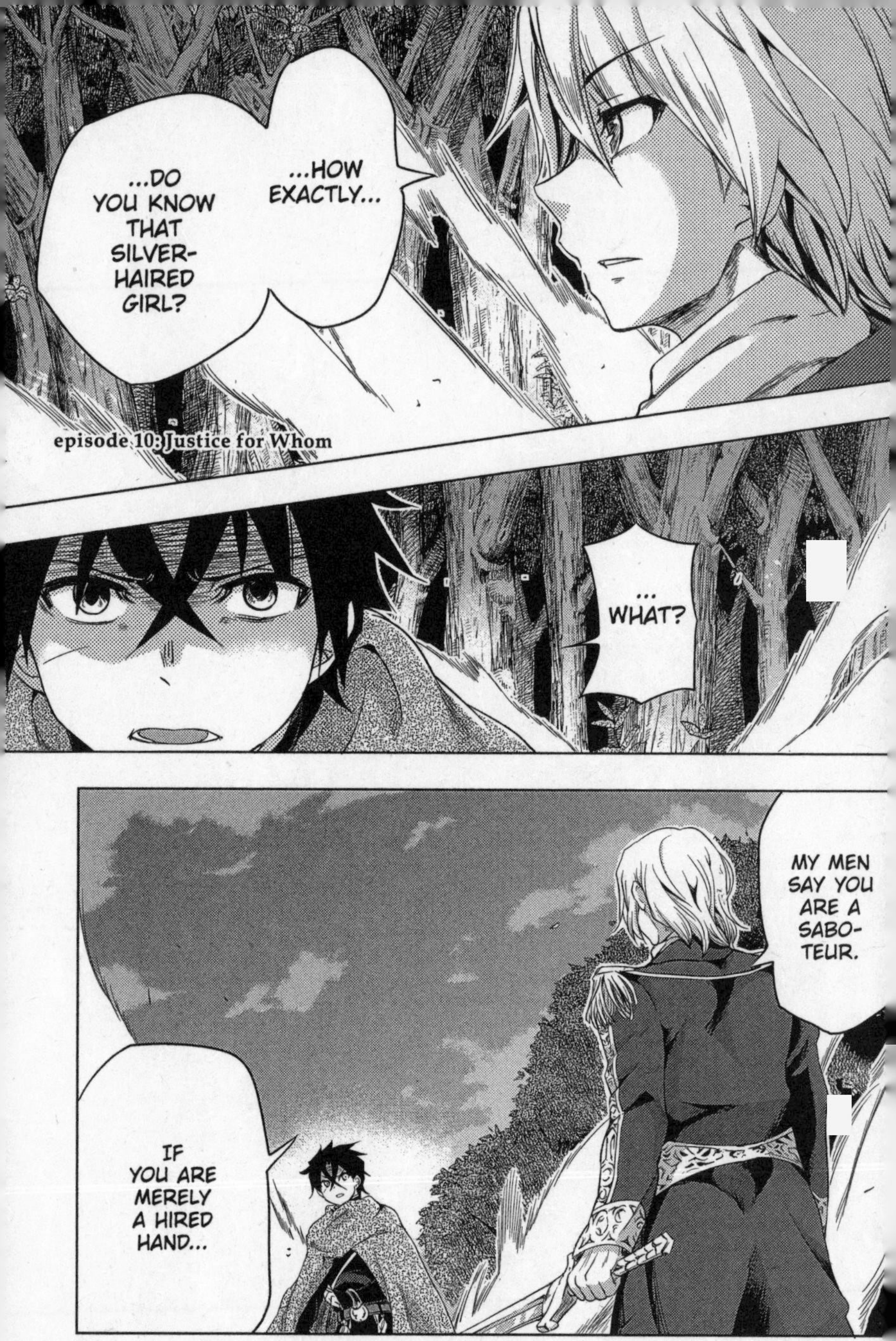
...HOW EXACTLY...
...DO YOU KNOW THAT SILVER-HAIRED GIRL?
episode 10: Justice for Whom
... WHAT?
MY MEN SAY YOU ARE A SABOTEUR.
IF YOU ARE MERELY A HIRED HAND...

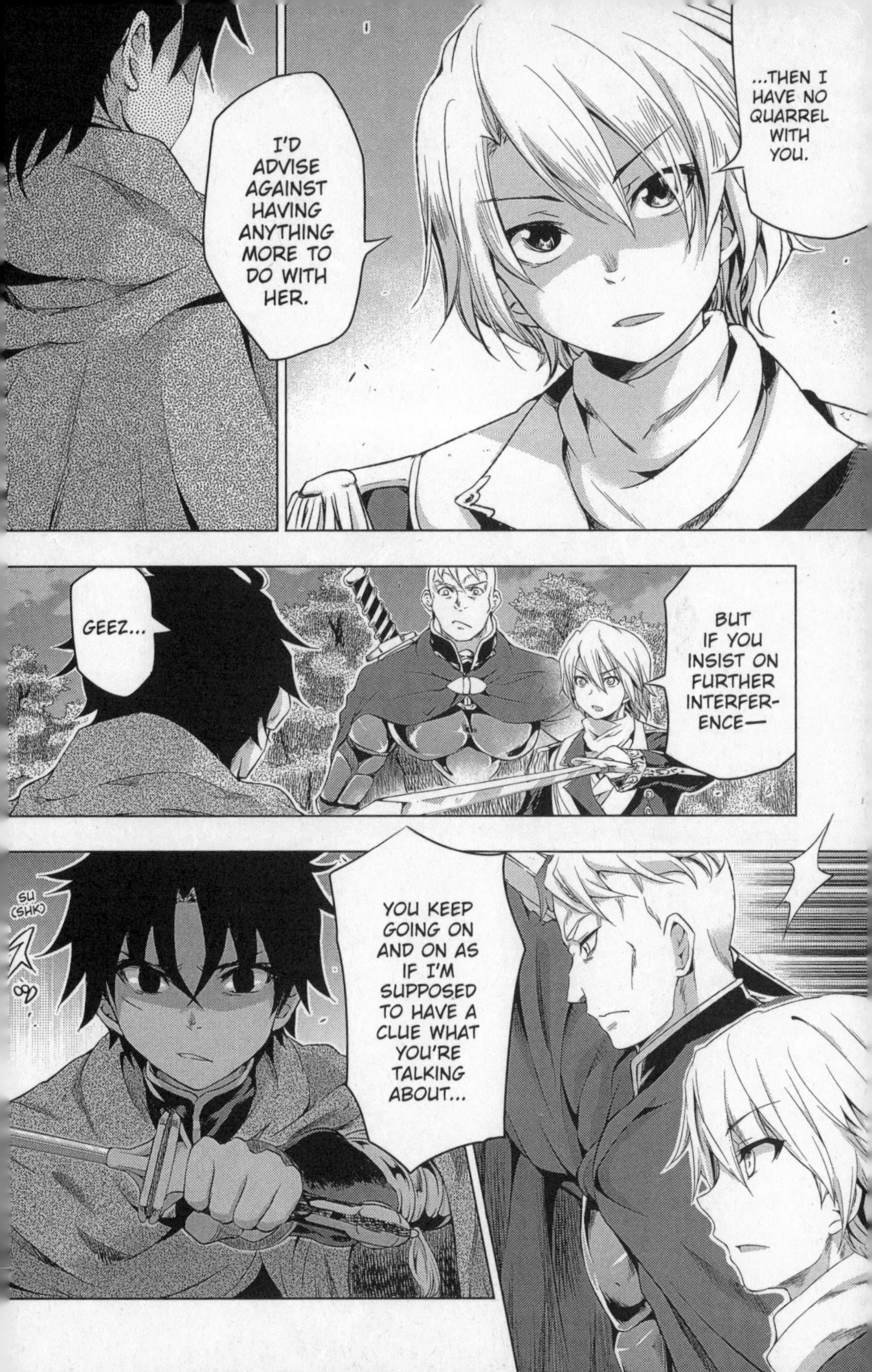
...THEN I HAVE NO QUARREL WITH YOU.
I'D ADVISE AGAINST HAVING ANYTHING MORE TO DO WITH HER.
BUT IF YOU INSIST ON FURTHER INTERFER-ENCE—
GEEZ...
YOU KEEP GOING ON AND ON AS IF I'M SUPPOSED TO HAVE A CLUE WHAT YOU'RE TALKING ABOUT...
SU (SHK)

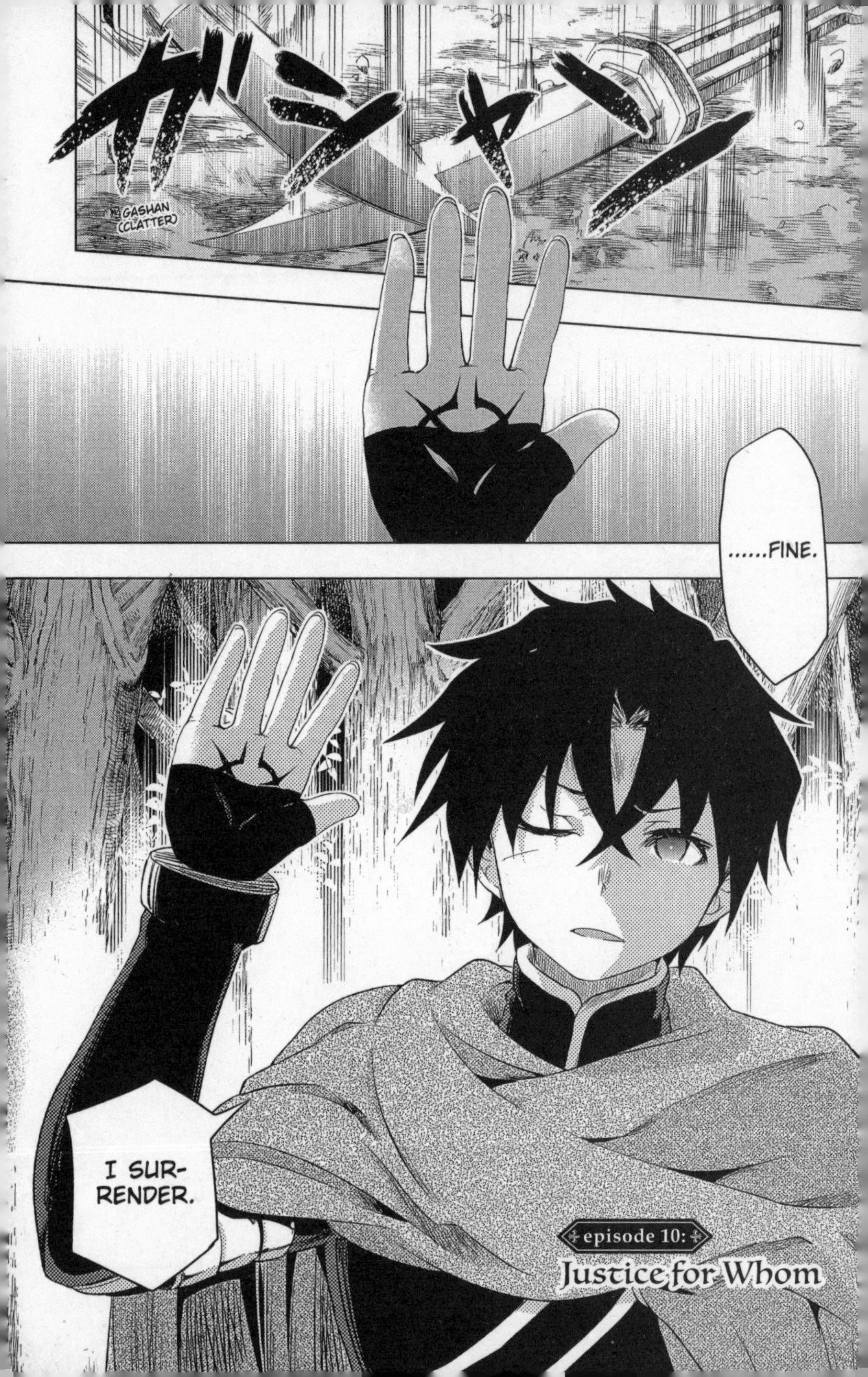
ガシャーン
GASHAN (CLATTER)
......FINE.
I SUR-RENDER.
episode 10:
Justice for Whom

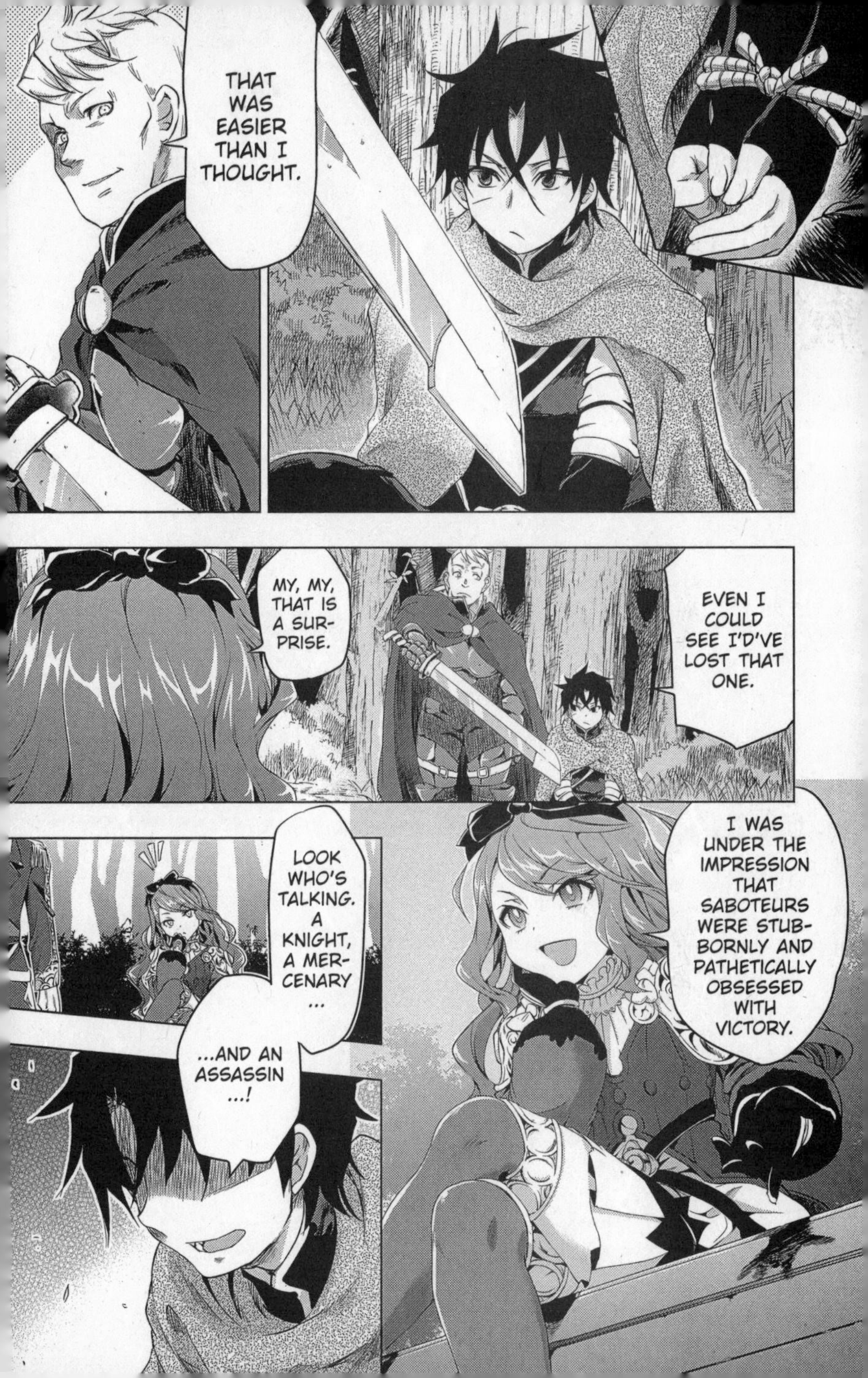
THAT WAS EASIER THAN I THOUGHT.
EVEN I COULD SEE I'D'VE LOST THAT ONE.
MY, MY, THAT IS A SURPRISE.
I WAS UNDER THE IMPRESSION THAT SABOTEURS WERE STUBBORNLY AND PATHETICALLY OBSESSED WITH VICTORY.
LOOK WHO'S TALKING. A KNIGHT, A MERCENARY...
...AND AN ASSASSIN...!

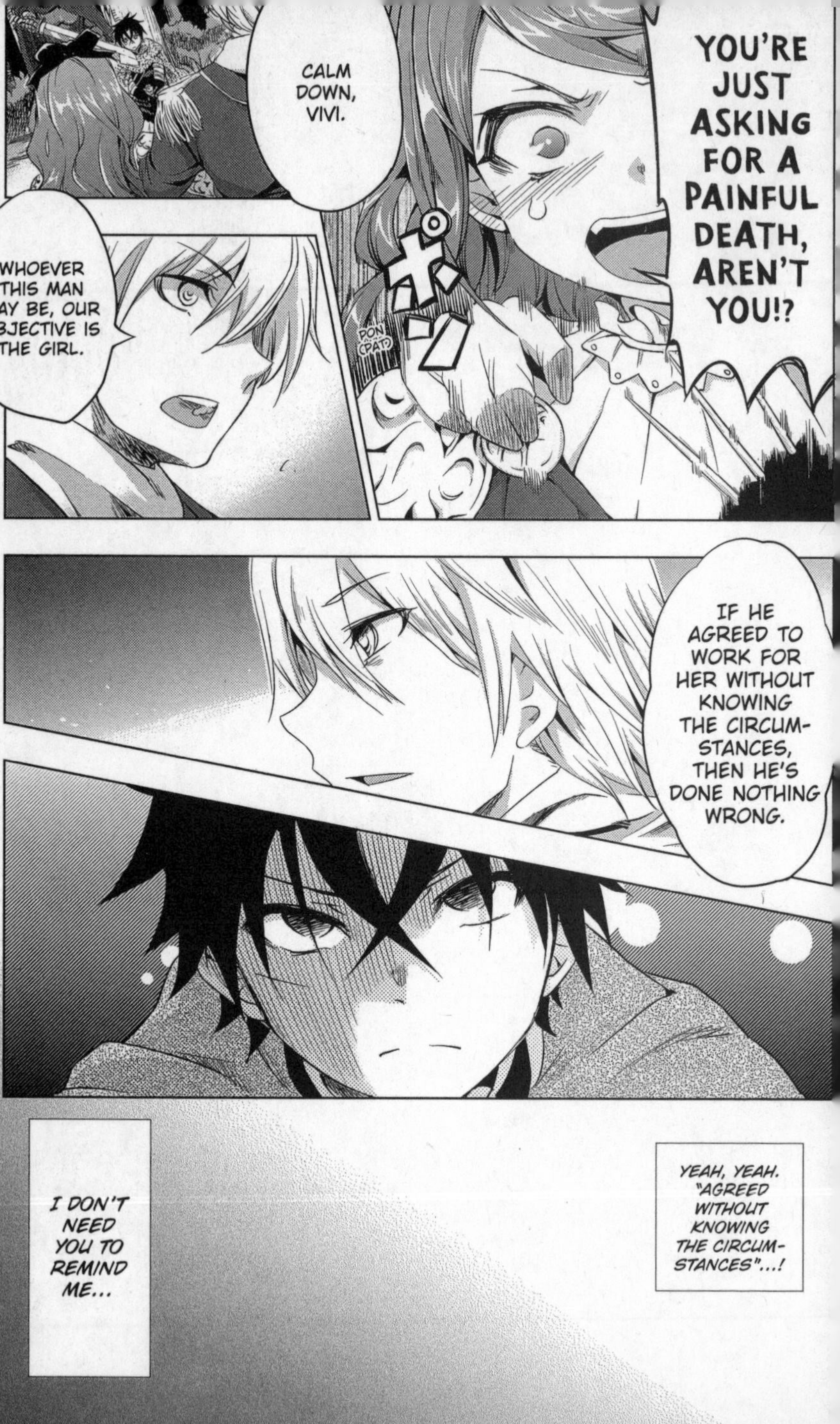
YOU'RE JUST ASKING FOR A PAINFUL DEATH, AREN'T YOU!?
CALM DOWN, VIVI.
PON (PAT)
WHOEVER THIS MAN MAY BE, OUR OBJECTIVE IS THE GIRL.
IF HE AGREED TO WORK FOR HER WITHOUT KNOWING THE CIRCUM-STANCES, THEN HE'S DONE NOTHING WRONG.
YEAH, YEAH. "AGREED WITHOUT KNOWING THE CIRCUM-STANCES"...!
I DON'T NEED YOU TO REMIND ME...

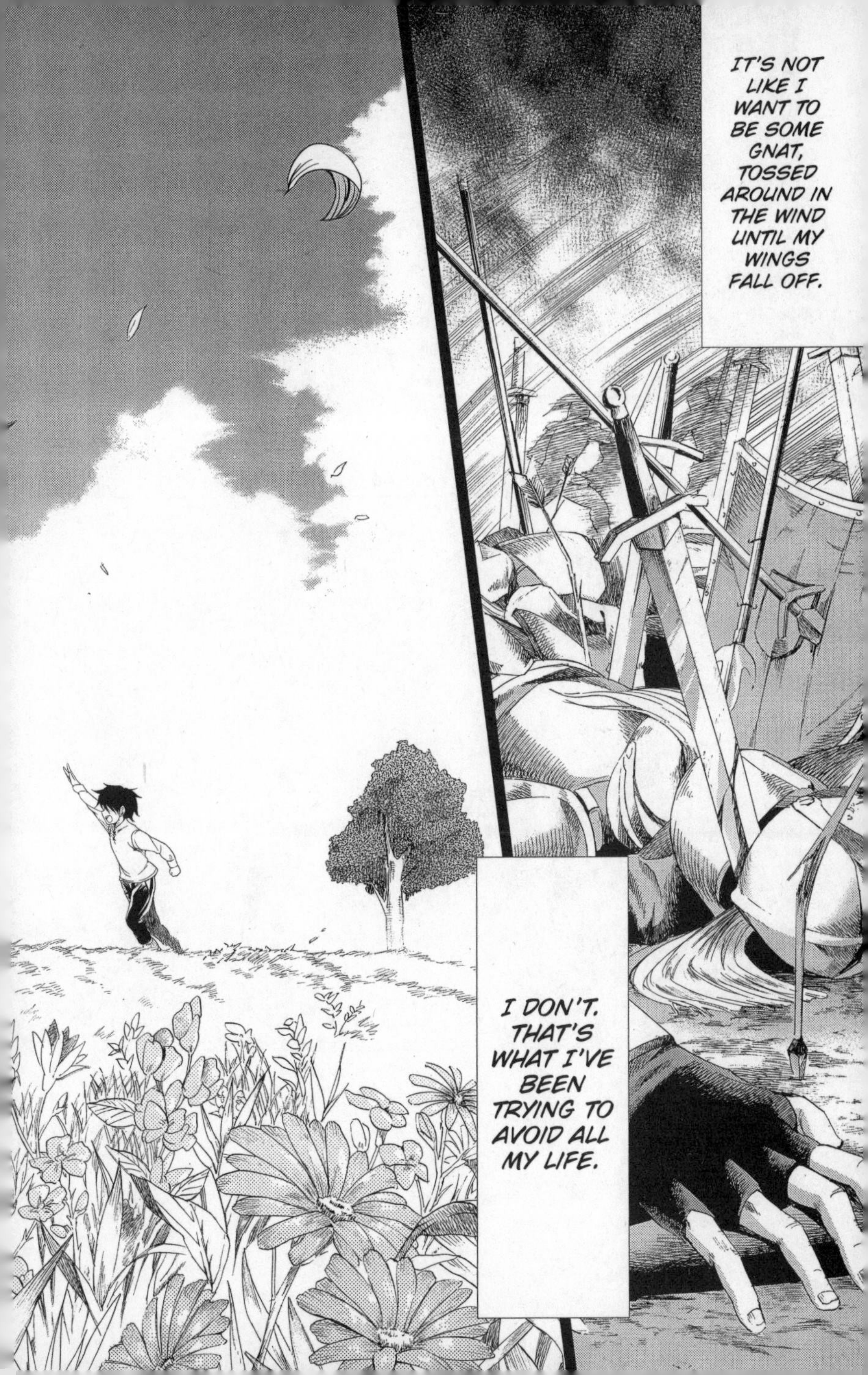
IT'S NOT LIKE I WANT TO BE SOME GNAT, TOSSED AROUND IN THE WIND UNTIL MY WINGS FALL OFF.
I DON'T. THAT'S WHAT I'VE BEEN TRYING TO AVOID ALL MY LIFE.

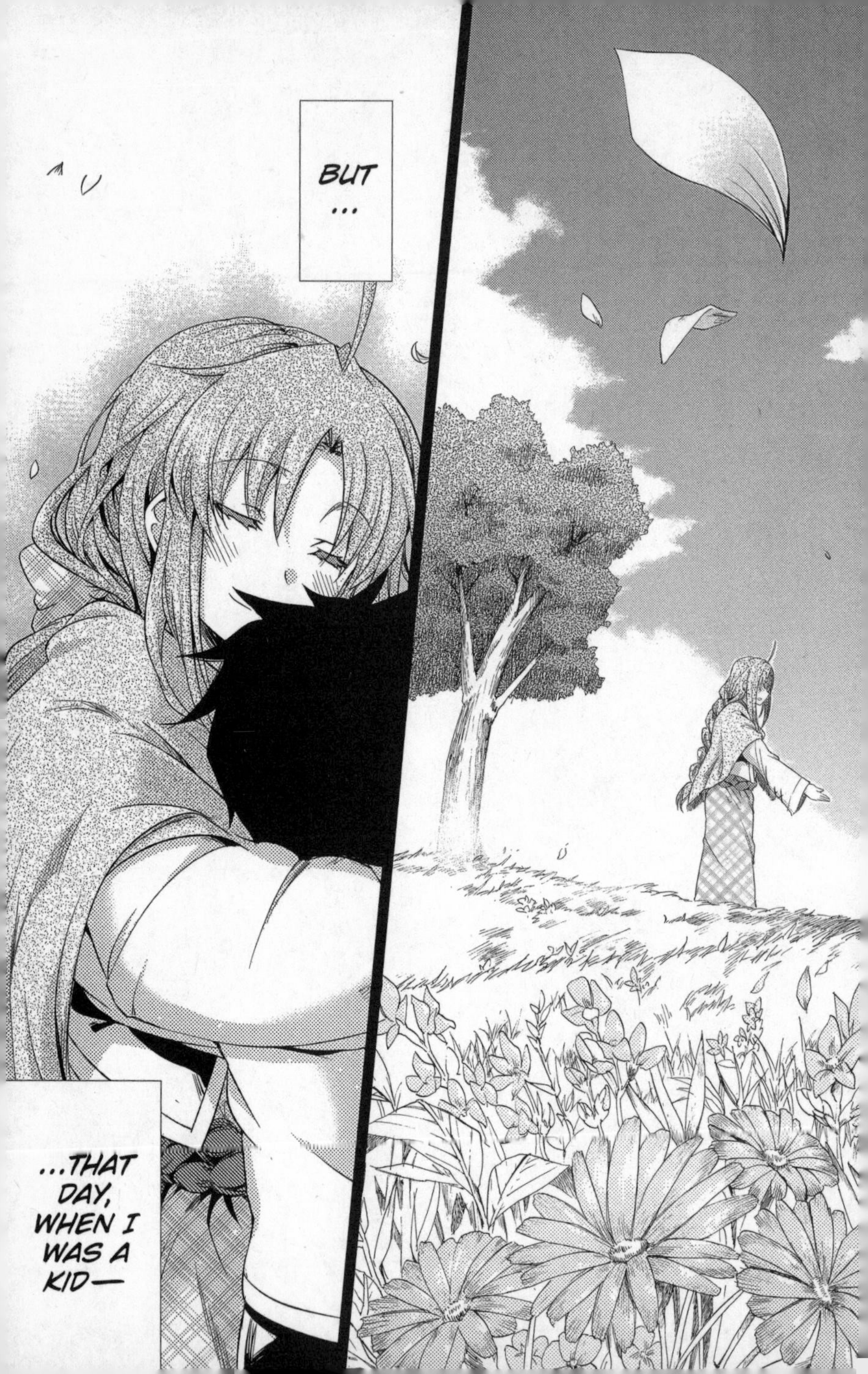
BUT ...
...THAT DAY, WHEN I WAS A KID—

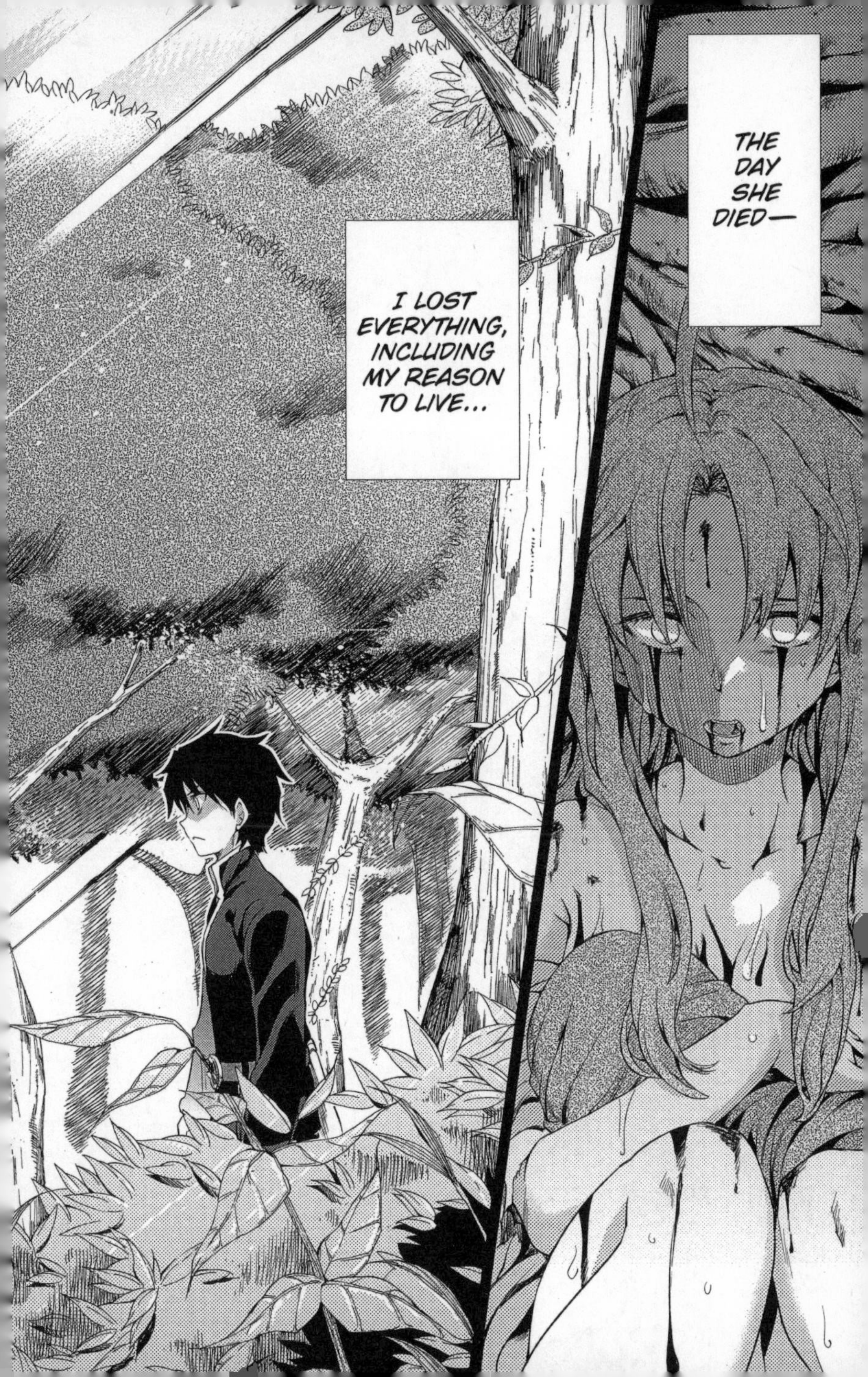
THE DAY SHE DIED—
I LOST EVERYTHING, INCLUDING MY REASON TO LIVE…

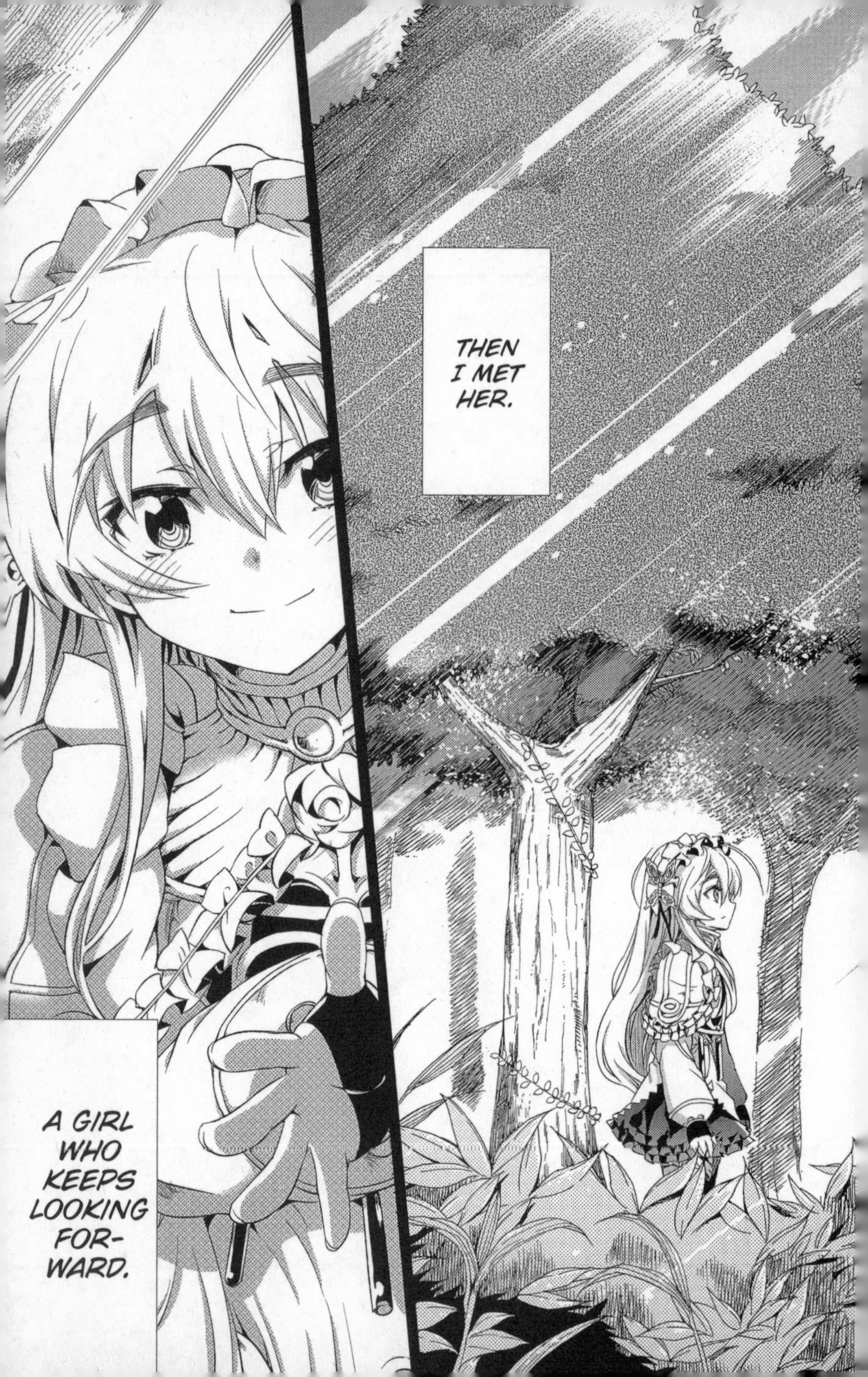
THEN I MET HER.
A GIRL WHO KEEPS LOOKING FOR-WARD.

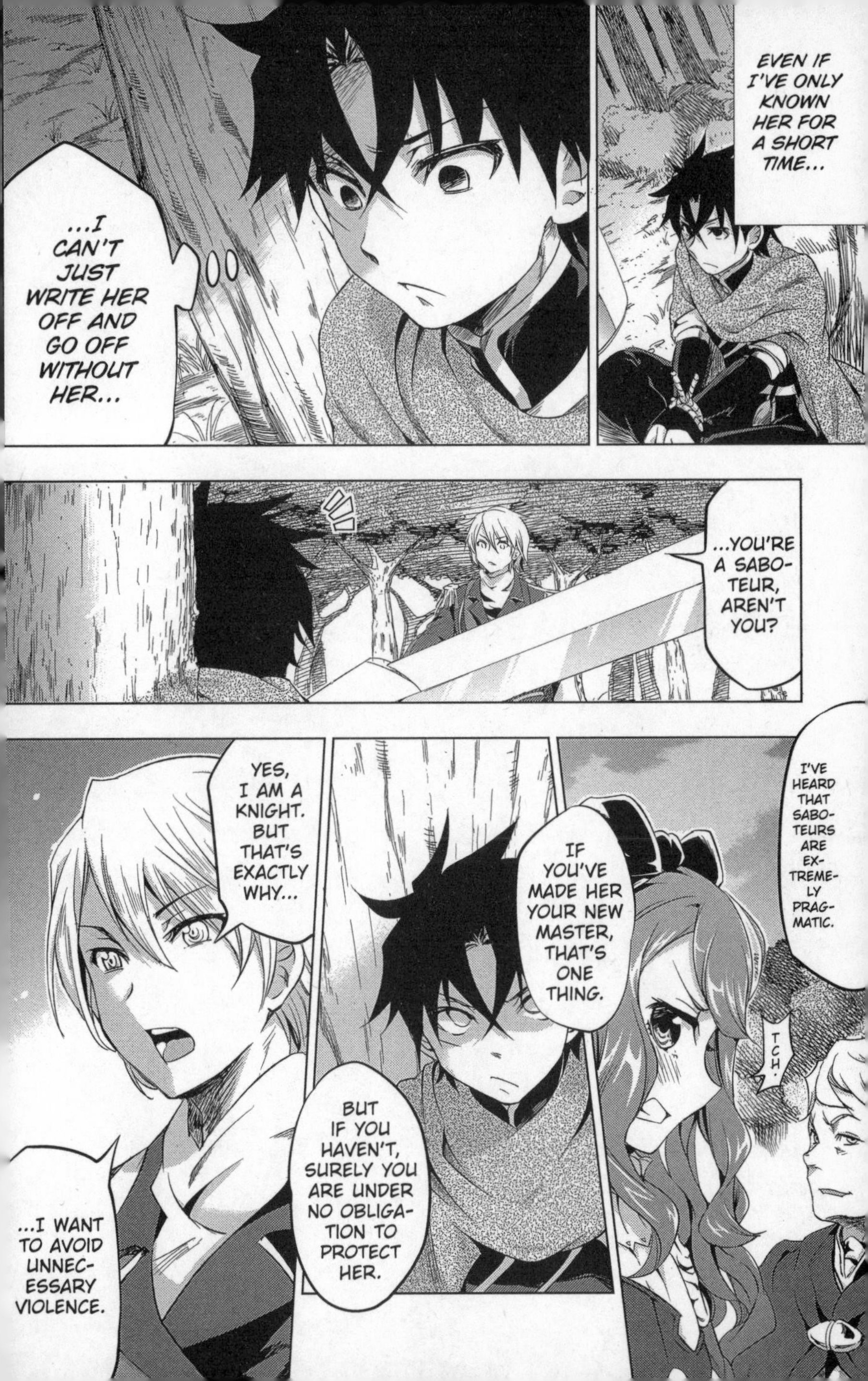
EVEN IF I'VE ONLY KNOWN HER FOR A SHORT TIME...
...I CAN'T JUST WRITE HER OFF AND GO OFF WITHOUT HER...
...YOU'RE A SABOTEUR, AREN'T YOU?
I'VE HEARD THAT SABOTEURS ARE EXTREMELY PRAGMATIC.
TCH.
IF YOU'VE MADE HER YOUR NEW MASTER, THAT'S ONE THING.
BUT IF YOU HAVEN'T, SURELY YOU ARE UNDER NO OBLIGATION TO PROTECT HER.
YES, I AM A KNIGHT. BUT THAT'S EXACTLY WHY...
...I WANT TO AVOID UNNECESSARY VIOLENCE.

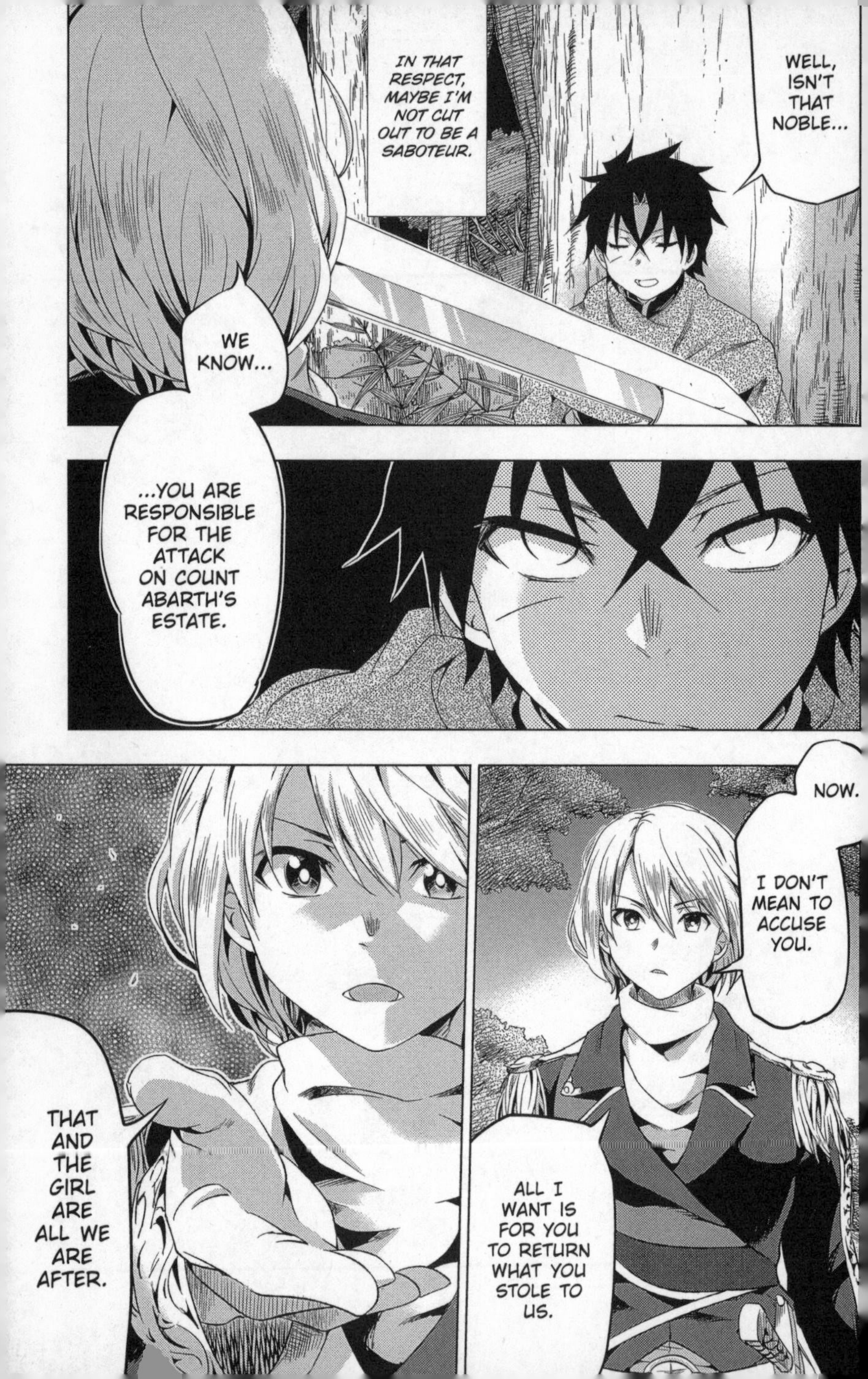
WELL, ISN'T THAT NOBLE...
IN THAT RESPECT, MAYBE I'M NOT CUT OUT TO BE A SABOTEUR.
WE KNOW...
...YOU ARE RESPONSIBLE FOR THE ATTACK ON COUNT ABARTH'S ESTATE.
NOW.
I DON'T MEAN TO ACCUSE YOU.
ALL I WANT IS FOR YOU TO RETURN WHAT YOU STOLE TO US.
THAT AND THE GIRL ARE ALL WE ARE AFTER.

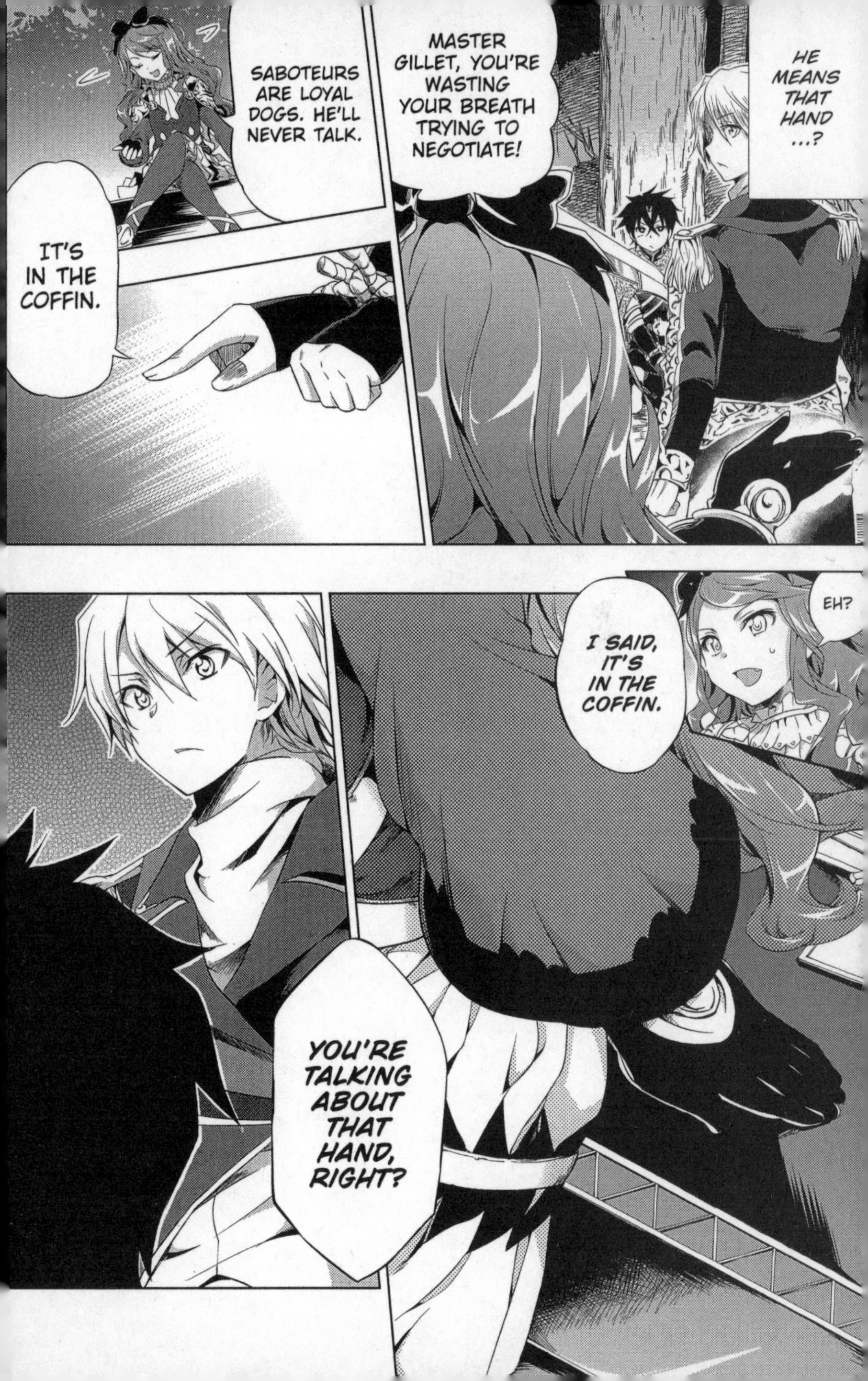
HE MEANS THAT HAND ...?
MASTER GILLET, YOU'RE WASTING YOUR BREATH TRYING TO NEGOTIATE!
SABOTEURS ARE LOYAL DOGS. HE'LL NEVER TALK.
IT'S IN THE COFFIN.
EH?
I SAID, IT'S IN THE COFFIN.
YOU'RE TALKING ABOUT THAT HAND, RIGHT?

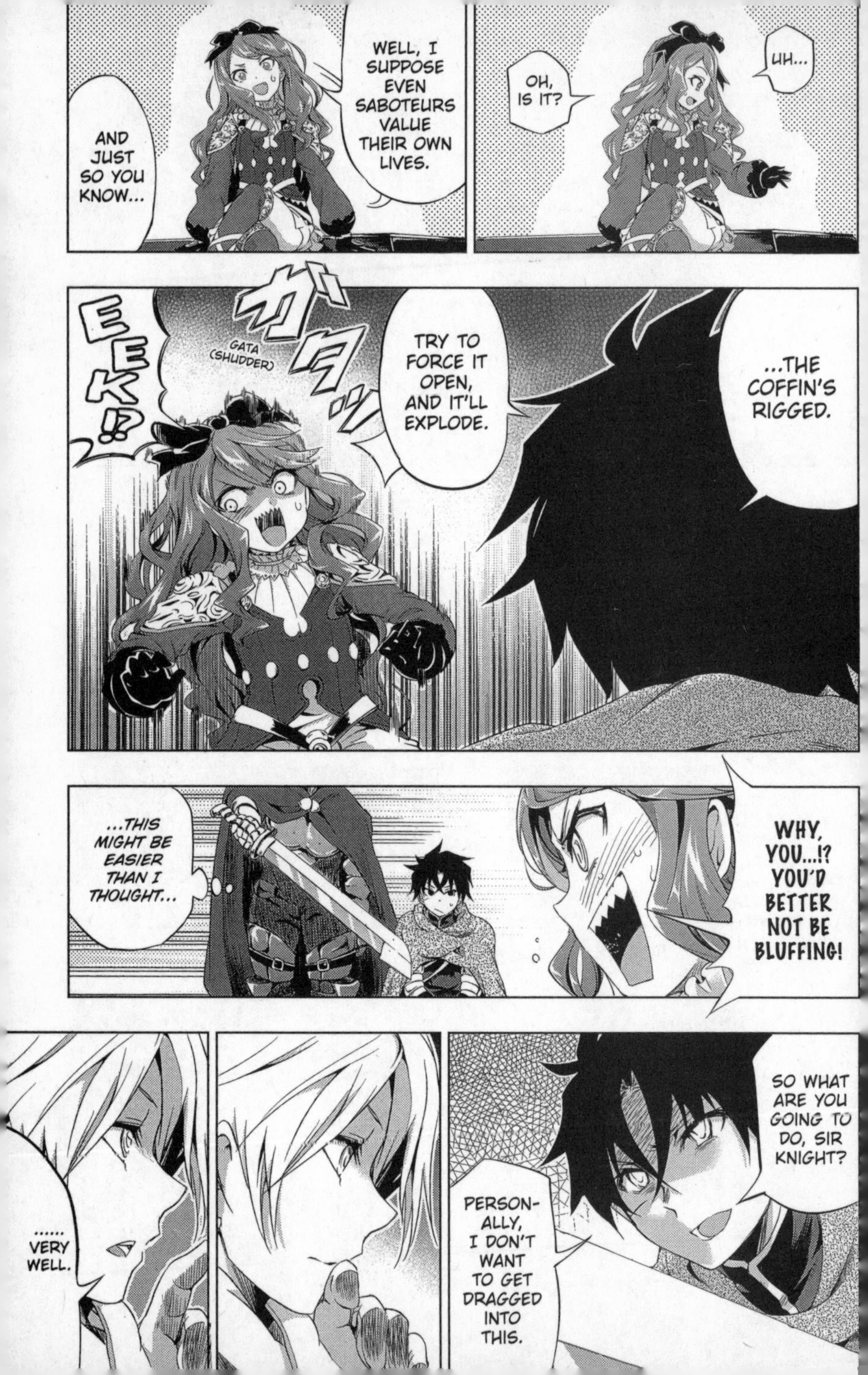
UH...
OH, IS IT?
WELL, I SUPPOSE EVEN SABOTEURS VALUE THEIR OWN LIVES.
AND JUST SO YOU KNOW...
...THE COFFIN'S RIGGED.
TRY TO FORCE IT OPEN, AND IT'LL EXPLODE.
GATA (SHUDDER)
EEK!?
WHY, YOU...!? YOU'D BETTER NOT BE BLUFFING!
...THIS MIGHT BE EASIER THAN I THOUGHT...
SO WHAT ARE YOU GOING TO DO, SIR KNIGHT?
PERSON-ALLY, I DON'T WANT TO GET DRAGGED INTO THIS.
...... VERY WELL.

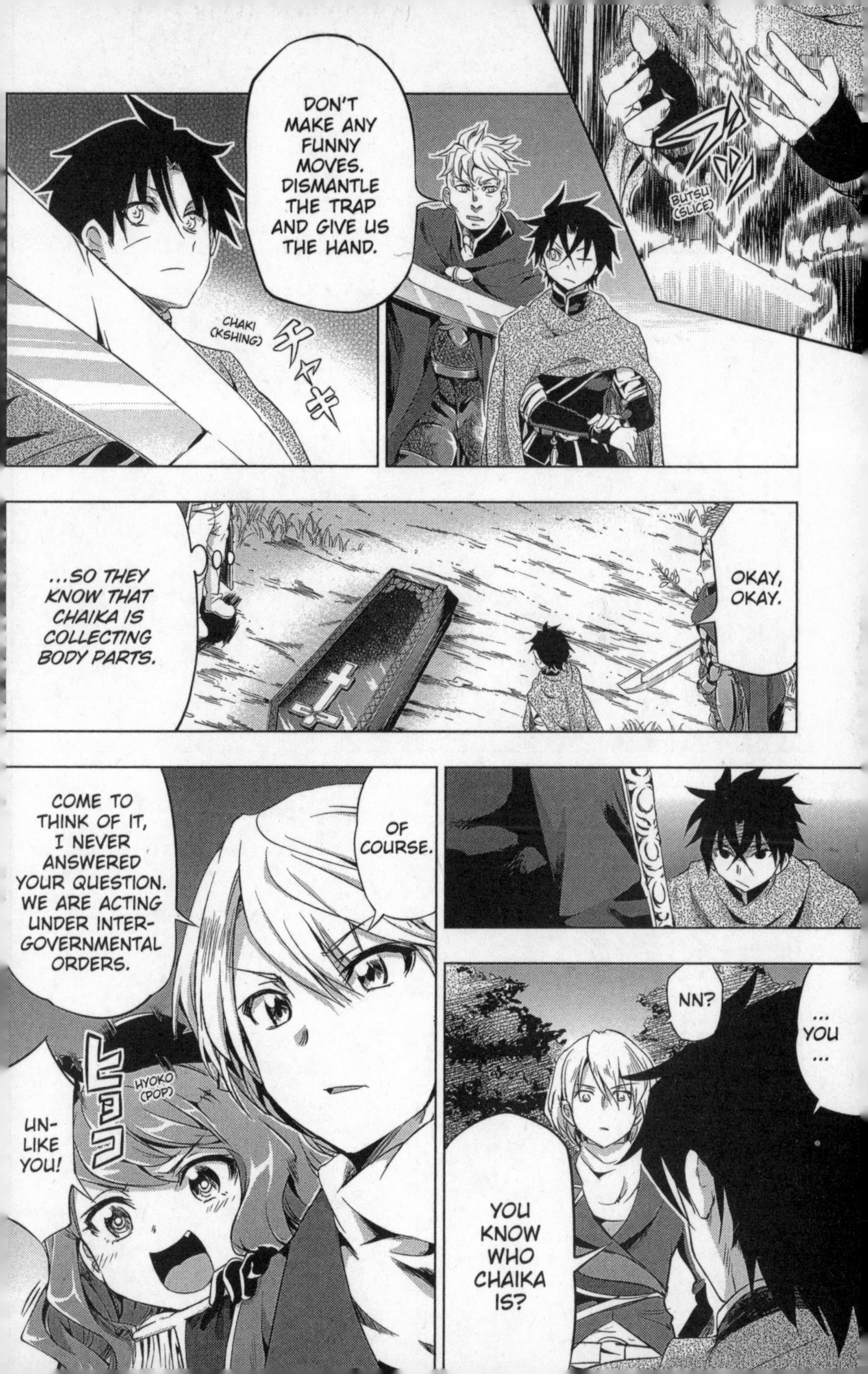
BUTSU (SLICE)
DON'T MAKE ANY FUNNY MOVES. DISMANTLE THE TRAP AND GIVE US THE HAND.
CHAKI (KSHING)
OKAY, OKAY.
...SO THEY KNOW THAT CHAIKA IS COLLECTING BODY PARTS.
... YOU ...
NN?
YOU KNOW WHO CHAIKA IS?
OF COURSE.
COME TO THINK OF IT, I NEVER ANSWERED YOUR QUESTION. WE ARE ACTING UNDER INTER-GOVERNMENTAL ORDERS.
HYOKO (POP)
UN-LIKE YOU!

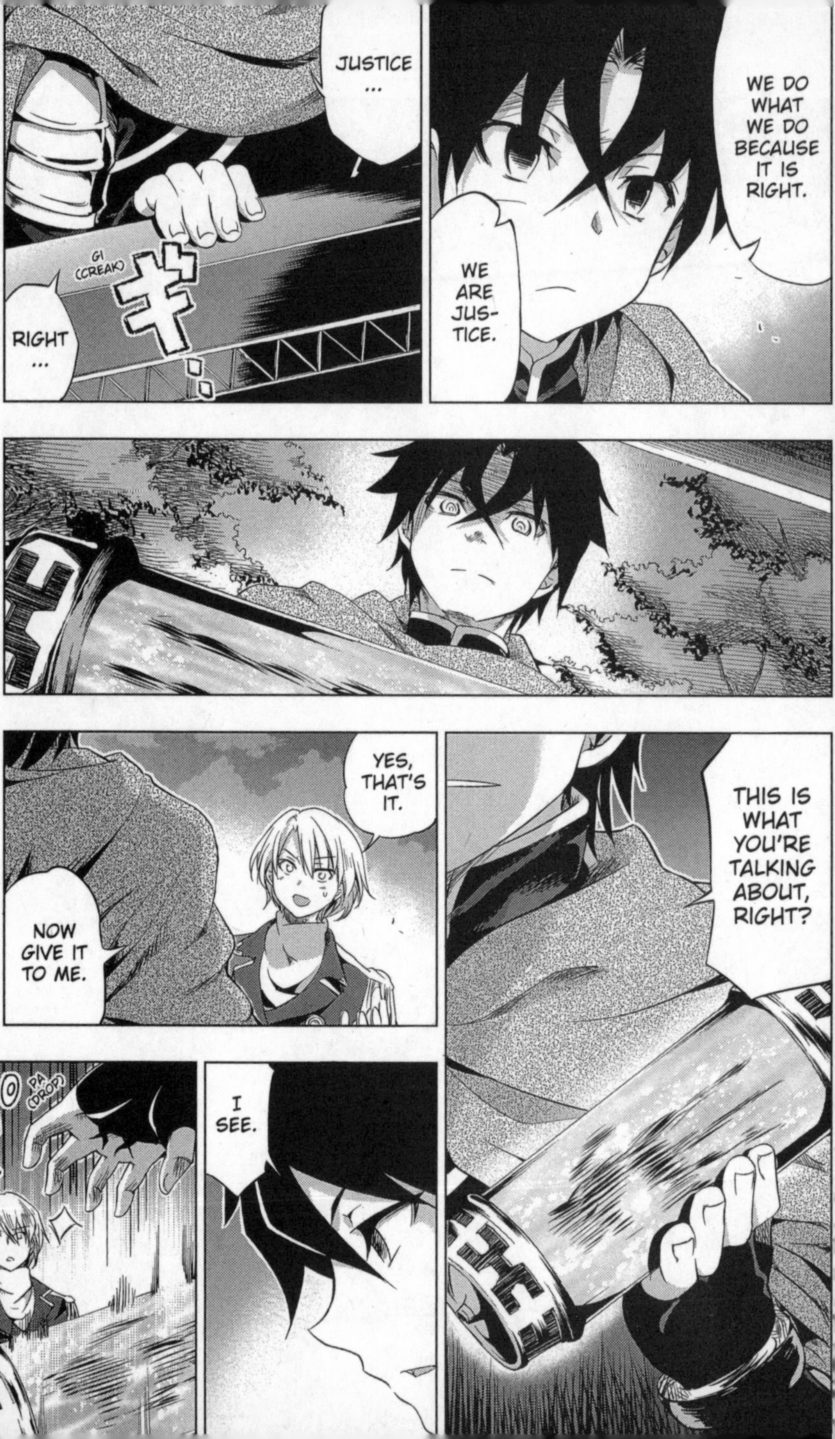
WE DO WHAT WE DO BECAUSE IT IS RIGHT.
WE ARE JUS-TICE.
JUSTICE ...
GI (CREAK)
RIGHT ...
THIS IS WHAT YOU'RE TALKING ABOUT, RIGHT?
YES, THAT'S IT.
NOW GIVE IT TO ME.
I SEE.
PA (DROP)

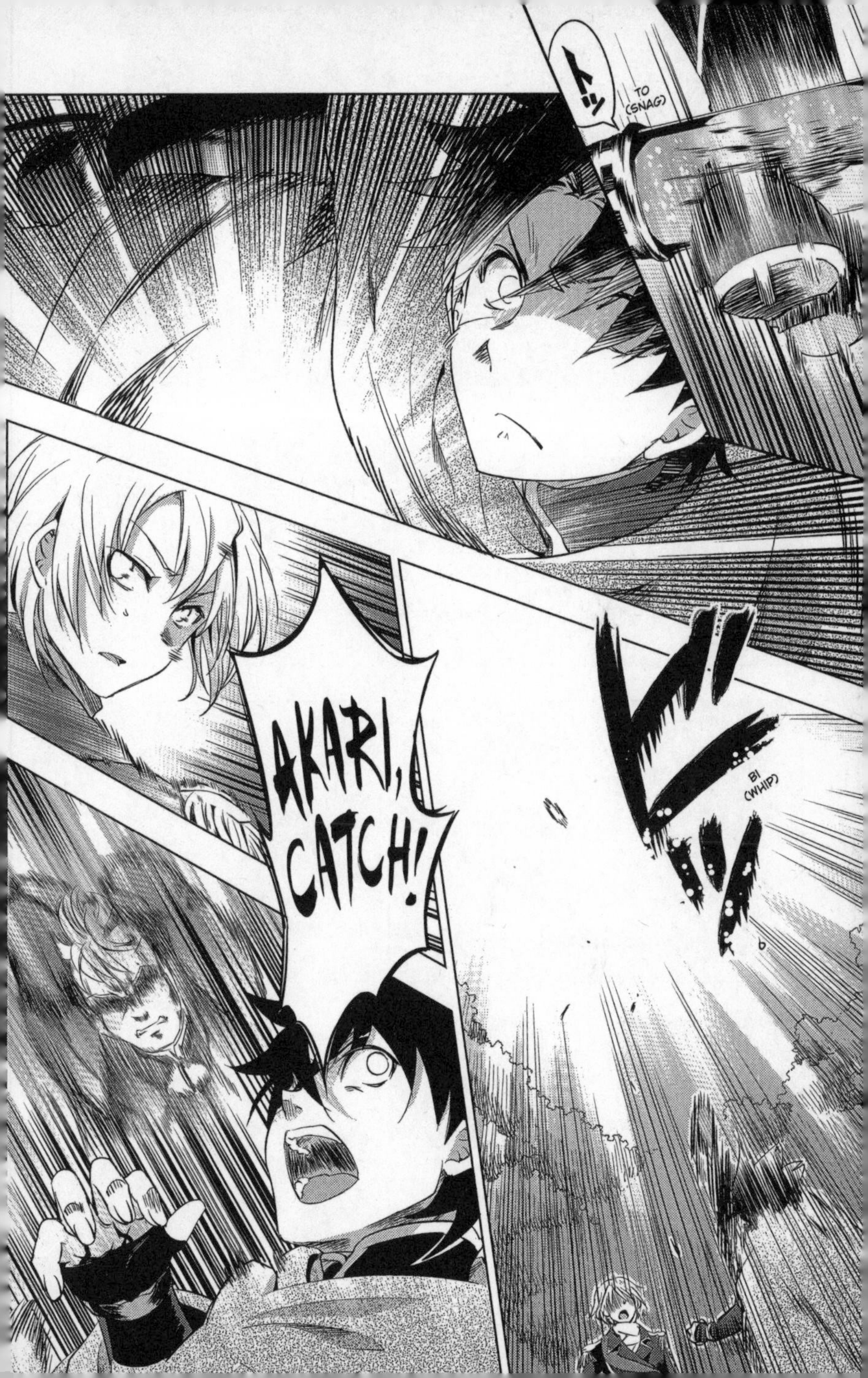
トッ
TO (SNAG)
ビッ
BI (WHIP)
AKARI, CATCH!

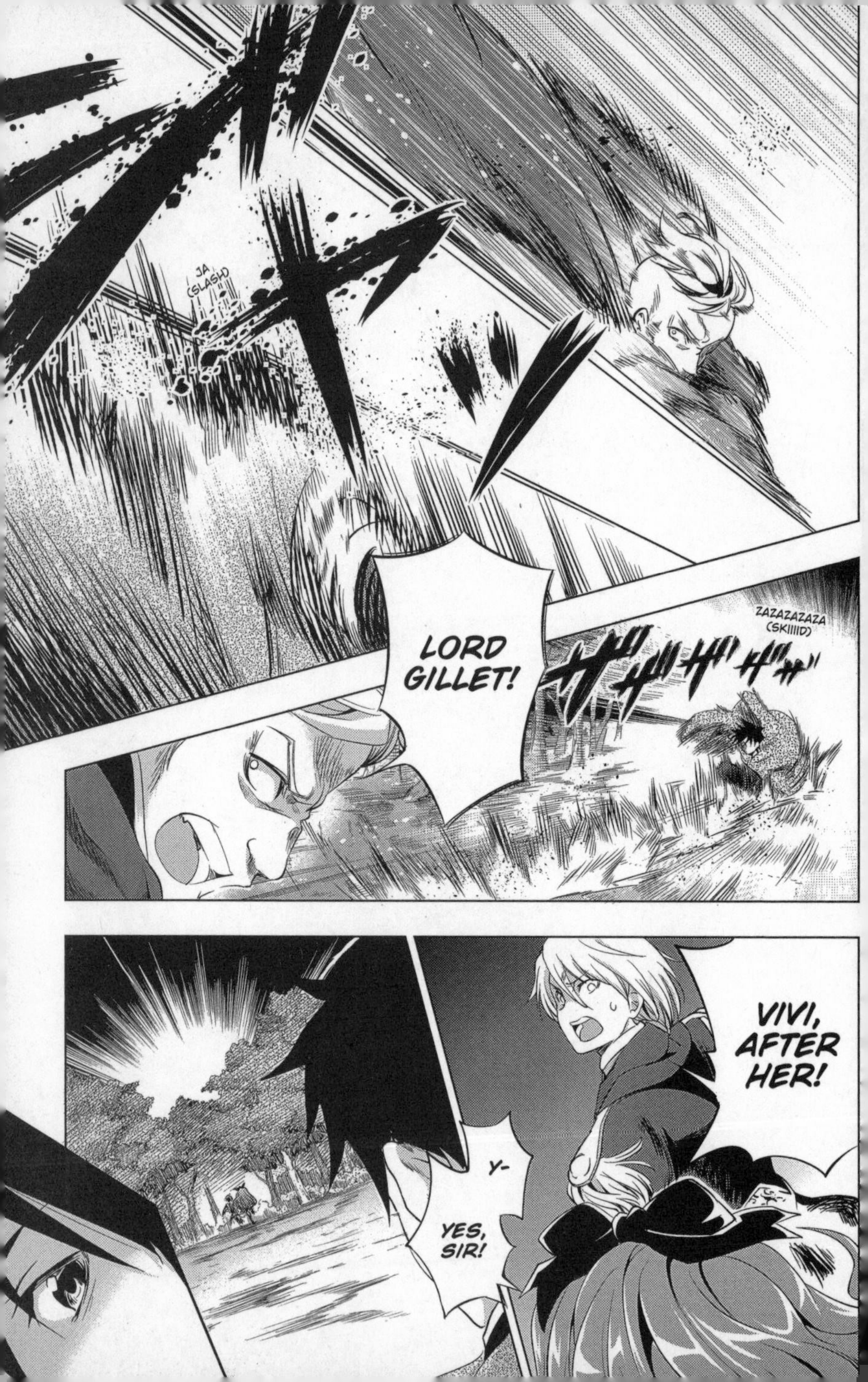
JA (SLASH)
ZAZAZAZA (SKIIIID)
LORD GILLET!
VIVI, AFTER HER!
Y-
YES, SIR!

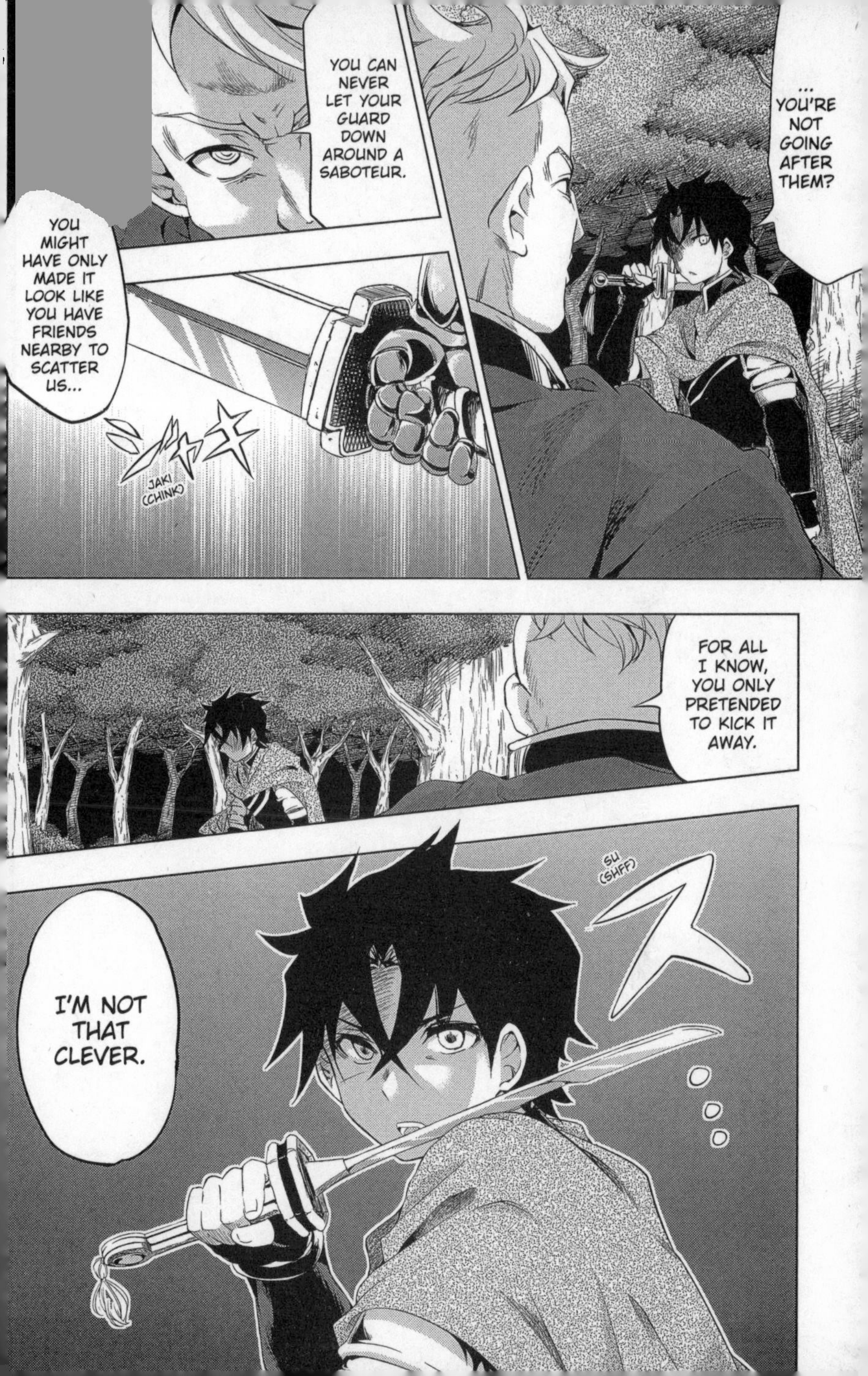

... YOU'RE NOT GOING AFTER THEM?
YOU CAN NEVER LET YOUR GUARD DOWN AROUND A SABOTEUR.
YOU MIGHT HAVE ONLY MADE IT LOOK LIKE YOU HAVE FRIENDS NEARBY TO SCATTER US...
JAKI (CHINK)
FOR ALL I KNOW, YOU ONLY PRETENDED TO KICK IT AWAY.
SU (SHFF)
I'M NOT THAT CLEVER.

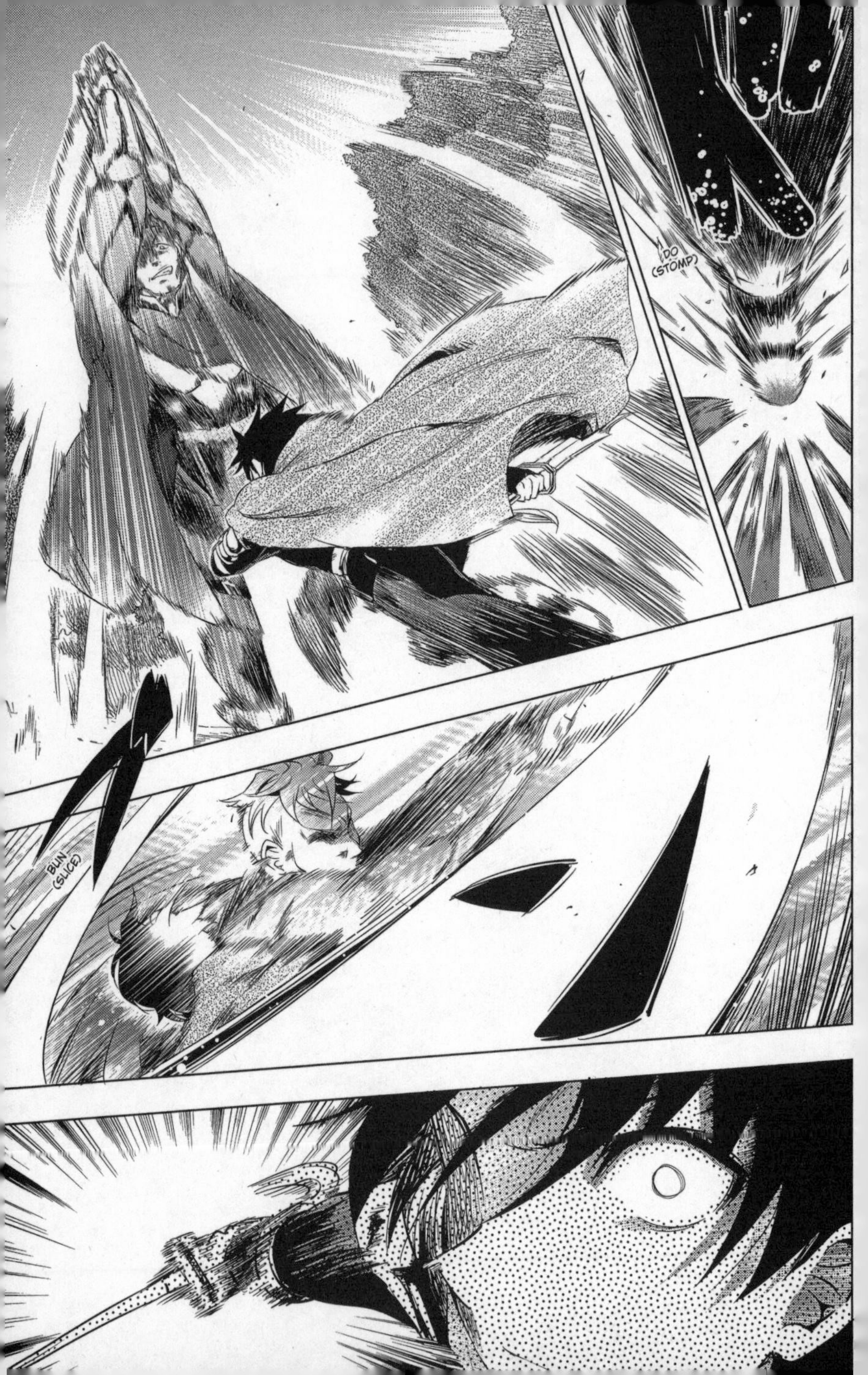
DO
(STOMP)
BUN
(SLICE)

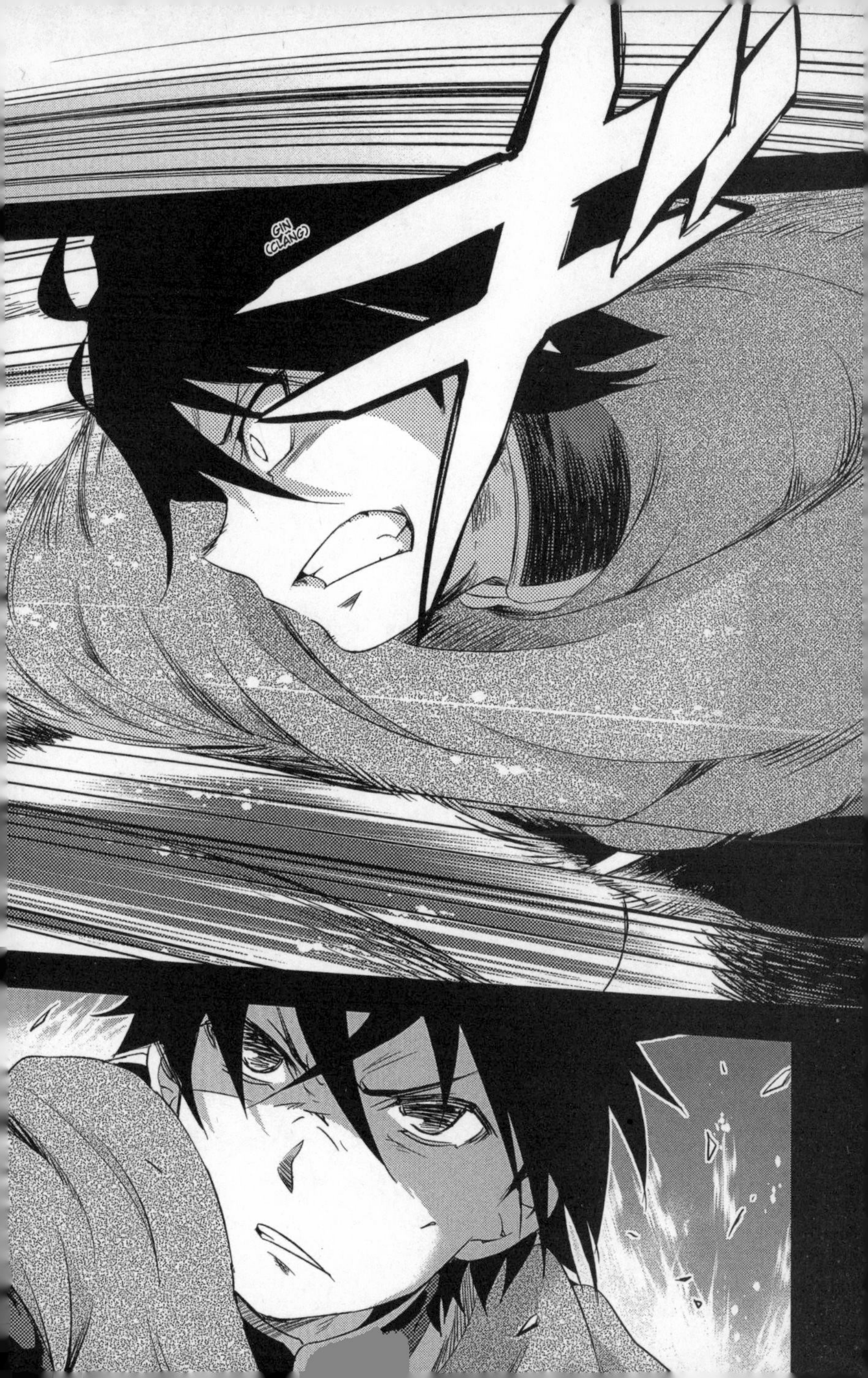
GIN
(CLANG)

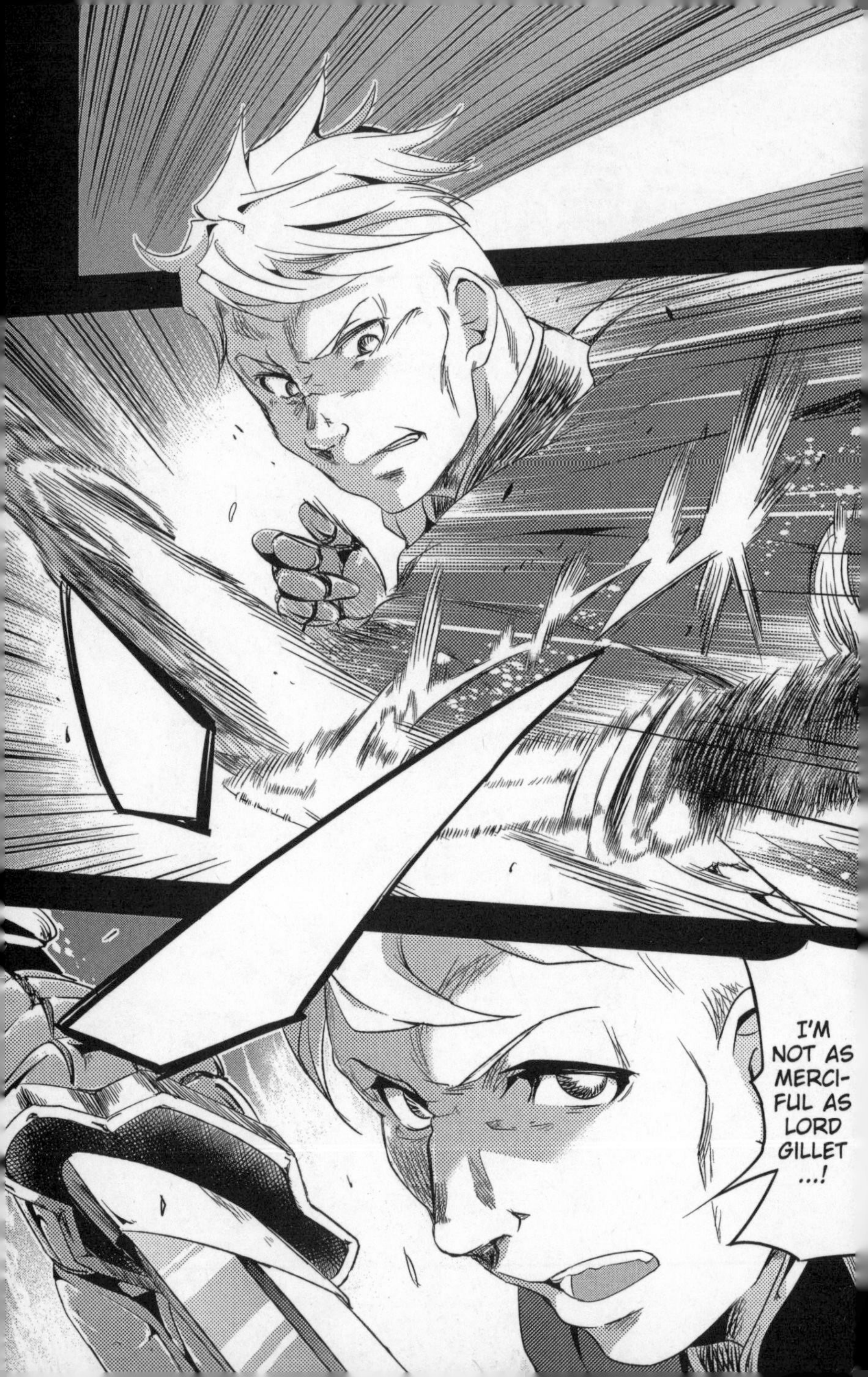
I'M NOT AS MERCI-FUL AS LORD GILLET ...!

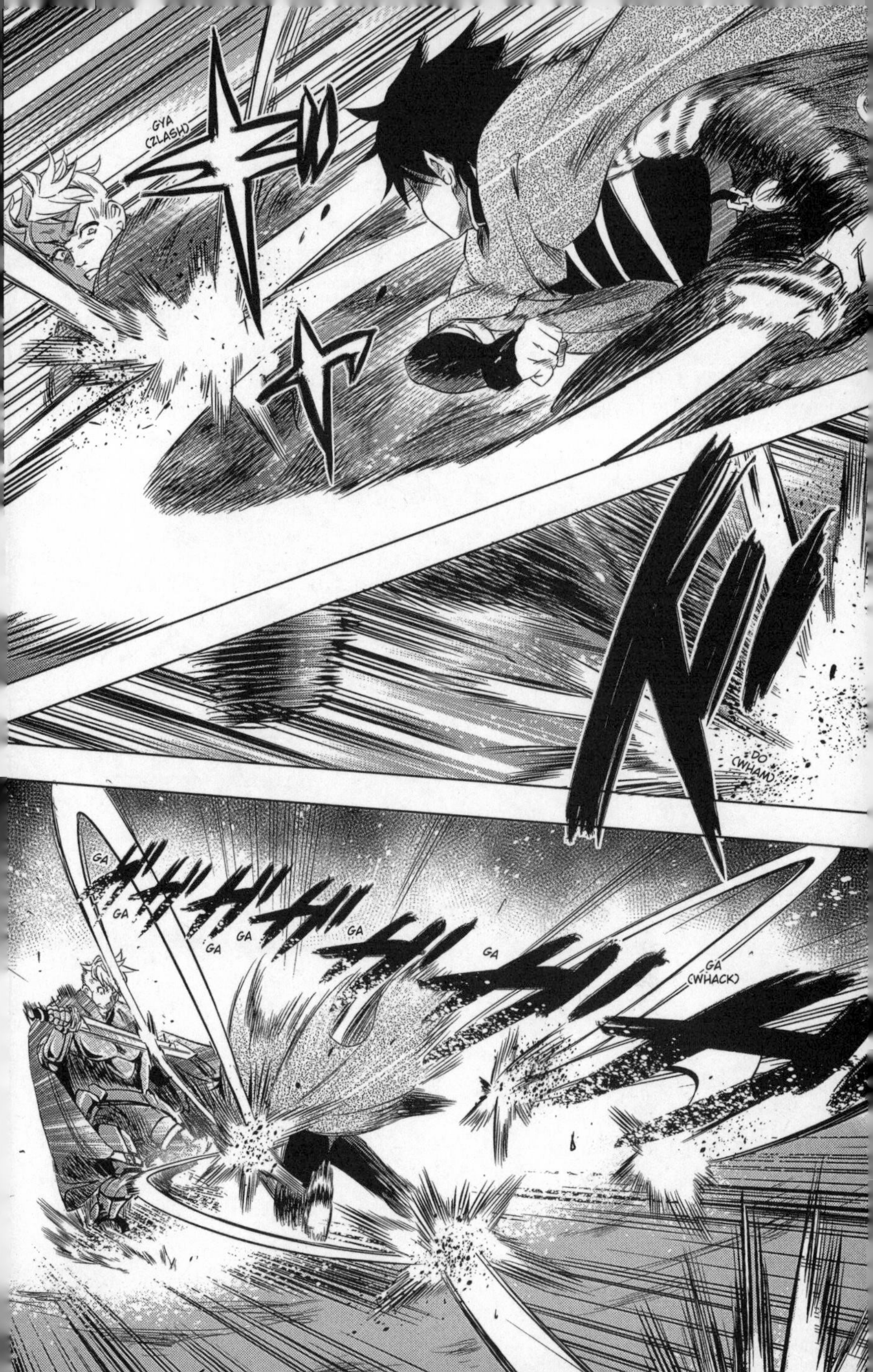
GYA
(ZLASH)
DO
(WHAM)
GA
(WHACK)
GA
GA
GA
GA
GA
GA

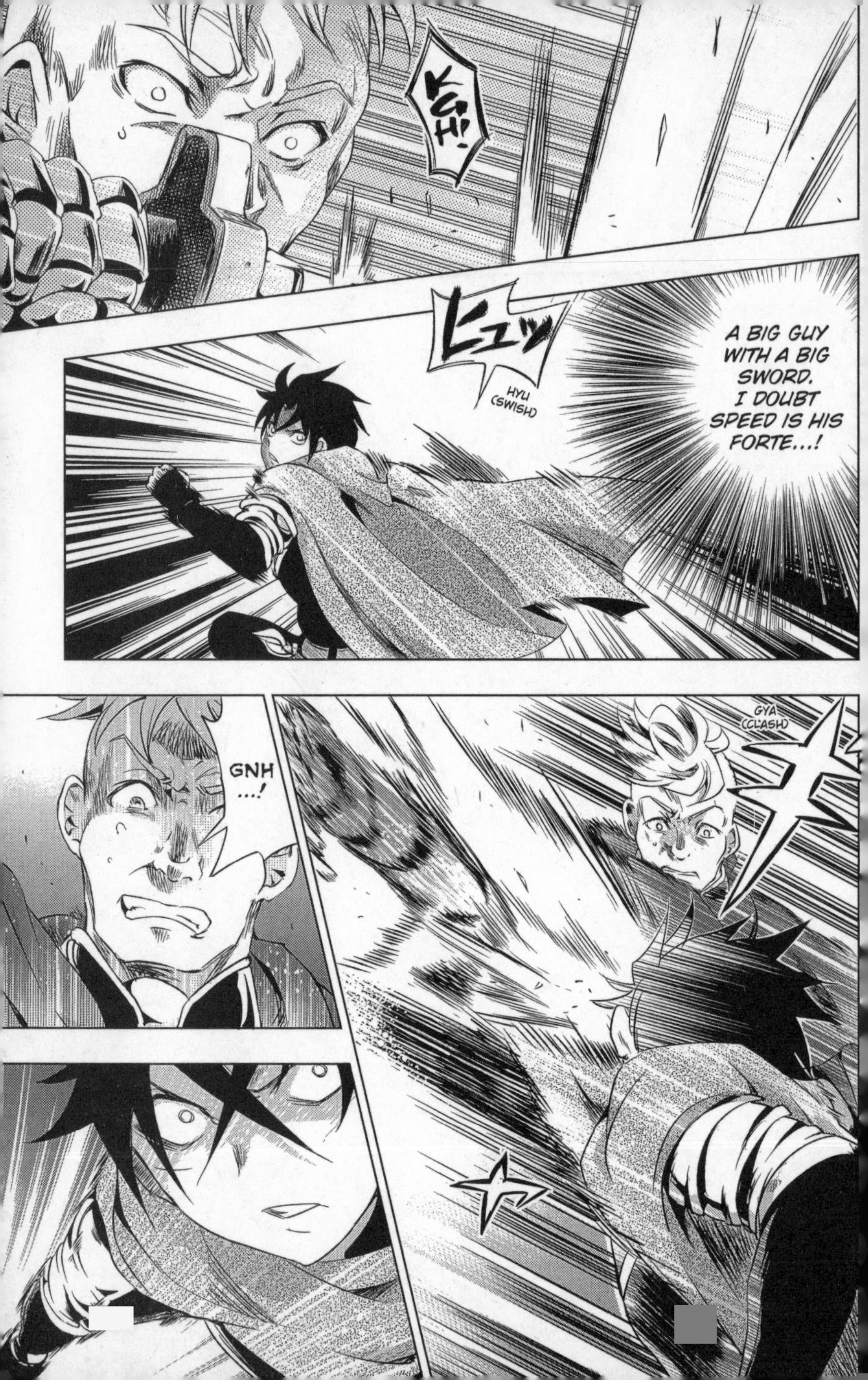
KGH!
ヒュッ
HYU (SWISH)
A BIG GUY WITH A BIG SWORD. I DOUBT SPEED IS HIS FORTE...!
GYA (CLASH)
GNH ...!

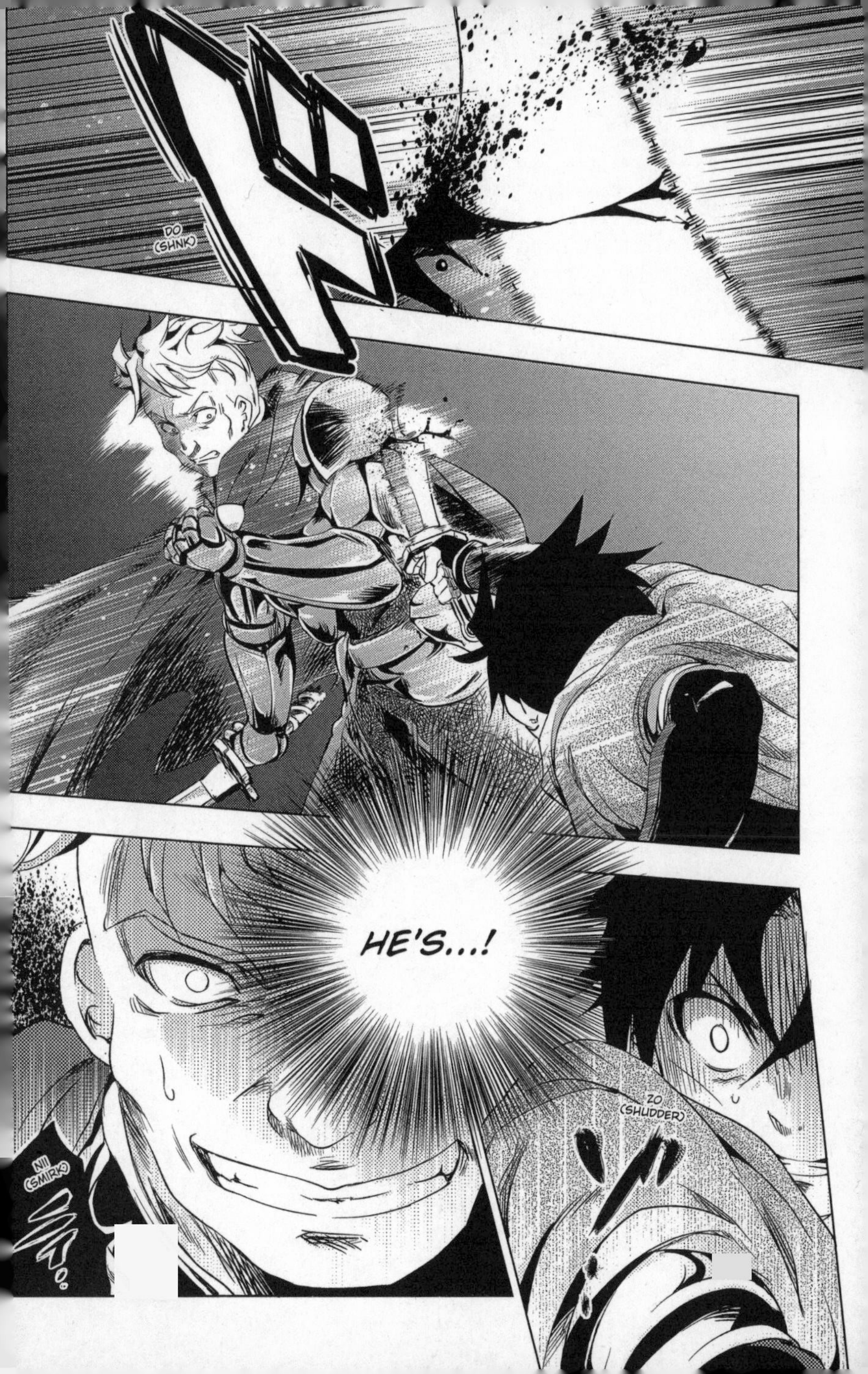
DO
(SHNK)
HE'S...!
ZO
(SHUDDER)
NII
(SMIRK)

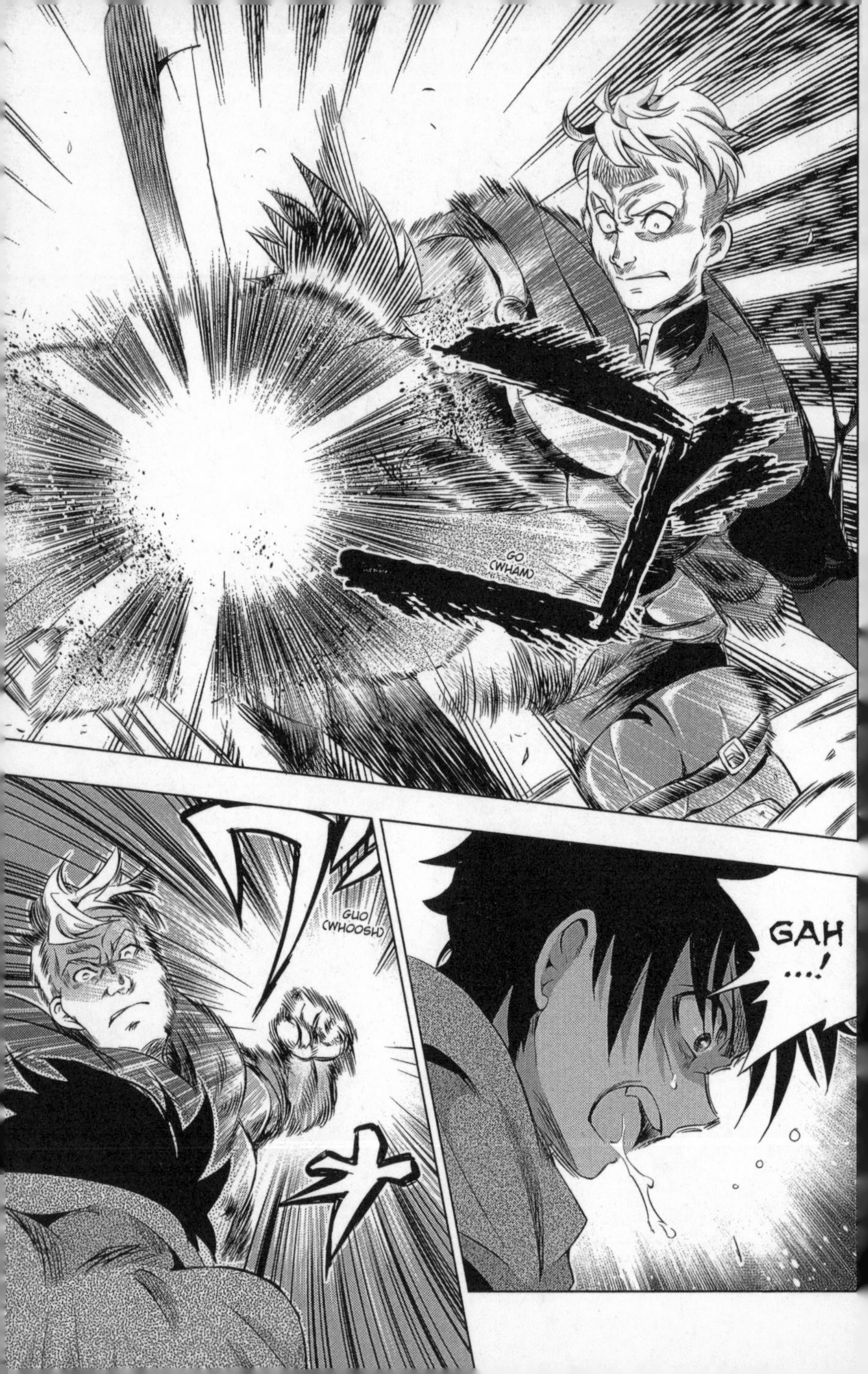
GO
(WHAM)
GAH
...!
GUO
(WHOOSH)

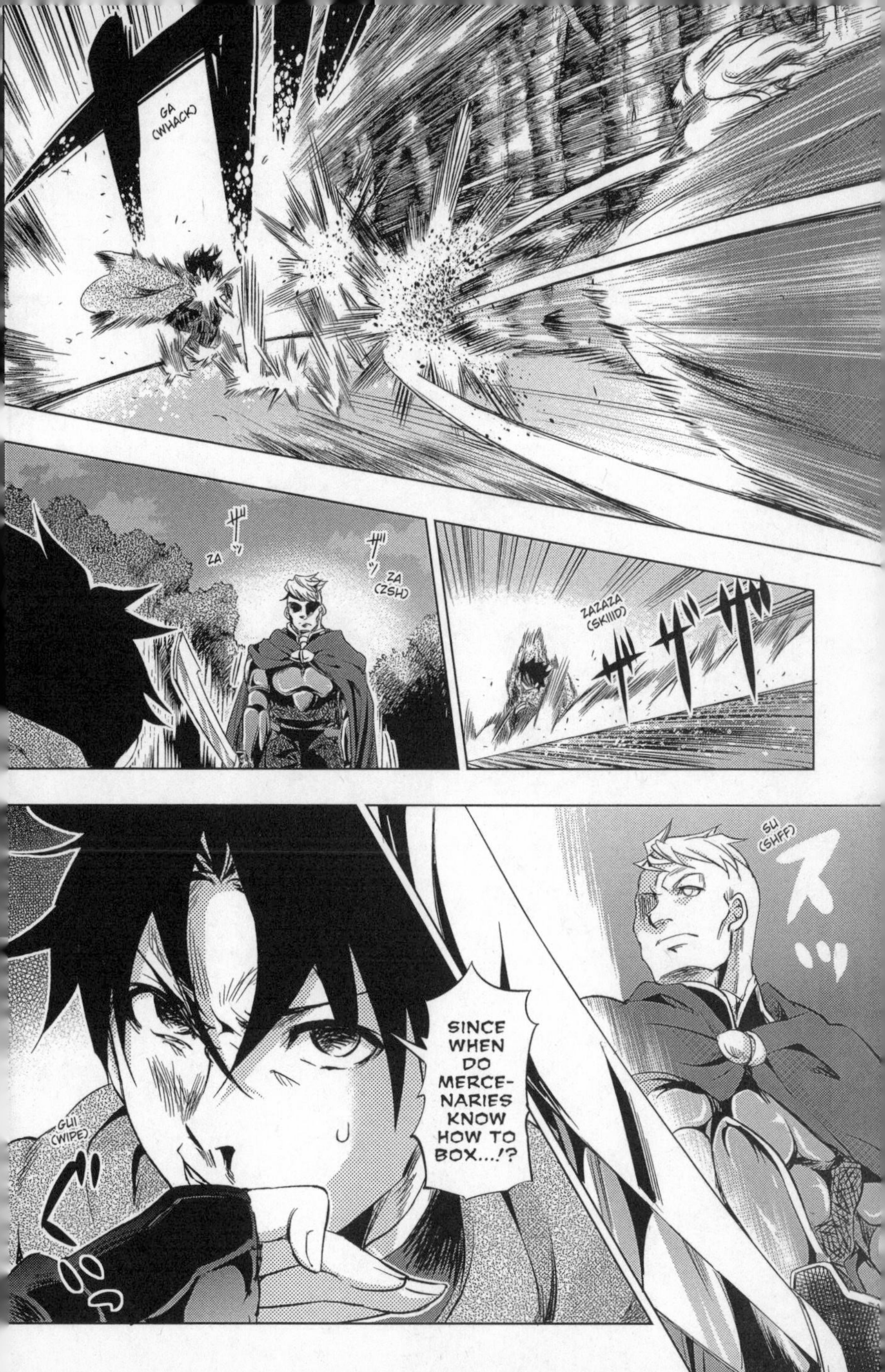
GA (WHACK)
ZAZAZA (SKIIID)
ZA (ZSH)
ZA
SU (SHFF)
SINCE WHEN DO MERCENARIES KNOW HOW TO BOX...!?
GUI (WIPE)

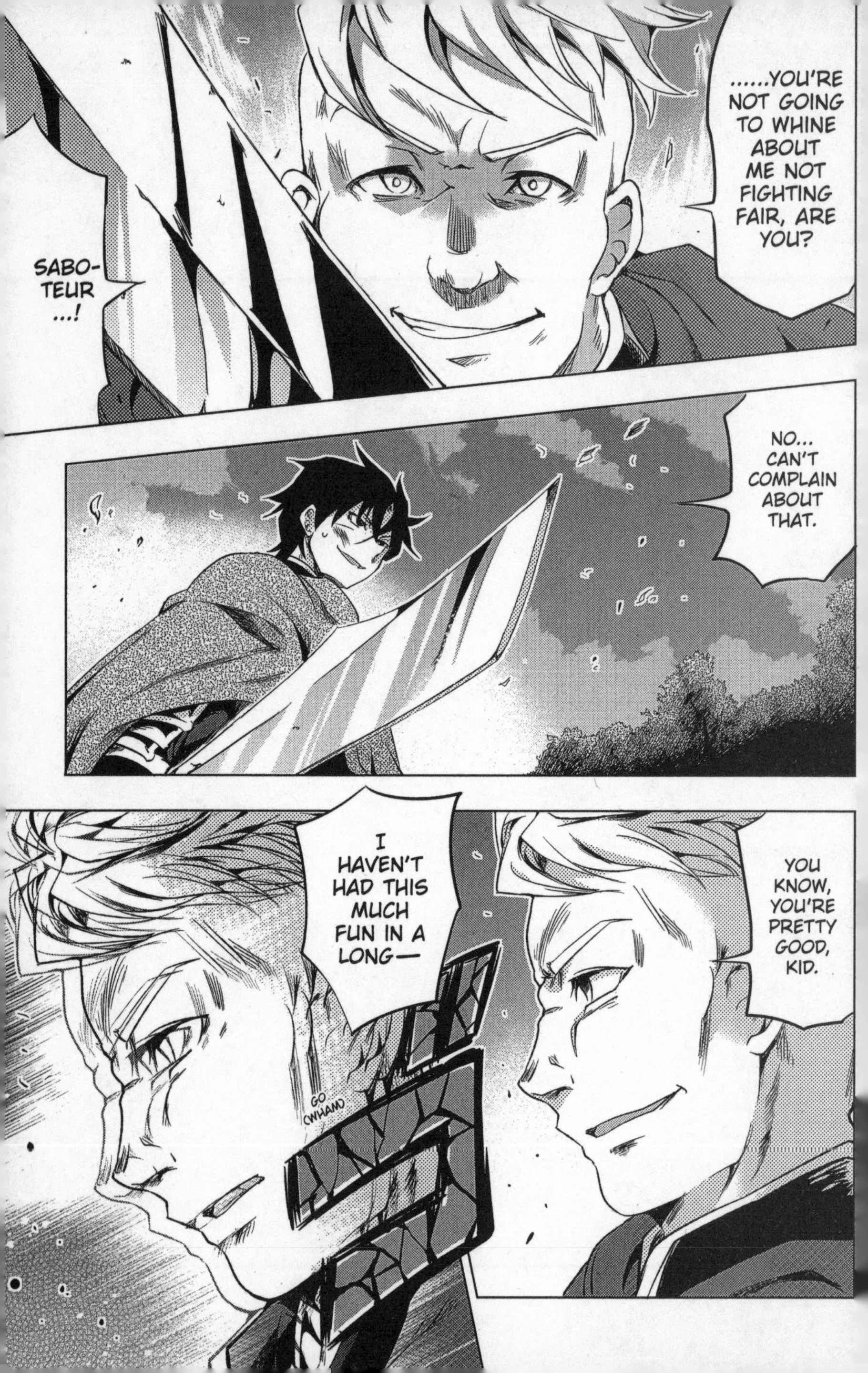
......YOU'RE NOT GOING TO WHINE ABOUT ME NOT FIGHTING FAIR, ARE YOU?
SABOTEUR ...!
NO... CAN'T COMPLAIN ABOUT THAT.
YOU KNOW, YOU'RE PRETTY GOOD, KID.
I HAVEN'T HAD THIS MUCH FUN IN A LONG—
GO (WHAM)

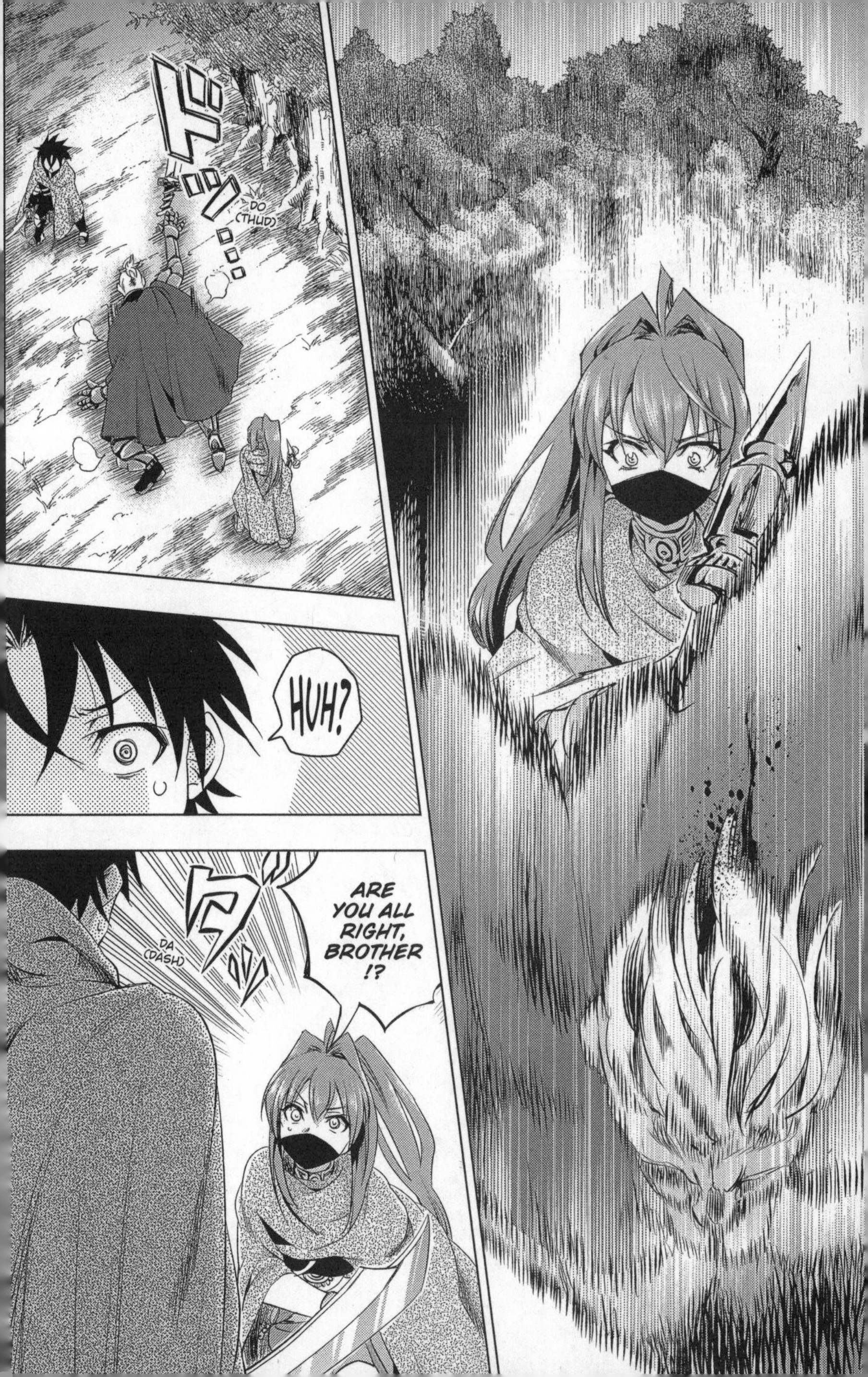
DO (THUD)
HUH?
DA (DASH)
ARE YOU ALL RIGHT, BROTHER!?

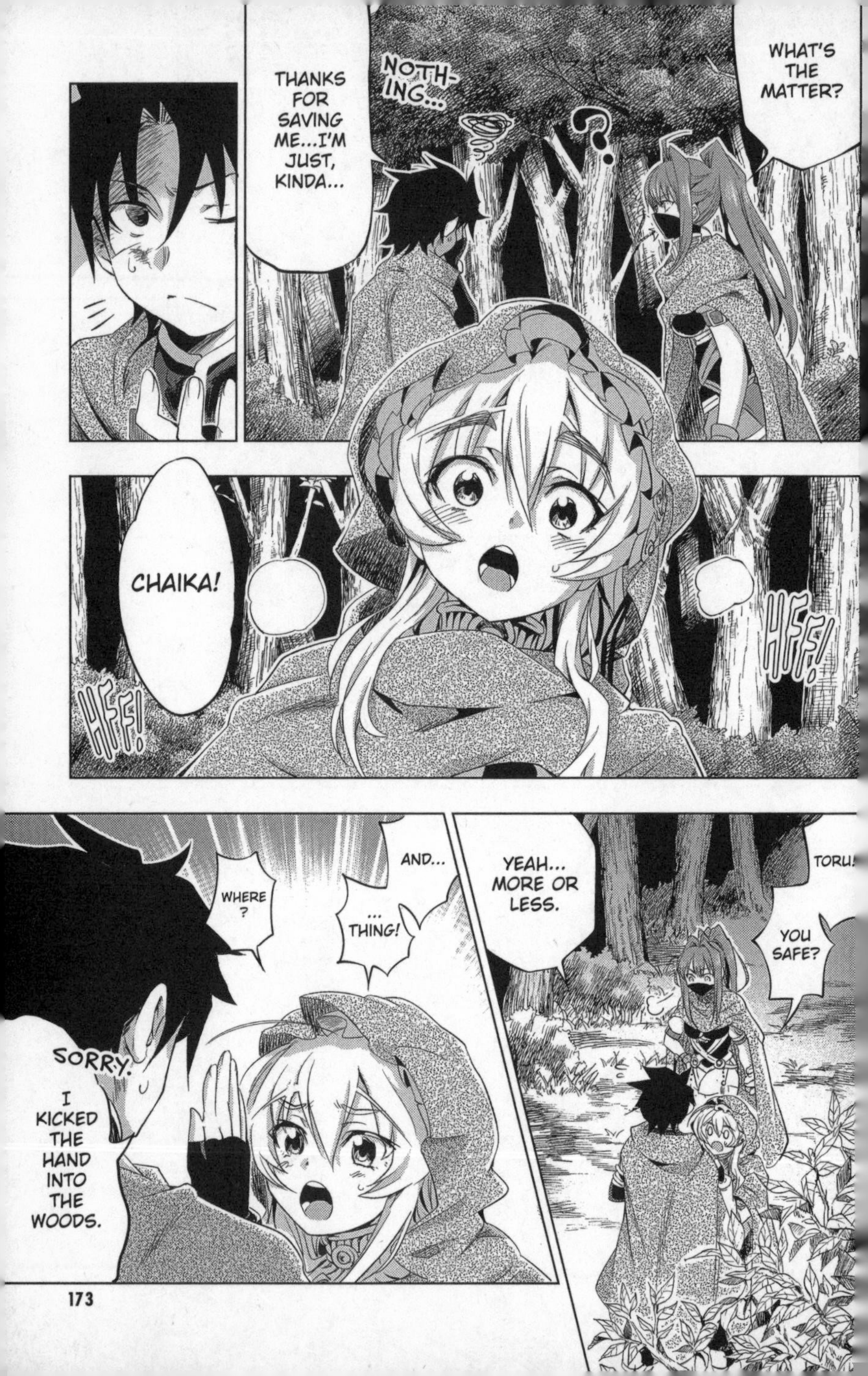
WHAT'S THE MATTER?
NOTH-ING...
THANKS FOR SAVING ME...I'M JUST, KINDA...
HFF!
CHAIKA!
HFF!
TORU!
YOU SAFE?
YEAH... MORE OR LESS.
AND...
... THING!
WHERE ?
SORRY.
I KICKED THE HAND INTO THE WOODS.

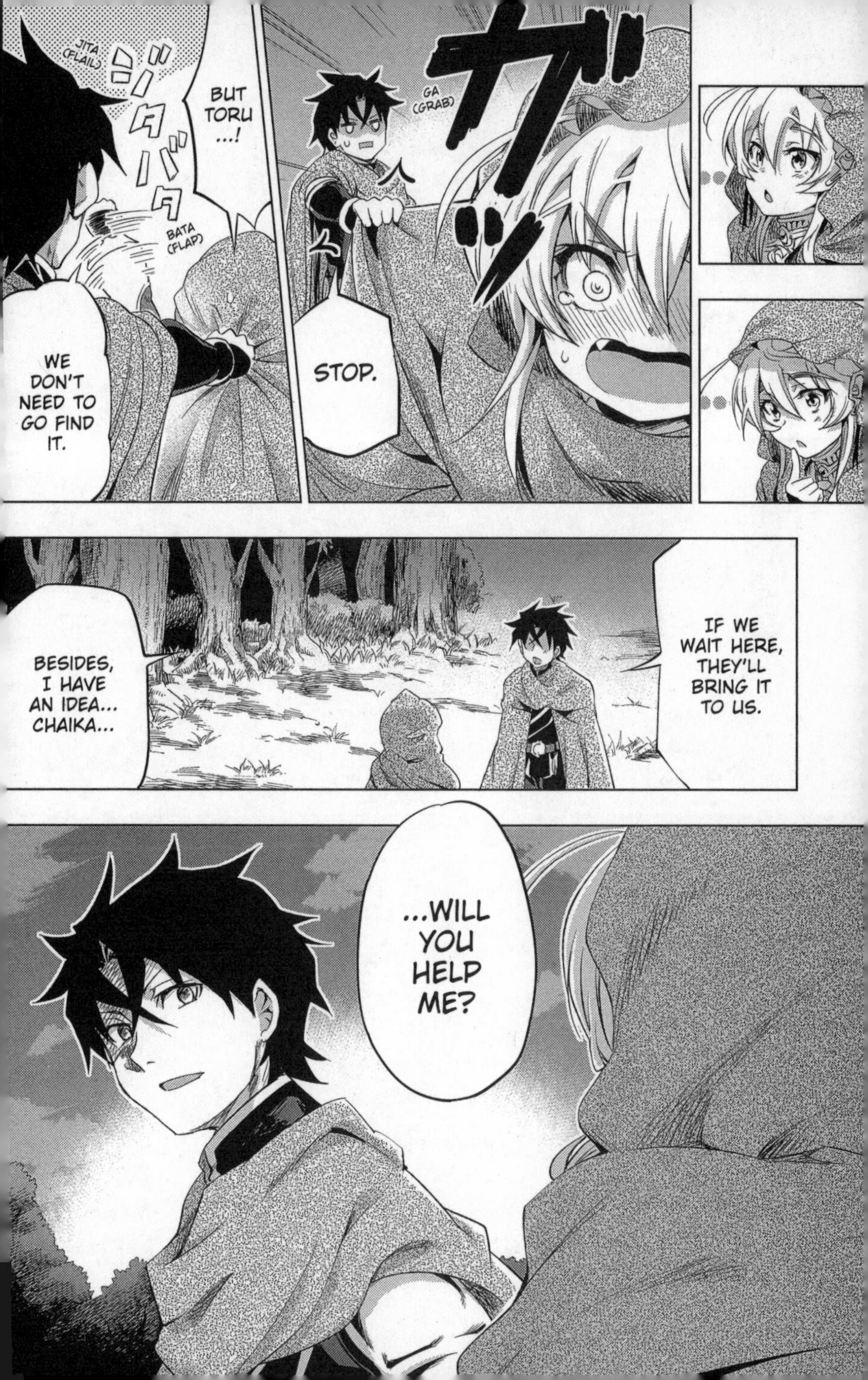
...
...
GA (GRAB)
STOP.
BUT TORU ...!
JITA (FLAIL)
BATA (FLAP)
WE DON'T NEED TO GO FIND IT.
IF WE WAIT HERE, THEY'LL BRING IT TO US.
BESIDES, I HAVE AN IDEA... CHAIKA...
...WILL YOU HELP ME?

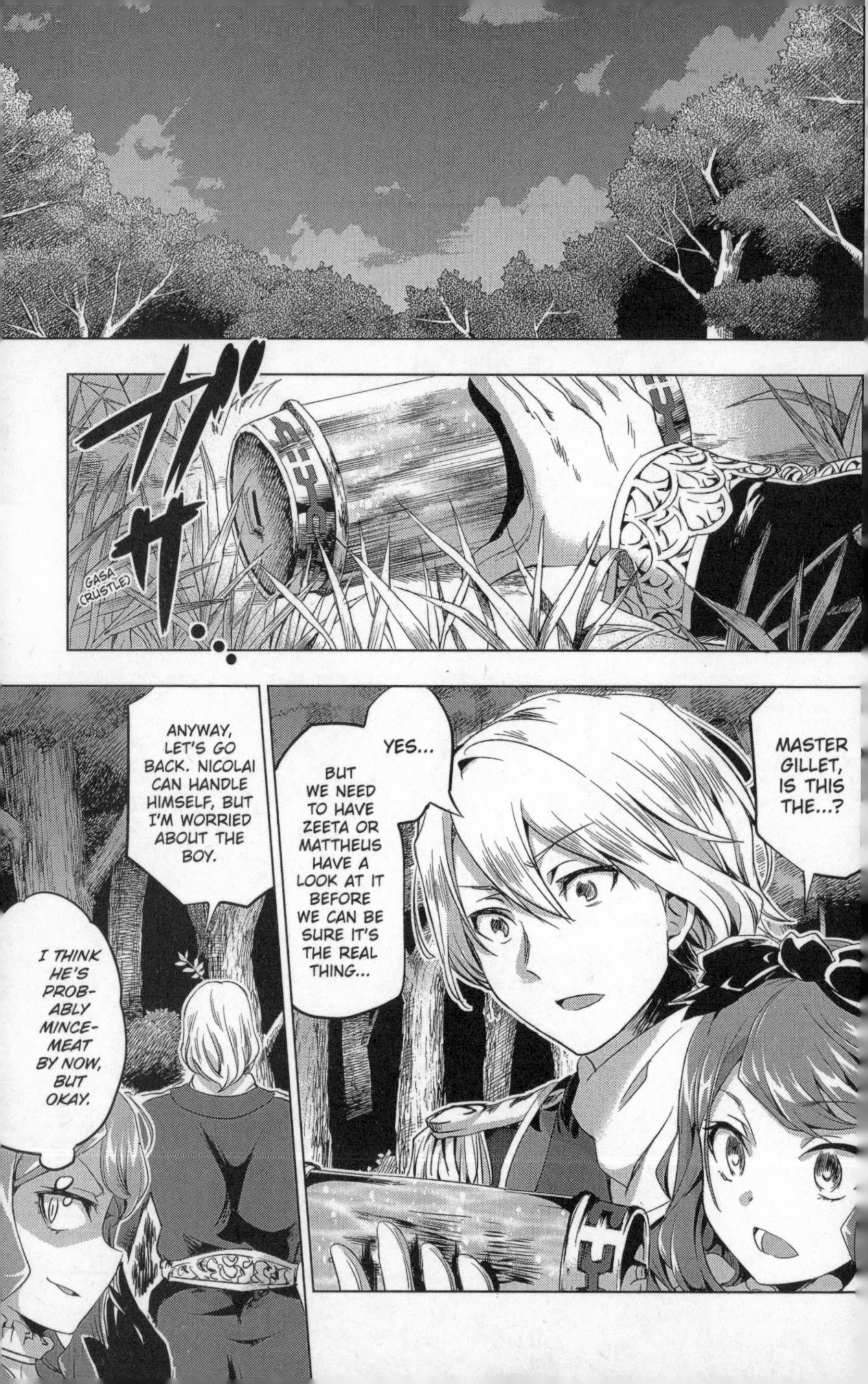
GASA (RUSTLE)
MASTER GILLET, IS THIS THE...?
YES...
BUT WE NEED TO HAVE ZEETA OR MATTHEUS HAVE A LOOK AT IT BEFORE WE CAN BE SURE IT'S THE REAL THING...
ANYWAY, LET'S GO BACK. NICOLAI CAN HANDLE HIMSELF, BUT I'M WORRIED ABOUT THE BOY.
I THINK HE'S PROBABLY MINCEMEAT BY NOW, BUT OKAY.

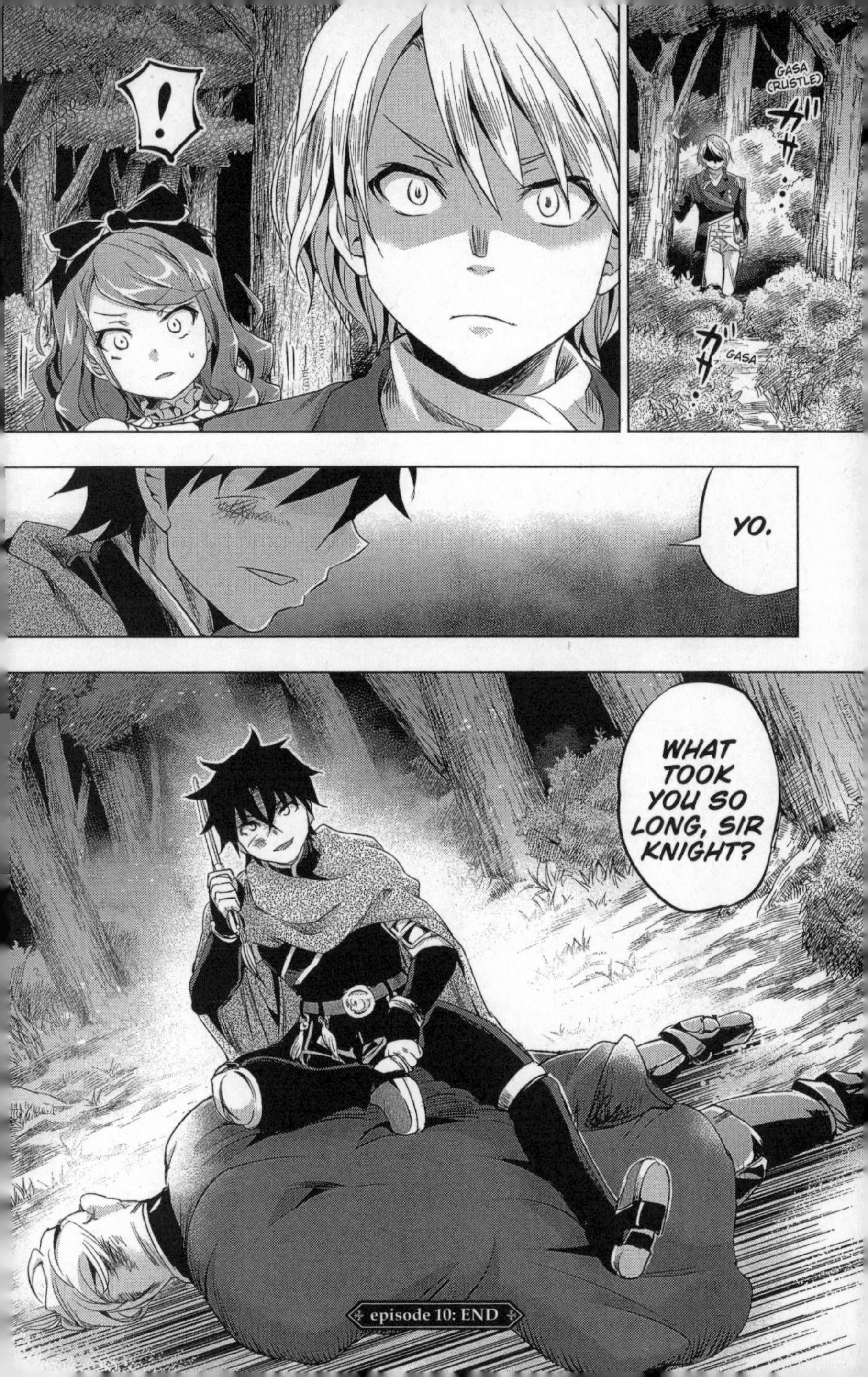
GASA (RUSTLE)
GASA
!
YO.
WHAT TOOK YOU SO LONG, SIR KNIGHT?
episode 10: END

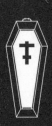

from Ichirou Sakaki

WHEN AN AUTHOR'S LIGHT NOVEL IS MADE INTO A MANGA, THE MANGA ALLOWS THE INCLUSION OF A LOT OF EXTRA MATERIAL THAT COULDN'T BE EXPRESSED IN THE ORIGINAL PROSE OR ILLUSTRATIONS, AND SO THE WRITER MAY VIEW IT AS A NICE COMPLEMENT TO THE NOVEL. BUT SOMETIMES THE MANGA ARTIST WILL PRODUCE A DIFFERENT INTERPRETATION OF THE SOURCE MATERIAL, AND TOTALLY NEW INFORMATION WILL POP UP, AND THAT'S FUN TOO. AS AN EXAMPLE OF SOMETHING THAT WASN'T IN THE NOVELS, LOOK AT THE SCENES WITH YOUNG TORU AND AKARI WITH JASMÍN—IN THE MANGA VERSION, TORU GRABS JASMÍN'S CHEST AND AKARI BEATS HIM UP. THOSE THINGS DON'T HAPPEN IN THE NOVEL, OR RATHER, THEY'RE DEPICTED SLIGHTLY DIFFERENTLY FROM THE NOVEL VERSIONS OF TORU AND AKARI. (TORU ISN'T OFTEN THE INSTIGATOR OF SUCH CRUDE ADULT HUMOR.) ON THE OTHER HAND, IMAGINING WAYS TO FILL IN THE GAPS—WHAT KINDS OF TWISTS AND TURNS HAPPENED ALONG THE WAY TO TURN THOSE TWO INTO THE PEOPLE THEY ARE NOW—IS ALSO FUN AND INTERESTING. FOR EXAMPLE, WHAT MADE TORU THE WAY HE IS NOW? WHY DOES HE SEEM SOMEWHAT DISINTERESTED IN NAUGHTY JOKES? OR, FOR EXAMPLE, IF AKARI WAS SO MUCH STRONGER BACK THEN, WHY ARE THEY ABOUT EQUAL NOW? MAYBE JASMÍN'S DEATH KILLED TORU'S INTEREST IN THE OPPOSITE SEX. AND AS A RESULT, MAYBE HE DEVOTED HIMSELF EXCESSIVELY TO HIS TRAINING SO THAT, WHILE HIS SKILL AS A SABOTEUR GREW EXPONENTIALLY, HIS MENTAL GROWTH STOPPED COMPLETELY. AND AKARI HAS BEEN BY HIS SIDE, WORRYING ABOUT THE IMBALANCE ALL THIS TIME. AND THEN, WHEN WE GET TO THE MAIN STORY, MAYBE TORU'S ENCOUNTER WITH CHAIKA REACTIVATED HIS ROMANTIC EMOTIONS, RESTARTING THEIR GRADUAL GROWTH. WHILE I CAN'T PUT THESE SPECULATIONS IN THE STORY PROPER (CHAIKA WOULDN'T BE IN THEM, SO IT WOULD GO AGAINST THE TITLE OF THE SERIES—HA-HA), THESE EPISODES DO FORM IN MY HEAD AS I READ THE MANGA, AND IT'S A LOT OF FUN. THEY'RE ALL MINOR DETAILS, BUT THESE ASPECTS—THIS PART OF THE ADAPTED MANGA—IS THE BEST PART OF MEDIA MIXING, AND THESE ARE THE THINGS I THINK ABOUT WHILE I READ THE MANGA VERSION.

ICHIROU SAKAKI

from Namaniku ATK

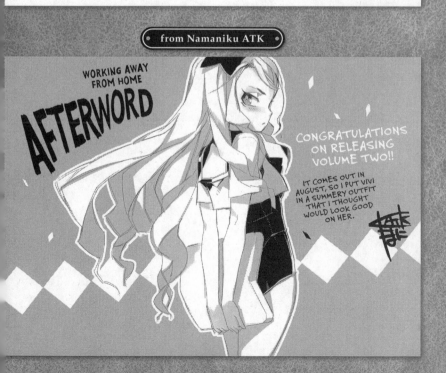

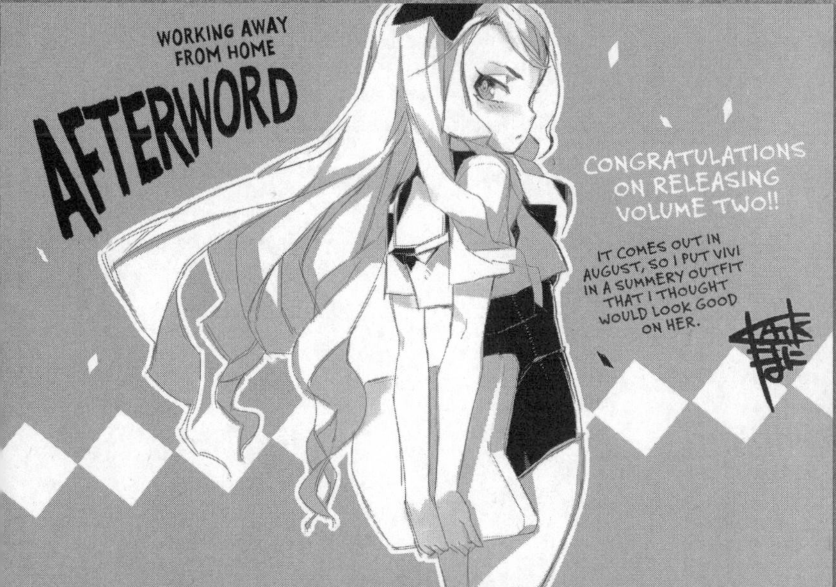
WORKING AWAY FROM HOME
AFTERWORD
CONGRATULATIONS ON RELEASING VOLUME TWO!!
IT COMES OUT IN AUGUST, SO I PUT VIVI IN A SUMMERY OUTFIT THAT I THOUGHT WOULD LOOK GOOD ON HER.

THANK YOU FOR BUYING VOLUME TWO OF CHAIKA: THE COFFIN PRINCESS.

WOW, BEFORE I EVEN KNEW WHAT WAS HAPPENING, VOLUME TWO IS ON SALE. TIME FLIES. THIS VOLUME INCLUDES THE STORY OF TORU'S PAST. I DID THE CHARACTER DESIGN FOR THE MANGA VERSION OF JASMÍN ALL BY MYSELF, SO I WAS NERVOUS ABOUT WHETHER OR NOT IT WOULD DESTROY EVERYONE'S IMAGE OF HER FROM THE NOVEL, BUT PERSONALLY I LIKE IT.

I'M REALLY HAPPY TO HAVE COMMENTS IN THIS VOLUME AND THE PREVIOUS ONE FROM SAKAKI-SENSEI AND NAMANIKU ATK-SAN. I WILL KEEP DOING MY BEST...! AND I HAVE THE UTMOST GRATITUDE FOR MY ASSISTANTS TOO.

AND OF COURSE... I WANT TO THANK ALL YOU READERS WHO PICKED UP THIS BOOK!

LET'S MEET AGAIN IN THE NEXT VOLUME.

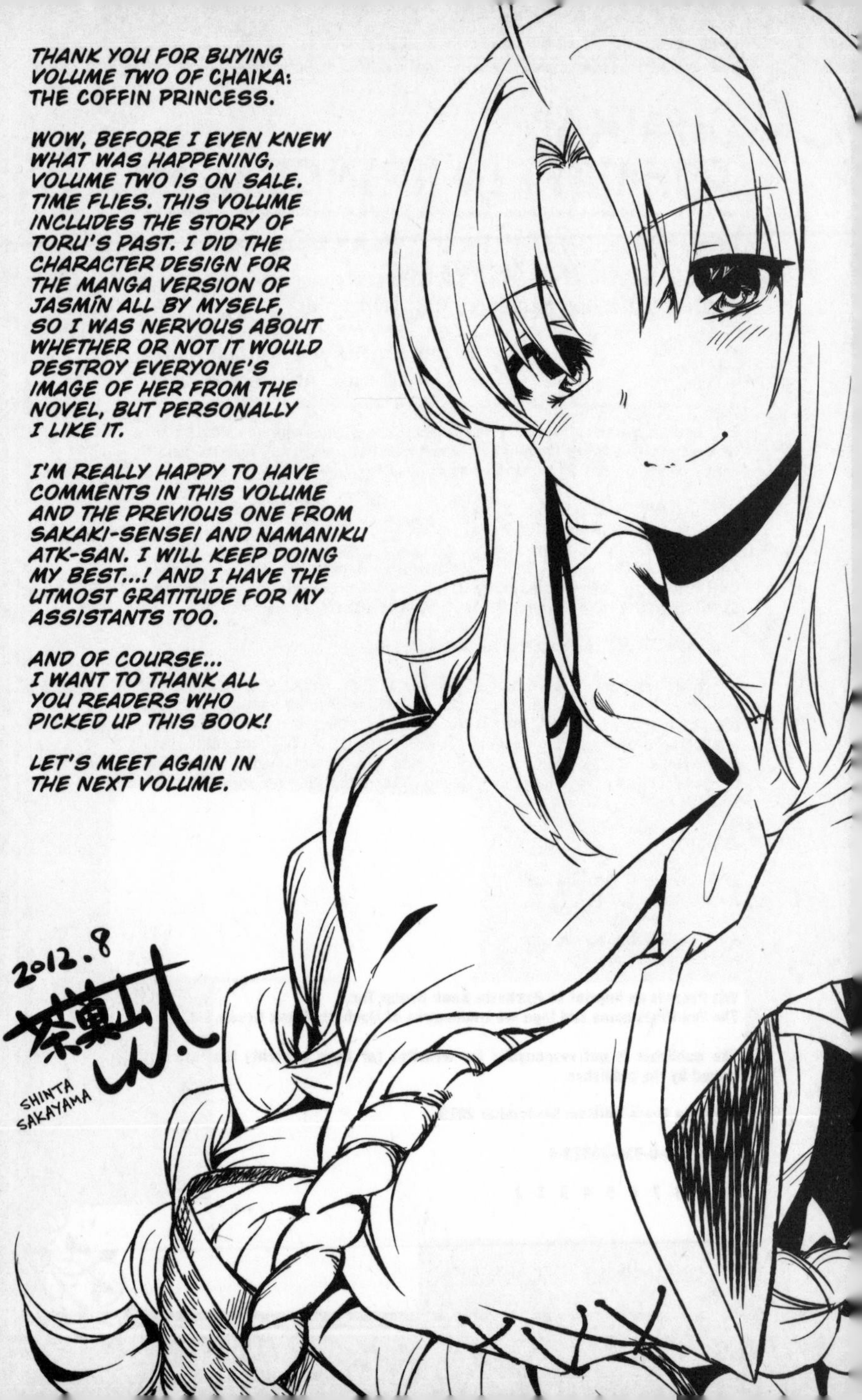

2012.8

SHINTA SAKAYAMA

CHAIKA: THE COFFIN PRINCESS ❷

Original Story By: ICHIROU SAKAKI
Manga: SHINTA SAKAYAMA
Character Design: Namaniku ATK (Nitroplus)

Translation: Athena and Alethea Nibley
Lettering: Abigail Blackman

HITSUGI NO CHAIKA Volume 2
©Ichirou Sakaki, Nitroplus 2012
©Shinta SAKAYAMA 2012
Edited by KADOKAWA SHOTEN. First published in Japan in 2012 by KADOKAWA CORPORATION, Tokyo. English translation rights arranged with KADOKAWA CORPORATION, Tokyo through TUTTLE-MORI AGENCY, INC., Tokyo.

Translation © 2015 by Hachette Book Group, Inc.

Yen Press
Hachette Book Group
1290 Avenue of the Americas
New York, NY 10104

www.hachettebookgroup.com
www.yenpress.com

D0002887

Inc.

t are not

Printed in the United States of America